# 𝔈nglish 𝔐en of 𝔄ction

# WARWICK THE KINGMAKER

WARWICK

FROM THE ROWS ROLL

# WARWICK

## THE KINGMAKER

BY

CHARLES W. OMAN

London

MACMILLAN AND CO.

AND NEW YORK

1891

# CONTENTS

# CHAPTER I

## THE DAYS OF THE KINGMAKER

OF all the great men of action who since the Conquest have guided the course of English policy, it is probable that none is less known to the reader of history than Richard Neville Earl of Warwick and Salisbury. The only man of anything approaching his eminence who has been treated with an equal neglect is Thomas Cromwell, and of late years the great minister of Henry the Eighth is beginning to receive some of the attention that is his due. But for the Kingmaker, the man who for ten years was the first subject of the English Crown, and whose figure looms out with a vague grandeur even through the misty annals of the Wars of the Roses, no writer has spared a monograph. Every one, it is true, knows his name, but his personal identity is quite ungrasped. Nine persons out of ten if asked to sketch his character would find, to their own surprise, that they were falling back for their information to Lord Lytton's *Last of the Barons* or Shakespeare's *Henry the Sixth.*

An attempt, therefore, even an inadequate attempt, to trace out with accuracy his career and his habits of

Œ                                    B

mind from the original authorities cannot fail to be of some use to the general reader as well as to the student of history. The result will perhaps appear meagre to those who are accustomed to the biographies of the men of later centuries. We are curiously ignorant of many of the facts that should aid us to build up a picture of the man. No trustworthy representation of his bodily form exists. The day of portraits was not yet come; his monument in Bisham Abbey has long been swept away; no writer has even deigned to describe his personal appearance—we know not if he was dark or fair, stout or slim. At most we may gather from the vague phrases of the chroniclers, and from his quaint armed figure in the Rous Roll, that he was of great stature and breadth of limb. But perhaps the good Rous was thinking of his fame rather than his body, when he sketched the Earl in that quaint pictorial pedigree over-topping all his race save his cousin and king and enemy, Edward the Fourth.

But Warwick has only shared the fate of all his con-temporaries. The men of the fifteenth century are far less well known to us than are their grandfathers or their grandsons. In the fourteenth century the chroni-clers were still working on their old scale; in the six-teenth the literary spirit had descended on the whole nation, and great men and small were writing hard at history as at every other branch of knowledge. But in the days of Lancaster and York the old fountains had run dry, and the new flood of the Renaissance had not risen. The materials for reconstructing history are both scanty and hard to handle. We dare not swallow Hall and Hollingshead whole, as was the custom for two

hundred years, or take their annals, coloured from end
to end with Tudor sympathies, as good authority for the
doings of the previous century. Yet when we have put aside
their fascinating, if somewhat untrustworthy, volumes,
we find ourselves wandering in a very dreary waste of
fragments and scraps of history, strung together on the
meagre thread of two or three dry and jejune compila-
tions of annals.  To have to take William of Worcester
or good Abbot Whethamsted as the groundwork of a
continuous account of the times is absolutely maddening.
Hence it comes to pass that Warwick has failed to receive
his dues.

Of all the men of Warwick's century there are only
two whose characters we seem thoroughly to grasp—the
best and the worst products of the age—Henry the Fifth
and Richard the Third.  The achievements of the one
stirred even the feeble writers of that day into a fulness of
detail in which they indulge for no other hero ; the other
served as the text for so many invectives under the Tudors
that we imagine that we see a real man in the gloomy
portrait that is set up before us.  Yet we may fairly ask
whether our impression is not drawn, either at first or at
second hand, almost entirely from Sir Thomas More's
famous biography of the usurper, a work whose literary
merits have caused it to be received as the only serious
source for Richard's history.  If we had not that work,
Richard of Gloucester would seem a vaguely-defined
monster of iniquity, as great a puzzle to the student of
history as are the other shadowy forms which move on
through those evil times to fall, one after the other, into
the bloody grave which was the common lot of all.

In spite, however, of the dearth of good chronicles,

and of the absolute non-existence of any contemporary writers of literary merit, there are authorities enough of one sort and another to make it both possible and profitable to build up a detailed picture of Warwick and his times. First and foremost, of course, come the invaluable Paston Letters, covering the whole period, and often supplying the vivid touches of detail in which the more formal documents are so lamentably deficient. If but half a dozen families, as constant in letter-writing as John and Margery Paston, had transmitted their correspondence to posterity, there would be little need to grumble at our lack of information. Other letters too exist, scattered in collections, such as the interesting scrawl from Warwick himself, in his dire extremity before Barnet fight, to Henry Vernon, which was turned up a year ago among the lumber at Belvoir Castle. Much can be gathered from rolls and inquests—for example, the all-important information as to centres and sources of local power can be traced out with perfect accuracy from the columns of the Escheats Roll, where each peer or knight's lands are carefully set forth at the moment of his decease. Joining one authority to another, we may fairly build up the England of the fifteenth century before our eyes with some approach to completeness.

The whole picture of the times is very depressing on the moral if not on the material side. There are few more pitiful episodes in history than the whole tale of the reign of Henry the Sixth, the most unselfish and well-intentioned king that ever sat upon the English throne —a man of whom not even his enemies and oppressors could find an evil word to say; the troubles came, as they confessed, "all because of his false lords, and never

of him." We feel that there must have been something
wrong with the heart of a nation that could see unmoved
the meek and holy King torn from wife and child, sent
to wander in disguise up and down the kingdom for
which he had done his poor best, and finally doomed to
pine for five years a prisoner in the fortress where he
had so long held his royal Court.    Nor is our first
impression concerning the demoralisation of England
wrong.    Every line that we read bears home to us more
and more the fact that the nation had fallen on evil
times.    First and foremost among the causes of its moral
deterioration was the wretched French War, a war begun
in the pure spirit of greed and ambition,—there was not
even the poor excuse that had existed in the time of
Edward the Third—carried on by the aid of hordes of de-
bauched foreign mercenaries (after Henry the Fifth's death
the native English seldom formed more than a third of
any host that took the field in France), and persisted in
long after it had become hopeless, partly from misplaced
national pride, partly because of the personal interests
of the ruling classes.    Thirty-five years of a war that
was as unjust as it was unfortunate had both soured and
demoralised the nation.    England was full of disbanded
soldiers of fortune; of knights who had lost the ill-gotten
lands across the Channel, where they had maintained a
precarious lordship in the days of better fortune; of
castellans and governors whose occupation was gone; of
hangers-on of all sorts who had once maintained themselves on the spoils of Normandy and Guienne.    Year
after year men and money had been lavished on the
war to no effect; and when the final catastrophe came,
and the fights of Formigny and Chatillon ended the

chapter of our disasters, the nation began to cast about
for a scapegoat on whom to lay the burden of its
failures. The real blame lay on the nation itself, not
on any individual; and the real fault that had been
committed was not the mismanagement of an enterprise
which presented any hopes of success, but a wrong-
headed persistence in an attempt to conquer a country
which was too strong to be held down. However, the
majority of the English people chose to assume firstly
that the war with France might have been conducted to
a prosperous issue, and secondly that certain particular
persons were responsible for its having come to the
opposite conclusion. At first the unfortunate Suffolk
and Somerset had the responsibility laid upon them. A
little later the outcry became more bold and fixed upon
the Lancastrian dynasty itself as being to blame not only
for disaster abroad, but for the "want of governance"
at home. If King Henry had understood the charge,
and possessed the wit to answer it, he might fairly have
replied that his subjects must fit the burden upon their
own backs, not upon his. The war had been weakly
conducted, it was true; but weakly because the men and
money for it were grudged. The England that could put
one hundred thousand men into the field in a civil broil
at Towton sent four thousand to fight the decisive battle
at Formigny that settled our fate in Normandy. At
home the bulwarks of social order seemed crumbling
away. Private wars, riot, open highway robbery, murder,
abduction, armed resistance to the law, prevailed on a scale
that had been unknown since the troublous times of Edward the Second—we might almost say since the evil days
of Stephen. But it was not the Crown alone that should

have been blamed for the state of the realm. The nation had chosen to impose over-stringent constitutional checks on the kingly power before it was ripe for self-government, and the Lancastrian house sat on the throne because it had agreed to submit to those checks. If the result of the experiment was disastrous, both parties to the contract had to bear their share of the responsibility. But a nation seldom allows that it has been wrong ; and Henry of Windsor had to serve as scapegoat for all the misfortunes of the realm, because Henry of Bolingbroke had committed his descendants to the unhappy compact.

Want of a strong central government was undoubtedly the complaint under which England was labouring in the middle of the fifteenth century, and all the grievances against which outcry was made were but symptoms of one latent disease.

Ever since the death of Henry the Fifth the internal government of the country had been steadily going from bad to worse. The mischief had begun in the young King's earliest years. The Council of Regency that ruled in his name had from the first proved unable to make its authority felt as a single individual ruler might have done. With the burden of the interminable French War weighing upon their backs, and the divisions caused by the quarrels of Beaufort and Gloucester dividing them into factions, the councillors had not enough attention to spare for home government. As early as 1428 we find them, when confronted by the outbreak of a private war in the north, endeavouring to patch up the quarrel by arbitration, instead of punishing the offenders on each side. Accounts of riotous assemblages in all parts of the country, of armed violence at parliamentary elections, of

party fights in London at Parliament time—like that
which won for the meeting of 1426 the name of the
Parliament of Bats (bludgeons)—grow more and
more common. We even find treasonable insurrection
appearing in the strange obscure rising of the political
Lollards under Jack Sharp in 1431, an incident which
shows how England was on the verge of bloodshed
twenty years before the final outbreak of civil war was
to take place.

But all these public troubles would have been of comparatively small importance if the heart of the nation
had been sound. The phenomenon which makes the
time so depressing is the terrible decay in private morals
since the previous century. A steady deterioration is
going on through the whole period, till at its end we
find hardly a single individual in whom it is possible to
interest ourselves, save an occasional Colet or Caxton,
who belongs in spirit, if not date, to the oncoming
renascence of the next century. There is no class
or caste in England which comes well out of the
scrutiny. The Church, which had served as the conscience of the nation in better times, had become dead
to spiritual things; it no longer produced either men of
saintly life or learned theologians or patriotic statesmen.
In its corporate capacity it had grown inertly orthodox.
Destitute of any pretence of spiritual energy, yet showing
a spirit of persecution such as it had never displayed in
earlier centuries, its sole activity consisted in hunting to
the stake the few men who displayed any symptoms of
thinking for themselves in matters of religion. So great
was the deadness of the Church that it was possible to
fall into trouble, like Bishop Pecock, not for defending

Lollardry, but for showing too much originality in attacking it.   Individually the leading churchmen of the day
were politicians and nothing more, nor were they as a
rule politicians of the better sort; for one like Beaufort,
who was at any rate consistent and steadfast, there are
many Bourchiers and George Nevilles and Beauchamps,
who merely sailed with the wind and intrigued for their
own fortunes or those of their families.

Of the English baronage of the fifteenth century we
shall have so much to say in future chapters that we
need not here enlarge on its characteristics.   Grown too
few and too powerful, divided into a few rival groups,
whose political attitude was settled by a consideration of
family grudges and interests rather than by any grounds
of principle, or patriotism, or loyalty, they were as unlike
their ancestors of the days of John or Edward the First as
their ecclesiastical contemporaries were unlike Langton or
even Winchelsey.   The baronage of England had often been
unruly, but it had never before developed the two vices
which distinguished it in the times of the Two Roses—a
taste for indiscriminate bloodshed and a turn for rapid
political apostasy.   To put prisoners to death by torture
as did Tiptoft Earl of Worcester, to desert to the enemy
in the midst of battle like Lord Grey de Ruthyn at
Northampton, or Stanley at Bosworth, had never before
been the custom of England.   It is impossible not to
recognise in such traits the results of the French War.
Twenty years spent in contact with French factions, and
in command of the godless mercenaries who formed the
bulk of the English armies, had taught our nobles lessons
of cruelty and faithlessness such as they had not before
imbibed.   Their demoralisation had been displayed in

France long ere the outbreak of civil war caused it to
manifest itself at home.

But if the Church was effete and the baronage
demoralised, it might have been thought that England
should have found salvation in the soundheartedness of
her gentry and her burgesses. Unfortunately such was
not to be the case. Both of these classes were growing
in strength and importance during the century, but when
the times of trouble came they gave no signs of aspiring
to direct the destinies of the nation. The House of Commons which should, as representing those classes, have
gone on developing its privileges, was, on the contrary,
thrice as important in the reign of Henry the Fourth as
in that of Edward the Fourth. The knights and squires
showed on a smaller scale all of the vices of the nobility.
Instead of holding together and maintaining a united
loyalty to the Crown, they bound themselves by solemn
sealed bonds and the reception of "liveries" each to the
baron whom he preferred. This fatal system, by which
the smaller landholder agreed on behalf of himself and
his tenants to follow his greater neighbour in peace and
war, had ruined the military system of England, and was
quite as dangerous as the ancient feudalism. The salutary old usage, by which all freemen who were not
tenants of a lord served under the sheriff in war, and not
under the banner of any of the baronage, had long been
forgotten. Now, if all the gentry of a county were bound
by these voluntary indentures to serve some great lord,
there was no national force in that county on which the
Crown could count, for the yeoman followed the knight
as the knight followed the baron. If the gentry constituted themselves the voluntary followers of the baronage,

and aided their employers to keep England unhappy, the class of citizens and burgesses took a very different line of conduct. If not actively mischievous, they were sordidly inert. They refused to entangle themselves in politics at all. They submitted impassively to each ruler in turn, when they had ascertained that their own persons and property were not endangered by so doing. A town, it has been remarked, seldom or never stood a siege during the Wars of the Roses, for no town ever refused to open its gates to any commander with an adequate force who asked for entrance. If we find a few exceptions to the rule, we almost always learn that entrance was denied not by the citizens, but by some garrison of the opposite side which was already within the walls. Loyalty seems to have been as wanting among the citizens as among the barons of England. If they generally showed some slight preference for York rather than for Lancaster, it was not on any moral or sentimental ground, but because the house of Lancaster was known by experience to be weak in enforcing "good governance," and the house of York was pledged to restore the strength of the Crown and to secure better times for trade than its rival.

Warwick was a strong man, born at the commencement of Henry the Sixth's unhappy minority, whose coming of age coincided with the outburst of national rage caused by the end of the disastrous French War, whose birth placed him at the head of one of the great factions in the nobility, whose strength of body and mind enabled him to turn that headship to full account. How he dealt with the problems which inevitable necessity laid before him we shall endeavour to relate.

# CHAPTER II

OF all the great houses of mediæval England, the Nevilles of Raby were incontestably the toughest and the most prolific. From the reign of John to the reign of Elizabeth their heritage never once passed into the female line, and in all the fourteen generations which lived and died between 1210 and 1600 there was only one occasion on which the succession passed from uncle to nephew, and not from father to son or grandson. The vitality of the Neville tribe was sufficient to bear them through repeated marriages with those only daughters and heiresses whose wedlock so often forebodes the extinction of an ancient house. Of four successive heads of the family between 1250 and 1350, all married ladies who were the last representatives of old baronial houses; but the Nevilles only grew more numerous, and spread into more and more branches, extending their possessions farther and farther from their original seat on the Durham moors till all the counties of the north were full of their manors.

The original source of the family was a certain Robert Fitz-Maldred, lord of Raby, who, in the reign of John, married Isabella de Neville, heiress of his neighbour

Geoffrey de Neville of Brancepeth. Robert's son Geoffrey, who united the Teesdale lands of his father with his mother's heritage hard by the gates of Durham, took the name of Neville, and that of Fitz-Maldred was never again heard in the family. The lords of Raby did not at first distinguish themselves in any way above the rest of the barons of the North Country. We find them from time to time going forth to the King's Scotch or French wars, serving in Simon de Montfort's rebel army, wrangling with their feudal superior the Bishop of Durham, slaying an occasional sheriff, and founding an occasional chantry, and otherwise conducting themselves after the manner of their kind. It was one of the house who led the English van against the Scots at the great victory of 1346, and erected the graceful monument which gave to the battlefield the name of Neville's Cross.     •

Only two characteristics marked these Nevilles of the thirteenth and fourteenth centuries; the largeness of their families—three successive lords of Raby boasted respectively of ten, eleven, and nine children—and their never-ending success in laying field by field and manor by manor. Robert Neville, who in the time of Henry the Third married Ida Mitford, added to his Durham lands his wife's broad Northumbrian barony in the valley of the Wansbeck. His son of the same name made Neville one of the greatest names in Yorkshire, when he wedded Mary of Middleham, and became in her right lord of Middleham Castle and all the manors dependent on it, reaching for a dozen miles along the Ure and running up to the farthest bounds of the forest of Coverdale. Robert the younger's heir, Ralph, emulated the good

fortune of his father and grandfather by securing as his
wife Euphemia, heiress of Clavering, who brought him
not only the half-hundred of Clavering in Essex, but the
less remote and more valuable lands of Warkworth on the
Northumbrian coast. Ralph's son John, though he
married as his first wife a younger daughter of the
house of Percy, secured as his second Elizabeth Latimer,
heiress of an old baronial house whose domains lay
scattered about Bucks and Bedfordshire.

Four generations of wealthy marriages had made the
Nevilles the greatest lords in all the North Country. Even
their neighbours, the Percies of Northumberland, were not
so strong. The "saltire argent on the field gules," and the
dun bull, the two Neville badges, were borne by hosts of
retainers. Three hundred men-at-arms, of whom fourteen
were knights and three hundred archers, followed the lord
of Raby even when he went so far afield as Brittany. For
home service against the Scots he could muster thrice as
many. More than seventy manors were in his hands, some
spread far and wide in Essex, Norfolk, Bedfordshire, and
Buckinghamshire, but the great bulk of them lying massed
in North Yorkshire and South Durham, around Raby and
Middleham, the two strong castles which were the centres
of his influence. Hence it was not surprising that King
Richard the Second, when he lavished titles and honours
broadcast on the nobility after his surprising *coup d'état*
of 1397, should have singled out the head of the Nevilles
for conciliation and preferment. Accordingly, Ralph
Neville, then in the thirty-fourth year of his age, was
raised to the dignity of an earl. Curiously enough, he
could not be given the designation of either of the
counties where the bulk of his broad lands lay. The

earldom of Durham was, now as always, in the hands of its bishop, *comes palatinus* of the county since the days of William the Conqueror.   The titles of York and of Richmondshire, wherein lay the other great stretch of Neville land, were vested in members of the royal house. The Percies had twenty years before received the title of Northumberland, the third county where the Nevilles held considerable property.   Hence Ralph of Raby had to be put off with the title of Westmoreland, though in that county he seems, curiously enough, not to have held a single manor.   The gift of the earldom was accompanied with the more tangible present of the royal honour of Penrith.

All these favours, however, did not buy the loyalty of Ralph Neville.  He was married to one of John of Gaunt's daughters by Katherine Swinford, and was at heart a strong partisan of the house of Lancaster.   Accordingly, when Henry of Bolingbroke landed at Ravenspur in July 1399, Westmoreland was one of the first to join him; he rode with him to Flint, saw the surrender of King Richard, and bore the royal sceptre at the usurper's coronation at Westminster.   Henry rewarded his services by making him Earl Marshal in place of the exiled Duke of Norfolk.

Earl Ralph went on in a prosperous career, aided King Henry against the rising of the Percies in 1403, and committed himself more firmly than ever to the cause of the house of Lancaster by putting down the insurrection which Scrope, Mowbray, and the aged Northumberland had raised in 1405.   Twice he served King Henry as ambassador to treat with the Scots, and twice the custody of the Border was committed to him as

warden.  When Bolingbroke died, and Henry of Mon-
mouth succeeded him, Earl Ralph was no less firm and
faithful.    At the famous Parliament of Leicester in
1414, when the glorious but fatal war with France was
resolved upon, he was one of the few who withstood the
arguments of Archbishop Chicheley and the appeals of
the Duke of Exeter and gave their voices against the
expedition.   He besought the King that, if he must
needs make war, he should attack Scotland rather than
France, the English title to that crown being as good,
the enterprise more hopeful, and the result more likely
to bring permanent profit, while—quoting an old popular
rhyme—he ended by saying that

He that wolde France win, must with Scotland first begin.

But all men cried "War! War! France! France!"  The
ambitious young King had his will; and the next spring
there sailed from Southampton the first of those many
gallant hosts of Englishmen who were to win so many
fruitless battles to their country's final loss, and leave
their bones behind to moulder in French soil, in the
trenches of Harfleur and Orleans or on the fields of
Beaugé and Patay.
    Every reader of Shakespeare has met Earl Ralph in
the English camp on the eve of the battle of Agincourt,
remembers his downhearted wish for a few thousands
of the "gentlemen of England now abed," and can
repeat by heart the young King's stirring reply to
his uncle's forebodings.  But, in fact, Earl Ralph was
not at Agincourt, nor did he even cross the sea.  He
had been left behind with Lord Scrope and the Baron
of Greystock to keep the Scottish March, and was far

away at Carlisle when Henry's little band of English
were waiting for the dawn on that eventful St. Crispin's
day.   Unless tradition errs, it was really Walter of
Hungerford who made the speech that drew down his
master's chiding.

Ralph was now growing an old man as the men of
the fifteenth century reckoned old age ; and while the bril-
liant campaigns of Henry the Fifth were in progress abode
at home, busied with statecraft rather than with war.
But his sons, and they were a numerous tribe, were one
after another sent across the seas to join their royal
cousin.   John, the heir of Westmoreland, was serving
all through the campaigns of 1417-18, and was made
governor of Verneuil and other places in its neighbourhood, after having held the trenches opposite the Porte
de Normandie during the long siege of Rouen, and
assisted also at the leaguer of Caen.   Ralph, Richard,
William, and George are found following in their elder
brother's footsteps as each of them arrived at the years
of manhood, and all earned their knighthood by services
done in France.

Meanwhile Earl Ralph, after surviving his royal nephew
some three years, and serving for a few months as one
of the Privy Council that governed in the name of the
infant Henry the Sixth, died on October 21st, 1425, at
the age of sixty-two, and was buried in the beautiful
collegiate church which he had founded at Staindrop,
hard by the gates of his ancestral castle of Raby.   There
his monument still remains, escaped by good fortune
from the vandalism of Edwardian and Cromwellian
Protestants.   He lies in full armour, wearing the peaked
basinet that was customary in his younger days, though

C

it had gone out of fashion ere his death. His regular features have little trace of real portraiture, and show no signs of his advancing years, so that we may conclude that the sculptor had never been acquainted with the man he was representing. Only the short twisted moustache, curling over the mail of the Earl's camail, has something of individuality, and must have corresponded to the life; for by 1425 all the men of the younger generation were close shaven, like King Henry the Fifth. On Earl Ralph's right hand, as befitted a princess of the blood royal, lies his second wife Joan of Beaufort; on his left Margaret Stafford, the bride of his youth and the mother of his heir.

# CHAPTER III

## RICHARD OF SALISBURY

EARL RALPH, surpassing all his keen and prolific ancestors not only in the success with which he pushed his fortunes, but in the enormous family which he reared, had become the father of no less than twenty-three children by his two wives. Nine were the offspring of Margaret of Stafford, fourteen of Joan of Beaufort. John, the heir of Westmoreland, had died a few years before his father, and the earldom passed to his son, Ralph the second, now a lad of about eighteen. But the greater number of the other twenty-two children still survived, and their fortunes influenced the after history both of the house of Neville and the kingdom of England to such an extent that they need careful statement.

The old Earl had turned all his energies into negotiating the marriages of his children, and partly by the favour of the two Henries, partly by judicious buying up of wardships in accordance with the practice of the fifteenth century, partly by playing on the desire of his neighbours to · be allied to the greatest house of the North Country, he had succeeded in establishing a compact family group, which was already by 1425 one of the factors to be reckoned with in English politics. The most important of these

connections by far was the wedding of his youngest
daughter Cecily to Richard Duke of York—a marriage
brought about by royal favour shortly before the Earl's
death, while both the contracting parties were mere
children; the Duke some eleven years old, the little bride
about nine.[1]  By this union Ralph of Westmoreland was
destined to become the ancestor of a score of kings and
queens of England.  It bound the house of Neville to
the Yorkist cause, and led away the children of Ralph
from that loyalty to Lancaster which had been the
cause of their father's greatness.  But at the time when
the marriage was brought about no one could well have
foreseen the Wars of the Roses, and we may acquit the
Earl of any design greater than that of increasing the
prosperity of his house by another marriage with a
younger branch of the royal stock.  His own union
with Joan of Beaufort had served him so well, that he
could desire nothing better for the next generation.
The elder brothers and sisters of Cecily of York,
if their alliances were less exalted than hers, were yet
wedded, almost without exception, to the most important
members of the baronage.

Of the elder family, the offspring of Earl Ralph
by Margaret of Stafford, the second son Ralph Neville
of Biwell married the co-heiress of Ferrers.  One sister
died young, another became a nun, but four of the
remaining five were married to the heirs of the houses
of Mauley, Dacre, Scrope of Bolton, and Kyme.  The

---

[1] Cecily is called Duchess of York in Earl's Ralph's will, so
the children must therefore have been already married; but the
consummation of the marriage was not till about 1438, when he
was twenty-six and she twenty-three years of age.

younger family, the children of Joan of Beaufort, made
even more fortunate marriages. Of the daughters, the
youngest, as we have stated above, wedded Richard of
York. Her elder sisters were united respectively to
John Mowbray Duke of Norfolk, Humphrey Stafford
Duke of Buckingham, and Henry Percy Earl of Northumberland—the grandson of Earl Ralph's old enemy
and the son of Hotspur. Of the six sons of Joan of
Beaufort, Richard the eldest married Alice Montacute, heiress of the earldom of Salisbury, and became
by her the father of the Kingmaker; with him we
shall have much to do. William, the second son, won
the heiress of Fauconbridge. George, the third son, was
made the heir of his half-uncle John Lord Latimer, and
by special grant succeeded to his uncle's barony. Robert
entered the Church, and by judicious family backing
became Bishop of Salisbury before he had reached his
twenty-fifth year, only to be transplanted ten years
later to Durham, the most powerful of the English
bishoprics, whose palatine rights he could thus turn to
the use of his numerous kindred. Finally, Edward, the
youngest brother, secured Elizabeth Beauchamp, heiress
of Abergavenny.

The numbers of the English baronage had been
rapidly decreasing since the reign of the third Edward,
and in the early years of Henry the Sixth the total number of peers summoned to a Parliament never exceeded
thirty-five. Among this small muster could be counted
one grandson, three sons, and five sons-in-law of Earl
Ralph.[1] A little later, one son and one grandson more

---

[1] The grandson was Ralph Earl of Westmoreland; the sons,
Richard of Salisbury, William of Fauconbridge, and George of

were added to the peers of the Neville kindred, and it
seemed probable that by the marriages of the next
generation half the English House of Lords would be
found to descend from the prolific stock of Raby.

In the first twenty years of the reign of Henry of
Windsor, while the young King's personal weakness was
not yet known, while his uncle of Bedford and his great-
uncle of Winchester stood beside the throne, and while
the war in France—though the balance had long turned
against England—was still far from its disastrous end,
the confederacies of the great baronial houses were of
comparatively little importance. The fatal question of
the succession to the Crown was still asleep, for the
young King was only just nearing manhood, and might,
for all that men knew, be the parent of as many warlike sons as his grandfather. It was not till Henry's
nine years of barren wedlock, from 1445 to 1454,
set the minds of his nobles running on the problem
of the succession, that the peace of England was really
endangered.

Richard Neville, the eldest of the sons of Earl Ralph's
second marriage, was born in 1399. He was too young
to follow King Henry to the siege of Harfleur and the
fight of Agincourt, but a few years later he accompanied
his half-brother John, the heir of Westmoreland, to the
wars of France. It was not in France, however, that the
years of his early manhood were to be spent, but on
the Scotch Border in the company of his father. When

Latimer; the sons-in-law, the Dukes of York, Norfolk, and
Buckingham, the Earl of Northumberland, and Lord Dacre.
Later, Edward Neville Lord Abergavenny, and Roger Lord Scrope,
appear; the first a son, the second a grandson.

he came of age and was knighted in 1420 he was made
the colleague of the old Earl in the wardenship of the
Western Marches.  This office he retained for several
years, and was in consequence much mixed up with
Scotch affairs, twice acting as commissioner to treat with
the Regent of Scotland, and escorting James the First to
the border of his kingdom when the English Council
released him from his long captivity.  We hear of him
occasionally at Court, as when, for example, he acted as
carver at the Coronation Banquet of the newly-wed
Queen Catherine, a ceremony which, according to
Monstrelet, "was performed with such splendid magni-
ficence that the like had never been seen since the time
of that noble knight Arthur, King of the English and
Bretons."

Richard had reached the age of twenty-six when, in
1425, he married Alice, the only child of Thomas Montacute Earl of Salisbury, who had just reached her
eighteenth year.  The Montacutes were not among the
wealthiest of the English earls—for his faithful adherence
to Richard the Second the last head of the house had lost
his life and his estates ; and although his son had been
restored in blood, and had received back many of the
Montacute lands, yet the list of his manors in the
Escheats Roll reads poorly enough beside those of the
Earls of Norfolk and Devon, March and Arundell.
Earl Thomas, in spite of his father's fate, had consented
to serve the house of Lancaster.

In 1425, as we have already mentioned, the old Earl,
Ralph of Westmoreland, died.  In his will, which has
been preserved, we find that he left his son Richard
little enough—"two chargers, twelve dishes, and a great

ewer and basin of silver, a bed of Arras, with red, white, and green hangings, and four untrained horses, the best that should be found in his stable." Evidently he thought that he need do nothing for this son on whom the earldom of Salisbury was bound to devolve. It was only to Ralph and Edward, the two among his surviving sons who had not yet inherited land from their wives, that the old Earl demised the baronies of Biwell and Winlayton, two of his outlying estates.

But in another respect the will of Earl Ralph was destined to prove a source of many heart-burnings in the house of Neville, and fated to break up the strict family alliance which made its strength. While he left the Durham lands of Neville, round his ancestral castle of Raby, to his grandson and heir, Ralph the second, he made over the larger part of his Yorkshire possessions not to the young Earl, but as jointure to his widow, Joan of Beaufort, the mother of Richard and the other thirteen children of his second family. The Countess, once mistress of Sherif Hoton Castle and the other North-Riding lands of Neville, had no thought of letting them pass away from her own sons to the descendants of her husband's first wife. They were destined to be diverted from the elder to the younger family. Here lay the source of many future troubles, but while the young Earl Ralph was still a minor the matter did not come to a head.

Three years after he lost his father, Richard Neville heard of the death of his father-in-law. The Earl of Salisbury had been appointed by John of Bedford Captain-General of all the English forces in France, and gathering together ten thousand men, all that the

Regent could spare, had marched to the fatal siege of
Orleans.   There in the early days of the leaguer, six
months before Joan the Maid came to the rescue of the
garrison, he had met his death.   As he watched the
walls from the tower on the bridge over the Loire, a
stone shot had torn away half his face; he died in a few
days, exhorting his officers with his last breath to per-
severe in the attack.

Thus Richard Neville became by the death of his
father-in-law Earl of Salisbury and master of the lands of
Montacute.   They lay, for the most part, on the borders
of Wiltshire and Hampshire, between Ringwood and
Amesbury, in the valleys of the Bourn and Avon.   The
castles of Christchurch and Trowbridge were the most
important part of the heritage from the military point of
view.   Some scattered manors in Berkshire, Dorset, and
Somerset served to swell its value.   Richard, now become
a considerable South Country baron, at once did homage
for his wife's lands, and was summoned as Earl of
Salisbury to the next Parliament, that of 1429.   At the
same meeting at which he took his seat his nephew,
Ralph the younger of Westmoreland, also appeared for
the first time, having now passed his minority and
entered into possession of such of the Neville lands as
had not been left to his step-mother.

It was beyond doubt the alienation of these lands
which led to the estrangement between the younger and
the elder Nevilles which we soon after find taking visible
form in troubles in the North.   Ralph, marrying a sister
of Henry Earl of Northumberland, became the firm
friend and ally of that house of Percy which his grandfather had done so much to humble.   Richard kept up

the old feud, and was always found on the opposite side
from his nephew. Presently (the exact year of the commencement of the quarrel is uncertain, but it was at its
height in 1435) we find them at actual blows in a manner
which brings out the fact that the "good and strong
governance," which Parliament after Parliament sighed
for in the reign of Henry the Sixth, had already become a
hopeless dream. Plaints come down from the North to the
Lord Chancellor that " owing to the grievous differences
which have arisen between Ralph Earl of Westmoreland,
and his brothers John and Thomas on the one hand,
and Joan Dowager-Countess of Westmoreland and her
son Richard Earl of Salisbury, on the other hand, have
of late assembled, by manner of war and insurrection,
great routs and companies upon the field, which have
done all manner of great offences as well in slaughter
and destruction of the King's lieges as otherwise, which
things are greatly against the estate and weal and peace
of this Royaume of England."

Of the details of this local war in Yorkshire we know
nothing. Some sort of accommodation was patched up,
by three arbitrators named by the Privy Council, for the
moment between uncle and nephew; but the grudge
rankled, and if ever England should be rent by civil
war, it took no prophet to foretell that the two Neville
earls would be found in opposite camps.

The old Countess Joan of Westmoreland died in 1440,
and left, as was natural, Middleham, Sherif Hoton,
and all the other lands of her jointure to her eldest son.
Richard of Salisbury thus became a much greater landholder in the North than he already was in the South.
His Hampshire and Wiltshire fiefs are for the future the

less important centre of his strength.   Sherif Hoton
becomes his favourite residence, and it is always as a
power in Yorkshire, not in Wessex, that he is mentioned
by the chroniclers of the day.

Neither of the Neville earls took any prominent part
in the never-ending French War.   Ralph of Westmoreland seems to have been wanting both in the appetite
for war and the keen eye for the main chance which had
hitherto distinguished the lords of Raby.   It was his
younger brother John who was the fighting man of the
older branch of Neville.   Earl Richard, on the other
hand, was energetic enough, but seems to have preferred
to push his fortunes at home, rather than to risk his
reputation in the unlucky wars where Somerset and
Suffolk and so many more earned ill-fame and unpopu-
larity.   We hear of him most often on the Scottish
Border, where he seems to have succeeded to the commanding position that had once been held by his father.
He was Captain of Berwick, and served as Warden both
of the Eastern and Western Marches, till at the end of
1435 he was sent as ambassador extraordinary to Edinburgh.   James the First, with whom he had to settle
some matters of Border feud, was his own connection, for
Salisbury's mother was aunt of Joan Beaufort, the young
Queen of Scots.   After quitting King James, only a few
months before his cruel murder at Perth, Earl Richard
went on an embassy of far greater importance, being
sent to France, along with his young brother-in-law the
Duke of York, to endeavour to patch up some agreement
that might end the series of disasters which had commenced with the death of the Duke of Bedford in the
previous year.   His mission failed, as indeed all missions

were bound to do that made after the treaty of Arras the same demands which the French had refused before it. Nevertheless, on his return, in 1437, Salisbury was made a member of the Privy Council, and took his seat in the body which ever since 1422 had been directing the fortunes of England.

This appointment fixed Salisbury in London for the greater part of the next ten years. We find from the records of the Privy Council that he was almost as regular an attendant at its meetings as was Cardinal Beaufort himself, the practical Prime Minister of the realm. His signature appears at the foot of countless documents, and his activity and appetite for business seem to have been most exemplary. So far as we can judge of his action, he appears to have sided with the great Cardinal, and not with the Opposition which centred round Humphrey Duke of Gloucester; but factions had not fully developed themselves as yet in the Council, and the definite parties which existed a few years later were only just beginning to sketch themselves out.

# CHAPTER IV

## THE KINGMAKER'S YOUTH

RICHARD, the second child but eldest son of Richard Neville of Salisbury and Alice Montacute, was born on November 22nd, 1428, just nineteen days after his grandfather had fallen at the siege of Orleans. We know absolutely nothing of his childhood—not even the place of his birth is recorded. We must suppose, but cannot prove, that his earliest days were passed on his mother's lands in Wessex, in moving about between Amesbury, Christchurch, and Ringwood as his parents' household made its periodical peregrinations from manor to manor according to the universal practice of the time. As a boy he must have visited his paternal grandmother, Joan of Beaufort, on her Yorkshire estates, when his father was fixed in the North as Warden of the Scotch Border. There probably he may have imbibed some of the old lady's dislike for her step-sons of the elder branch of the Nevilles, with whom she and his father were now at open variance. A little later he must have spent much time in London, when his father became a member of the Council of Regency, lodged at the "Tenement called the Harbour in the Ward of Dowgate," which his father and grandmother had received by will from his grandfather when the larger London house of the family, "Neville's Inn in Silver Street," passed with the Westmoreland earldom to the elder branch.

The fortunes of the house of Neville, as we have told them hitherto, have consisted of one interminable story of fortunate marriages. The reader must now be asked to concentrate his attention on another group of these alliances, a group which settled the whole history of the Kingmaker, and gave him the title of the earldom by which he is always named.

The Beauchamps of Warwick held one of the oldest English earldoms; they represented in direct descent the Henry of Newburgh to whom William Rufus had granted the county in 1190.[1] Richard Beauchamp, the head of the family at this time, was perhaps the worthiest and the most esteemed of the English nobles of his day. The "gracious Warwick," the "father of courtesy" as the Emperor Sigismund called him, had been through all the wars of Henry the Fifth, and won therein a name only second to that of the King himself. He had seen many cities and men in every land that lay between England and Palestine, and left everywhere behind him a good report. His virtues and accomplishments had caused him to be singled out as tutor and governor to the young King, Henry the Sixth; no better model, as all agreed, could be found for the ruler of England to copy. Nor did Warwick belie his task; he made Henry upright, learned, painstaking, conscientious to a fault. If he

---

[1] The Beauchamps came into the title in 1268, William de Beauchamp having married the grand-daughter of Henry of Newburgh, whose male issue had died out.

could but have made him as strong in body and spirit as he was morally, he would have given England the best king that ever she possessed.

Richard Beauchamp had married Isabel, heiress of Despenser, and widow of Richard, Lord of Abergavenny. Their family consisted of a son, Henry, a boy of ten, and a daughter, Anne, three years younger. In addition, the Countess of Warwick had an only daughter by her first husband, who was heiress of Abergavenny. Beauchamp and Richard Neville of Salisbury were the best of friends, and had determined to seal their friendship by intermarriage between their families. The alliance was destined to be complicated; each earl married his heir to his friend's daughter. The boy Henry, heir of Warwick, was affianced to Cecily Neville, Salisbury's six-year-old daughter; the boy Richard, heir of Salisbury, to Anne Beauchamp, daughter of Warwick. Nor was this all; the family relations were complicated by the marriage of Warwick's step-daughter Elizabeth, the heiress of Abergavenny, to Edward Neville the younger brother of Salisbury.

The boy Richard Neville received a competent dowry with his wife, but nothing more was expected to follow from the marriage. Fate, however, decreed otherwise.

The old Earl of Warwick died in 1439, full of years and honours. To him succeeded his son Henry, the husband of Cecily Neville, now sixteen years of age, and "a seemly lord of person." He had been brought up with the young King, a lad of his own years, and was Henry of Lancaster's bosom friend. When the King came of age he heaped on the young Beauchamp every honour that his affection could devise. Not only was he made Knight of the Garter and a Privy Councillor before he was nineteen, but he was created Duke of Warwick, and invested by the King's own hands with the lordship of the Isle of Wight. If Henry Beauchamp had lived, it would have been he, and not Suffolk and Somerset, who in a few years would have ruled England. But his career was broken in its earliest promise. Ere he had finished his twenty-third year Henry Beauchamp was cut off from the land of the living, and his lands and duchy devolved on his only child, a little girl but four years of age. Her wardship fell to William de la Pole Earl of Suffolk, already the declared adversary of Salisbury and the Neville family.

By the wholly unexpected death of Henry Beauchamp only this one frail life lay between the lad Richard Neville—he was sixteen when his brother-in-law died—and the earldom of Warwick. Nor was that life to continue long. The child Anne Beauchamp survived for three years more, and then died, aged seven, on June 23rd, 1449. She was buried by her grandam Constance, daughter of Edmund Duke of York, before the high altar of Reading Abbey.

The heiress of Warwick was now the elder Anne, Richard Neville's young wife,[1] and in her right Richard received the Beauchamp lands from the unwilling hands of the little countess's guardian, Suffolk. The patent which created him Earl of Warwick, and joined his wife in the grant, was dated July 23rd, 1449.

---

[1] Anne was the only heir of the full blood to Henry Duke of Warwick, but he had several half-sisters, to whom the reversion of the title was left by the patent which gave Richard and Anne Neville the earldom.

Thus, in the year in which he reached his twenty-first birthday, the future Kingmaker became "Earl of Warwick, Newburgh, and Aumarle, Premier Earl of England, Baron of Elmley and Hanslape, and Lord of Glamorgan and Morgannoc." He was now a much more important personage than his own father, for the Beauchamp and Despenser manors in the West Midlands and the Welsh Marches were broader by far than the Montacute lands in Wessex, or the Neville holding round Middleham.

A short survey of the items of the Beauchamp heritage is necessary to show how wide-spread was the power which was now placed in the hands of the young Richard Neville. Perhaps the most compact block of his new possessions was the old Despenser holding in South Wales and Herefordshire, which included the castles of Cardiff, Neath, Caerphilly, Llantrussant, Seyntweonard, Ewyas Lacy, Castle-Dinas, Snodhill, Whitchurch, and Maud's Castle. Caerphilly alone was a stronghold fit to resist ten thousand men, with its tremendous rings of concentric fortification; and the massive Norman masonry of Cardiff was still ready for good service. Between Neath and Ewyas Lacy lay no less than fifty manors of the Despenser heritage. In Gloucestershire was another group of estates which the Beauchamps had got from the Despensers —of which the chief were the wide and populous manors of Tewkesbury, Sodbury, Fairford, Whittington, Chedworth, Wickwar, and Lydney. In Worcestershire there was a compact block of land along the Severn and on both its banks; the largest manors included in it were Upton-on-Severn, Hanley Castle, and Bewdley, but there were twenty-four more estates of less importance, together with the Castle of Elmley, which had given the Beauchamps a

D

baron's title.   In Warwickshire, beside the fair town and
castle which went with the earldom, there were not any
very broad tracts of land—only nine manors in all, but
one of these was the wealthy manor of Tamworth.
Going farther south in the Midlands we find in Oxfordshire five manors and the forest of Wychwood reckoned
to the Beauchamps, and in Buckinghamshire the baronial
seat of Hanslape and seven manors more.   Nor was it
only in central England that Richard Neville could
count his estates; there were scattered holdings accru-
ing to him in Kent, Hampshire, Sussex, Essex, Hertford-
shire, Suffolk, Norfolk, Berkshire, Wiltshire, Somerset,
Devon, Cornwall, Northampton, Stafford, Cambridge,
Rutland, and Nottingham, amounting in all to forty-
eight manors.   Even in the distant North one isolated
possession fell to him—the castle of Barnard's-Castle on
the Tees.   If in addition to the manors we began to
count up the scattered knights' fees, the advowsons of
churches, the chantries, the patronage of abbeys, and
the tenements in towns, which formed part of the
Beauchamp heritage, we should never be done; but
these are all written in the Escheats Roll, whence the
antiquary may excavate them at his will.

The year 1449, in which Richard Neville attained
his majority and gathered in his wife's heritage, was the
turning-point in the reign of Henry the Sixth.   No more
critical time could have been found in the whole century
in which to place power and influence in the hands of a
young, able, and ambitious man.   For it was in 1449 that
the doom of the house of Lancaster was settled by the
final collapse of the English domination in France.   In
March came the fatal attack on Fougères which reopened

the war, an attack of which it is hard to say whether it was more foolish or wicked. In August, September, and October occurred with bewildering rapidity the fall of the great towns of eastern and central Normandy, ending with the capitulation of Rouen after a siege of only nineteen days.

It was this unparalleled series of disasters which made the existing Lancastrian rule unbearable to the English nation. Suffolk, the minister whose policy had led up to the disaster, and Somerset, the governor whose avarice had depleted the Norman garrisons, and whose rashness and ill faith had precipitated the outbreak of hostilities, were henceforth pursued by the bitter hatred of the majority of Englishmen. When it was found that King Henry identified their cause with his own, he himself— against whom no one had previously breathed a word— found for the first time that the current of public opinion was setting against him.

It was now that the final scission of the two parties that were afterwards to be known as Yorkist and Lancastrian took place. Every man of note in England had now to make his choice whether his personal loyalty to the King should lead him into acquiescing in the continuance in office of the ministers whom Henry openly favoured, or whether he would set himself in opposition to the Court faction, even though he was thereby led into opposition to the King.

From the first moment there was no doubt which of the two courses would be adopted by the two Neville earls of the younger branch. Warwick, now as always, acted in strict union with his father, and Salisbury had never been a friend of Suffolk. Moreover, they were both concerned in behalf of their relative the Duke of York, who by Somerset's contrivance had been sent into a kind of honorary exile in Ireland. When the crisis should come, it was already pretty certain that Salisbury and Warwick would be found on the side of York, and not on that of Suffolk and Somerset. But as yet, though men were growing excited and preparing for evil times, no one foresaw the exact shape which the troubles were to take. One thing only was certain, that Suffolk and Somerset were growing so hateful to the nation that an explosion against them would soon take place, and that when the explosion came there would be a large party among the leading men of England who would rejoice in its effects.

The most ominous sign of the times was that the great barons on both sides were already quietly arming, seeing to the numbers of their retainers, and concluding agreements to take their neighbours into their livery if the worst should come to the worst.

Nothing can be a more typical sign of the times than the treaty which Salisbury entered into with a Westmoreland knight, whose lands lay not far from his great holding in the North-Riding, as early as September 1449, the very month when Somerset was losing Normandy.

"This indenture made between Richard Earl of Salisbury, on the one part, and Walter Strykelande knight, on the other, beareth witness that the said Walter is retained and withholded with the said Earl for the term of his life, against all folk, saving his allegiance to the King. And the said Walter shall be well and conveniently horsed, armed, and arrayed, and always ready to bide come and go with to and for the said Earl, at all times and places, as well in time of peace as time of war, at the wages of the same Earl." Walter's following was worth having, being "servants, tenants, and inhabitants within the county of Westmoreland ; bowmen with horse and harness, sixty-nine ; billmen horsed and harnessed, seventy-four ; bowmen without horses, seventy-one ; bill-men without horses, seventy-six "—in fact a little army of two hundred and ninety men. The existence of a few such treaties as this between Salisbury and his northern neighbours shows clearly enough how the Neville power was built up, and how formidable to the public peace it might become. If once such treaties were in existence, how long would it be before the single clause "saving his allegiance" would begin to drop into oblivion ?

# CHAPTER V

## THE CAUSE OF YORK

IF 1449, the year of Warwick's accession to his wife's heritage, was a time of trouble for England, the year which immediately followed was far worse. The loss of the Norman fortresses was followed in a few months by the sporadic outbreaks of popular rage which might have been expected—outbreaks directed against all who could in any way be connected with the evil governance of the realm. Bishop Moleyns, the Keeper of the Privy Seal, was murdered by a mob of mutinous sailors at Portsmouth in January. But this blow was only a premonitory symptom of the storm which was brewing against Suffolk, the head of the Government. Four months later—the fatal battle of Formigny had been fought meanwhile, and the last English foothold in Northern France lost—he was driven from power by an irresistible demonstration of wrath, in which the whole nation, from the House of Lords to the London mob, took its part. Protected from legal punishment by the King's pardon, Suffolk fled over-sea; but some London ships waylaid him in the Straits of Dover, and he was seized and put to death after a mock trial by the captain of the *Nicholas of the Tower*. So well hated was he that his tragic end was received with exultation instead of remorse, and the political ballad-mongers of the day wrote many an insulting rhyme over his headless corpse.

Instead of mending matters, Suffolk's death was only the signal for worse troubles. Two months after his death came the great rebellion of the Kentishmen under Cade, accompanied by various other outbreaks in the southern counties. The insurgents were inspired by the same impulse which had slain Suffolk; they were set on making an end of all who had been responsible for the late disaster abroad and misgovernment at home. In London, Lord Say the Treasurer was caught and slain; in Wiltshire, Bishop Ayscough was beheaded by a mob of his own tenantry. But the rising, being but a sudden ebullition of rage with no plan or programme of reform, and being headed not by any respectable leader but merely by the disreputable adventurer Cade, died down of its own accord, without leaving any permanent effect on the governance of the realm. To make its power felt, the national discontent had to look for a responsible leader and a definite programme.

Both the Court party and the people knew where that leader might be found. Richard Duke of York, the heir-apparent to the childless King, lay across the sea in Ireland. He was an able soldier, much tried in the French wars, a firm and successful administrator—he had even succeeded in winning popularity in Ireland—and a man of blameless character, who had completely won the nation's confidence. Moreover, he was a man with a grievance; though the first prince of the blood, he was deliberately excluded from all place in the King's councils or share in the administration of the realm.

While in the midst of a successful campaign in France
he had been superseded by the unlucky Somerset, and
sent off to Ireland, apparently in the idea that like most
other rulers of that distressful country he would wreck
his reputation there.   But he had been fortunate, and
only increased his fame by the administration of the
island.   Already the Court party were murmuring
against him once more, and the people believed that
some other exile would ere long be found for him.   As
the ballad-monger sang—

> The falcon flies and has no rest
> Till he wot where he may build his nest.

Cade's rebels had used the Duke's name largely in
their proclamations, but there seems no real ground for
supposing that they had held any communication with
him.   The only evidence against him was that all discontented parties and persons spoke of him as the man
that should right them some day.   Nevertheless threats
were made that he should be indicted for high treason,
and action against him was apparently imminent.   Then
at last York took the initiative.   He threw up the
government of Ireland, crossed over to Wales, and came
up to London with a considerable body of his tenants
from the Marches at his back.   There he claimed and
obtained an interview with the King, in which he
declared his loyalty, and received Henry's assurance
that no harm was intended against him.   This done, he
retired to his estates on the Welsh border.   But he had
now definitely put himself at the head of the opposition
to the Court party, whom he had bitterly rated in his
remonstrance to the King.

The discontent of England had found its mouthpiece and its leader in this resolute prince, "a man of low stature, with a short square face, and somewhat stout of body," like his uncle Edmund of York, who had fallen at Agincourt rather stifled in his armour than slain by his wounds.

Our whole view of the conduct of Warwick in the ten years between 1450 and 1460 must be determined by our decision as to the designs and conduct of his uncle of York during that period. If we conclude that the Duke was aiming at the crown from the first, then we cannot but believe that his brother-in-law Salisbury and his nephew Warwick must have known or guessed his wishes, and on them must rest almost as great a share of blame for the outbreak of the Civil War as lies on the head of York himself. For the gain of their family we must believe that they sacrificed the peace of their country. This view has been commonly adopted by historians; it was set forth in every Lancastrian manifesto of the time; it was repeated by the historians who wrote under the Tudors, and it still prevails.

Another view, however, was taken by the majority of the English people in York's own day. Wherever in England public spirit ran strong, wherever wealth had accumulated and civilisation had advanced, a sympathy for the Yorkist party manifested itself. Kent, London, and East Anglia were always strongly on the Duke's side. But if York had been an ambitious schemer, deliberately upsetting the peace of the realm for his own ends, we should not expect to find his supporters among those parts of the nation to whom peace and good governance were above all things profitable.

A glance through the pages of the chroniclers who were contemporary with the war, Harding, Gregory, William of Worcester, Whethamsted, the anonymous English chronicler in the Camden Series, shows that to the majority of the English people York passed not as a disturber of the peace, but as a wronged and injured man, goaded into resistance by the machinations of the Court party. In one aspect he was regarded as a great lord of the royal blood excluded from his rightful place at the Council board, and even kept out of the country by his enemies who had the King's ear. In another he was regarded as the leader and mouthpiece of the Opposition of the day, of the old and popular war-party which inherited the traditions of Henry the Fifth and Humphrey of Gloucester—a party, indeed, whose views (as we have said elsewhere) were unwise and even immoral, but one which might reasonably ask to be taken into consideration by those who managed the affairs of the realm. In these days of ours when Ministries prove incapable and grow discredited the Opposition has its turn at the helm in the natural course of things. In the fifteenth century the old methods which had served Simon de Montfort, and the Lords Ordainers of 1322, were still the only ones which could be used against ministers who were out of sympathy with the nation. York was doing at St. Albans much what Earl Simon had done at Lewes.

This too must be said, that if disaster without and disorder within are to be held sufficient to discredit any rule, there had never been a time since the evil days of Bannockburn when England had more right to be discontented with her rulers. Moreover, there was no

chance that things would grow better; as long as the
Queen and her friends ruled the King, so long would
things continue as they were.  Men thought at one
moment that with the removal of Suffolk the evil times
would come to an end.  But when an outburst of
popular fury swept Suffolk to his end—and be it remembered that there is no evidence to connect York with
Suffolk's tragic death—the ascendency of Somerset proved
as disastrous and as hopeless as that of his predecessor.
And when Somerset fell at St. Albans men hoped once
more that matters would right themselves; but the less-
known ministers who soon succeeded to the helm—Beaumont and the Earl of Wiltshire—proved quite as unprofit-
able servants to the nation.  As long as the Queen was
at the King's side to choose his councillors for him, so
long would the discontent of England continue to in-
crease.  Margaret's misfortunes make us loath to speak
evil of her, but in fairness to the Yorkists it must be
remembered that she was the most detestable politician.
that England had known.  It is usual to call the dislike
of the nation for her a stupid prejudice against a
foreigner; but there was surely some reason for hating
the woman who sold Berwick to the Scots and Calais to
the French, who reintroduced the hateful practice of
sweeping attainders in the Parliament of 1459, who succeeded in turning loyalty into a party-cry by making the
King a party-leader.  Well might she confess to a
foreign friend on one occasion "that if the great lords
of her own party knew what she was doing, they would
themselves be the first to rise and put her to death," for
she it was who committed that foulest treason of all—
which consists in sending secretly to tell a foreign enemy

where to strike, in order that by his blow a party-end
may be served. In 1457, when the realm was for a
moment at peace, she deliberately incited the French
admirals to make their great descent on the Kentish
coast which ended in the fearful sack of Sandwich,
merely because she knew that such a disaster would be
counted against her political enemies the Yorkists. There
is nothing to be compared to it in English history except
the conduct of the arch-traitor Marlborough in 1694 over
the affair of Brest.

·The English hatred of Queen Margaret was no prejudice, but a wholesome instinct which led the English
nation to recognise its enemy. She made herself a
party-leader, and as a party-leader she had to be treated.
York's ten years' strife with her must be regarded not
so much as the rebellion of a subject against his
sovereign, but as the struggle of one party-leader against
another with the primitive weapons which alone were
possible in the constitutional crises of that day. But
even if we grant that York had his excuses, and that
his general attitude does not stand self-condemned at
the first glance, it remains to be seen how far his programme was justifiable, and how far he honestly endeavoured to carry it out to the best of his abilities.
That he was an able, self-confident, ambitious man, with
the fixed idea that he was the victim of the intrigues of
the Court party, and that but for those intrigues he would
be able to assume the position in the King's Council to
which his birth entitled him, we know well. That when
the King remained childless for nine years after his
marriage, York could not help dwelling on the near
prospect of his accession to the throne, was matter of

notoriety. When that prospect was suddenly taken from him by the unexpected birth of an heir to the crown, York's spirits were deeply dashed, and his friends murmured in secret about changelings and bastards. But his own attitude and language were still everything that could be required by the most exacting critic; he shared in the rejoicings at the birth of Prince Edward, and joined the Commission which was appointed to confer on the infant the title of Prince of Wales. All his speeches and manifestoes for the next six years were full even to satiety of professions of loyalty to the King, and no claims on his own part were ever made for anything more than that right of access to the King's ear to which he was obviously entitled. The Yorkist declarations are always statements of grievance and demands for reform, set forth on public grounds; they show no traces of dynastic claims. The actions of the party, too, are quite in keeping with their declarations. That they would take the King into their own hands, and not leave him in those of the Somersets or Wiltshire or Beaumont, they had always stated, and they attempted no more when they had the chance. The best criterion of York's honesty is his conduct after the first battle of St. Albans, when the fortune of war had placed the King's person in his power. He then proceeded to give Henry new ministers, but did absolutely nothing more. No word about the succession was breathed, nor was it even attempted to punish those who had previously ruled the kingdom so ill. With a wise moderation all the blame was heaped on Somerset—and Somerset was dead, and could suffer no harm whatever might be laid to his charge.

It may then fairly be argued that Warwick and all
those who followed Richard of York in peace and war
down to the year 1460 had an honest programme, and
could in all sincerity trust their leader, when he assured
them that his ends were national and not personal,—the
reform of the governance of England, not the establishment of the house of York on the throne.   We shall see
that when, after enduring and inflicting many evils, York
did at last lay claim to the throne, his own party, headed
by Warwick, firmly withstood him and compelled him, in
adherence to his and their original pledges, to leave King
Henry his throne and content himself with the prospect
of an ultimate succession.

This being so, it is only just to Warwick and the
other Yorkist leaders to give them the benefit of the
doubt wherever their conduct admits of an honourable
explanation, and not to judge their earlier assertions or
claims or complaints in the light of later events.   On
these lines we shall proceed to describe the young Earl's
actions down to the final outbreak of war in 1459.

# CHAPTER VI

## THE BEGINNING OF THE CIVIL WAR: ST ALBANS

FROM the moment when York returned from Ireland without the King's permission, and commenced to expostulate with his royal kinsman against the doings of Somerset and the rest of the Court party, the progress of events was sure and steady. Nothing save some extraordinary chance could have warded off the inevitable Civil War. That it did not break out sooner was only due to the fact that York was as cautious as he was determined, and was content to wait for the crown which the King's sickly constitution and long-barren wedlock promised him. Moreover, the Court party themselves had no desire to push matters to extremities against the man who was in all probability to become their king at no very distant date. For more than four years the struggle between York and Somerset proceeded before swords were actually drawn; they fought by manifestoes and proclamations, by Acts of Parliament, by armed demonstrations, but neither would actually strike the first blow.

The final crisis was brought about by the juxtaposition of two events of very different character. In August 1453 the King fell into a melancholy madness, exactly

similar to that which had afflicted his unfortunate grandfather Charles the Sixth of France. He sat for days without moving or speaking; whatever was said to him he
cast down his eyes and answered nought. The King's
insanity was a deadly blow to Somerset, for he was
helpless without the royal name to back him. York, on
the other hand, with the general consent of the nation,
assumed the direction of affairs, and became the King's
lieutenant. He was afterwards made Protector of the
Realm. This promised a final termination to the civil
troubles of the realm.

But a few months after the King had become deranged,
the whole face of affairs was changed by the birth of an
heir to the crown. The Queen was delivered of a
son on October 13th. This unexpected event—for
the royal pair had been childless for nine years—was of
fatal import to York. It took away the safety that had
proceeded from the fact that his enemies believed that
he was one day to reign over them, and it made York
himself desperate. He came to the conclusion that he
must be either regent or nothing; to save his head he
must resort to desperate measures, and no more shrink
from arms.

It is at this moment that Warwick begins to come to
the front. In the earlier phases of York's struggle with
Somerset he and his father had avoided committing
themselves unreservedly to their kinsman's party; when
he made his armed demonstration in 1452 they had not
appeared at his side, but had negotiated in his favour
with the King. In the Parliament of January 1454
they took part more decidedly in his favour. Mischief
was brewing and every peer came up to London with

hundreds of retainers in his train. It was then noticed that Warwick "with a goodly fellowship at his back" rode up in company with his uncle of York, and that Salisbury with sevenscore men-at-arms joined him in London.

York's preponderance in the councils of the realm was at once followed by the promotion of his Neville kinsmen. In December Warwick, now aged twenty-five, was made a member of the Privy Council. In April, after York had been made Protector, Salisbury was made Chancellor of the Realm; it was forty-four years since a layman had held the post.

The King was insane for sixteen months, and for that time York governed the realm with discretion and success. His conduct with regard to the question of the succession was scrupulously correct. The infant Prince Edward was acknowledged heir to the throne, and York, Warwick, and Salisbury were all members of the Commission which in April invested him with the title of Prince of Wales. The Court party were treated with leniency; only Somerset, against whom the popular outcry was as loud as ever (he had nearly been torn to pieces by a London mob in 1453), was committed to custody in the Tower, where he lay all the time of the King's madness. The country seemed satisfied and the prospect was fair.

To the Nevilles these two last years of promotion and success had only been clouded by a fierce quarrel with the house of Percy. In 1453 Salisbury had been celebrating the marriage of his fourth son, Thomas, to a niece of Lord Cromwell at Tattershall in Yorkshire. As he left the feast his retainers fell into an affray with some followers of Thomas Percy Lord Egremont, a

E

younger son of the Earl of Northumberland. Out of
this small spark sprung a sudden outbreak of private
war all over the counties of York and Northumberland,
in which the Nevilles were headed by John, Salisbury's
second son, and the Percies by Egremont. The trouble
lasted more than a year, and was only ended by York
going in person, after he had been made Protector, to
pacify the combatants. In this he succeeded, but the
Percies maintained that they had been wronged, and were
ever afterwards strong supporters of Somerset and the
Queen.

In December 1454 King Henry came to his senses,
and York resigned the protectorate. The King's recovery was in every way unfortunate; the moment that
he was himself again he fell back into the hands of the
Court party. His first act was to release Somerset from
the Tower, and declare him a true and faithful subject.
His next was to dismiss York and Salisbury from all
their offices, and with them several other high function-
aries who were enemies of Somerset, including Tiptoft
Earl of Worcester, the Lord Treasurer. The disgraced
peers retired to their estates—York to Sendal, Salisbury
to Middleham.

But worse was to come. In May a Council, to which
were summoned neither York, Salisbury, Warwick, nor
any other of the old councillors who were their friends,
met at Westminster. This body summoned a Parliament to meet at Leicester, "for the purpose of providing
for the safety of the King's person against his enemies."
Who would be declared the enemies York and Salisbury
could guess without difficulty; and what would be done
with these enemies they knew well enough. Imprison-

ment would be the least evil to be feared at the hands of Somerset.

The fatal moment had come. York was desperate, and resolved to anticipate the vengeance of his adversaries. The moment that the news came, he called out his Yorkshire retainers, and sent to ask the aid of his friends all over England. Salisbury joined him at once with the Neville tenants from his North-Riding estates, and without a moment's delay York and his brother-in-law marched on London. Warwick fell in with them on the way, but no other friend came to their aid, though the Duke of Norfolk was getting together a considerable force on their behalf in East Anglia.

York's little army marched down the Ermine Street; on May 20th he lay at Royston in Cambridgeshire. Beside the two Nevilles he had only one other peer in his company, Lord Clinton, and the knights present were merely the personal followers of York and Salisbury. Except a few of Warwick's Midland tenants, the whole army was composed of the Yorkshire retainers of York and Salisbury, and the chroniclers speak of the whole army as the Northern Men. More troops could have been had by waiting, but the Duke knew that if he delayed, the enemy would also gain time to muster in strength. At present the lords of the King's Council were quite unprepared for war, and the rapid march of York's little army had not allowed them time for preparation.

On the 21st the Duke felt his way southward along the line of the Ermine Street, and lay at Ware. There he and the two Earls indited a laborious apology for their arrival in arms to "their most redoubted sovereign Lord the King." They were "coming in grace, as true and humble liegemen, to declare and show at large their loyalty," and sought instant admission to the royal presence that they might convince him of the "sinister, malicious, and fraudulent reports of their enemies."

Somerset read clearly enough the meaning of York's march on London, and even before the Duke's manifesto was received, had stirred up the King to have recourse to arms. Many of the great lords of the King's party were in London, but they were surprised by the sudden approach of the enemy, and had brought few followers with them. Thus it came to pass that although the King marched out of Westminster on the 21st with many of the greatest lords of England at his back, he had less than three thousand combatants in his host. With him went forth his half-brother Jasper of Pembroke, the Dukes of Somerset and Buckingham, the Earls of Northumberland, Devon, Stafford, Wiltshire, and Dorset, and Lords Clifford, Dudley, Berners, and Roos, nearly a quarter of the scanty peerage of England. York's manifesto reached the King as he marched through Kilburn, but Somerset sent it back without allowing it to reach the royal hands. That night the army turned off the Roman road to shelter themselves in the houses of Watford; but next morning very early all were afoot again, and long before seven o'clock King Henry and his host reached St. Albans. The royal banner was pitched in St. Peter's Street, at the northern end of the straggling little town, the outlets of the streets were barricaded, and then the troops dispersed to water their horses and prepare breakfast. An hour

later York and his forces appeared, advancing cautiously
from the east along the Hertford Road.   Hearing of
the King's march on Watford, the Duke had left the
direct line of advance on London, and set out to seek
his enemies.   When St. Albans was found to be strongly
held, York, Salisbury, and Warwick drew up their four
thousand men in battle array, in a field called Keyfield
to the east of the town, and paused before attacking.
They were hardly arrived before the Duke of Buckingham was seen emerging with a herald from the barricade
which closed the eastern outlet of the town.   This
elderly nobleman was Salisbury's brother-in-law and
Warwick's uncle; he was sure of a fair hearing from
the insurgents, for he had never been identified with
the party of Suffolk and Somerset, and was in arms out
of pure loyalty to the King.   Arrived in the presence
of the rebel leaders, Humphrey of Buckingham demanded the cause of their coming and the nature of
their intentions.   The Duke of York replied by charging
his master's envoy with a message for the royal ears,
which began with all manner of earnest protestations
of loyalty, proceeded with a vague declaration that the
intent of his coming in arms was righteous and true,
and ended with a peremptory demand that it would
please the King "to deliver up such persons as he
might accuse, to be dealt with like as they have deserved."   Buckingham brought the message back and repeated it to the King, as he sat in the house of Westley,
the Hundredman of the town of St. Albans, whither
he had retired after his arrival.   When the Duke's
demand was made known, for once in his life the saintly
King burst out into a fit of passion.   "Now I shall

know," he cried, "what traitors are so bold as to raise a
host against me in my own land.   And by the faith
that I owe to St. Edward and the Crown of England, I
will destroy them every mother's son, to have example
to all traitors who make such rising of people against
their King and Governour.   And for a conclusion, say
that rather than they shall have any lord here with me
at this time, I will this day for his sake and in this
quarrel stand myself to live or die."

When this answer came to the Duke of York he
made no immediate attack on the town, but turned to
harangue his troops.   He told them that the King refused
all reformation or reparation, that the fate of England
lay in their hands, and that at the worst an honourable
death in the field was better than the shame of a traitor's
end, which awaited them if they lost the day.   Then he
launched the whole body in three divisions against
the barricades which obstructed the northern, southern,
and eastern exits of the town.

The hour was half-past eleven o'clock, for the inter-
change of messages between the King and York had
consumed four hours of the morning.   The royal troops,
seeing Buckingham coming and going between the two
armies, had believed that an agreement would be patched
up without fighting.   Many had left their posts, and
some had disarmed themselves.   When the Duke's men
were seen in motion every man ran to arms, and the
bells of the abbey and the churches ringing the alarm
set monks and townsmen to prayers, in good hope that the
shield of their warrior-patron would be stretched over them
to ward off the plundering bands from the North, the

Gens Boreæ, gens perfidiæ, gens prona rapinæ,

whose advent always sent Abbot Whethamsted into an
ecstasy of bad Latin verses.

The first rush of the Yorkists was beaten off at all
the three points which they attacked.   Lord Clifford on
the London Road "kept the barriers so strongly that the
Duke might not in any wise, for all the power he had,
break into the streets."   Warwick too, who led the left
division of the Yorkist host, was repulsed in his attack
on the southern exit of the town.   But the Earl's quick
military eye, now for the first time exercised, had
marked that the Lancastrians, though strong enough to
hold the barricades, had not enough men to defend the
long straggling line of houses which formed the southern
extension of the town.   Gathering together his repulsed
retainers, he broke into the gardens which lay behind the
houses of Holywell Street, and bursting open the back-
doors of several dwellings, ran out into the main thorough-
fare of the town, "between the sign of the Chequers and
the sign of the Key, blowing up his trumpets and shouting with a great voice, A Warwick !   A Warwick !"—a
cry destined to strike terror into Lancastrian ears on
many a future battlefield.   Warwick's sudden irruption
took the defenders of the barricades in the rear, but
they faced about and stood to it manfully in the streets.
The Lancastrian line was broken, and the Yorkist centre,
where Sir Robert Ogle led on the Duke's own followers
from the Northern Marches, now burst into the market-
place in the centre of the town to aid Warwick.

For one wild half-hour the arrows flew like sleet up
and down St. Peter's Street, and the knights fought
hand to hand in the narrow roadway.   But the Lancastrians were overmatched.   The King received an arrow

in the neck, and was led bleeding into the house of a
tanner. Somerset, the cause of the battle, was stricken
dead on the doorstep of an inn named the Castle. Sir
Philip Wentworth, the King's standard-bearer, threw
down his banner and fled away. James of Ormond the
Irish Earl of Wiltshire, and Thorpe the Speaker of the
House of Commons, followed him. But the other
leaders of the King's army were less fortunate. The
Earl of Northumberland and Lord Clifford were slain.
The Earl of Dorset was desperately wounded, and left
for dead in the street. The Duke of Buckingham, with
an arrow sticking in his face, took sanctuary in the
abbey. The Earls of Stafford and Devon, both wounded,
and Lord Dudley, yielded themselves prisoners. Only
sixscore men had been slain in the King's army, but
the larger part were persons of mark, for, as was often
the case in that century, the lightly-equipped archers
and billmen could fling down their arms and get away
with ease, while the knights and nobles, fighting on foot
in their cumbrous armour, could not make speed to fly
when the day was lost. So it came to pass that of the
one hundred and twenty Lancastrians who fell, only
forty-eight were common men, the rest were nobles,
knights, and squires, or officers of the King's household.
On the next day the victors marched on London, vainly
hoping, perhaps, that with the death of Somerset and
the capture of the King the days of the weak government of Lancaster were over.

The Duke and his followers thought, as yet, of nothing
more than a change of ministry. Their conduct shows
that they had nothing more in hand than the replacing
of the Court party in the great offices of State by persons

who should be more in touch with their own views and
the will of the nation. The Chancellorship was left in
the hands of Archbishop Bourchier, whom the Yorkists
felt that they could trust; but the Earl of Wiltshire
was replaced as Treasurer by Lord Bourchier, the Archbishop's brother. The Duke of York became Constable;
Warwick superseded the dead Somerset as Captain of
Calais; Salisbury was made Steward of the Duchy of
Lancaster. A little later Warwick's younger brother
George Neville was given the wealthy bishopric of
Exeter, though he had only just reached his twenty-
sixth year. A Parliament summoned in July ratified
these appointments, and chose as its Speaker Sir John
Wenlock, of whom we shall frequently hear again as one
of Warwick's firmest friends and adherents. A strongly-
worded oath of allegiance to King Henry was taken by
the Duke of York, and all the House of Lords with him,
and the new ministry started on its career with favourable prospects. The only trouble for the moment came
from an ill-judged attempt in Parliament to fix the
responsibility for the "Ill Day of St. Albans" on definite
persons. Warwick named Lord Cromwell as one of
those most to blame, and when Cromwell gave an angry
reply, there sprang up such an altercation between them
that men feared a breach of the peace. That night
Cromwell borrowed the Earl of Shrewsbury's men-at-
arms to guard his house; but Warwick had cooled down
and no more came of the quarrel, for the Parliament
very wisely concluded to lay all the responsibility for the
Civil War on Somerset, who was dead and could not
reply.

York's authority in the kingdom was made more

secure for the moment when King Henry fell once again into one of his fits of melancholy madness in October. The Parliament reassembled and appointed the Duke Regent, but on February 25th Henry came to his senses, and at once relieved York of his office. There followed a time of unrest and rumours of war, but for some months longer the Duke succeeded in maintaining his place at the helm. But trouble was always impending. Warwick, whose trained and paid soldiery in the garrison of Calais were the only permanent military force belonging to the Crown, had to come over on several occasions to back his uncle. At one time we hear that York feared to be waylaid on his way to Parliament, and got Warwick with three hundred men "all in jacks or brigandines" to escort him thither, "saying that if he had not come so strong he would have been distressed, but no man knew by whom, for men think verily that there is no man able to undertake any such enterprise."

York was not wrong, however, in thinking that there were those who were ready to risk much to get him out of power. Since Somerset was dead, the leadership of the Court party had fallen into very firm and determined hands, those of Margaret of Anjou, and the Queen had resolved to exercise the unbounded influence that she enjoyed over her husband to make him evict his Yorkist ministers the moment that it seemed safe so to do. For her resolve she had this much excuse, that the new government was at first no more fortunate than the old in enforcing order in the kingdom, for into the period of York's ascendency fell the worst private war that had been seen for a generation. Courtney Earl of Devon and Lord Bonville fell to blows in the West, and

fought a battle outside Exeter with four thousand men
a side ; the Earl won, and signalised his victory by ran-
sacking the cathedral and carrying off several of the
canons as prisoners.   Yet he was not brought to justice
for this abominable sacrilege, even though he was of the
party which was opposed to York.   But Margaret was
not entitled to blame York for the state of the kingdom,
for we find that she deliberately went to work to give
the Duke trouble, by stirring up foreign enemies against
England.   A Scotch raid in the summer of 1456 was
more than suspected to be due to her intrigues ; and it
is certain that while the Duke was officially taking the
Scots to task in the King's name, the King was disavow-
ing York's warlike despatches in private letters to James
the Second.   When we know that a year later Margaret
was not above setting on the French to ravage the
Kentish sea-ports for her own private purposes, we can
understand a little of the hatred with which she was
followed by the Commons of the south-eastern counties.

# CHAPTER VII

IT was in the four years which lay between the fight of
St. Albans and the second outbreak of the Civil War
in 1459 that Warwick made his reputation and won
his popularity. Up to 1455 he had been known merely
as a capable young nobleman who followed in all things
the lead of his father Salisbury. He had not as yet
been given any independent command, nor trusted
alone in any business of importance, though he was
already far beyond the age at which many personages
of the fifteenth century began to take a prominent part
in politics. He was now twenty-seven years old, eleven
years older than Henry the Fifth when he took over the
government of Wales, nine years older than Edward the
Fourth when he won the fight of Mortimer's Cross.
There were no signs in Warwick of that premature development which made so many of his contemporaries
grown men at sixteen, and worn-out veterans at forty.

Unlike most of his house, Warwick had not been
blessed with a large family. Anne Beauchamp had borne
him two daughters only, both of them delicate girls who
did not live to see their thirtieth year. No male offspring was ever granted him, and it seemed evident

that the lands of Warwick and Despenser were destined to pass once more into the female line.  But
the day was far distant when this was to be, and
Richard Neville's sturdy frame and constitution,—his
*altitudo animi cum paribus corporis viribus*, to quote Polidore Vergil,—promised many a long year of vigorous
manhood.

Warwick had already become a prominent figure in
English politics, not so much from the breadth of his
lands or from the promise of military prowess that he
had shown at St. Albans, as from the almost universal
popularity which he enjoyed.  He was far from being
the haughty noble, the Last of the Barons, whom later
writers have drawn for us.  His contemporaries speak
of him rather as the idol of the Commons and the
people's friend: "his words were gentle, and he was
affable and familiar with all men, and never spoke of
his own advancement, but always of the augmentation
and good governance of the realm."  There never was
any peer who was a better lord to his own retainers,
nor was there any who bore himself more kindly
towards the Commons; hence he won a personal popularity to which his father Salisbury never attained,
and which even his uncle of York could not rival.

As a school for a man of action there could have
been no better post than the governorship of Calais.
The place had been beset by the French ever since the
loss of Normandy in 1450, and was never out of danger
of a sudden attack.  Three times in the last six years
considerable armies had marched against it, and had
only been turned away by unexpected events in other
quarters.  Bickering with the French garrisons of

Boulogne and other neighbouring places never ended,
even in times of nominal truce.    To cope with the
enemy the Captain of Calais had a garrison always
insufficient in numbers, and generally in a state of
suppressed mutiny; for one of the chief symptoms of
the evil rule of Suffolk and Somerset had been the
impotence of the central government to find money for
the regular war-expenses of the realm.    The garrison of
Calais was perpetually in arrears of pay, and successive
governors are found complaining again and again that
they were obliged to empty their own pockets to keep
the soldiers to their post.    Even the town-walls had
been allowed to fall into disrepair for want of money to
mend them.

Besides his military duties the Captain of Calais had
other difficult functions.    He lay on the frontier of
Flanders, and a great part of the trade between England
and the dominions of the house of Burgundy passed
through his town, for Calais was the "staple" for that
branch of commerce.    Hence he had to keep on good
terms with the neighbouring Burgundian governors,
and also—what was far more difficult—to endeavour to
sweep the Straits of Dover clear of pirates and of French
privateers, whenever there was not an English fleet at
sea.    This was no sinecure, for of late English fleets had
been rarely seen, and when they did appear had gone
home without effecting anything useful.    The man who
could with a light heart undertake to assume the post
of Captain of Calais must have been both able and
self-confident.

Warwick held the place from August 1455 to August
1460, and combined with it the post of "Captain to guard

the Sea" from October 1457 to September 1459.   His
tenure of office was in every way successful.  The garrison
was brought up to its full strength, and put in good
discipline—largely, we may suspect, at the expense of
the Earl's own pocket, for after October 1456, when the
Duke of York ceased to be Protector, Warwick got little
money or encouragement from England.   He raised
the strength of his troops to about two thousand men,
and was then able to assume the offensive against the
neighbouring French garrisons.   His greatest success
was when, in the spring of the third year of his office, he
led a body of eight hundred combatants on a daring raid
as far as Étaples, forty miles down the coast of Picardy,
and took the town together with a fleet of wine-ships
from the south of France, which he put up to ransom,
and so raised a sum large enough to pay his men for
some months.   Falling into a disagreement also with
the Burgundian governors in Flanders, he made such
havoc in the direction of Gravelines and St. Omer that
Duke Philip was obliged to strengthen his garrisons
there, and finally was glad to consent to a pacification.
The negotiations were held in Calais and came to a
successful conclusion, for a commercial treaty was concluded with Flanders as well as a mere suspension
of arms.

   While Warwick lay at Calais he could not pay very
frequent visits to England, for French alarms were
always abounding.  In June 1456, for example, "men
said that the siege should come to Calais, for much
people had crossed the water of Somme, and great
navies were on the sea."   Again, in May 1457, another
threatened attack caused the Earl to lay in great stores,

for which he had to draw on Kent: "so he had the folks of Canterbury and Sandwich before him, and thanked them for their good hearts in victualling of Calais, and prayed them for continuance therein." That those rumours of coming trouble were not all vain was shown a few months later, for a Norman fleet under Peter de Brézé threw four thousand men ashore near Sandwich in August, and the French stormed the town from the land side, held it for a day, and sacked it from garret to cellar. It was this disaster which England owed to Margaret of Anjou, for she had deliberately suggested the time and place of attack to de Brézé, in order to bring discredit on the government of the Duke of York.

It is curious to note how the work of the day of St. Albans was undone, without any violent shock, during the earlier years of Warwick's rule at Calais. The Queen played her game more cautiously than usual. First, York's protectorate was ended, on the excuse that the King, whose mind had failed him again after St. Albans, was now himself once more. Then, eight months later, a great Council was summoned, not at London, where York was too popular, but at Coventry. The meeting was packed with the men-at-arms of the Queen's adherents, and at it King Henry dismissed the two Bourchier brothers, York's firm supporters, from their offices of Chancellor and Treasurer, and replaced them by the Earl of Shrewsbury, a strong adherent of the Court party, and by Wainfleet Bishop of Winchester. It was widely believed that York, who had come to the Council with no knowledge of the Queen's intended *coup d'état*, would have met with an ill end if his kinsman the Duke of Buckingham had not succeeded in aiding him

to escape.  Of all the offices bestowed as the result of
St. Albans fight, Warwick's post at Calais was the only
one which was not now forfeited.  Probably the Queen
and her friends preferred to keep him over-sea as much
as possible.

It is a good testimony to the loyalty of the Duke and
his friends that they made no stir on their eviction from
office.  York retired to Wigmore, and for the next year
abode quietly upon his estates.  Salisbury went to
Middleham and remained in the North.  Meanwhile the
country showed its discontent with the renewed rule of
the Queen.  Tumultuous gatherings took place in Oxfordshire and Berkshire, and again on the Welsh Border,
although no leading Yorkist was implicated in them.
The temper of London was so discontented that the
Queen would not allow the King to approach it for a
whole year.

The ascendency of the Earls of Wiltshire, Beaumont,
Shrewsbury, Exeter, and the other lords who ruled in
the King's name and by the Queen's guidance, proved as
unfortunate and as unpopular as any of the other periods
during which Margaret's friends were at the helm.  Men
felt that civil war was destined to break out once more,
as soon as York should be pressed too hard and find his
patience at an end.  Hence general joy was felt when in
January 1458 the King, taking the initiative for once,
announced that he was about to reconcile all the private
grievances of his lords, and invited York, Salisbury, and
Warwick, with the rest of their party, to attend a great
Council at Westminster.  They came, but fearing some
snare of the Queen's, came with a numerous following—
York with a hundred and forty horse, Salisbury with

four hundred, Warwick with six hundred men of the
Calais garrison all apparelled in red jackets emblazoned
with the Beauchamp badge of the ragged staff. There
was no snare in the King's invitation, and all precautions
were taken to prevent affrays. The Yorkist lords and
their retainers were lodged within the city, while the
Queen's friends, who appeared in great force—the Earl
of Northumberland alone brought three thousand
men—were provided for in the suburbs. The Mayor
of London—Godfrey Bulleyn, Anne Bulleyn's ancestor
—with five thousand citizens arrayed in arms kept the
streets, to guard against brawling between the retainers
of the two parties.

The King at once set forth his purpose of a general
pacification, and found York and his friends very ready
to fall in with his views. More trouble was required to
induce the sons of those who had fallen at St. Albans—
the young Somerset, Clifford, and Northumberland—to
pardon those on whose swords was their fathers' blood.
But the King's untiring efforts produced the desired
result. York, Salisbury, and Warwick promised to
endow the Abbey of St. Albans with a sum of £45 a
year, to be spent in masses for the souls of the slain, and
to make large money payments to their heirs—York
gave the young Duke of Somerset and his mother five
thousand marks, and Warwick made over one thousand
to the young Clifford. After this curious bargain had
been made, and a proclamation issued to the effect that
both the victors and the vanquished of St. Albans had
acted as true liegemen of the King, a solemn ceremony
of reconciliation was held. The King walked in state
to St. Paul's, behind him came the Queen, led by the

Duke of York; then followed Salisbury hand in hand with
Somerset, Warwick hand in hand with the Duke of
Exeter, and after them their respective adherents two
and two. The sight must have gladdened the King's
kindly heart, but no one save his own guileless self could
have supposed that such a reconciliation was final;
almost the whole of his train were destined to die by
each other's hands. The Queen and Somerset were one
day to behead York and Salisbury; Warwick was
destined to slay Exeter's son; and so all down the long
procession.

As one of the tokens of reconciliation, Warwick was
created "Chief Captain to guard the Sea," a post wherein
centred the ambition of his unwilling partner in the
great procession, the Duke of Exeter. The office was not
one with many attractions. The royal navy comprised
no more than the *Grace Dieu* and two or three more
large carracks. When a fleet was required, it was made
up by requisitioning hastily-armed merchant-vessels
from the maritime towns. Of late years, whenever such
an array was mustered, the sailors had gone unpaid, and
the command had been entrusted to some unskilled
leader from the ranks of the Court party. England had
entirely ceased to count as a naval power; her coasts
were frequently ravaged by French expeditions, such as
that which had burnt Sandwich in 1457, and pirates
and privateers of all nations swarmed in the Channel.

In his capacity as Captain of Calais, Warwick had
been compelled to learn something of the Channel, but
we should never have guessed that he had accumulated
enough of the seaman's craft to make him a competent
admiral. Nevertheless, his doings during the twenty

months of his command at sea entitle him to a respectable
place by the side of Blake and Monk and our other
inland-bred naval heroes. He not merely acquired
enough skill to take the charge of a fleet in one of the
rough and ready sea-fights of the day, but actually
became a competent seaman. At a pinch, as he showed
a few years later, he could himself take the tiller and
pilot his ship for a considerable voyage.

The tale of Warwick's first naval venture has been
most fortunately preserved to us by the letter of an
actor in it.

On Trinity Sunday (May 28th) in the morning [writes
John Jernyngan] came tidings unto my Lord of Warwick
that there were twenty-eight sail of Spaniards on the sea,
whereof sixteen were great ships of forecastle; and then my
Lord went and manned five ships of forecastle and three
carvells and four pinnaces, and on the Monday we met together before Calais at four of the clock in the morning, and
fought together till ten. And there we took six of their
ships, and they slew of our men about fourscore and hurt
two hundred of us right sore. And we slew of them about
twelvescore, and hurt a five hundred of them. It happed
that at the first boarding of them we took a ship of three
hundred tons, and I was left therein and twenty-three men
with me. And they fought so sore that our men were fain
to leave them. Then came they and boarded the ship that
I was in, and there was I taken, and was prisoner with them
six hours, and was delivered again in return for their men
that were taken at the first. As men say, there has not
been so great a battle upon the sea these forty winters. And,
to say sooth, we were well and truly beaten: so my Lord
has sent for more ships, and is like to fight them again in
haste.

Such a hard-fought struggle against superior numbers
was almost as honourable to Warwick's courage and

enterprise as a victory, and the indomitable pluck which
he displayed seems to have won the hearts of the sailors,
who were ever after, down to the day of his death,
faithful to his cause.  But his later undertakings were
fortunate as well as bold.

The best known of them took place in the spring of
1458.  Sweeping the Channel with fourteen small vessels,
Warwick came on five great ships—"three great Genoese
carracks, and two Spaniards far larger and higher than
the others."  For two days Warwick fought a running
fight with the enemy, "hard and long, for he had no
vessel that could compare in size with theirs."  Finally
he took three of the carracks and put the other two to
flight.  Nearly a thousand Spaniards were slain, and
the prisoners were so many that the prisons of Calais
could hardly contain them.  The prizes were richly
laden, and their contents were valued at no less than
£10,000.  The markets of Calais and Kent were for
the moment so charged with Southern goods that a
shilling bought that year more than two would have
bought the year before.

This fight naturally made Warwick popular with
merchants and sailors, but it was less liked at Westminster; for although at odds with the King of Castile,
England was not at this moment engaged in hostilities
with the Genoese, though there was a dispute in progress
about the ill-treatment of some British merchants by
them.  Another feat of Warwick's, however, was to get
him into worse trouble.  Early in the autumn of the
same year he had an engagement in the Straits of Dover
with a great fleet of Hanseatic vessels from Lubeck, who
were sailing southward to France.  From them he took

five ships which he brought into Calais. Now England
had signed a commercial treaty with the Hansa only two
years before, and this engagement was a flagrant violation of it. It led Warwick's enemies on the Continent
to call him no better than a pirate. What was his plea
of justification we do not know. It may be, as some
have alleged, that he mistook the Germans at first for
Spaniards or Frenchmen. It may be that he fell out
with them on some question as to the rights of the
English admiral in the narrow seas, such as gave constant
trouble in later centuries, and were the forerunners of
the famous quarrels over the "right of search" and "the
right of salute."

But about Warwick's capture of the Hanseatic vessels
there was no doubt. A month later a board was
appointed, consisting of Lord Rivers, Sir Thomas Kyrriel,
and seven other members, to investigate the matter.

On November 8th Warwick came over from Calais
to lay his defence before the King and Council. Henry
received him courteously enough, and there was much
sage talk about the marches of Picardy, "but the Earl
could judge well enough by the countenances of many
who sat in the Council Chamber that they bore him
hatred, so that he bethought him of the warnings that
his father had lately written him about the Queen's
friends."

Next day when Warwick again came into the royal
presence, the Council had hardly begun when a great
tumult arose in the court, "the noise was heard over
the whole palace, and every one was calling for Warwick."
What had happened was, that the retainers of Somerset
and Wiltshire had fallen on the Earl's attendants and

were making an end of them. Warwick ran down to see what was the matter, but the moment that he appeared in the court he was set on by a score of armed men, and it was only by the merest chance that he was able to cut his way down to the water-stairs, and leap with two of his men into a boat. He escaped with his life to the Surrey side, but his followers were not so lucky; three were slain and many wounded.

Warwick declared that the whole business had been a deliberate plot to murder him, and he was probably right; but the lords of the Queen's party maintained that the affray had been a chance medley between the two bands of retainers, and that the first blow had been struck by one of Warwick's men. But whatever was the truth about the matter, Warwick could not be blamed if he swore never to come to Court again without armed men at his heels. The sequel of the quarrel shows what had really been intended. Next day the Queen and her friends represented to the King that the quarrel had been due to brawling on Warwick's part, and procured an order for committing him to the Tower. Warned of this by a secret friend in the Council, the Earl rode off in haste to Warwick Castle, and sent to his father and the Duke of York. The three held a conference, in which they resolved that at the next hostile move of their enemies they would repeat the line of conduct which had been so successful four years before—they would muster their retainers and deliver the King by force out of the hands of the Court party.

Meanwhile Warwick retired to Calais, where he called together the officers of the garrison, and the Mayor and aldermen, set forth to them the attempt upon his life, and begged them to be true to him and guard him against the machination of his enemies.

The next attack of the Queen on the followers of York was long in coming; nine months elapsed between the affray at Westminster and the final outbreak of Civil War.

Meanwhile [says the chronicler] the realm of England was out of all good governance, as it had been many days before; for the King was simple, and led by covetous counsel, and owed more than he was worth. His debts encreased daily, but payment was there none; for all the manors and lordships that pertained to the Crown the King had given away, so that he had almost nought to live on. And such impositions as were put on the people, as taxes, tallages, and 'fifteenths,' all were spent in vain, for the King held no household and maintained no wars. So for these misgovernances the hearts of the people were turned from them that had the land in governance, and their blessing was turned to cursing. The Queen and her affinity ruled the realm as they liked, gathering riches innumerable. The officers of the realm, and specially the Earl of Wiltshire, the Treasurer, for to enrich themselves pilled the poor people, and disherited rightful heirs, and did many wrongs. The Queen was sore defamed, and many said that he that was called the Prince was not the King's son, but gotten in adultery.

The name of Wiltshire, "the best-favoured knight in the land, and the most feared of losing his beauty," was united with that of Margaret by many tongues, and the Queen's behaviour was certainly curious; for instead of staying with her husband, she was continually absent from his side, busied in all manner of political intrigues, and only visiting King Henry when some grant or signature had to be wrung out of him.

All the summer of 1459 she was in Lancashire and Cheshire "allying to her the knights and squires in those parts for to have their benevolence, and held open household among them, and made her son give a livery blazoned with a swan to all the gentlemen of the country, trusting through their strength to make her son King; for she was making privy means to some lords of England for to stir the King to resign the crown to his son; but she could not bring her purpose about."

The exact details of the outbreak of the war are hard to arrange chronologically. Writs were being sent about by the Queen in the King's name ordering every one to be ready to assemble "with as many men as they might, defensibly arrayed," as early as May. But no such muster seems to have taken place, and it was not till September that a blow was struck. In the middle of that month an army was raised in the Midlands with which the King took the field. A summons was then sent to Salisbury, who lay at Sherif Hoton in his northern lands, bidding him come to London. Remembering what had happened to his son on his last visit to the King, Salisbury went not, but took the summons, combined with the mustering of the King's forces, as an alarm of war. Collecting some three thousand of his Yorkshire tenants, he marched off to seek his brother-in-law York, who was lying at Ludlow. At the same time he sent messengers to his son at Calais, bidding him cross over at once to join him.

Warwick, seeing that the crisis was come, took two hundred men-at-arms and four hundred archers of the garrison of Calais, under Sir Andrew Trollope a veteran of the French War, and crossed to Sandwich. He left

Calais, where lay his wife and his two daughters, in
charge of his uncle, William Neville Lord Fauconbridge,
"a little man in stature but a knight of great reverence."
Warwick marched quietly through London, and crossed
the Midlands as far as Coleshill in Warwickshire without meeting an enemy. There he just avoided a battle,
for Somerset, with a great force from his Wessex lands,
was marching through the town from south-west to
north-east the same day that Warwick traversed it
from south-east to north-west; but as it happened they
neither of them caught any sight or heard any rumour
of the other.

While Warwick was taking his way through the
Midlands, decisive events had been occurring. When
the Queen, who lay at Eccleshall in Staffordshire, heard
that Salisbury was on his way to York's castle of
Ludlow, she called out all her new-made friends of the
north-west Midlands, and bade them intercept the Earl.
Lord Audley their leader was given a commission to
arrest Salisbury and send him to the Tower of London.
All the knighthood of Cheshire and Shropshire came
together and joined Audley, who was soon at the head
of nearly ten thousand men. With this force he threw
himself across Salisbury's path at Blore Heath near
Market Drayton on September 23rd. The old Earl refused
to listen to Audley's summons to surrender, entrenched
himself on the edge of a wood and waited to be attacked.
Audley first led two cavalry charges against the Yorkist
line, and when these were beaten back by the arrows of
the northern archers, launched a great column of billmen
and dismounted knights against the enemy. After hard
fighting it was repulsed, Audley himself was slain, and

the Lancastrians drew back, "leaving dead on the field most of those notable knights and squires of Chesshire that had taken the badge of the Swan."

In the night Salisbury drew off his men and marched round the defeated enemy, who still lay in front of his position. A curious story is told of his retreat by the chronicler Gregory. "Next day," he says, "the Earl of Salisbury, if he had stayed, would have been taken, so great were the forces that would have been brought up by the Queen, who lay at Eccleshall only six miles from the field." But the enemy knew nothing of Salisbury's departure, "because an Austin friar shot guns all night in the park at the rear of the field, so that they knew not the Earl was departed. Next morrow they found neither man nor child in that park save the friar, and he said that it was for fear that he abode in that park, firing the guns to keep up his heart."

Salisbury was now able to join York at Ludlow without further molestation, and Warwick came in a few days later without having seen an enemy. The Duke and the younger Earl called out their vassals of the Welsh March, and their united forces soon amounted to twenty thousand men. They made no hostile movement however, though the Lancastrian force defeated at Blore Heath was now being joined by new reinforcements and lay opposite them in great strength. But the Duke and the two Earls went forward to Worcester, and there in the cathedral took a solemn oath that they meant nothing against the King's estate or the common weal of the realm. They charged the Prior of Worcester and Dr. William Lynwood to lay before the King a declaration "that they would forbear and avoid all things that might serve to the effusion of Christian blood," and would not strike a blow except in self-defence, being only in arms to save their own lives.

The refusal of the Yorkist lords to assume the offensive, if creditable to their honesty, was fatal to their cause. For the next three weeks the levies of Northern and Central England came pouring into the Queen's camp, and the King himself, waking up for once, assumed the command in person. A curious record in the preamble of an Act of Parliament of this year tells us how he buckled on his armour, "and spared not for any impediment or difficulty of way, nor intemperance of weather, but jeopardied his royal person, and continued his labour for thirty days, and sometimes lodged in the bare field for two nights together, with all his host, in the cold season of the year, not resting in the same place more than one night save only on the Sundays." About October 12th, the King, whose army now amounted to as many as fifty thousand men, pushed slowly forward on to Ludlow, putting out as he went strongly-worded proclamations which stigmatised the Duke and the Earls as traitors, and summoned their followers to disperse, promising free pardon to all save Salisbury and the others who had fought at Blore Heath.

York and Warwick had, of course, no intention of abandoning their kinsman; they paid no heed to the royal proclamation, but they soon found that their followers were far from holding it so lightly. The Yorkists were so manifestly inferior in numbers to the enemy, less than half their force indeed, that the men's

hearts were failing them. Their position on the Welsh
Border, with the King's army cutting them off from
England, and with the Welsh in arms behind them, was
unsatisfactory, and none of the Yorkist barons had
succeeded in joining them except Lord Clinton and Lord
Grey of Powis. The inaction of their leaders had
allowed them time to think over their position, and it
would appear that the news of the King's proclamation
had reached them, and the announcement of pardon
worked its effect. York seems to have recognised that
the use of the royal name against him was the fatal
thing, and proceeded to spread a rumour through his
camp that King Henry was really dead. He even
ordered his chaplains to celebrate the mass for the dead
in the midst of the camp. But the stratagem recoiled
on his head next day, when the truth became known,
and the King was seen, with his banner displayed at
his side, leading forward in person the van of the Lancastrian army. At nightfall on October 13th the armies
were only separated by the Teme, then in flood and
covering the fields for some way on each side of its
course. The Duke set some cannon to play upon the
King's line, but the darkness or the distance kept them
from doing any hurt. This was all the fighting that
was destined to take place.

That night demoralisation set in among the Yorkist
ranks. It commenced with the veteran Trollope, who
secretly led off his six hundred Calais troops from
their place in the Yorkist line and joined the enemy.
Lord Powis followed his example, and at dawn the
whole army was melting away. York bade the bridges
be broken down, and began to draw off, but nothing

could keep his men together; they were dispersing with such rapidity that he could no longer hope to fight. Accordingly he bade those who still followed him to save themselves, and made off with his two sons Edward and Edmund, Warwick and Salisbury, and a few devoted retainers, to seek some place of refuge.

Thus by the Rout of Ludford all the work of Blore Heath and St. Albans was entirely undone.

# CHAPTER VIII

THE adventures of Warwick after the army of York broke up have luckily been preserved to us in some detail. He and his father, together with the Duke and his two sons· Edward and Edmund, fled southwards together with a few score of horse, hotly pursued by Sir Andrew Trollope and his men. So close was the chase that John and Thomas Neville, who lingered behind their brother and father—both having been wounded at Blore Heath—were taken prisoners. Presently the party was forced to break up by the imminence of their peril. The Duke of York and his second son Edmund turned off into Wales, with the design of taking ship for Ireland. Salisbury, Warwick, and Edward Plantaganet, the young Earl of March, York's eldest son and Salis-bury's god-child and nephew, accompanied by Sir John Dynham and only two persons more, fled across Here-fordshire by cross-roads, avoiding the towns, and then by a hazardous journey through Gloucestershire and Somersetshire reached the coast of Devon, apparently somewhere near Barnstaple. There the fugitives turned into a fishing village, where Sir John Dynham bought for two hundred and twenty-two nobles—the sum of the

party's resources—a one-masted fishing-smack. He gave
out that he was bound for Bristol, and hired a master
and four hands to navigate the little vessel.

When they had got well out from land Warwick asked
the master if he knew the seas of Cornwall and the
English Channel. The man answered that he was quite
ignorant of them, and had never rounded the Land's
End. "Then all that company was much cast down:
but the Earl seeing that his father and the rest were
sad, said to them that by the favour of God and St.
George he would himself steer them to a safe port. And
he stripped to his doublet, and took the helm himself,
and had the sail hoisted, and turned the ship's bows westward," much to the disgust, we doubt not, of the master and
his four hands, who had not counted on such a voyage
when they hired themselves to sail to Bristol town.

It was not for nothing that Warwick had ranged the
Channel for two years. He now proved that he was a
competent seaman, by navigating the little vessel down
the Bristol Channel, round the Land's End, and across
to Guernsey. Here they were eight days wind-bound,
but putting forth on the ninth ran safely up the Channel
and came ashore at Calais on November 3rd, just twenty
days after the rout of Ludford. Counting the crew,
they had been eleven souls in the vessel.

Warwick found Calais still safe in the hands of his
uncle Fauconbridge, whom he had left in charge of the
town and of his own wife and daughters when he went
to England two months before. Overjoyed at the news,
Fauconbridge came to meet him on the quay, and fell
on his neck. "Then all those lords went together in
pilgrimage to Notre Dame de St. Pierre, and gave thanks

for their safety. And when they came into Calais, the
Mayor and the aldermen and the merchants of the Staple
came out to meet them, and made them good cheer.
And that night they were merry enough, when they
thought they might have found Calais already in the
hands of their enemies."

· Such indeed might well have been their fortune, for
the Duke of Somerset was already at Sandwich, with
some hundreds of men-at-arms. The King had appointed
him Captain of Calais, and he was on his way to remove
Fauconbridge and get the town into his own keeping.
But the south-west wind which blew Warwick up from
Guernsey had kept Somerset on shore.

That very evening the wind shifted, and late at night
Somerset's herald appeared before the water-gate to
warn the garrison that his master would arrive to take
command next day. "Then the guard answered the
herald that they would give his news to the Earl of
Warwick, who was their sole and only captain, and that
he should have Warwick's answer in a few minutes.
The herald was much abashed, and got him away, and
went back that same night to his master."

No one in England knew what had become of Warwick or Salisbury, and Somerset's surprise was as great
as his wrath when he found that they had anticipated
him at Calais. Next morning he set sail with his forces,
of which the greater part were comprised of Sir Andrew
Trollope's soldiers, making for Guisnes, with the intention of attacking Calais from the land side. But a
tempest rose up while he was at sea, and though he and
most of his men came ashore at Guisnes, the vessels that
contained their horses and stores and armour were

G

driven into Calais harbour for safety, and compelled
to surrender to Warwick. The Earl "thanked Pro-
vidence for the present, and not the Duke of Somerset,"
and was much pleased at the chance, for his men were
greatly in want of arms. He had the prisoners forth,
and went down their ranks ; then he picked out those
that had been officers under him and had sworn the
oath to him as Captain of Calais and threw them into
prison, but the rest he sent away in safety, saying that
they had but served their King to the best of their
knowledge; only Lord Audley, Somerset's second in
command, son to the peer whom Salisbury had slain at
Blore Heath, was not permitted to depart, and was con-
signed to the castle. But the men who had broken
their oath to Warwick were brought out into the market-
place next day, and beheaded before a great concourse
of the citizens.

Somerset and Sir Andrew Trollope had been received
into Guisnes, and made it their headquarters. But for
some time they could do nothing against Calais, because
they were in want of arms and horses. It was not till
they had got themselves refitted by help of the French
of Boulogne that they were able to harm Warwick.
Meanwhile they were practically cut off from England,
for Warwick's ships held the straits, and neither news
nor men came across to them. Presently Somerset set to
work to intercept Warwick's supply of provisions, which
was drawn mainly from Flanders, and the Earl had to
arrange that every market-day parties of the garrison
should ride out to escort the Flemings and their waggons.
It might have gone hard with Calais if this source of
supply had been cut off, but Warwick had concluded a

secret agreement with Duke Philip, by which the introduction of food into the town was to be winked at by
the Flemish officials, notwithstanding any treaties with
England that might exist. Neither Somerset nor Warwick got much profit out of the continual skirmishes
that resulted from the attempts of the Lancastrians to
cut off the waggon-trains from Dunkirk and Gravelines.

So passed the months of November and December
1459, with no stirring incidents but plenty of bickering.
But Christmastide brought with it abundant excitement:
the Queen had at last taken measures to reinforce
Somerset, and Lord Rivers with his son Sir Antony
Woodville had come down to Sandwich with a few
hundred men to take the first safe opportunity of
crossing to Guisnes. But the time was stormy and the
troops mutinous; they got little or no pay, and scattered
themselves over the neighbourhood to live at free
quarters, so that Rivers lay in Sandwich almost un-
attended.

"So at Christmastide the Earl called together his
men-at-arms, and asked whether it was not possible to
get back his great ship that he had used when he was
admiral, for it lay at Sandwich in Lord Rivers' hands
with several ships more. And Sir John Dynham
answered 'yea,' and swore to take it back with God's
aid if the Earl would give him four hundred men to sail
with him. So the Earl bade his men arm, and fitted out
his vessels, and he gave the charge of the business to
Sir John Dynham, and Sir John Wenlock that wise
knight, who had done many feats of arms in his day."
They set out at night, and arrived off Sandwich before
dawn. Waiting for the tide to rise, they ran into the

harbour at five in the morning. No one paid any attention to them, for the men of Sandwich thought they were but timber-ships from the Baltic, as all the men-at-arms were kept below hatches.

There was no stir in the town, and Wenlock was able to seize the ships and fit them out in haste, while Dynham swept the streets and caught Lord Rivers' men-at-arms as they turned out to see what was the matter. Sir Antony Woodville was captured one hour later, as he rode into the town from London, whither he had gone to ask the Queen for a supply of money. Lord Rivers himself was found, still asleep, in his bed at the Black Friars, and carried on board his own ship before he could realise what was happening.

The men of Sandwich, like the rest of the Kentishmen, had no desire to harm the Yorkists, so that there was no fighting, and Dynham and Wenlock sailed home at their ease, without striking a single blow, with their prisoners and all the war-ships in the port save the *Grace Dieu* alone, which was found quite unready for the sea.

That evening they were again in Calais, and landed in triumph to deliver their spoils to Warwick. A quaint and undignified scene followed when the prisoners were brought out. "So that evening Lord Rivers and his son were taken before the three Earls, accompanied by a hundred and sixty torches. And first the Earl of Salisbury rated Lord Rivers, calling him a knave's son, that he should have been so rude as to call him and these other lords traitors, for they should be found the King's true lieges when he should be found a traitor indeed. And then my Lord of Warwick rated him,

and said that his father was but a squire, and that he
had made himself by his marriage, and was but a made
lord, so that it was not his part to hold such language
of lords of the King's blood. And then my Lord of
March rated him in like wise. Lastly Sir Antony was
rated for his language of all three lords in the same
manner."

If Rivers had any sense of humour, he must have felt
the absurdity of being rated by the Nevilles—who more
than any other race in England had risen by a series of
wealthy alliances—for having "made himself by his
marriage." But probably anger and fear were sufficient to keep him from any such reflections. We
could wish that Warwick had been less undignified in
the hour of his triumph; but if his words were rough
his actions were not: Rivers and his son were sent to
join Lord Audley in the castle, but they were well
treated in their captivity and came to no harm. Before
many months were out they joined their captor's cause.

It would have been hard for the actors in the scene
to foresee the changes that ten years were to make in
their relations to each other. By 1470 Rivers was
destined to find himself the father-in-law of the young
Earl of March, who was now exercising his tongue
against him in imitation of the Nevilles, and to lose
his life in the service of the house of York. Warwick,
on the other hand, was to become the deadly enemy of
the young Prince whom he was now harbouring and
training to arms, and to adopt the Lancastrian cause
which Rivers had deserted.

The months of January and February passed in
continual skirmishing with Somerset and the garrison

of Guisnes, which led to no marked result; but about
the beginning of Lent news arrived at Calais that the
Duke of York, of whom nothing definite had been heard
since October, was now in great force in Ireland, where
he had got possession of Dublin, "and was greatly
strengthened by the earls and homagers of that country."
Warwick at once resolved to sail to Ireland to concert
measures with his uncle, and to learn if it would be
possible to invade England; for it was obvious that
unless some vigorous offensive action were taken in the
spring, the Lancastrians would finally succeed in bringing
enough men across to form the siege of Calais, and then
the town could not hold out for ever.

Accordingly, though the storms of March were at
their highest, Warwick equipped his ten largest ships,
manned them with one thousand five hundred sailors
and men-at-arms, "the best stuff in Calais," and sailed
down the Channel for Ireland.   The voyage was undisturbed by the enemy, but terribly tempestuous and
protracted.   However, the Earl reached Waterford at last,
and found there not only York and his son Rutland,
but his own mother, the Countess of Salisbury, who had
fled over to Ireland when she heard that her name was
inserted among the list of persons attainted by the
Lancastrian Parliament which met at Leicester in
December 1459.

Warwick found the Duke in good spirits, and so
hopeful that he was ready to engage to land in Wales
in June with all the force that could be raised in
Ireland, if Warwick would promise to head a descent on
Kent at the same moment.   This plan was agreed upon
and the Earl set sail to return about May 1st, taking

with him his mother, who was anxious to rejoin her husband whom she had not seen for nearly a year.

Meanwhile the news of Warwick's departure for Ireland had reached the Lancastrian government, and the Duke of Exeter, Warwick's successor in the office of admiral, had sworn to prevent him from returning to Calais. Accordingly Exeter "with the great ship called the *Grace Dieu*, and three great carracks, and ten other ships all well armed and ordered," was now besetting the Channel. When Warwick was off Start Point the vessel which sailed in advance of his squadron to reconnoitre the way returned in haste, with the news that a squadron was lying off Dartmouth and that some fishing-boats, with whom communication had been held, reported the Duke of Exeter to be in command.

Warwick was resolved to fight, though the enemy was considerably superior in force. He sent for his captains on board his carvel "and prayed that they would serve him loyally that day, for he had good hope that God would give him the victory," to which they answered that they were well disposed enough for a fight and that the men were in good heart. Accordingly the Earl's ten ships formed line and bore down on the Duke's fourteen. A fight appeared imminent, when suddenly the whole Lancastrian fleet went about, and fled in disorder into Dartmouth harbour, which lay just behind them. This unexpected action was caused by mutiny on board. When the Duke had given orders to prepare for action, his officers had come to him in dismay, to announce that the men would not arm to fight their old commander, and that if he came any nearer to the Earl, the crews would undoubtedly rise

and deliver them over to the enemy. Accordingly
Exeter gave orders to retire into harbour.

Warwick, however, could not know of the cause of
the enemy's retreat, and having a good west wind behind
him and a great desire to get back to Calais, from
which he had now been absent more than ten weeks,
pursued his journey without attempting anything against
Dartmouth. He reached Calais in safety on June 1st,
and was proud to restore his mother, "who had suffered
grievously from the sea during her voyage," to his
father's arms. Salisbury and Fauconbridge had been
much alarmed at the length of his absence, and the
more faint-hearted of the garrison had begun to murmur
that he had deserted them for good, and had fled to
foreign parts to save his own person.

Now, however, all was stir and bustle in Calais, for
Salisbury and Fauconbridge thoroughly approved of the
plan of invasion which had been concerted at Dublin.
The news from England indeed was all that could be
desired. The reckless attainting of all the Yorkists by
the Parliament of Leicester had met with grave disapproval. The retainers of the Lancastrian lords had
been committing all sorts of misdoings, chief among
which was the unprovoked sack of the town of Newbury
by the followers of Ormond Earl of Wiltshire. London
was murmuring savagely at the execution of seven
citizens who, in company with a gentleman of the
house of Neville, had been caught in the Thames on
their way to Calais to join the Earls. The "unlearned
preachers" whom the Government put up to preach
against York at Paul's Cross were hooted down by the
mob. The Commons of Kent were signifying in no

doubtful terms their willingness to join the Earls, the
moment that the banner of the White Rose should be
unfurled in England.   A fragment of a ballad hung by
an unknown hand on the gate of Canterbury in June is
worth quoting as an expression of their feelings.

> Send home, most gracious Jesu most benigne,
> Send home the true blood to his proper vein,
> Richard Duke of York thy servant insigne,
> Whom Satan not ceaseth to set at disdain,
> But by thee preserved he may not be slain.
> Set him 'ut sedeat in principibus' as he did before,
> And so to our new song Lord thyne ear incline,
> Gloria, laus et honor tibi sit Christe redemptor !

> Edward the Earl of March, whose fame the earth
>         shall spread,
> Richard Earl of Salisbury, named Prudence,
> With that noble knight and flower of manhood
> Richard Earl of Warwick, shield of our defence,
> Also little Faulconbridge, a knight of grete reverence,
> Jesu ! restore them to the honour they had before !

Nor was it only the Commons that were ready to join
in a new appeal to arms.   The partisans of York among
the great houses, who had not definitely committed
themselves at the time of the rout of Ludford, and so
had escaped arrest and attainder, let it be known at
Calais that they were ready for action.   Chief among
them were the Duke of Norfolk and the two brothers
Lord Bourchier and Bourchier Archbishop of Canterbury,
who pledged themselves to put their retainers in motion
the moment that Warwick should cross the sea.

It was in no spirit of recklessness then that Warwick
resolved to cross into Kent in the last week of June,
with every man that could be spared from Calais.   As

a preliminary to his advance, he had resolved to clear
away the only Lancastrian force that was watching him—
a body of five hundred men-at-arms which had been sent
down to Sandwich, to replace Lord Rivers' troops and
to endeavour to communicate with Somerset at Guisnes.
This body was commanded by Osbert Mundeford, one of
the officers of the Calais garrison who had deserted
Warwick in company with Sir Andrew Trollope.

Accordingly, on June 25th Sir John Dynham, the
captor of Rivers, sailed over to Sandwich for the second
time, and fell on Mundeford's force. There was a hot
skirmish, for on this occasion the Lancastrians were not
caught sleeping; but again the Yorkists won the day.
Dynham indeed was wounded by a shot from a bombard,
but his men stormed the town, routed the enemy, and
took Mundeford prisoner. He was sent over to Calais,
where he was tried for deserting his captain, as the
prisoners of November 3rd had been, and beheaded next
day outside the walls.

On the 27th Warwick himself, his father, the Earl
of March, Lord Fauconbridge, Wenlock, and the rest of
the leaders at Calais, crossed over to Sandwich with
two thousand men in good array, leaving in the town
the smallest garrison that could safely be trusted with
the duty of keeping out Somerset. They had published
before their landing a manifesto, which set out the
stereotyped Yorkist grievances once more—the weak
government, the crushing taxes, the exclusion of the
King's relatives from his Council, the diversion of the
revenue into the pockets of the courtiers, the misdoings
of individual Lancastrian chiefs, the oppression of the
King's lieges, and all the other customary complaints.

The three Earls had only been in Sandwich a few hours when, as had been agreed, the Archbishop of Canterbury came to join them with many of the tenants of the see arrayed in arms. They then moved forward, with numbers increasing at every step, for the Kentishmen came to meet them by thousands, and no one raised a hand against them.

The Lancastrians had been caught wholly unprepared. They seem to have been expecting raids from Warwick on the eastern coast, not on the southern, and except Mundeford's routed force there was no one in arms south of the Thames. The King and Queen were at Coventry, and most of the Lancastrian lords scattered each in their own lands. Lord Scales and Lord Hungerford were in command of London, where there were present a few other notables—Lord Vesey, Lord Lovell, and John de Foix titular Earl of Kendal. These leaders endeavoured to fortify the city, posting guns on London Bridge and placing their retainers in the Tower. But the aspect of the citizens was threatening, and Warwick was known to be coming on fast. The landing had taken place on the 27th, and on July 1st the three Earls and the Archbishop of Canterbury were already before the walls of London. They had marched over seventy miles in four days, taking the route of Canterbury, Rochester, and Dartford, and were at hand long before they were expected.

When the Archbishop's herald summoned the town there was some attempt made by the Lancastrian lords to offer resistance, but the mob rose and drove them into the Tower, while a deputation of aldermen went forth to offer a free entry to the Yorkist army.

On July 2nd the three Earls entered London in state, conducted by the Archbishop and a Papal Legate, a certain Bishop of Teramo who had been sent by Pius the Second to endeavour to reconcile the English factions and to get them to join in a crusade. He had allowed himself to be talked over by Warwick, and did all in his power to further the cause of York.

The Earls rode to St. Paul's and there before a great multitude, both clerical and lay, Warwick "recited the cause of their coming in to the land, how they had been put out from the King's presence with great violence, so that they might not come to his Highness to excuse themselves of the accusations laid against them. But now they were come again, by God's mercy, accompanied by their people, for to come into his presence, there to declare their innocence, or else to die upon the field. And there he made an oath upon the Cross of Canterbury, that they bore true faith and liegeance to the King's person, whereof he took Christ and His Holy Mother and all the Saints of Heaven to witness." We shall see that this last promise was not an entirely unmeaning formula in Warwick's mouth, and that his oath was not like the deliberate perjuries to which others of his contemporaries—notably Edward the Fourth—were prone.

# CHAPTER IX

WHEN the arrival of the three Earls in London was
known, all the Yorkist peers who were within touch of
London came flocking in with their retainers. Thither
came Warwick's uncle Edward Neville Lord Abergavenny, and his brother George Neville Bishop of Exeter,
and his cousin Lord Scrope, and Clinton one of the
victors of St. Albans, and Bourchier and Cobham and Say,
and the Bishops of Ely, Salisbury, and Rochester. It is
strange to read that Audley, who had been Warwick's
prisoner in Calais ever since last November, also joined
the Yorkists in arms. He had come to terms with his
captor, and had agreed to forget the death of his father
at Blore Heath and to serve the cause of York. In a
few days an army of more than thirty thousand men
had been gathered together.

The first task of the Yorkists was to provide for the
blockade of the Tower of London, where Hungerford and
Scales abode in great wrath, "shooting wild-fire into the
town every hour, and laying great ordnance against it."
Salisbury agreed to remain in charge of the city and to
undertake the siege. With him were left Lord Cobham,

Sir John Wenlock, and the greater part of the levy of London, commanded by the Lord Mayor and by one Harrow, a mercer. They brought batteries to bear on the Tower from the side of St. Katherine's wharf, "so they skirmished together daily, and much harm was done."

Meanwhile Warwick and the young Earl of March set out on Saturday July 5th, having with them the other Yorkist lords, "and much people out of Kent, Sussex, and Essex with much great ordnance." Marching by the great north road, past St. Albans and Towcester, they made for Northampton, where they heard that the King was collecting his host.

The invasion of England had been so sudden and its success so rapid that the Lancastrians had not had time to call in all their strength, more especially as it lay to a great extent in the extreme North and West. But the Midlands were well roused, and, if a Yorkist chronicler is to be believed, the Queen "had it proclaimed in Cheshire and Lancashire that if so the King had the victory of the Earls, then every man should take what he might, and make havoc in Kent, Essex, Middlesex, Surrey, and Sussex." The Duke of Buckingham had the chief command, though he was not of the Court party nor a great lover of the Queen's, but out of sheer loyalty he now—as formerly at St. Albans—came out with all his retainers when he received the King's missive. With him were Egremont and Beaumont, both deadly enemies of the Nevilles and favourites of the Queen, the Earl of Shrewsbury, Lord Grey de Ruthyn, and many more. Their forces, though very considerable, were still somewhat inferior to those of the Yorkists.

The King's camp was pitched just outside Northampton town, in the meadows south of the Nen, near
the Nunnery between Sandiford and Hardingstone.
The position had been strongly entrenched, and the
earthworks were lined with a numerous artillery; the
river covered both flanks, the lines being drawn from
point to point in a broad bend of its course.

Warwick, in accordance with his declaration at St.
Paul's on the previous Thursday, made three separate
attempts to secure permission to approach the King's
person; but Buckingham sternly refused to listen to his
envoys, the Bishops of Rochester and Salisbury. "You
came here not as bishops to treat of peace, but as men-
at-arms," he said, pointing to the squadrons arrayed
under the bishops' banners in the Yorkist host. Negotiations were fruitless, and at two in the afternoon
Warwick drew out his army on the rising ground by the
old Danish camp, the Hunsborough, which overlooks
the water-meadows, and descended to the attack.
Fauconbridge led the vanguard on the left, the Earl
himself the centre, Edward of March, now seeing his
first stricken field, conducted the right wing. Before
the attack it was proclaimed that every man should
spare the Commons, and slay none but the knights and
lords, with whom alone lay the blame for the shedding
of all the blood that might fall that day.

The first assault on the Lancastrian lines failed completely. The obstacles were far greater than Warwick
had imagined; it was six feet from the bottom of the
ditch to the top of the rampart, and the trenches were
full of water, for it had rained heavily in the morning.
How the day would have gone if treachery had not come

to the succour of the Yorkists it is impossible to say; but only a few minutes after the first gun had been fired, Lord Grey de Ruthyn on the Lancastrian left mounted the badge of the Ragged Staff, and his men were seen beckoning to the Yorkists to approach, and leaning over the rampart to reach their hands to pull them up. Assisted in this way, the Earl of March's column got within the entrenchments, and sweeping along their front cleared a space for Warwick to burst in. All was over in half an hour and with very little bloodshed. Only three hundred men fell, but among them were nearly all the Lancastrian leaders. On foot and in their heavy armour the lords and knights could not get away. The aged Buckingham fell at the door of his own tent, and Beaumont, Egremont, and Shrewsbury close to the King's quarters, as they strove to protect his retreat. But the King, helpless as ever, was too late to fly, and fell into the hands of an archer named Henry Montford. His capture, however, was not so important so long as his wife and child remained at large; and Margaret—as adroit as her husband was shiftless—was already speeding away with the young Prince, bound for North Wales.

Warwick and March conducted King Henry back with all respect to London, where he was lodged in the palace at Westminster. They had done their work so rapidly that they had not needed the assistance of the Duke of York, whose arrival from Ireland—he was two months later than his promise—was just announced from the West. Even before he appeared the victors of Northampton had begun to reconstitute the King's ministry. Henry was made to sign patents appointing Salisbury Lieutenant in the six northern counties; his son, George Bishop of Exeter, received the Chancellorship; John Neville another son was made the King's Chamberlain, and Lord Bourchier got the Treasury. Warwick himself was re-established *de jure* in the position he had been so long holding *de facto*, the captainship of Calais.

The garrison of the Tower of London surrendered nine days after the battle of Northampton. Most of the defenders went away in safety, but Lord Scales, who was much hated by the populace of London, was not so fortunate. He took boat for the sanctuary of Westminster, but was recognised as he rowed along by some water-men, who gave chase to him and slew him on the river "just under the river wall of Winchester House." His body was stripped and thrown ashore into the cemetery of St. Mary Overy, whence it was removed and honourably buried by the Earls of March and Warwick that night. "Great pity was it that so noble a knight, so well approved in the wars of France and Normandy, should die so mischievously," adds the chronicler.

A Parliament was summoned by the Yorkists to meet on October 9th. Meanwhile Warwick was well employed. When August came round he ran across to Calais to see to his old antagonist at Guisnes. Somerset was now in low spirits, and willingly met the Earl at Newnham Bridge, there to be reconciled to him and make peace. But after he had embraced Warwick and assented to all his conditions, he secretly departed with his follower Trollope, fled through Picardy to Dieppe, and took refuge in his own south-western county. Meanwhile the Earl conducted his mother and wife in great state back to London, and re-established them in their old dwelling of

H

"the Harbour." He spent September in going on a
pilgrimage with the Countess to the shrine of the Virgin
at Walsingham in Norfolk. On this journey he ran
great peril, for Lord Willoughby, an unreconciled Lancastrian, lay in wait for him near Lichfield on his return,
and was within an ace of making him prisoner.

So Warwick came at last to his own Midland estates.
And there all the knights and ladies of his lands came
to him "complaining of the evils that they had suffered
in the past year from the Duke of Somerset, who had
pilled and robbed them, and sacked their towns and
manors, and usurped the Earl's castles; but notwithstanding all their troubles they praised Heaven for the
joyous return of their lord."

York had reached Chester early in September, and
had marched slowly through his estates in the Welsh
March towards London. When he came to Abingdon
"he sent for trompeteres and claryners from London,
and gave them banners with the royal arms of England
without distinction or diversity, and commanded his
sword to be borne upright before him, and so he rode till
he came to the gates of the palace of Westminster."
This assumption of royal state was the beginning of evils.

Meanwhile the Parliament was already sitting before
the Duke's arrival. King Henry opened it with due
solemnity, and heard it commence its work by repealing
all the Acts of the Lancastrian Parliament of Leicester,
and by removing the attainders of the Yorkist lords.
On the third day of the session, Richard of York came
up in the evening, and entered the palace, where he
rudely took possession of the royal apartments. "He
had the doors broken open, and King Henry hear-

ing the great noise gave place, and took him another chamber that night."

This unceremonious eviction of his sovereign was only the beginning of the Duke's violent conduct. Next morning he went to the House of Lords, and approaching the throne laid his hand on the cushion as if about to take formal possession of the seat. Archbishop Bourchier asked him what he would do, and the Duke then made a lengthy reply "challenging and claiming the realm and crown of England as male heir of King Richard the Second, and proposing without any delay to be crowned on All Hallows' Day then following." The lords listened with obvious disapproval and dismay, and York did not even venture to seat himself on the throne. The meeting broke up without further transaction of business.

"Now when the Earl of Warwick, who had not been present that day, heard this, he was very wroth, and sent for the Archbishop and prayed him to go to the Duke and tell him that he was acting evilly, and to remind him of the many promises he had made to King Henry." Warwick in short remembered his oath of July 4th, and was determined that Henry should not be despoiled of his throne, but only placed in the hands of Yorkist ministers. The Archbishop refused to face the Duke.

Then the Earl sent for his brother Thomas Neville, and entered into his barge, and rowed to the palace. It was all full of the Duke's men-of-arms, but the Earl stayed not, and went straight to the Duke's chamber, and found him standing there, leaning against a side-board. And there were hard words between them, for the Earl told him that neither the lords nor the people would suffer him to strip the King of his crown. And as they wrangled, the Earl of Rutland came in and said to his cousin, "Fair sir be not angry, for you know that we have the true right to the crown, and that my Lord and Father here must have it." But the Earl of March his brother stayed him and said, " Brother, vex no man, for all shall be well." But the Earl of Warwick would stay no longer when he understood his uncle's intent, and went off hastily to his barge, greeting no one as he went save his cousin of March.

Next day, when his wrath had cooled down, the Earl sent to his uncle the Bishops of Ely and Rochester, Lord Audley, and a London citizen named Grey, to beg and beseech him to give up his enterprise. The Duke sent them away, with the answer that he would be crowned the very next Monday, the day of the translation of St. Edward the Confessor (October 13th). The preparations for the coronation were actually made, and the crowd was mustering in the Abbey, when on a last appeal made by Sir Thomas Neville in the name of his brother and of all the lords and commonalty of England, the Duke wavered. Fearing to offend his greatest supporters beyond redemption he temporised, put off his coronation, and began to negotiate.

Richard Neville, in fact, had matched his will against that of his imperious uncle and had won. The Duke was never crowned. The arrangement at which the parties arrived was that Henry should be King for life, that York should be made Protector, named Prince of Wales, Duke of Cornwall, and Earl of Chester, and should be acknowledged as heir to the crown. The Duke, on the other hand, swore to be faithful to the King so long as he should live. On All Saints' Day the agreement was solemnly ratified at St. Paul's, whither the lords went in procession, Warwick bearing the sword before the King, and Edward of March bearing the King's mantle. " And the crowd shouted 'Long live King Henry and the Earl of Warwick,' for the said Earl had the good voice of the people, because he knew how to give them fair words, showing himself easy and familiar with them, for he was very subtle at gaining his ends, and always spoke not of himself but of the augmentation and good governance of the kingdom, for which he would have spent his life: and thus he had the goodwill of England, so that in all the land he was the lord who was held in most esteem and faith and credence."

The Act of Parliament which recorded the agreement of York and King Henry made no mention of Queen Margaret or of the Prince her son. But it was of little use passing Acts of Parliament while she was at large and the Lancastrian lords of the North and West unsubdued. Margaret's first move had been to stir up the Scots, and at her bidding James the Second crossed the Border and laid siege to Roxburgh, which was then an English town. Fauconbridge, Warwick's uncle, was sent north to defend the place, but later events deprived him of aid from England, and he was forced to surrender, though not till after the King of Scots had fallen, slain by the bursting of one of his own siege guns.

But the Scotch invasion was only one of Margaret's schemes. Her main hope lay in a rising of the Lancastrians who had not suffered at Northampton; and from her retreat at Harlech in North Wales she sent to summon them together. Their mustering-place was in the North, where the Earl of Northumberland and Lord Neville, brother of Ralph Earl of Westmoreland, and Clifford son of the Clifford who fell at St. Albans, united their retainers as the nucleus of an army. To them fled Somerset, regardless of his oath at Calais, and Exeter the late Admiral, and Courtney Earl of Devon, and Willoughby and Roos and Hungerford, and many more.

The danger was so imminent that the Duke of York, after wearing the honours of the protectorate for no more than three weeks, resolved to march north and disperse the gathering of the Queen's friends. He took with him his second son Edmund of Rutland, a boy of seventeen; Salisbury accompanied him, and he also left his first-born at home and went out with his fourth son Thomas Neville. The Duke and the Earl raised about six thousand men, and proceeded on their way, unopposed save by a small Lancastrian force which they beat at Worksop, till they reached Sandal Castle, one of York's family strongholds, close beside the town of Wakefield. When they arrived there, about Christmas Eve, they learnt that the Queen's army was much stronger than they had reckoned, and sent south for reinforcements. But on December 30th they were themselves assailed by forces tripling their own small host, under Somerset and Clifford. The Duke rashly fought in the open, though many of his men were scattered over the country-side foraging. It is said that he relied on help treacherously promised him by some of the Lancastrian leaders; but he was disappointed. No one played for his benefit the part that Grey de Ruthyn had carried out at Northampton.

The defeat of the Yorkists was decisive. Two thousand two hundred men out of their five thousand were slain. The fate of war fell heavily on the leaders, hardly one of whom escaped. The Duke fell on the

field, with Thomas Neville and William Lord Harington.
The Earl of Rutland, "the best-disposed young gentleman in England," was slain in the pursuit as he fled
across Wakefield Bridge. Salisbury's fate was more
unhappy still; he was taken prisoner, and beheaded
next day at Pontefract by the Bastard of Exeter,
"though he offered great sums of money that he should
have grant of his life." The heads of Salisbury and
his son, of Harington, and of five knights, were set on
spikes over the gate of York, with that of Duke Richard
in the midst, crowned with a paper crown in mockery
of the prospective kingship that he had never enjoyed.

All the Lancastrians of the North and the Midlands
rose at once to join the Queen. She was soon at the
head of forty thousand men, largely composed of the
lawless moss-troopers of the Scotch Border, who looked
upon war as a mere excuse for raids, and boasted that
everything beyond the Trent was in an enemy's country.
Before moving south they harried most thoroughly the
estates of the northern Yorkists. Salisbury's patrimony
about Middleham and Sherif Hoton bore the brunt of
the plunder, at the hands of the retainers of the elder
branch of Neville, whose head, Earl Ralph of Westmoreland, put his men under the charge of his brother
Thomas, one of the most rabid Lancastrians in the
North Country.

About the middle of January the Queen's army began
to roll southward, pillaging recklessly on all sides, and
sacking from roof to cellar the towns of Grantham,
Stamford, Peterborough, Huntingdon, Royston, Mel-
bourn, and Dunstable, as they passed down the Ermine
Street.

The news of the battle of Wakefield reached London about January 5th, and set the whole South Country in dismay. Warwick, who had been keeping his Christmas on his own estates, was forced to ride up to the capital at full speed, and assume the direction of affairs, for there was now no one to share the responsibility with him. His uncle, in whose cause he had fought so long, and his father, whose prudent counsels had guided the party, were both gone; his cousin of March, the head of the family, was no more than nineteen years of age, and was moreover at this moment far away by the Severn, looking after the Welsh March. It devolved on Warwick to assume the responsibility for the government of the kingdom and the safety of the Yorkist party.

Though there were traitors enough ready to change to the winning side, as was always the case in this unhappy war, the south-eastern counties were firm to York even in the darkest hour. Warwick found ready assistants in the Duke of Norfolk, the Archbishop of Canterbury, the Earl of Arundel, the Lords Bonville, Cobham, Fitzwalter, and the Commons of Kent and London. "In this country," wrote a partisan of York, "every man is well willing to go with my Lords here, and I hope God shall help them, for the people of the North rob and steal, and are appointed to pillage all this country, and give away men's goods and livelihood in all the South Country, and that shall be a mischief."

To resist the advance of the Queen on London, Warwick marched out to St. Albans and arrayed some thirty thousand men to cover the London road. His army was drawn up not in the great masses which were usual at this time, but in detachments scattered along a

front of three miles; the right on a heath called No
Man's Land, the left in St. Albans town.  The country-
side was full of woods and hedges, which were manned
by archers, supported by a body of Burgundian hand-
gun-men whom Warwick had hired in Flanders.  King
Henry was taken along with the army, and stationed in
the rear, in charge of Lord Bonville.  The position was
strong, but the communication between its various parts
was bad, and the whole force of Warwick's men seems
to have been ill placed for concentration.  Owing to
some mismanagement of the officer commanding the
mounted scouts, the Lancastrians attacked before they
were expected.  "The Queen's men were at hands with
the Earl's in the town of St. Albans while all things
were set to seek and out of order, for the prickers came
not home to bring tidings that the Queen was at hand,
save one, and he came and said that she was yet nine
mile off."  The first Lancastrian attack on the left, in
St. Albans town, was beaten back, but in another part
of the field a fatal disaster took place.  A Kentish
squire named Lovelace, who led a company in the right
wing, went over to the enemy, and let the Lancastrians
through the Yorkist line.  King Henry was captured
by his wife's followers "as he sat under a great oak,
smiling to see the discomfiture of the army."  When
the news ran along the front that treachery was at
work, and that the King was taken, the bulk of the
Yorkists broke up and fled.  Not more than three
thousand were slain or taken, but the whole force was
irretrievably scattered, and the greater part of the
leaders fled home to their own lands as if the war was
over.

Queen Margaret showed her joy at the recovery of her husband's person by an exhibition of savage cruelty. Lord Bonville and Sir Thomas Kyrriel, who had been in charge of Henry and had been captured with him, were brought before her. "So she told them they must die, and sent for her son the Prince of Wales, and said that he should choose what death they should suffer. And when the boy—he was eight years old—was brought into the tent, she said 'Fair son, what manner of death shall these knights, whom you see here, die?' And the young child answered 'Let them have their heads taken off.' Then said Sir Thomas, 'May God destroy those who taught thee this manner of speech,' but immediately they drew them out and cut off both their heads" (February 17th, 1461).

# CHAPTER X

THE dispersion of the Yorkist army seems to have been so complete that Warwick could not gather together more than four or five thousand of the thirty thousand men who had stood in line at St. Albans. With this small force he considered himself unable to protect London, and he therefore retreated not southward but westward, intending to fall back on his own Midland estates, to raise fresh troops, and join the Earl of March in the west. He only sent to London to order that his young cousins George and Richard of York— now boys of eleven and nine respectively—should be sent over-sea to take refuge in Flanders.

Accordingly Warwick now marched by vile cross-country roads, and in the worst days of a February which was long remembered for its rains and inundations, across Buckinghamshire and Oxfordshire to Chipping Norton. Here he met with the Earl of March, whose proceedings during the last month require a word of notice.

Edward was at Gloucester when the news of Wakefield reached him, and saw at once that troops must be raised to help Warwick to defend London. Accordingly

he moved into the Welsh Marches, and hastily called
together some ten or eleven thousand men. With these
he would have marched east, if it had not been that
Mid Wales had risen in behalf of Queen Margaret, and
that he himself was beset by forces headed by Jasper
Earl of Pembroke, Jasper's father Owen Tudor, the
husband of the Queen Dowager, and James Earl of
Wiltshire. Before he could move to succour Warwick,
he must free himself from these adversaries in his rear.
The campaign in the West was short and sharp. The
Earl of March met the Welsh at Mortimer's Cross, in
north Herefordshire near Wigmore, on February 2nd,
and gave them a crushing defeat. Owen Tudor was
taken prisoner and beheaded, and his head was set on
the highest step of the market-cross at Hereford. "And
a mad woman combed his hair and washed away the
blood from his face, and got candles, and set them about
the head burning, more than a hundred, no one hinder-
ing her." The Earls of Pembroke and Wiltshire
escaped, and joined Queen Margaret with the wrecks of
their army.

The moment that he had crushed the Welsh Lancastrians and settled the affairs of the March, Edward had
set out for London, hoping to arrive in time to aid
Warwick. He could not achieve the impossible, but he
had passed the Severn, crossed the bleak Cotswolds,
and reached Chipping Norton by February 22nd.
Having left some of his troops behind in Wales, he had
not more than eight or nine thousand of his Marchmen
with him, under Hastings—destined one day to be the
victim of Richard of Gloucester—Sir John Wenlock, and
William Herbert the future Earl of Pembroke.

The news that reached Warwick and the Earl of
March at Chipping Norton was so startling that it caused
them to change their whole plan of operations, and to
march straight upon London, instead of merely gathering fresh strength to make head in a new campaign in
the west Midlands.

The course of events after the fight of St. Albans had
been exactly the reverse of what might have been expected from the Queen's fiery temper and the reckless
courage of the Northern bands that followed her.

The battle had been fought upon February 17th,
the troops of Warwick had retired westward on the
18th, the victorious army was within thirteen miles
of London, and there was nothing to prevent the Queen
from entering the city next day.  It is one of the most
curious problems of English history to find that the
Lancastrians lay for eight days quiescent, and made no
endeavour to replace the King in his capital.  Knowing
the extraordinary apathy which the citizens displayed
all over England during the Wars of the Roses, we may
be sure that the Londoners, in spite of their preference
for York, would not have ventured to exclude the
Northern army when it claimed admittance at their
gates.

But on this one occasion Queen Margaret displayed
not only her usual want of judgment, but a want of
firmness that was foreign to her character.  King Henry,
asserting for once some influence on politics, and asserting it to his own harm, had determined to spare London
and the home counties the horrors of plunder at the
hands of the Northern hordes.  Not an armed force
but a few envoys were sent to London, while the main

body of the troops were held back, and the van pushed no farther than Barnet. Simultaneously the King issued strenuous proclamations against raiding of any kind. This ordinance caused vast murmuring among the Northern Men, observes the Abbot of St. Albans, on whom the King was quartered, but had not the least effect in curbing their propensity to plunder.

The Londoners had quite made up their minds to submit; their only thought was to buy their pardon as cheaply as possible at the King's hands. On the 20th they sent the Duchesses of Bedford and Bucking-ham—the widows of the great Regent of France and of the Lancastrian Duke slain at Northampton—together with certain aldermen, to plead for grace and peace at the hands of the Queen. The King and Queen were found at Barnet, whither they had moved from St. Albans, and gave not unpropitious answers, although that very morning Margaret had doomed to execution the unfortunate Bonville and Kyrriel. As a proof of their good intentions they undertook to move back their army out of reach of the city; accordingly on Thursday the 25th the Northerners, in a state of deep disgust, were sent back to Dunstable.

The first demand which the Queen had made on London was for a supply of provisions for her army; and on Friday the 26th the Mayor and aldermen gathered a long train of waggons, laden with "all sorts of victuals, and much Lenten stuff," and prepared to despatch it northward. The city, however, was in a great state of disturbance. Public feeling was excited by the plundering of the Lancastrians, and news had arrived that the cause of York was not lost, and that a

Yorkist army was marching to the relief of London. To the horror of the more prudent citizens, a mob, headed by Sir John Wenlock's cook, stopped the carts at Newgate, plundered the provisions, and drove the waggoners away.

Such an act was bound to draw down punishment, and that same afternoon a great body of Lancastrian men-at-arms, under Sir Baldwin Fulford, was pushed up to Westminster to overawe the city. The Londoners had to make up their minds that Friday evening whether they would fight or submit, and many were the heart-searchings of the timid aldermen; but on Saturday morning their grief was turned into joy. News arrived that Warwick and the Earl of March were at hand: Fulford's men abandoned Westminster and fell back northward; and ere the day was out the travel-stained troops of the Yorkist lords were defiling into the city. By nightfall ten thousand men were within the gates, and all thought of surrender was gone.

Thus King Henry's good intentions and Queen Margaret's unexpected irresolution had lost London to the Lancastrians. But their army still lay in a threatening attitude at Dunstable, and it seemed inevitable that the Earl of March would have either to fight a battle or to stand a siege before he was a week older.

But before the fate of England was put to the arbitrament of combat there was one thing to be done. The cruel deaths of York and Salisbury had driven the quarrel between York and Lancaster beyond the possibility of accommodation. In spite of all the personal respect that was felt for King Henry, it was no longer possible that the heir of Duke Richard should be content to pose merely as the destined successor to the throne. Now that Henry was again in the hands of his wife and the Beauforts, it was certain that the royal name would be used to the utmost against the Yorkists. They must have some cry to set against the appeal to national loyalty which would be made in the name of King Henry.

No doubt Warwick and Edward had settled the whole matter on their ride from Chipping Norton to London, for their action showed every sign of having been long planned out. On the Sunday morning, within twenty-four hours of their arrival in the city, their army was drawn out "in the great field outside Clerkenwell," and while a great multitude of Londoners stood by, George Bishop of Exeter, the orator of the Neville clan, made a solemn statement of Edward's claim to the throne. At once soldiers and citizens joined in the shout, "God save King Edward!" and there was no doubt of the spontaneity of their enthusiasm. The heart of the people was with York, and it only remained necessary to legalise their choice by some form of election.

Save the three Nevilles, Warwick, Fauconbridge, and Bishop George, there seems to have been no peer with Edward at the moment. Warwick felt that it would not look well that his cousin should ostensibly receive his crown from the Nevilles alone, whatever might be the reality of the case. Accordingly the few Yorkist peers within reach were hastily summoned. The Archbishop of Canterbury came in from Kent, where he had been "waiting for better times." The Duke of Norfolk, Lord Fitzwalter, Lord Ferrers of Chartley, and the Bishop of Salisbury appeared ere two days were out. Then these eight peers, spiritual and temporal, with a dozen or so of knights, and a deputation of London citizens, solemnly met at Baynard's Castle and declared Edward King. There had not been an instance of the election of a monarch by such a scanty body of supporters since the meeting of the Witan that chose Henry the First. The house of Neville and their cousin of Norfolk were practically the sole movers in the business.

Next day, Thursday March 4th, Edward rode in state to Westminster with his scanty following of notables. There before the high altar he declared his title, and sat on his throne, with the sceptre of Edward the Confessor in his hand, beneath a canopy, receiving the homage and fealty of his adherents. Then embarking in a state barge he returned by water to the Tower where he fixed his abode, deserting the York family mansion of Baynard's Castle. Meanwhile the heralds proclaimed him at every street corner as Edward the Fourth, King of France and England, and Lord of Ireland.

Every one had been expecting that the coronation would be interrupted by the news that Queen Margaret's army was thundering at the gates; but no signs of the approach of an enemy appeared, and that same day it was known that the Queen had broken up from Dunstable and marched away northward. Her troops were in a state of incipient disbandment: they had refused to obey the King's proclamation against plunder, and had melted away by thousands, some to harry the Home Counties, some to bear off booty already obtained. The men that still adhered to the standards were so few and so discontented that the Lancastrian lords begged the Queen to retreat. They had heard exaggerated

rumours of the strength of King Edward, and dared
not fight him. Accordingly Henry, his wife and son,
and his nobles, with their whole following, rode off
along the Watling Street, sending before them messengers to raise the whole force of the North, and to
bid it meet their retiring army on the borders of
Yorkshire.

The festivities of the coronation had not prevented the
Yorkist lords from keeping the imminence of their danger
close before their eyes. The ceremony had taken place on
Thursday afternoon; by early dawn on Friday Mowbray
had ridden off eastward to array his followers in Norfolk
and Suffolk. On the Saturday Warwick himself marched
out by the great North road, with the war-tried troops
who had fought under him at St. Albans and accompanied his retreat to Chipping Norton. He moved on
cautiously, gathering in the Yorkist knights of the Midlands and his own Warwickshire and Worcestershire
retainers, till he had been joined by the whole force of
his party. For four or five days after Warwick had set
forth, the levies of the Southern Counties continued to
pour into London. On the 10th the main body of in-
fantry marched on to unite with the Earl; they were
some fifteen thousand strong, Marchmen from the
Welsh Border and Kentishmen; for Kent, ever loyal to
York, had turned out its archers in full force, under a
notable captain named Robert Horne. Finally, King
Edward—who had remained behind till the last available
moment, cheering the Londoners, bidding for the support of doubtful adherents, getting together money, and
signing the manifold documents which had to be drawn
up on his accession—started with his personal following,

amid the cheers of the citizens and cries for vengeance on King Henry and his wife.

Warwick had pushed forward cautiously, keeping in his front some light horse under John Ratcliff, who claimed the barony of Fitzwalter. King Edward, on the other hand, came on at full speed, and was able to overtake his vanguard at Leicester. Mowbray, with the troops from the Eastern Counties, was less ready; he was several days behind the King, and, as we shall see, did not come up till the actual eve of battle.

There had been some expectation that the Lancastrians would fight on the line of the Trent, for the Northern lords tarried some days at Nottingham. But as Warwick pushed on he had always found the enemy retreating before him. Their route could be traced by the blazing villages on each side of their path, for the Northern men had gone homewards excited to bitter wrath by the loss of the plunder of London. They had eaten up the whole countryside, swept off the horses, pulled the very houses to pieces in search of hidden goods, stripped every man, woman, and child they met of purse and raiment, even to the beggars who came out to ask them for charity, and slain every man that raised a hand against them. Beyond the Trent, they said, they were in an enemy's country. In the eyes of every Southern man the measure of their iniquities was full.

When Warwick and King Edward learnt that the Queen and the Northern lords had drawn their plundering bands north of the Trent, they had not much difficulty in settling the direction of their march. It was practically certain that the Lancastrians would be found on one of the positions across the Great North Road which cover the approach to York. Now, as in every age since the Romans built their great line of communication between north and south, it would be on the line between York and Lincoln that the fate of Northern England would be decided. The only doubt was whether the Lancastrians would choose to defend the Don or the Aire or the Wharfe, behind each of which they might take up their position.

On the Friday, March 26th, the Yorkists crossed the Don unmolested, but the news was not long in reaching them that the enemy lay behind the next obstacle, the Aire, now swollen to a formidable torrent by the spring rains, and likely to cause much trouble ere it could be crossed. King Henry with his wife and son lay at York, but all his lords with their retainers lay in the villages about Tadcaster and Cawood midway between the Wharfe and Aire, with their central camp hard by the church of Towton, which was destined to give its name to the coming battle.

To secure the passage of the Aire was now the task that was incumbent on the Yorkists. Accordingly their vanguard under Lord Fitzwalter was sent forward in haste on to Ferrybridge, where the Roman road crosses the stream. Contrary to expectation the place was found unoccupied, and its all-important bridge secured. The line of the Aire was won; but the Friday was not destined to pass without bloodshed. The Northern lords, cursing the carelessness which had lost them their line of defence, determined to fall on the advanced guard of the enemy, and beat it out of Ferry-bridge before the main body should come up. Lord

Clifford, who commanded the nearest detachment, rode off at once from Towton, and charged into Ferrybridge while the newly-arrived Yorkists were at their meal. Fitzwalter had kept as careless a watch as his enemies; he was taken unprepared, his men were routed, and he himself slain as he tried to rally them. At nightfall Clifford held the town, and slept there undisturbed.

Next morning, however, the situation was changed. Somerset, or rather the council of the Lancastrian lords, had taken no measures to support Clifford. He was left alone at Ferrybridge with the few thousand men of his original force, while the main army was slowly gathering on Towton hill-side eight miles to the rear. Meanwhile the Yorkist main body was approaching Ferrybridge from the south, and a detached column under Lord Fauconbridge, stoutest of Warwick's many uncles, was trying the dangerous passage at Castleford, three miles away, where there was no one to resist them. Hearing that Fauconbridge was already across, and was moving round to cut him off from his base, Clifford evacuated Ferry-bridge and fell back towards his main body. He had already accomplished six of the eight miles of his journey, when near Dintingdale Fauconbridge suddenly came in upon his flank with a very superior force. Clifford had so nearly reached his friends that he was marching in perfect security. The Yorkists scattered his men before they could form up to fight, and killed him ere he had even time to brace on his helmet. The survivors of his detachment were chased in upon the Lancastrian main army, which was so badly served by its scouts that it had neither heard of Fauconbridge's approach nor taken

any measures to bring in Clifford's party in safety.
Nay, so inert were the Lancastrian commanders, that
they did not, after the skirmish, march out to beat off
Fauconbridge, whose friends were still miles away,
painfully threading the bridge of Ferrybridge or the
ford at Castleford.

All through Saturday the Yorkists were slowly coming
up to reinforce their vanguard, but the roads and the
weather were so bad that the rear was still on the other
side of the Aire when night fell.  However, the main body
was safely concentrated on a ridge south of Saxton village,
and probably thirty-five thousand out of Edward's forty-
eight thousand men were in line, though much famished
for victuals.   The belated rear-guard, which was destined
to form the right wing of the army on the morrow, was
composed of the troops from the Eastern Counties under
Mowbray; with him were Sir John Wenlock and Sir
John Dynham, two of Warwick's most trusted friends.
They were not expected to come up till some hours after
daybreak on Sunday morning.   With the Yorkist main
body were the King, Warwick, his brother John, his
uncle Fauconbridge, Lord Scrope, Lord Berners, Lord
Stanley, Sir William Hastings, Sir John Stafford, Sir
Walter Blunt, Robert Horne, the leader of the
Kentishmen, and many other South-Country knights
and squires.

Two miles north of the Yorkist camp at Saxton, the
Lancastrians lay in full force on Towton hill-side.   They
had with them the largest army that was ever put into
the field during the whole war.   Somerset, Exeter,
James Butler the Irish Earl who had endeavoured to
rival Warwick's power in Wiltshire, Courtney Earl of

Devon, Moleyns, Hungerford, and Willoughby had
brought in the South-Country adherents of Lancaster,
those at least of them whom the fields of St. Albans and
Northampton had left unharmed and unabashed. Sir
Andrew Trollope was there, with the remnant of the
trained troops from Calais who had deserted York at
Ludford in the previous year. But the bulk of the
sixty thousand men who served under the Red Rose
were the retainers of the Northern lords. Henry Percy
of Northumberland appeared in person with all his
following. The Durham vassals of the elder house of
Neville were arrayed under John Lord Neville, the
younger brother of Ralph of Westmoreland, though the
Earl himself was (now as always) not forthcoming in
person. Beside the Neville and Percy retainers were
the bands of Lords Dacre, Welles, Roos, Beaumont,
Mauley, and of the dead Clifford—of all the barons and
knights indeed of the North Country save of the younger
house of Neville.

· The Lancastrian position was very strong. Eight
miles north of Ferrybridge the Great North Road is
flanked by a long plateau some hundred and fifty feet
above the level of the surrounding country, the first
rising ground to the west that breaks the plain of York.
The high road to Tadcaster creeps along its eastern foot,
and then winds round its northern extremity; its
western side is skirted by a brook called the Cock,
which was then in flood and only passable at a few
points beside the bridge where the high road crosses it.
The Lancastrians were drawn up across the plateau,
their left wing on the high road, their right touching
the steep bank of the Cock. One flank was completely

covered by the flooded stream, while the other, the one
which lay over the road, could only be turned by the
enemy if he went down into the plain and exposed himself to a flank attack while executing his movement.
The ground, however, was very cramped for an army of
sixty thousand men; it was less than a mile and a half
in breadth, and it seems likely that the Lancastrians
must, contrary to the usual English custom, have formed
several lines, one in rear of the other, in order to crowd
their men on to such a narrow space.

The Yorkists at Saxton lay just on the southern
declivity of the plateau, within two miles of the
Lancastrian line of battle, whose general disposition
must have been rendered sufficiently evident by the
countless watchfires along the rising ground.

Although they knew themselves to be outnumbered
by the enemy, Warwick and King Edward were
determined to attack. Each of them had a father to
revenge, and they were not disposed to count heads.
Before it was dawn, at four o'clock on the morning of
that eventful Palm Sunday, the Yorkist army was
drawn out. The King rode down the line bidding them
remember that they had the just cause, and the men
began to climb the gentle ascent of the Towton plateau.
The left wing, which was slightly in advance of the
main body, was led by Fauconbridge; the great
central mass by Warwick in person; the King was in
command of the reserve. Of the details of the
marshalling we know no more, but the Yorkist line,
though only thirty-five thousand strong, was drawn up
on a front equal to that which the sixty thousand
Lancastrians occupied, and must therefore have been

much thinner. When Norfolk and the missing right wing should appear, it was obvious that they would outflank the enemy on the side of the plain. Warwick's plan, therefore, was evidently to engage the Lancastrians so closely and so occupy their attention that Norfolk should be able to take them in flank without molestation on his arrival.

In the dusk of the March morning, with a strong north wind blowing in their faces, the clumps of Yorkist billmen and archers commenced to mount the hill. No opposition was made to their approach, but when they had advanced for one thousand yards along the summit of the plateau, they dimly descried the Lancastrian host in order of battle, on the farther side of a slight dip in the ground called Towtondale. At the same moment the wind veered round, and a heavy fall of snow commenced to beat in the faces of the Lancastrians. So thick was it that the two armies could only make out each other's position from the simultaneous shout of defiance which ran down each line. Fauconbridge, whose wing lay nearest to the enemy, determined to utilise the accident of the snow in a manner which throws the greatest credit on his presence of mind. He sent forward his archers to the edge of the dip in the plateau, with orders to discharge a few flights of arrows into the Lancastrian columns, and then to retire back again to the line of battle. This they did; the wind bore their arrows into the crowded masses, who with the snow beating into their eyes could not see the enemy that was molesting them, and considerable execution was done. Accordingly the whole Lancastrian line of archers commenced to reply; but as they were shooting against the

wind, and as Fauconbridge's men had withdrawn after
delivering their volley, it resulted that the Northeners
continued to pour a heavy flight of arrows into the
unoccupied ground forty yards in front of the Yorkist
position. Their fire was so fast and furious that ere
very long their shafts began to run short. When this
became noticeable, Fauconbridge led his men forward
again to the edge of Towtondale, and recommenced his
deadly volleys into the enemy's right wing. The
Lancastrians could make little or no reply, their store of
missiles being almost used up; their position was
growing unbearable, and with a simultaneous impulse
the whole mass facing Fauconbridge plunged down into
Towtondale, to cross the dip and fall on the enemy at
close quarters. The movement spread down the line
from west to east, and in a few minutes the two armies
were engaged along their whole front. Thus the
Lancastrians, though fighting on their own chosen ground,
had to become the assailants, and were forced to incur
the disadvantage of having the slope against them, as
they struggled up the southern side of the declivity of
Towtondale.

Of all the battles of the Wars of the Roses, perhaps
indeed of all the battles in English history, the fight of
Towton was the most desperate and the most bloody.
For sheer hard fighting there is nothing that can compare to it; from five in the morning to mid-day the
battle never slackened for a moment. No one ever again
complained that the Southern men were less tough than
the Northern. Time after time the Lancastrians rolled
up the southern slope of Towtondale and flung themselves on the Yorkist host; sometimes they were driven

down at once, sometimes they pushed the enemy back
for a space, but they could never break the King's line.
Each time that an attacking column was repelled, newly-
rallied troops took its place, and the push of pike never
ceased. We catch one glimpse of Warwick in the midst
of the tumult. Waurin tells how "the greatest press
of the battle lay on the quarter where the Earl of Warwick
stood," and Whethamsted describes him "pressing on like
a second Hector, and encouraging his young soldiers;"
but there is little to be gathered about the details of the
fight.[1] There cannot have been much to learn, for each
combatant, lost in the mist and drifting snow, could tell
only of what was going on in his own immediate neighbourhood. They have only left us vague pictures of
horror, "the dead hindered the living from coming to
close quarters, they lay so thick," "there was more red
than white visible on the snow," are the significant
remarks of the chronicler. King Henry, as he heard
his Palm-Sunday mass in York Minster ten miles away
—"he was kept off the field because he was better at
praying than at fighting," says the Yorkist chronicler—
may well have redoubled his prayers, for never was there
to be such a slaughter of Englishmen.

At length the object for which Warwick's stubborn
billmen had so long maintained their ground against
such odds was attained. The column under the Duke
of Norfolk, which was to form the Yorkist right
wing, began to come up from Ferrybridge. Its route

---

[1] There is nothing authentic to be discovered of the story mentioned by Monstrelet, and popularised in Warwickshire tradition,
that the Earl slew his charger at Towton to show his men that he
would not fly.

brought it out on the extreme left flank of the Lancastrians, where the high road skirts the plateau.  Too heavily engaged in front to suspect that all the army of York was not yet before them, Somerset and his colleagues had made no provision against a new force appearing beyond their left wing.  Thus Norfolk's advancing columns were able to turn the exposed flank, open an enfilading fire upon the enemy's left rear, and, what was still more important, to cut him off from all lines of retreat save that which led across the flooded Cock.  The effect of Norfolk's advance was at once manifest; the battle began to roll northward and westward, as the Lancastrians gave back and tried to form a new front against the unsuspected enemy.  But the moment that they began to retire the whole Yorkist line followed them.  The arrival of Norfolk had been to Warwick's men what the arrival of Blücher was to Wellington's at Waterloo; after having fought all the day on the defensive they had their opportunity at last, and were eager to use it.  When the Lancastrians had once begun to retire they found themselves so hotly pushed on that they could never form a new line of battle.  Their gross numbers were crushed more and more closely together as the pressure on their left flank became more and more marked, and if any reserves yet remained in hand, there was no way of bringing them to the front.  Yet, as all the chroniclers acknowledge, the Northern men gave way to no panic; they turned again and again, and strove to dispute every step between Towtondale and the edge of the plateau.  It took three hours more of fighting to roll them off the rising ground; but when once they were driven down

their position became terrible. The Cock when in
flood is in many places unfordable; sometimes it
spreads out so as to cover the fields for fifty yards
on each side of its wonted bed; and the only safe
retreat across it was by the single bridge on the
Tadcaster road. The sole result of the desperate
fighting of the Lancastrians was that this deadly obstacle
now lay in their immediate rear. The whole mass was
compelled to pass the river as best it could. Some
escaped by the bridge; many forded the Cock where its
stream ran shallow; many yielded themselves as
prisoners — some to get quarter, others not, for the
Yorkists were wild with the rage of ten hours' slaughter.
But many thousands had a worse fortune; striving to
ford the river where it was out of their depth, or trodden
down in the shallower parts by their own flying comrades, they died without being touched by the Yorkist
steel. Any knight or man-at-arms who lost his footing
in the water was doomed, for the cumbrous armour
of the later fifteenth century made it quite impossible
to rise again. Even the billman and archer in his
salet and jack would find it hard to regain his feet.
Hence we may well believe the chroniclers when they
tell us that the Cock slew its thousands that day, and
that the last Lancastrians who crossed its waters
crossed them on a bridge composed of the bodies of
their comrades.

Even this ghastly scene was not to be the end of the
slaughter; the Yorkists urged the pursuit for miles from
the field, nearly to the gates of York, still slaying as
they went. The hapless King Henry, with his wife and
son, were borne out of the town by their flying followers,

who warned them that the enemy was still close behind,
and were fain to take the road for Durham and the
Border. Only Richard Tunstal, the King's Chamberlain, and five horsemen more guarded them during the
flight.

When Warwick and King Edward drew in their men
from the pursuit, and bade the heralds count the slain,
they must have felt that their fathers were well avenged.
Nearly thirty thousand corpses lay on the trampled
snow of the plateau, or blocked the muddy course of the
Cock, or strewed the road to Tadcaster and York; and
of these only eight thousand were Yorkists. The sword
had fallen heavily on the Lancastrian leaders. The Earl
of Northumberland was carried off by his followers
mortally wounded, and died next day. Of the barons,
Dacre, Neville, Mauley, and Welles, lay on the field.
Thomas Courtney the Earl of Devon was taken
alive—a worse fate than that of his fellows, for the
headsman's axe awaited him. Of leaders below the
baronial rank there were slain Sir Andrew Trollope, the
late Lieutenant of Calais, Sir Ralph Grey, Sir Henry
Beckingham, and many more whom it would be tedious
to name. The slaughter had been as deadly to the
Northern knighthood as was Flodden a generation later
to the noble houses of Scotland; there was hardly a
family that had not to mourn the loss of its head or
heir.

The uphill fight which the Yorkists had to wage
during the earlier hours of the day had left its mark in
their ranks; eight thousand had fallen, one man for
every six in the field. But the leaders had come off
fortunately; only Sir John Stafford and Robert

Horne, the Kentish captain, had fallen. So long indeed as the fight ran level, the knights in their armour of proof were comparatively safe; it was always the pursuit which proved so fatal to the chiefs of a broken army.

# CHAPTER XI

ON the evening of that bloody Palm Sunday, King Edward, Warwick, and the other Yorkist chiefs, slept in the villages round the battle-field. Next morning, however, they set their weary army on the march to reap the fruits of victory. In the afternoon they appeared before the gates of York, where the heads of York and Salisbury, bleached with three months of winter rains, still looked southward from the battlements. The citizens had, as was usual in the time, not the slightest intention of offering resistance, but they must have felt many a qualm as Edward's men, drunk with slaughter and set on revenging the harrying of the South by the Queen's army, drew up before their walls.

Edward, however, had already fixed on the policy from which he ·never swerved throughout his reign— hard measure for the great and easy measure for the small. The Mayor and citizens were allowed to "find means of grace through Lord Berners and Sir John Neville, brother to the Earl of Warwick"—doubtless through a sufficient gift of rose nobles. These two lords led the Mayor and Council before the King, who promptly granted them grace, and was then received into the town "with great solemnity and processions." There Edward kept his Easter week, and made every arrangement for the subjugation of the North. His first act was to take down the heads of his father and his uncle from over the gate, and provide for their reverent burial. His next was to mete out to his Lancastrian prisoners the measure that York and Salisbury had received. The chief of them, Courtney Earl of Devon and the Bastard of Exeter, were decapitated in the market-place, and their heads sent south to be set up on London Bridge. James Earl of Wiltshire—long Salisbury's rival in the South—was caught a few days later, and suffered the same fate.

The submission of the various Yorkshire towns was not long in coming in, and it was soon ascertained that no further resistance was to be looked for south of the Tees. The broken bands of the Lancastrians had disappeared from Yorkshire, and Warwick's tenants from Middleham and Sherif Hoton were now able to come in to explain to their lord how they had fared during the Lancastrian ascendency at the hands of his cousins of Westmoreland. In common with the few other Yorkists of the North, they had received hard measure; they had been well plundered, and probably constrained to pay up all that the Westmorelands could wring out of them, as arrears for the twenty years during which the Yorkshire lands of Neville had been out of the hands of the senior branch.

A few days after Easter, Warwick and Edward moved out of York and pushed on to Durham. On the way they were entertained at Middleham with such cheer as the place could afford after its plunder by the Lancas-

trians.   Nowhere did they meet with any resistance, and
the task of finishing the war appeared so simple that
the King betook himself homeward about May 1st,
leaving Warwick with a general commission to pacify
the North.   John Neville remained behind with his
brother, as did Sir Robert Ogle and Sir John Coniers,
the only two Yorkists of importance in the North outside
the Neville family.   The King took with him the rest
of the lords, who were wanted for the approaching
festivals and councils in London, and with them the
bulk of the army.

The task which Warwick had received turned out to
be a much more formidable matter than had been
expected.   King Henry, Queen Margaret, the Dukes of
Somerset and Exeter, Lords Hungerford and Roos, with
the other surviving Lancastrian leaders, had fled to
Scotland, where they had succeeded in inducing the
Scotch regents—Kennedy, Boyd, and their fellows—to
continue the policy of the late King, and throw themselves heartily into the war with the Yorkists.   The
inducement offered was the cession of Berwick and
Carlisle, and the former town was at once handed over
"and well stuffed with Scots."   Nor was it only on
Scotch aid that the Lancastrians relied; they had determined to make application to the King of France, and
Somerset and Hungerford sailed for the Continent at
the earliest opportunity.   They were stayed at Dieppe
by orders of the wily Louis the Eleventh, who was
averse to committing himself to either party in the
English struggle while his own crown was hardly three
months old; but their mission was not to be without its
results.   Putting aside the hope of assistance from France

and Scotland, the Lancastrians had still some resources of their own on which they might count. A few scattered bands of Percy retainers still kept the field in Northumberland, and the Percy crescent still floated over the strong castles of Alnwick, Bamborough, and Dunstanburgh.

The problem which fell into Warwick's hands was to clear the routed Lancastrians out of Northumberland, and at the same time to keep good watch against the inroads of the Scotch and the English refugees who were leagued with them. Defensive and offensive operations would have to be combined, for, on the one hand, the siege of the Percy castles must be formed—and sieges in the fifteenth century were slow and weary work—while, on the other, the raids of the lords of the Scotch Border might occur at any time and place, and had to be met without delay. Warwick was forced to divide his troops, undertaking himself to cover the line of the Tyne and observe the Northumbrian castles, while his brother John, who for his services at Towton had just been created Lord Montagu, took charge of the force which was to fend off Scotch attacks on the Western Marches.

In June the Scots and the English refugees crossed the Border in force; their main body made a push to seize Carlisle, which the Lancastrian chiefs, the Duke of Exeter and Lord Grey de Rougemont, promised to deliver to them as they had already delivered Berwick. The town, however, shut its gates; and the invaders were constrained to content themselves with burning its suburbs and forming a regular siege. But as they lay before it they were suddenly attacked by Montagu, who came up long before he was expected, and beat them

back over the Border with the loss of several thousand
men; among the slain was John Clifford, brother to the
peer who had fallen at Towton.

Almost simultaneously another raiding party, led by
Lord Roos and Sir John Fortescu, the late Chief-Justice,
and guided by two of the Westmoreland Nevilles,
Thomas and Humphrey, slipped down from the Middle
Marches and attempted to raise the county of Durham.
But as they drew near to the ancestral Neville seat of
Brancepeth, they were fallen upon by forces brought
up by Warwick, and were driven back on June 26th as
disastrously as the main army for which they had been
making a diversion.

These two defeats cooled the ardour of the Scotch
allies of the house of Lancaster. Moreover, trouble was
soon provided for them on their own side of the Border.
There were always discontented nobles to be found in
the North, and King Edward was able to retaliate on
the Scotch regents by concluding a treaty with the Earl
of Ross, which set a considerable rebellion on foot in the
Highlands and the Western Isles. By the time that the
autumn came there was no longer any immediate danger
to be apprehended on the Borders, and Warwick was
able to relinquish his northern viceroyalty and come
south, to pay his estates a flying visit, and to obey
the writ which summoned him in November to King
Edward's first Parliament at Westminster.

While Warwick had been labouring in the North, the
King had been holding his Court at London, free to rule
after his own devices. At twenty Edward the Fourth
had already a formed character, and displayed all the
personal traits which developed in his later years.

The spirit of the fifteenth century was strong in him. Cultured and cruel, as skilled as the oldest statesman in the art of cajoling the people, as cool in the hour of danger as the oldest soldier, he was not a sovereign with whom even the greatest of his subjects could deal lightly.   Yet he was so inordinately fond of display and luxury of all sorts, so given to sudden fits of idleness, so prone to sacrifice policy to any whim or selfish impulse of the moment, that he must have seemed at times almost contemptible to a man who, like Warwick, had none of the softer vices of self-indulgence.   Still in mourning for a father and brother not six months dead, with a kingdom not yet fully subdued to his fealty, with an empty exchequer, with half the nobles and gentry of England owing him a blood-feud for their kinsmen slain at Towton, Edward had cast. aside every thought of the past and the morrow, and was bearing himself with all the thriftless good-humour of an heir lately come to a well-established fortune.   It seems that the splendours of his coronation-feasts were the main things that had been occupying his mind while Warwick had been fighting his . battles in the North. Reading of his jousts and banquets and processions, his gorgeous reception by the city magnates, and his lavish distributions of honours and titles, we hardly remember that he was no firmly-rooted King, but the precarious sovereign of a party, surrounded by armed enemies and secret conspirators.

In the lists of honours which Edward had distributed after his return homeward from Towton field, Warwick found that he had not been neglected.   The offices which he had held in 1458-59 had been restored to him ;

he was again Captain of the town and castle of Calais,
Lieutenant of the March of Picardy, Grand Chamberlain
of England, and High Steward of the Duchy of
Lancaster.  In addition he was now created Constable
of Dover and Warden of the Cinque Ports, and made
Master of the Mews and Falcons, and Steward of the
Manor and Forest of Feckenham.  His position in the
North, too, was made regular by his appointment as
Warden and Commissary General of the East and West
Marches, and Procurator Envoy and Deputy for all
negotiations with the Scots.

Nor had the rest of the Neville clan been overlooked.
John Neville had, as we have already mentioned,
received the barony of Montagu.  George Neville the
Bishop of Exeter was again Chancellor.  Fauconbridge,
who had fought so manfully at Towton, was created
Earl of Kent.  Moreover, Sir John Wenlock, Warwick's
most faithful adherent, who had done him such good
service at Sandwich in 1459, was made a baron.  We
shall always find him true to the cause of his patron
down to his death at Tewkesbury field.  Although
several other creations swelled the depleted ranks of
the peerage at the same time, the Nevilles could not
complain that they had failed to receive their due share
of the rewards.

Nor would it seem that at first the King made any
effort to resent the natural ascendency which his cousin
exercised over his counsels.  The experienced warrior
of thirty-three must still have overborne the precocious
lad of twenty when their wills came into contact.  The
campaigns of 1459-60, in which he had learnt soldiering
under Warwick, must have long remained impressed

on Edward's mind, even after he had won his own
laurels at Mortimer's Cross and shared with equal
honours in the bloody triumph of Towton. So long as
Richard Neville was still in close and constant contact
with the young King, his ascendency was likely to
continue. It was when, in the succeeding years, his
duties took him for long periods far from Edward's
side, that the Earl was to find his cousin first growing
indifferent, then setting his own will against his
adviser's, then deliberately going to work to override
every scheme that came to him from any member of
the Neville house.

We have no particular notice of Warwick's personal
doings in the Parliament which sat in November and
December 1461 ; but the language of his brother
George the Chancellor represents, no doubt, the attitude which the whole family adopted. His text was
"Amend your ways and your doings," and the tenor
of his discourse was to point out that the ills of England
during the last generation came from the national
apostasy in having deserted the rightful heirs so long
in behalf of the usurping house of Lancaster. Now
that a new reign had commenced, a reform in national
morality should accompany the return of the English
to their lawful allegiance. The sweeping acts of
attainder against fourteen peers and many scores of
knights and squires which the Yorkist Parliament
passed might not seem a very propitious beginning for
the new era, but at any rate it should be remembered
to the credit of the Nevilles that the King's Council
under their guidance tempered the zeal of the Commons
by many limitations which guarded the rights of numer-

ous individuals who would have been injured by the
original proposals.

Moreover, the Government allowed the opportunity
of reconciliation to many of the more lukewarm
adherents of Lancaster, who had not been personally
engaged in the last struggle. It is to Warwick's credit
that his cousin Ralph of Westmoreland was admitted
to pardon, and not taken to task for the doings of his
retainers, under the conduct of his brother, in the
campaign of Wakefield and St. Albans. Ralph was
summoned to the Parliament, and treated no worse
than if he had been a consistent adherent of York.
The same favour was granted to the Earl of Oxford,
till he forfeited it by deliberate conspiracy against the
King. Sanguine men were already beginning to hope
that King Edward and his advisers might be induced
to end the civil wars by a general grant of amnesty,
and might invite his rival Henry to return to England
as the first subject of the Crown. Such mercy and
reconciliation, however, were beyond the mind of the
ordinary partisan of York; and the popular feeling of
the day was probably on the side of the correspondent
of the Pastons, who complained "that the King receives
such men as have been his great enemies, and great
oppressors of his Commons, while such as have assisted
his Highness be not rewarded; which is to be considered,
or else it will hurt, as seemeth me but reason."

# CHAPTER XII

WHATEVER the partisans of peace may have hoped in the winter of 1461-62, there was in reality no prospect of a general pacification so long as the indomitable Margaret of Anjou was still at liberty and free to plot against the quiet of England. The defeats of her Scotch allies in the summer of 1461 had only spurred her to fresh exertions. In the winter, while Edward's Parliament was sitting at Westminster, she was busy hatching a new scheme for simultaneous risings in various parts of England, accompanied by descents from France and Brittany aided by a Castilian fleet. Somerset and Hungerford had got some countenance from the King of France, and Margaret's own hopeful heart built on this small foundation a great scheme for the invasion of England. A Scotch raid, a rising in Wales, a descent of Bretons upon Guernsey and Jersey, and a great French landing at Sandwich, were to synchronise: "if weather and wind had served them, they should have had one hundred and twenty thousand men on foot in England upon Candlemass Day." But weather and wind were unpropitious, and the only tangible result of the plan was to cost the life of the Earl of Oxford, who had been told

off to head the insurgents of the Eastern Counties.  He
had been taken into favour by King Edward, and we
need have small pity for him when he was detected in
correspondence with the Queen at the very time that he
was experiencing the clemency of her rival.   But it was
an evil sign of the times that he and his son were
executed, not after a regular trial before their peers, but
by a special and unconstitutional court held by the Earl
of Worcester as Constable of England.   For this evil
precedent Warwick must take the blame no less than
Edward.

But Margaret of Anjou had not yet exhausted her
energy.   So soon as the storms of winter were over
and Somerset returned from France without the promised
succours, she resolved to set out in person to stimulate
the zeal of Louis the Eleventh, and to gather help from her
various relatives on the Continent.   Escaping from Scotland by the Irish Sea, she rounded the Land's End and
came ashore with her young son in Brittany.   The Duke
gave her twelve thousand crowns, and passed her on to her
father Réné in Anjou.   From his Court she went on to
King Louis, who lay at Rouen.   With him she had more
success than might have been expected, though far less
of course than she had hoped.   Louis was able to show
that he had already got together a fleet, reinforced by
some Breton and Castilian vessels, in the mouth of the
Seine.   In return for an agreement by which Margaret
promised the cession of Calais, and perhaps that of the
Channel Isles, he undertook to engage frankly in the
war, and to put at Margaret's disposition a force for the
invasion of England.   The way in which Louis chose a
leader for this army was very characteristic of the man.

He had in close confinement at the time a favourite of
his father and an enemy of his own, Peter de Brézé,
Count of Maulévrier and Seneschal of Normandy.  De
Brézé was a gallant knight and a skilled leader; only a
few years before he had distinguished himself in the
English war, and among other achievements had taken
and sacked Sandwich.  The King now offered him the
choice of staying in prison or of taking charge of an
expedition to Scotland in aid of Margaret.  De Brézé
accepted with alacrity the latter alternative, as much,
we are told, from chivalrous desire to assist a distressed
Queen as from dislike for the inside of the dungeons of
Loches.  Quite satisfied, apparently, at getting an enemy
out of the country on a dangerous quest, Louis gave
him twenty thousand livres in money, forty small vessels,
and about two thousand men, and bade him take the
Queen whither she would go.

While Louis and Margaret were negotiating, their
English enemies had been acting with their accustomed
vigour.  When May came round Warwick again resumed
command of the Northern Border, and marched out to
finish the work that had been begun in the previous
year.  He was already on Scottish ground, and had
taken at least one castle north of the Border, when he
received a herald from the Scotch regents offering to
treat for peace.  By his commission, drawn up in the
last year, Warwick was authorised to act as pleni-
potentiary in any such matter.  Accordingly he sent
back his army and went himself to Dumfries, where
he met Mary, the Dowager Queen of Scotland, and
the majority of the regents.  They concluded an armis-
tice to last till St. Bartholomew's Day, and then set

to work to discuss terms of peace. The common report ran that the Scots were ready not only to give up the Lancastrian cause, but even to deliver over the person of King Henry. Moreover, there was talk of an alliance by marriage between the English King and a Scotch Princess. This new departure, mainly brought about by the Queen-Dowager's influence,[1] was not without its effect on the Lancastrian partisans, who found themselves left unsupported to resist Warwick's army, which was, during the negotiations, put under the command of his brother Montagu and set to reduce the Northumbrian fortresses. King Henry fled from the Scotch Court and took refuge in one of the castles of the Archbishop of St. Andrews, the chief member of the regency who opposed peace with England. Lord Dacre, brother of the peer who fell at Towton, surrendered himself to Montagu, and was sent to London, where King Edward received him into grace. Even Somerset himself, the chief of the party, lost heart, and began to send secret letters to Warwick to ascertain whether there was any hope of pardon for him. Meanwhile Naworth Castle was surrendered to Montagu, and the more important stronghold of Alnwick yielded itself to Lord Hastings, who had been detached to form its siege. Bamborough was given up by Sir William Tunstal, and of all the Northern fortresses only Dunstanburgh remained in Lancastrian hands, and it seemed that this place must fall ere the year was out.

Believing that the war was practically at an end, Warwick now turned south, and rode up to London to

---

[1] Queen Mary had, so the story runs, shown overmuch favour to the Duke of Somerset. He openly boasted of his success in love, and the Queen was ever after his deadly enemy.

lay the Scotch proposal before the King. But he had not long left the Border when the whole aspect of affairs was once more transformed by the reappearance of Queen Margaret on the scene.

While Montagu and Warwick had been in the North, King Edward had been sorely vexed by rumours of French invasion. Seventy French and Spanish ships were roaming the Channel, and Fauconbridge, who had set out to find them with a hastily-raised fleet, came home without success. A French force had mustered in Picardy, and Queen Margaret lay all the summer at Boulogne, tampering with the garrison of Calais, who had fallen into mutiny on account of long arrears of pay. But Calais failed to revolt, Louis made no serious attempt on England, and the Queen at last grew impatient and determined to start herself for England, though she could only rely on the assistance of Peter de Brézé and his two thousand men. Setting sail early in October, she passed up the eastern coast, and landed in Northumberland, expecting that all the North Country would rise to her aid. No general insurrection followed, but Margaret's arrival was not without effect. Both Alnwick and Bamborough fell into her hands—the former by famine, for it was wholly unvictualled and could not hold out a week; the latter betrayed by the governor's brother. Nor was this all; the presence of the Queen moved the Scotch regents to break off their negotiations with England, and denounce the truce which they had so recently concluded. All that the statesmanship of Warwick and the sword of Montagu had done for England in the year 1462 was lost in the space of a week.

The moment that the unwelcome news of Margaret's advent reached London, Warwick flew to repair the disaster. Only eight days after the fall of Bamborough he was already at the head of twenty thousand men, and hastening north by forced marches. The King, ill-informed as to the exact force that had landed in Northumberland, had sent out in haste for every man that could be gathered, and followed himself with the full levy of the Southern Counties.

The nearer the Yorkists approached to the scene of action the less formidable did their task appear. The approach of winter had prevented the Scots from putting an army into the field, and the Lancastrians and their French allies had made no attempt to push out from their castles. All that they had done was to strengthen the three strongholds and fill them with provisions. In Alnwick lay Peter de Brézé's son and some of the Frenchmen, together with Lord Hungerford. Somerset, who had dropped his secret negotiations with Warwick when his mistress returned from France, held Bamborough; with him were Lord Roos and Jasper Earl of Pembroke. Sir Ralph Percy, the fighting-man of the Percy clan—for his nephew the heir of Northumberland was a minor—had made himself strong in Dunstanburgh. Meanwhile the Queen, on the approach of Warwick, had quitted her adherents and set sail for Scotland with her son and her treasure, under convoy of de Brézé and the main body of the French mercenaries. But the month was now November, the seas were rough, and off Bamborough she was caught in a storm; her vessel, with three others, was driven against the iron-bound coast, and she herself barely escaped with her life in a fishing-

boat which took her into Berwick. Her treasures went
to the bottom; and of her French followers four hundred were cast ashore on Holy Island, where they were
forced to surrender next day to. a force sent against
them by Montagu.

Warwick had now arrived at Newcastle, and King
Edward was but a few days' march behind him. Though
the · month was November, and winter campaigns,
especially in the bleak and thinly-populated North, were
in the fifteenth century as unusual as they were miserable, Warwick had determined to make an end of the
new Lancastrian invasion before the Scots should have
time to move. Luckily we have a full account of his
dispositions for the simultaneous siege of the three
Percy castles, from the pen of one who served on the
spot.

The army was arranged as follows. King Edward
with the reserve lay at Durham, in full touch with York
and the South. The Duke of Norfolk held Newcastle,
having as his main charge the duty of forwarding convoys of victuals and ammunition to the front, and of
furnishing them with strong escorts on their way, to
guard against any attempts made by roving bands of
Scots or Percy retainers to break the line of communi-
cations, thirty miles long, which connected Newcastle
with the army in the field. The force under Warwick's
immediate command, charged with the reduction of
the fortresses, was divided into four fractions. The
castles lie at considerable intervals from each other:
first, Bamborough to the north on a bold headland
projecting into the sea, a Norman keep surrounded
with later outworks; next Dunstanburgh, nine miles

farther south, and also on the coast; lastly, Alnwick, five miles south-west of Dunstanburgh, on a hill, three miles from the sea-coast, overlooking the river Alne. Dunstanburgh and Bamborough, if not relieved from the sea, could be surrounded and blockaded with comparative ease; Alnwick, the largest and strongest of the three castles, required to be shut in on all sides, and was likely to prove by far the hardest task. Luckily for Warwick the Roman road known as the Devil's Causeway was available for the connection of his out-lying forces, as it runs almost by the walls of Alnwick and within easy distance of both Dunstanburgh and Bamborough. To each castle its own blockading force was attached. Opposite Bamborough, the one of the three which was nearest to Scotland and most exposed to attack by a relieving army, lay Montagu and Sir Robert Ogle, both of whom knew every inch of the Border. Dunstanburgh was beleaguered by Tiptoft Earl of Worcester and Sir Ralph Grey. Alnwick was ob-served by Fauconbridge and Lord Scales. Warwick himself, with the general reserve, lay at Warkworth, three miles from Alnwick, ready to transfer himself to any point where his aid might be needed.

The forces employed were not less than thirty thou-sand men, without counting the troops on the lines of communication at Newcastle and Durham. To feed such a body in the depth of winter, in a sparsely-peopled and hostile country and with only one road open, was no mean task. Nevertheless the arrangements of Warwick worked with perfect smoothness and accur-acy,—good witness to the fact that his talent for organisation was as great as his talent for the use of

troops in the field. Every morning, we are told, the
Earl rode out and visited all the three sieges "for to
oversee; and if they wanted victuals or any other thing
he was ready to purvey it to them with all his power."
His day's ride was not less than thirty miles in all.
The army was in good spirits and sure of success. "We
have people enow here," wrote John Paston, whose
duty it was to escort Norfolk's convoys to and fro,
"so make as merry as ye can at home, for there is no
jeopardie toward."

A siege at Christmastide was the last thing that the
Lancastrians had expected at the moment of their
rising; they had counted on having the whole winter
to strengthen their position. No hope of immediate
aid from Scotland was forthcoming, and after three
weeks' blockade the spirits of the defenders of Bamborough and Dunstanburgh sank so low that they
commenced to think of surrender. Somerset, as we have
already mentioned, had been in treaty with Warwick
six months before, with the object of obtaining grace
from King Edward. He now renewed his offer to
Warwick, pledging himself to surrender Bamborough in
return for a free pardon. Ralph Percy, the commander
of Dunstanburgh, professed himself ready to make
similar terms.

It is somewhat surprising to find that Warwick
supported, and Edward granted, the petitions of
Somerset and Percy. But it was now two years since
the tragedy of Wakefield, both the King and his cousin
were sincerely anxious to bring about a pacification, and
they had resolved to forget their blood feud with the
Beauforts. On Christmas Eve 1462, therefore, Bam-

borough and Dunstanburgh threw open their gates,
such of their garrisons as chose to swear allegiance to
King Edward being admitted to pardon, while the rest,
headed by Jasper of Pembroke and Lord Roos, were
allowed to retire to Scotland unarmed and with white
staves in their hands.   Somerset and Percy went on to
Durham, where they swore allegiance to the King.
Edward took them into favour and "gave them his own
livery and great rewards," to Somerset in especial a
grant of twenty marks a week for his personal expenses,
and the promise of a pension of a thousand marks a year.
As a token of his loyalty Somerset offered to take the
field under Warwick against the Scots, and he was
accordingly sent up to assist at the siege of Alnwick.
Percy was shown equal favour; as a mark of confidence
the King made him Governor of Bamborough which
Somerset had just surrendered.

After the yielding of his chief adversary, King
Edward thought that there was no further need for his
presence in the North.   Accordingly he returned home
with the bulk of the army, leaving Warwick with ten
thousand men, commanded by Norfolk and the Earl of
Worcester, to finish the siege of Alnwick.   Somerset lay
with them, neither overmuch trusted nor overmuch
contemned by his late enemies.   Warwick's last siege,
however, was not destined to come to such an uneventful
close as those of Bamborough and Dunstanburgh.   Lord
Hungerford and the younger de Brézé made no signs of
surrender, and protracted their defence till January 6th
1463.

On that day, at five o'clock in the dusk of the winter
morning, a relieving army suddenly appeared in front of

Warwick's entrenchments. Though it was midwinter, Queen Margaret had succeeded in stirring up the Earl of Angus—the most powerful noble in Scotland and at that moment practical head of the Douglases—to lead a raid into England. Fired by the promise of an English dukedom, to be given when King Henry should come to his own again, Angus got together twenty thousand men, and slipping through the Central Marches, and taking to the Watling Street, presented himself most unexpectedly before the English camp. With him was Peter de Brézé, anxious to save his beleaguered son, and the Queen's French mercenaries.

For once in his life Warwick was taken by surprise. The Scots showed in such force that he thought himself unable to maintain the whole of his lines, and concentrated his forces on a front facing north-west between the castle hill and the river. Here he awaited attack, but nothing followed save insignificant skirmishing; Angus had come not to fight, but only to save the garrison. When the English blockading force was withdrawn, a party of Scotch horse rode up to the postern-gate of the castle and invited the besieged to escape; accordingly Lord Hungerford, the younger de Brézé, Sir Richard Tunstal, and the great majority of the garrison, hastily issued forth and joined the relieving force. Then Angus, to the surprise of the English, drew off his men, and fell back hastily over the Border.

Warwick had been quite outgeneralled; but the whole of his fault seems to have been the neglect to keep a sufficient force of scouts on the Border. If he had known of Angus's approach, he would have been able to take proper measures for protecting the siege.

But the main feeling in the English army was rather relief at the departure of the Scots than disgust at the escape of the garrison. "If on that day the Scots had but been bold as they were cunning, they might have destroyed the English lords, for they had double their numbers," writes the chronicler. The thing which attracted most notice was the fact that the renegade Somerset showed no signs of treachery, and bore himself bravely in the skirmish, "proving manfully that he was a true liegeman to King Edward." Henceforth he was trusted by his colleagues.

Some of the Alnwick garrison had been either unwilling or unable to escape with Angus. These protracted the defence for three weeks longer, but on January 30th they offered to surrender, and were allowed to depart unharmed to Scotland. The castle was garrisoned for the King, and entrusted to Sir John Ashley, to the great displeasure of Sir Ralph Grey to whom it had been promised. We shall see ere long what evils came from this displeasure.

It seemed now as if the war could not be far from its end. No single place now held out for Lancaster save the castle of Harlech in North Wales, where an obscure rebellion had been smouldering ever since 1461. We must not therefore blame Warwick for want of energy, when we find that in March he left the indefatigable Montagu in command, and came up to London to attend the Parliament which King Edward had summoned to meet in April. Nevertheless, as we shall see, his absence had the most unhappy results on the Border.

We have no definite information as to Warwick's doings in the spring of 1463, but we cannot doubt that it was by his counsel and consent that in April his brother the Chancellor and his friend Lord Wenlock, in company with Bourchier Earl of Essex, went over-sea to Flanders, and contracted with Philip Duke of Burgundy a treaty of commercial intercourse and a political alliance. Philip then conveyed the English ambassadors to the Court of Louis of France, who was lying at Hesdin, and with him they negotiated a truce to last from October 1st till the new year. This was to be preliminary to a definite peace with France, a plan always forward in Warwick's thoughts, for he was convinced that the last hope of Lancaster lay in the support of Louis, and that peace between Edward and the French King would finally ruin Queen Margaret's plans.

But while George Neville and the Burgundians were negotiating, a new and curious development of this period of lingering troubles had commenced. Once more the Lancastrians were up in arms, and again the evil began in Northumberland. Sir Ralph Grey had been promised, as we mentioned above, the governorship of Alnwick, and had failed to receive it when the castle fell. This so rankled in his mind that he determined to risk his fortunes on an attempt to seize the place by force and deliver it up again to the Queen. In the end of May he mastered the castle by treachery, and sent for the Lancastrians from over the Border. Lord Hungerford came up, and once more received command of the castle which he had evacuated five months before. The news of this exploit of Grey's was too much for the loyalty of Sir Ralph Percy, the renegade governor of Bamborough. When de Brézé and Hungerford came before his gates he deliberately surrendered the castle to them without resistance.

The exasperating news that the North was once more aflame reached Warwick as he banqueted with King Edward at Westminster on May 31st. With his customary energy the Earl set himself to repair the mischief before it should spread farther. On June 2nd he was once more marching up the Great North Road, with a new commission to act as the King's lieutenant in the North, while his brother Montagu was named under him Lord Warden of the Marches. Warwick's plan of campaign this time was not to reduce the castles at once, but to cut off the Lancastrians from their base by forcing the Scots to conclude peace. Accordingly he left the strongholds on his right and made straight for the Border. His first exploit was to relieve Norham Castle, on the English side of the Tweed, which was beset by four thousand Scotch borderers, aided by Peter de Brézé and his mercenaries. Queen Margaret herself was in their camp, and had dragged her unfortunate consort down to the seat of war. When the English appeared, the Scots and French raised the siege and retired behind the Tweed, where they set themselves to guard the ford called the Holybank. But Warwick was determined to cross; he won the passage by force of arms, and drove off its defenders. A few miles across the Border he found de Brézé's Frenchmen resting in an abbey, and fell on them with such vehemence that several hundreds were taken prisoners, including the Lord of Graville and Raoul d'Araines, de Brézé's chief lieutenants.

One chronicler records a curious incident at this fight.

"At the departing of Sir Piers de Bressy and his fellow-ship, there was one manly man among them, that pur-posed to meet with the Earl of Warwick; he was a taberette (drummer) and he stood upon a little hill with his tabor and his pipe, tabering and piping as merrily as any man might. There he stood by himself; till my lord Earl came unto him he would not leave his ground." Warwick was much pleased with the Frenchman's pluck, bade him be taken gently and well treated, "and there he became my lord's man, and yet is with him, a full good servant to his lord."

The moment that Warwick was actually across the Tweed, the Scotch regents offered him terms of peace. To prove their sincerity they agreed to send off Queen Margaret. Such pressure was accordingly put upon her that "she with all her Council, and Sir Peter with the Frenchmen, fled away by water in four balyngarys, and they landed at Sluis in Flanders, leaving all their horses and harness behind them, so sorely were they hasted by the Earl and his brother the Lord Montagu."[1] With the horses and harness was left poor King Henry, who for the next two years wandered about in an aim-less way on both sides of the Border, a mere meaningless shadow now that he was separated from his vehement consort.

Now at last the Civil War seemed at an end. With Margaret over-sea, Somerset a liegeman of York, the Northumbrian castles cut off from any hope of succour,

---

[1] The famous story of the robber and Queen Margaret, placed by so many writers after the battle of Hexham, seems quite impos-sible. If the incident took place at all, it happened on the other side of the Channel.

and the Scots suing humbly for peace, Warwick might
hope that his three years' toil had at last come to an
end. That, after all, the struggle was to be protracted
for twelve months more, was a fact that not even the
best of prophets could have predicted.

After the raid which drove Queen Margaret away,
and turned the hearts of the Scots toward peace, we lose
sight of Warwick for some months. We only know
that, for reasons to us unknown, he did not finish his
exploits by the capture of the Northumbrian castles, but
came home in the autumn, leaving them still unsubdued.
Perhaps after the winter campaign of 1462-63 he wished
to spend Christmas for once in his own fair castle of
Warwick. His estates indeed in Wales and the West
Midlands can hardly have seen him since the Civil War
recommenced in 1459, and must have required the
master's eye in every quarter. His wife and his daughters
too, now girls growing towards a marriageable age as
ages were reckoned in the fifteenth century, must long
have been without a sight of him.

While Warwick was for once at home, and King
Edward was making a progress round his kingdom with
much pomp and expense, it would seem that Queen
Margaret, from the retreat in Lorraine to which she had
betaken herself, was once more exerting her influence
to trouble England. At any rate a new Lancastrian
conspiracy was hatched in the winter of 1463-64,
with branches extending from Wales to Yorkshire.
The outbreak commenced at Christmas by the wholly
unexpected rebellion of the Duke of Somerset. Henry
of Beaufort had been so well treated by King Edward
that his conduct appears most extraordinary. He

had supped at the King's board, slept in the King's
chamber, served as captain of the King's guard, and
jousted with the King's favour on his helm; yet at midwinter he broke away for the North, with a very small
following, and made for the garrison at Alnwick.
Probably Somerset's conscience and his enemies had
united to make his position unbearable.   The Yorkists
were always taunting him behind his back, and when
he appeared in public in the King's company a noisy
mob rose up to stone him, and Edward had much ado to
save his life.   But whether urged by remorse for his
desertion of Lancaster, or by resentment for his treatment by the Yorkists, Somerset set himself to join the
sinking cause at one of its darkest hours.

His arrival in the North, where he came almost alone,
for his followers were wellnigh all cut off at Durham,
was the signal for the new Lancastrian outbreak.
Simultaneously Jasper of Pembroke endeavoured to stir
up Wales.   A rising took place in South Lancashire and
Cheshire, in which at one moment ten thousand men are
said to have been in the field: a band set out from Alnwick,
pushed by the Yorkist garrison at Newcastle, and seized
the Castle of Skipton in Craven, hard by Warwick's
ancestral estates in the North Riding; and Norham on
the Border was taken by treachery.

In March Warwick set out once more to regain the
twice-subdued North.   The rising in Cheshire collapsed
without needing his arms to put it down, and he was
able to reach York without molestation.   From thence
he sent to Scotland to summon the regency to carry out
the terms of pacification which they had promised in
the previous year.   The Scots made no objection, and

offered to send their ambassadors to York if safe escort
was given them past the Lancastrian fortresses. Accordingly Montagu started from Durham to pick up his
troops at Newcastle, where Lord Scrope was already
arrayed with the levies of the Northern Counties. This
journey was near being Montagu's last, for a few miles
outside Newcastle he was beset by his cousin Sir Humphrey Neville, the Earl of Westmoreland's nephew, who
fell on his escort with eighty spears as he passed through
a wood. Montagu, however, escaped by a detour and
came safely into Newcastle, where he took charge of
Scrope's force and marched for the Scotch Border.

At Hedgeley Moor he found Somerset with all the
Lancastrian refugees barring the way. There had
mustered all the survivors of the campaigns of 1461-2-3,
Roos and Hungerford, and Tailboys Lord of Kyme, and
the two traitors Ralph Grey and Ralph Percy. On April
15th their five thousand men fell on Montagu, whose
forces were probably about equal. The shock was
sharp but short; and when Ralph Percy, who led their
van, was struck down, the Lancastrians dispersed.
Percy, if the tale be true, refused to fly with the rest,
and died crying, "I have saved the bird in my bosom,"
meaning his loyalty to Henry. He should have remembered his faith a year before, when he swore fealty to
Edward at Durham.

Montagu was now able to reach Scotland unmolested.
He brought the Scots Commissioners back to York, and
a fifteen years' peace was safely concluded, the Scots
promising to give no further shelter to the Lancastrians,
and the English to disavow the Earls of Ross and Douglas
whom they had armed against the Scotch regency.

"An the Scots be true, the treaty may continue fifteen years," said the chronicler, "but it is hard to trust Scots : they be ever full of guile and deceit."

Somerset and his followers were now without hope. Their refuge in Scotland was cut off and their Northumbrian strongholds doomed to a speedy fall, for King Edward had been casting all the winter a train of great ordnance such as England had never seen before, and the pieces were already on their way north. Nevertheless the desperate adherents of Lancaster hardened their hearts, gathered their broken bands, and made one last desperate stand for the mastery of the North. On the Linhills, by the town of Hexham, they arrayed themselves against Montagu on May 13th. But when the Yorkists came in sight the hearts of the followers of Somerset failed them. All save five hundred melted away from their banners, and the small band that stayed to fight was broken, beaten, surrounded, and captured by Montagu's four thousand men with perfect ease.

The Lancastrian lords had fought their last field ; one and all were slain or captured on the hill a mile outside Hexham town, where they had made their stand. Montagu marked his triumph by the most bloody executions that had been seen throughout the whole war. At Hexham, next day, he beheaded Somerset, Sir Edmond Fitzhugh, a moss-trooping captain called Black Jack, and three more. On the next day but one he slew at Newcastle Lord Roos, Lord Hungerford, and three others. Next day he moved south to his brother's ancestral seat of Middleham, and executed Sir Philip Wentworth and six squires. Finally, he conducted to York and beheaded there Sir Thomas Hussey and thirteen more, the remainder of the prisoners of rank who had come into his hands.

For these sweeping executions Warwick must take part of the blame. But there is this to be said in defence of Montagu's stern justice, that Somerset and three or four others of the victims were men who had claimed and abused Edward's pardon, and that Roos and several more had been spared at the surrender of Bamborough in 1462. The whole body had shown that they could never be trusted, even if they professed to submit to York; and the practical justification of their death lies in the fact that with their execution ceased all attempts to raise the North in favour of the house of Lancaster. Public opinion among the Yorkists had nothing but praise for Montagu. "Lo, so manly a man is this good Lord Montagu," wrote a London chronicler, "he spared not their malice, nor their falseness, nor their guile, nor their treason, but slew many, and took many, and let smite off their heads"!

Even before the battle of Hedgeley Moor King Edward had set out to reinforce Warwick and Montagu. The news of their victories reached him on the way, but he continued to advance, bringing with him the great train of artillery destined for the siege of the Northumbrian fortresses. This journey was important to King Edward in more ways than one. How he spent one day of it, May 1st, when he lay at Stony Stratford, we shall presently see. If Warwick had but known of his master's doings on that morning, we may doubt if he would have been so joyous over his brother's victories or so remorseless with his captured enemies.

The King came up to York in the end of May, "and

kept his estate there solemnly in the palace, and there
he created John Lord Montagu Earl of Northumberland," in memory of his good service during the
last few months, handing over to him, together with
the Percy title, the greater part of the great Percy
estates—Alnwick and Warkworth and Langley and
Prudhoe, and many more fiefs between Tyne and Tweed.

Warwick now advanced northward to complete the
work which his brother had begun in the previous month,
while the King remained behind in Yorkshire and
occupied himself in the capture of Skipton Castle in
Craven. On June 23rd the Earl appeared before
Alnwick and summoned the place. The Lancastrians
had lost their leaders at Hexham, there was no more
fight in them, and they surrendered at once on promise
of their lives. Dunstanburgh and Norham followed the
example of Alnwick. Only Bamborough held out, for
there Sir Ralph Grey had taken refuge. He knew that
his treachery at Alnwick in the last year could never be
pardoned, and utterly refused to surrender. With him
was Sir Humphrey Neville, who had so nearly destroyed Montagu two months before.

We happen to have an account of the siege of Bamborough which is not without its interest. When the
army appeared before the castle Warwick's herald summoned it in form—

Offering free pardon, grace, body, and livelihood to all,
reserving two persons, Sir Ralph Grey and Sir Humphrey
Neville. Then Sir Ralph clearly determined within himself
to live or die within the place, though the herald charged
him with all inconvenience and shedding of blood that might
befall: saying in this wise: "My Lord ensureth you upon
his honour to sustain this siege before you these seven years

so that he win you : and if ye deliver not this jewel, which
the King our dread Sovereign Lord hath greatly in favour,
seeing it marches so nigh unto his enemies of Scotland, whole
and unbroken with ordnance, and if ye suffer any great guns
to be laid against it, it shall cost you a head for every gun
shot, from the head of the chief man to the head of the least
person within." But Sir Ralph departed from the herald,
and put him in endeavour to make defence.

Warwick was therefore compelled to have recourse to
his battering train, the first that had been used to effect
in an English siege.

So all the King's guns that were charged began to shoot
upon the said castle." " Newcastle, the King's greatest gun,
and "London," the second gun of iron, so betide the place
that the stones of the walls flew into the sea. " Dijon," a
brass gun of the King's, smote through Sir Ralph Grey's
chamber oftentimes, and "Edward" and "Richard," the
bombardels, and other ordnance, were busied on the place.
Presently the wall was breached, and my lord of Warwick,
with his men-at-arms and archers, won the castle by assault,
maugre Sir Ralph Grey, and took him alive, and brought
him to the King at Doncaster. And there the Earl of Worcester, Constable of England, sat in judgment on him.

Tiptoft was a judge who never spared, and Grey
a renegade who could expect no mercy. The prisoner
was sentenced to be beheaded, and only spared degrada-
tion from his knighthood " because of his noble ancestor, who suffered at Southampton for the sake of the
King's grandfather, Richard Earl of Cambridge." His
head was sent to join the ghastly collection standing
over the gate on London Bridge.

With the fall of Bamborough the first act of King
Edward's reign was at an end.

# CHAPTER XIII

WITH Hedgeley Moor and Hexham and the final surrender of the Northumbrian castles ended the last desperate attempt of the Lancastrians to hold their own in the North. The few surviving leaders who had escaped the fate of Somerset and Hungerford left Scotland and fled over-sea. Philip de Commines soon after met the chief of them in the streets of Ghent "reduced to such extremity of want and poverty that no common beggar could have been poorer. The Duke of Exeter was seen (though he concealed his name) following the Duke of Burgundy's train begging his bread from door to door, till at last he had a small pension allowed him in pity for his subsistence." With him were some of the Somersets, John and Edmund, brothers of the Duke who had just been beheaded. Jasper of Pembroke made his way to Wales and wandered in the hills from county to county, finding friends nowhere. No one could have guessed that the cause of Lancaster would ever raise its head again.

The times of war were at length over, and Warwick, like the rest of Englishmen, might begin to busy himself about other things than battles and sieges. In

July he was at last free, and was able to think of
turning southward to seek for more than a passing
visit the Midland estates of which he had seen so
little for the last five years.    After a short inter-
val of leisure, we find him in September sitting in
the King's Council, and urging on two measures
which he held necessary for the final pacification of the
realm.    The first was the conclusion of a definite treaty
of peace with France.    It was from King Louis that
the Lancastrians had been accustomed to draw their
supplies of ships and money, and while England and
France were still at war it was certain that King
Edward's enemies would continue to obtain shelter and
succour across the Channel.    Accordingly the Earl urged
on the conclusion of a treaty, and finally procured the
appointment of himself and his friend and follower
Wenlock as ambassadors to Louis.    The second point
of his schemes was connected with the first.    It was
high time, as all England had for some time been saying, that the King should marry.[1]    Edward was now
in his twenty-fourth year, "and men marvelled that he
abode so long without any wife, and feared that he was
not over chaste of his living."    Those, indeed, who were
about the King's person knew that some scandal had
already been caused by his attempts, successful and
unsuccessful, on the honour of several ladies about the
Court.    Rumour had for some time been coupling
Edward's name with that of various princesses of a

---

[1] There seems to be no foundation for the theory that Warwick
wished the King to marry his daughter Isabel.    The Earl moved
strongly in favour of the French marriage, and his daughter was
too young, being only thirteen years of age, for a king desirous of
raising up heirs to his crown.

marriageable age among foreign royal families. Some
had said that he was about to marry Mary of Gueldres,
the Queen Dowager of Scotland, and others had specu-
lated on his opening negotiations for the hand of Isabel
of Castile, sister of the reigning Spanish King. But
there had been no truth in these reports. Warwick's
scheme was to cement the peace with France by a
marriage with a French princess, and in the preliminary
inquiries which the King permitted him to send to
Louis the marriage question was distinctly mentioned.
Louis' sisters were all married, and his daughters were mere
children, so that their names were not brought forward,
for King Edward required a wife of suitable years, "to
raise him goodly lineage such as his father had reared."
The lady whom Warwick proposed to the King was
Bona of Savoy, sister to Charlotte Queen of France, a
princess who dwelt at her brother-in-law King Louis'
Court and in whose veins ran the blood both of the
Kings of France and the Dukes of Burgundy.

King Edward made no open opposition to Warwick's
plans. The project was mooted to King Louis, safe
conducts for the English Embassy were obtained, and
Warwick and Wenlock were expected at St. Omer about
October 3rd or 4th. But at the last moment, when
Warwick attended at Reading on September 28th to
receive his master's final instructions, a most astounding
announcement was made to him. We have an account
of the scene which bears some marks of truth.

The Council met for the formal purpose of approving
the marriage negotiations. A speaker, probably Warwick,
laid before the King the hope and expectation of his
subjects that he would deign to give them a Queen.

M

Then the King answered that of a truth he wished to marry, but that perchance his choice might not be to the liking of all present. Then those of his Council asked to know of his intent, and would be told to what house he would go. To which the King replied in right merry guise that he would take to wife Dame Elizabeth Grey, the daughter of Lord Rivers. But they answered him that she was not his match, however good and however fair she might be, and that he must know well that she was no wife for such a high prince as himself; for she was not the daughter of a duke or earl, but her mother the Duchess of Bedford had married a simple knight, so that though she was the child of a duchess and the niece of the Count of St. Pol, still she was no wife for him. When King Edward heard these sayings of the lords of his blood and his Council, which it seemed good to them to lay before him, he answered that he should have no other wife and that such was his good pleasure.

Then came the clinching blow; no other wife could he have—for he was married to Dame Elizabeth already !

In fact, five months before, on May 1st, when he ought to have been far on his way to the North, King Edward had secretly ridden over from Stony Stratford to Grafton in Northamptonshire, and wedded the lady. No one had suspected the marriage, for the King had had but a short and slight acquaintance with Elizabeth Grey, who had been living a retired life ever since her husband, a Lancastrian knight, fell in the moment of victory at the second battle of St. Albans. Edward had casually met her, had been conquered by her fair face, and had made hot love to her. Elizabeth was clever and cautious; she would hear of nothing but a formal offer of marriage, and the young King, perfectly infatuated by his passion, had wedded her in secret at Grafton in the presence of no one save her mother and two other witnesses. This was the urgent private business which had kept him from appearing to open his Parliament at York.

The marriage was a most surprising event. Lord Rivers, the lady's father, had been a keen Lancastrian. He it was who had been captured at Sandwich in 1460, and brought before Warwick and Edward to undergo that curious scolding which we have elsewhere recorded. And now this "made lord, who had won his fortune by his marriage," had become the King's father-in-law. Dame Elizabeth herself was seven years older than her new husband, and was the mother of children twelve and thirteen years of age. The public was so astonished at the match that it was often said that the Queen's mother, the old Duchess of Bedford, must have given King Edward a love philtre, for in no other way could the thing be explained.

Warwick and the rest of the lords of the Council were no less vexed than astonished by this sudden announcement. The Earl had broached the subject of the French marriage to King Louis, and was expected to appear within a few days to submit the proposal for acceptance. The King, knowing all the time that the scheme was impossible, had allowed him to commit himself to it, and now left him to explain to King Louis that he had been duped in the most egregious way, and had been excluded from his master's confidence all along. Very naturally the Earl let the embassy drop; he could not dare to appear before the French King to ask for peace, when the bond of union which he had promised to cement it was no longer possible.

But vexed and angered though he must have been at
the way in which he had been treated, Warwick was too
loyal a servant of the house of York to withdraw from
his master's Council. He bowed to necessity, and
acquiesced in what he could not approve. Accordingly
Warwick attended next day to hear the King make
public announcement of his marriage in Reading Abbey
on the feast of St. Michael, and he himself, in company with George of Clarence the King's brother,
led Dame Elizabeth up to the seat prepared for her
beside her husband, and bowed the knee to her as
Queen.

For a few months it seemed as if the King's marriage
had been a single freak of youthful passion, and the
domination of the house of Neville in the royal Councils
appeared unshaken. As if to make amends for his late
treatment of Warwick, Edward raised his brother
George Neville the Chancellor to the vacant Arch-
bishopric of York, and in token of confidence sent the
Earl as his representative to prorogue a Parliament
summoned to meet on November 4th.

But these marks of regard were not destined to
continue. The favours of the King, though there was
as yet no open breach between him and his great
Minister, were for the future bestowed in another
quarter. The house of Rivers was almost as prolific as
the house of Neville; the Queen had three brothers,
five sisters, and two sons, and for them the royal influence was utilised in the most extraordinary way
during the next two years. Nor was it merely inordinate affection for his wife that led King Edward to
squander his wealth and misuse his power for the

benefit of her relatives. It soon became evident that he
had resolved to build up with the aid of the Queen's
family one of those great allied groups of noble houses
whose strength the fifteenth century knew so well—a
group that should make him independent of the control
of the Nevilles. A few days after the acknowledgment
of the Queen, began a series of marriages in the Rivers
family, which did not cease for two years. In October
1464, immediately after the scene at Reading, the
Queen's sister Margaret was married to Thomas Lord
Maltravers, the heir of the wealthy Earl of Arundel.
In January 1465 John Woodville, the youngest of her
brothers, wedded the Dowager Duchess of Norfolk.
This was a disgraceful match: the bridegroom was just
of age, the bride quite old enough to be his grandmother;
but she was a great heiress, and the King persuaded
her to marry the sordid young man. Within eighteen
months more, nearly the whole of the family had been
married off: Anne Woodville to the heir of Bourchier
Earl of Essex; Mary Woodville to the eldest son of
Lord Herbert, the King's most intimate counsellor after
Warwick in his earlier years; Eleanor Woodville to
George Grey heir of the Earl of Kent; and Catherine
Woodville, most fortunate of all, to the young Duke of
Buckingham, grandson of the old Duke who had fallen
at Northampton. To end the tale of the alliances of
this most fortunate family, it is only necessary to add
that even before Queen Elizabeth's marriage her eldest
brother Anthony had secured the hand of Elizabeth,
heiress of the Lord Scales who was slain on the Thames
in 1460. Truly the Woodville marriages may compare
not unfavourably with those of the Nevilles!

While the King was heaping his favours on the house of Rivers, Warwick was still employed from time to time in the service of the Crown. But he could no longer feel that he had the chief part in guiding his monarch's policy. Indeed, the King seems to have even gone out of his way to carry out every scheme on a different principle from that which the Earl adopted. In the spring of 1465, at the time of the Queen's formal coronation in May—a ceremony which he was glad enough to escape—Warwick went over-sea to conduct negotiations with the French and Burgundians. He met the Burgundian ambassadors at Boulogne, and those of France at Calais. It was a critical time for both France and Burgundy, for the War of the Public Weal had just broken out, and each party was anxious to secure the friendship, or at least the neutrality of England. With the Burgundians, whom Warwick met first, no agreement could be made, for the Count of Charolois, who had now got the upper hand of his aged father Duke Philip, refused to make any pledges against helping the Lancastrians. He was at this very time pensioning the exiled Somersets and Exeter, and almost reckoned himself a Lancastrian prince, because his mother, Isabel of Portugal, was a granddaughter of John of Gaunt. Warwick and Charles of Charolois were quite unable to agree. Each of them was too much accustomed to have his own way, and though they held high feasts together at Boulogne, and were long in council, they parted in wrath. There would seem to have been something more than a mere difference of opinion between them, for ever afterwards they regarded each other as personal enemies. King Louis, whose

ambassadors met Warwick a month later, proved far
more accommodating than the hot-headed Burgundian
prince. He consented to forget the matter of the marriage, and agreed to the conclusion of a truce for
eighteen months, during which he engaged to give no
help to Queen Margaret, while Warwick covenanted
that England should refrain from aiding the Dukes of
Burgundy and Bretagne, now in full rebellion against
their sovereign.

    Late in the summer of 1465 Warwick returned home
just in time to hear of a new stroke of fortune which
had befallen his master. Henry the Sixth had just been
captured in Lancashire. The ex-king had wandered
down from his retreat in Scotland, and was moving
about in an aimless way from one Lancastrian household
to another, accompanied by no one but a couple of
priests. One of Henry's entertainers betrayed him, and
he was seized by John Talbot of Basshall as he sat at
meat in Waddington Hall, and forwarded under guard
to London. At Islington Warwick rode forth to meet
his late sovereign, and by the King's orders led him
publicly through the city, with his feet bound by leather
straps to his stirrups. Why this indignity was inflicted
on the unfortunate Henry it is hard to say ; there cannot possibly have been any fear of a rescue, and Warwick
might well have spared his late master the shame of
bonds. Henry was led along Cheapside and Cornhill
to the Tower, where he was placed in honourable custody,
and permitted to receive the visits of all who wished to
see him.

    That Warwick was not yet altogether out of favour
with King Edward was shown by the fact that he was

asked to be godfather to the Queen's first child, the
Princess Elizabeth, in the February of the following
year 1466.    But immediately afterwards came the
succession of events which marked the final breach
between the King and the Nevilles.   In March Edward
suddenly dismissed from the office of Treasurer Lord
Mountjoy, a friend of Warwick's, and gave the post to
his wife's father Lord Rivers, whom he soon created
an earl.   The removal of his friend was highly displeas-
ing to Warwick; but worse was to follow.   Warwick's
nephew George Neville, the heir of his brother John,
had been affianced to Anne heiress of the exiled Duke
of Exeter; but the Queen gave the Duchess of Exeter
four thousand marks to break off the match, and the
young lady was wedded to Thomas Grey, Elizabeth's
eldest son by her first marriage.   This blow struck the
Nevilles in their tenderest point; even the marriages
which had made their good fortune were for the future
to be frustrated by royal influence.

The next slight which Warwick received at the
hands of his sovereign touched him even more closely.
His eldest daughter Isabel, who had been born in 1451,
was now in her sixteenth year, and already thoughts
about her marriage had begun to trouble her father's
brain.   The Earl counted her worthy of the highest
match that could be found in the realm, for there was
destined to go with her hand such an accumulation of
estates as no subject had ever before possessed—half
of the lands of Neville, Montacute, Despenser, and Beauchamp.   The husband whom Warwick had hoped to
secure for his child was George Duke of Clarence, the
King's next brother, a young man of eighteen years.

Clarence was sounded, and liked the prospect well enough, for the young lady was fair as well as rich. But they had not reckoned with the King. After a long visit which Clarence and his younger brother Richard of Gloucester had paid to Warwick in the end of 1466, Edward got wind of the proposed marriage. " When the King knew that his brothers had returned from their visit to the Earl at Cambridge, he asked them why they had left his Court, and who had given them counsel to visit the Earl. Then they answered that none had been the cause save they themselves. And the King asked whether there had been any talk of affiancing them to their cousins, the Earl's daughters; and the Duke of Clarence "—always prompt at a lie— "answered that there was not. But the King, who had been fully informed of all, waxed wroth, and sent them from his presence." Edward strictly forbade the marriage, and for the present there was no more talk of it; but Clarence and Warwick understood each other, and were always in communication, much to the King's displeasure. It did not please him to find his heir presumptive and his most powerful subject on too good terms.

The King waited a few months more, and then proceeded to put a far worse insult on his old friends and followers. In May 1467 he sent Warwick over-sea, with a commission to visit the King of France, and turn the eighteen months truce made in 1465 into a permanent peace on the best terms possible. The errand seemed both useful and honourable, and Warwick went forth in good spirits; but it was devised in reality merely to get him out of the kingdom, at a time when the King was about to cross all his most cherished plans.

Louis was quite as desirous as Warwick himself to conclude a permanent peace. It was all-important to him that England should not be on the side of Burgundy, and he was ready to make the Earl's task easy. The reception which he prepared for Warwick was such as might have been given to a crowned head. He went five leagues down the Seine to receive the English embassy, and feasted Warwick royally on the river bank. When Rouen was reached "the King gave the Earl most honourable greeting; for there came out to meet him the priests of every parish in the town in their copes, with crosses and banners and holy water, and so he was conducted to Notre Dame de Rouen, where he made his offering. And he was well lodged at the Jacobins in the said town of Rouen. Afterward the Queen and her daughters came to the said town that he might see them. And the King abode with Warwick for the space of twelve days communing with him, after which the Earl departed back into England." And with him went as Ambassadors from France the Archbishop of Narbonne, the Bastard of Bourbon (Admiral of France), the Bishop of Bayeux, Master Jean de Poupencourt, and William Monipenny, a Scotch agent in whom the King placed much confidence.

Warwick and the French Ambassadors landed at Sandwich, where they had a hearty reception; for the people of Sandwich, like all the men of Kent, were great supporters of the Earl. Posts were sent forward to notify their arrival to the King, and the party then set out to ride up to London. As they drew near the city

the Earl was somewhat vexed to find that no one came
forth to welcome them on the King's behalf; but presently the Duke of Clarence came riding alone to meet
him, and brought him intelligence which turned his
satisfaction at the success of the French negotiations
into bitter vexation of spirit.

When Warwick had got well over-sea, the King had
proceeded to work out his own plans, secure that he
would not be interrupted. He had really determined to
make alliance with Burgundy and not with France; and
the moment that the coast was clear a Burgundian
emissary appeared in London. Antony "the Grand
Bastard," the trusted agent of the Court of Charolois,
ascended the Thames at the very moment that Warwick
was ascending the Seine. Ostensibly he came on a
chivalrous errand, to joust with the Queen's brother
Lord Scales in honour of all the ladies of Burgundy.
The passage of arms was duly held, to the huge delight
of the populace of London, and the English chroniclers
give us all its details—instead of relating the important
political events of the year. But the real object of the
Bastard's visit was to negotiate an English alliance for
his brother; and he was so successful that he returned to
Flanders authorised to promise the hand of the King's
sister Margaret to the Count of Charolois.

But Warwick had not merely to learn that the King
had stultified his negotiations with France by making an
agreement with Burgundy behind his back. He was
now informed that, only two days before his arrival,
Edward had gone, without notice given or cause assigned,
to his brother the Archbishop of York, who lay ill at his
house by Westminster Barrs, and suddenly dismissed him

from the Chancellorship and taken the great seal from
him. Open war had been declared on the house of
Neville.[1]

But bitterly vexed though he was at his sovereign's
double dealing, Warwick proceeded to carry out the
forms of his duty. He called on the King immediately
on his arrival, announced the success of his embassy, and
craved for a day of audience for the French Ambassadors.
"When the Earl spoke of all the good cheer that King
Louis had made him, and how he had sent him the keys
of every castle and town that he passed through, he perceived from the King's countenance that he was paying
no attention at all to what he was saying, so he betook
himself home, sore displeased."

Next day the French had the audience. The King
received them in state, surrounded by Rivers, Scales,
John Woodville, and Lord Hastings. "The Ambassadors were much abashed to see him, for he showed himself a prince of a haughty bearing." Warwick then
introduced them, and Master Jean de Poupencourt,
as spokesman for the rest, laid the proposals of Louis
before the King. Edward briefly answered that he had
pressing business, and could not communicate with them
himself; they might say their say to certain lords whom
he would appoint for the purpose. Then they were
ushered out of his presence. It was clear that he would
do nothing for them; indeed the whole business had

---

[1] It seems impossible to work out to any purpose the statement
of Polidore Vergil and others that Warwick's final breach with the
King was caused by Edward's offering violence to a lady of the
house of Neville. Lord Lytton, of course, was justified in using
this hint for his romance, but the historian finds it too vague and
untrustworthy.

only been concocted to get Warwick out of the way. It
was abortive, and had been intended to be so.

The Earl on leaving the palace was bursting with
rage; his ordinary caution and affability were gone, and
he broke out in angry words even before the foreigners.
" As they rowed home in their barge the Frenchmen had
many discourses with each other.    But Warwick was so
wroth that he could not contain himself, and he said to
the Admiral of France, ' Have you not seen what traitors
there are about the King's person ?'    But the Admiral
answered, ' My Lord, I pray you grow not hot; for
some day you shall be well avenged.'    But the Earl
said, ' Know that those very traitors were the men who
have had my brother displaced from the office of Chancellor, and made the King take the seal from him.' "

Edward went to Windsor next day, taking no further
heed of the Ambassadors.   He appointed no one to treat
with them, and they remained six weeks without hearing
from him, seeing no one but Warwick, who did his best
to entertain them, and Warwick's new ally the Duke
of Clarence.    At last they betook themselves home,
having accomplished absolutely nothing.    On the eve of
their departure the King sent them a beggarly present
of hunting-horns, leather bottles, and mastiffs, in return
for the golden hanaps and bowls and the rich jewellery
which they had brought from France.

Warwick would have nothing more to do with his
master.   He saw the Ambassadors back as far as Sandwich, and then went off in high dudgeon to Middleham.
There he held much deep discourse with his brothers,
George the dispossessed Chancellor, and John of Montagu the Earl of Northumberland.    At Christmas the

King summoned him to Court; he sent back the reply
that "never would he come again to Council while all
his mortal enemies, who were about the King's person,
namely, Lord Rivers the Treasurer, and Lord Scales
and Lord Herbert and Sir John Woodville, remained
there present." The breach between Warwick and his
master was now complete.

# CHAPTER XIV

## PLAYING WITH TREASON

GREAT ministers who have been accustomed to sway the destinies of kingdoms, and who suddenly find themselves disgraced at their master's caprice, have seldom been wont to sit down in resignation and accept their fall with equanimity. Such a line of conduct requires a self-denial and a high-flown loyalty to principle which are seldom found in the practical statesman. If the fallen minister is well stricken in years, and the fire has gone out of him, he may confine himself to sermons on the ingratitude of kings. If his greatness has been purely official, and his power entirely dependent on the authority entrusted to him by his master, his discontent may not be dangerous. But Warwick was now in the very prime of his life,—he was just forty,—and he was moreover by far the most powerful subject within the four seas. It was sheer madness in King Edward to goad such a man to desperation by a series of deliberate insults.

This was no mere case of ordinary ingratitude. If ever one man had made another, Richard Neville had made Edward Plantagenet. He had taken charge of him, a raw lad of eighteen, at the moment of the

disastrous rout of Ludford, and trained him in arms
and statecraft with unceasing care. Twice had he
saved the lost cause of York, in 1459 and in 1461. He
had spent five years in harness, in one long series of
battles and sieges, that his cousin might wear his crown
in peace. He had compassed sea and land in embassies
that Edward might be safe from foreign as well as from
domestic foes. He had seen his father and his brother
fall by the axe and the sword in the cause of York. He
had seen his mother and his wife fugitives on the face
of the earth, his castles burnt, his manors wasted, his
tenants slain, all that the son of Richard Plantagenet
might sit on the throne that was his father's due.

Warwick then might well be cut to the heart at his
master's ingratitude. It was no marvel if, after the
King's last treachery to him in the matter of the French
embassy, he retired from Court and sent a bitter answer
to Edward's next summons. After the open breach
there were now two courses open to him : the first to
abandon all his schemes, and betake himself in silent
bitterness to the management of his vast estates ; the
second was to endeavour to win his way back to power
by the ways which medieval England knew only too
well—the way which had served Simon de Montfort,
and Thomas of Lancaster, and Richard of York ; the
way that had led Simon and Thomas and Richard to
their bloody graves. The first alternative was no doubt
the one that the perfect man, the ideally loyal and
unselfish knight, should have chosen. But Richard
Neville was no perfect man ; he was a practical statesman—"the cleverest man of his time," says one who
had observed him closely ; and his long tenure of

power had made him look upon the first place in the Council of the King as his right and due. His enemies the Woodvilles and Herberts had driven him from his well-earned precedence by the weapons that they could use—intrigue and misrepresentation; what more natural than that he should repay them by the weapon that he could best employ, the iron hand of armed force?

Hitherto the career of Warwick had been singularly straightforward and consistent. Through thick and thin he had supported the cause of York and never wavered in his allegiance to it. It must not be supposed that he changed his whole policy when his quarrel with the King came to a head. As his conduct in 1469, when his ungrateful master was in his power, was destined to show, he had no further design than to reconquer for himself the place in the royal Council which had been his from 1461 to 1464. Later events developed his plans further than he had himself expected, but it is evident that at first his sole design was to clear away the Woodvilles. The only element in his programme which threatened to lead to deeper and more treasonable plans was his connection with his would-be son-in-law George of Clarence. The handsome youth who professed such a devotion to him, followed his advice with such docility, and took his part so warmly in the quarrel with the King, seems from the first to have obtained a place in his affections greater than Edward had ever won. But Clarence had his ambitions; what they were and how far they extended the Earl had not as yet discovered.

Warwick had now the will to play his master's new ministers an ill turn; that he had also the power to do

N

so none knew better than himself.   The lands of Neville
and Montacute, Beauchamp and Despenser united could
send into the field a powerful army.   Moreover, his
neighbours, in most of the counties where his influence
prevailed, had bound themselves to him by taking his
livery; barons as well as knights were eager ·to be of
his "Privy Council," to wear his Ragged Staff and ride in
his array.   The very aspect of his household seemed to
show the state of a petty king.   Every one has read
Hollingshead's famous description, which tells how the
little army of followers which constituted his ordinary
retinue eat six oxen daily for breakfast.

Nor was it only in the strength of his own retainers
that Warwick trusted; he knew that he himself was the
most popular man in the kingdom.   Men called him ever
the friend of the Commons, and "his open kitchen persuaded the meaner sort as much as the justice of his cause."
His adversaries, on the other hand, were unmistakably
disliked by the people.   The old partisans of York still
looked on the Woodvilles as Lancastrian renegades, and
the grasping avarice of Rivers and his family was stirring
up popular demonstration against them even before
Warwick's breach with the King.   A great mob in Kent
had sacked one of Rivers' manors and killed his deer in
the autumn of 1467, and trouble was brewing against
him in other quarters.   A word of summons from
Warwick would call· rioters out of the ground in half
the shires of England.   Already in January 1468 a
French ambassador reports: "In one county more than
three hundred archers were in arms, and had made
themselves a captain named Robin, and sent to the
Earl of Warwick to know if it was time to be busy, and

to say that all their neighbours were ready.  But my Lord answered, bidding them go home, for it was not yet time to be stirring.  If the time should come, he would let them know."[1]

It was not only discontented Yorkists that had taken the news of the quarrel between Warwick and his master as a signal for moving.  The tidings had stirred the exiled Lancastrians to a sudden burst of activity of which we should hardly have thought them capable.  Queen Margaret borrowed ships and money from Louis, and lay in force at Harfleur.  Sir Henry Courtney, heir of the late Earl of Devon, and Thomas Hungerford, son of the lord who fell at Hexham, tried to raise an insurrection in the South-West; but they were caught by Lord Stafford of Southwick and beheaded at Salisbury.  As a reward the King gave Stafford his victim's title of Earl of Devon.  In Wales the long-wandering Jasper Tudor suddenly appeared, at the head of two thousand men, supported by a small French fleet. He took Harlech Castle and sacked Denbigh; but a few weeks later Warwick's enemy, Lord Herbert, fell upon him at the head of the Yorkists of the March, routed his tumultuary army, retook Harlech, and forced him again to seek refuge in the hills.  Herbert, like Lord Stafford, was rewarded with the title of the foe he had van-quished, and became Earl of Pembroke.  While these risings were on foot, Lancastrian emissaries were busy all over England; but their activity only resulted in a series

[1] Letter of William Monipenny to Louis the Eleventh.  He calls it *le pays de Surforkshire*, a cross between Suffolk and York-shire.  But the latter must be meant, as Warwick had no interest in Suffolk, and the captain is obviously Robin of Redesdale.

of executions. Two gentlemen of the Duke of Norfolk's
retinue were beheaded for holding secret communication
with the Beauforts while they were in Flanders, following the train which escorted the Princess Margaret at
her marriage with Charles of Charolois, who had now
become Duke of Burgundy. In London more executions took place, and Sir Thomas Cooke, late Lord
Mayor, had all his goods confiscated for misprision of
treason. Two of the Lancastrian emissaries alleged,
under torture, the one, that Warwick had promised aid
to the rising, the other, that Lord Wenlock, Warwick's
friend and supporter, had guilty knowledge of the
scheme; but in each case the King himself acknowledged that the accusation was frivolous—the random
imagining of men on the rack, forced to say something
to save their own bones. It was not likely that Warwick
would play the game of Queen Margaret, the slayer of
his father and brother, and the instigator of attempts on
his own life.

Startled by the sudden revival of Lancastrian energy,
but encouraged by the easy way in which he had
mastered it, King Edward determined to give the warlike impulses of his subjects vent by undertaking in the
next year a great expedition against France. He had the
example of Henry the Fifth before his eyes, and hoped
to stifle treason at home by foreign war. Among his
preparations for leaving home was a determined attempt
to open negotiations with Warwick for a reconciliation.
The King won over the Archbishop of York to plead
his cause, by restoring to him some estates which he
had seized in 1467; and about Easter George Neville
induced his brother to meet the King at Coventry.

Warwick came, but it is to be feared that he came fully
resolved to have his revenge at his own time, with his
heart quite unsoftened toward his master; yet he spoke
the King fair, and even consented to be reconciled to
Lord Herbert, though he would have nothing to say to
the Woodvilles. He was also induced to join the company which escorted the Princess Margaret to the coast,
on her way to her marriage in Flanders. After this
Warwick paid a short visit to London, where he sat
among the judges who in July tried the Lancastrian
conspirators of the city. Clarence accompanied him,
and sat on the same bench. He had spent the last few
months in moving the Pope to grant him a disposition
to marry Isabel Neville,[1] for they were within the pro-
hibited degrees; but under pressure from King Edward
the Curia had delayed the consideration of his re-
quest.

The autumn of 1468 and the spring of 1469 passed
away quietly. Warwick made no movement, for he
was still perfecting his plans. He saw with secret
pleasure that the French, with whom peace would have
been made long ago if his advice had been followed,
kept the King fully employed. It must have given him
peculiar gratification when his enemy Anthony Woodville, placed at the head of a large fleet, made two most
inglorious expeditions to the French coast, and returned
crestfallen without having even seen the enemy.

Meanwhile the Earl had been quietly measuring his
resources. He had spoken to all his kinsmen, and
secured the full co-operation of the majority of them.
George the Archbishop of York, Henry Neville heir to

[1] Clarence's mother was Isabel's great aunt.

Warwick's aged uncle Lord Latimer, Sir John Coniers of Hornby, husband of his niece Alice Neville, his cousin Lord Fitzhugh, and Thomas "the bastard of Faucon-bridge," natural son to the deceased peer who had fought so well at Towton, were his chief reliance. His brother John of Montagu, the Earl of Northumberland, could not make up his mind; he did not reveal Warwick's plans to the King, but he would not promise any aid. William Neville of Abergavenny was now too old to be taken into account. The rest of Warwick's uncles and brothers were by this time dead.

By April 1469 the preparations were complete. Every district where the name of Neville was great had been carefully prepared for trouble. Kent, Yorkshire, and South Wales were ready for insurrection, and yet all had been done so quietly that the King, who ever since he had thrown off the Earl's influence had been sinking deeper and deeper into habits of careless evil-living and debauchery, suspected nothing.

In April Warwick took his wife and daughters across to Calais, apparently to get them out of harm's way. He himself, professing a great wish to see his cousin Margaret, the newly-married Duchess of Burgundy, went on to St. Omer. He there visited Duke Charles, and was reconciled to him in spite of the evil memories of their last meeting at Boulogne. To judge from his conduct, the Earl was bent on nothing but a harmless tour; but, as a matter of fact, his movements were but a blind destined to deceive King Edward. While he was feasting at St. Omer he had sent orders over-sea for the commencement of an insurrection. In a few days it was timed to break out. Meanwhile Warwick returned to

Calais, and lodged with Wenlock, who was in charge of the great fortress.

His orders had had their effect. In the end of June grave riots broke out in the neighbourhood of York. Ostensibly they were connected with the maladministration of the estates of St. Leonard's hospital in that city; but they were in reality political and not agrarian. Within a few days fifteen thousand men were at the gates of York, clamorously setting forth a string of grievances, which were evidently founded on Cade's manifesto of 1450. Once more we hear of heavy taxation, maladministration of the law, the alienation of the royal estates to upstart favourites, the exclusion from the royal Councils of the great lords of the royal blood. Once more a demand is made for the punishment of evil counsellors, and the introduction of economy into the royal household, and the application of the revenue to the defence of the realm. The first leader of the rioters was Robert Huldyard, known as Robin of Redesdale, no doubt the same Robin whom the Earl had bidden in 1468 to keep quiet and wait the appointed time. John Neville the Earl of Northumberland lay at York with a large body of men-at-arms, for he was still Lieutenant of the North. Many expected that he would join the rioters; but, either because he had not quite recognised the insurrection to be his brother's work, or because he had resolved to adhere loyally to Edward, Montagu surprised the world by attacking the band which beset York. He routed its vanguard, captured Huldyard, and had him beheaded.

But this engagement was far from checking the rising. In a week the whole of Yorkshire, from Tees

to Humber, was up, and it soon became evident in
whose interest the movement was working. New leaders
appeared. Sir John Coniers, the husband of Warwick's
niece, and one of the most influential Yorkists of the
North, replaced Huldyard, and assumed his name of
Robin of Redesdale, while with him were Henry
Neville of Latimer and Lord Fitzhugh. Instead of
lingering at the gates of York, the great body of insurgents—rumour made it more than thirty thousand
strong—rolled southward into the Midlands. They
were coming, they said, to lay their grievances before
the King; and in every place that they passed they
hung their articles, obviously the work of some old
political hand, on the church doors.

King Edward seems to have been taken quite un-
awares by this dangerous insurrection. He had kept
his eye on Warwick alone, and when Warwick was over-
sea he thought himself safe. At the end of June he
had been making a progress in Norfolk, with no force
at his back save two hundred archers, a bodyguard
whom he had raised in 1468 and kept always around
him. Hearing of the stir in Yorkshire, he rode northward to Nottingham, calling in such force as could be
gathered by the way. As he went, news reached him
which suddenly revealed the whole scope of the insurrection.

The moment that his brother's attention was drawn
off by the Northern rising, the Duke of Clarence had
quietly slipped over to Calais, and with him went George
Neville the Archbishop of York. This looked suspicious,
and the King at once wrote to Clarence, Warwick, and
the Archbishop, bidding them all come to him without

delay. Long before his orders can have reached them, the tale of treason was out. Within twelve hours of Clarence's arrival at Calais the long-projected marriage between him and Isabel Neville had been celebrated, in full defiance of the King. Warwick and Clarence kept holiday but for one day; the marriage took place on the 11th, and by the 12th they were in Kent with a strong party of the garrison of Calais as their escort.

The unruly Kentishmen rose in a body in Warwick's favour, as eagerly as when they had mustered to his banner in 1460 before the battle of Northampton. The Earl and the Duke came to Canterbury with several thousand men at their back. There they revealed their treasonable intent, for they published a declaration that they considered the articles of Robin of Redesdale just and salutary, and would do their best to bring them to the King's notice. How the King was to be persuaded was indicated clearly enough, by a proclamation which summoned out the whole shire of Kent to join the Earl's banner. Warwick and his son-in-law then marched on London, which promptly threw open its gates. The King was thus caught between two fires—the open rebels lay to the north of him, his brother and cousin with their armed persuasion to the south.

Even before Warwick's treason had been known, the King had recognised the danger of the northern rising, and sent commissions of array all over England. Two considerable forces were soon in arms in his behalf. Herbert, the new Earl of Pembroke, raised fourteen thousand Welsh and Marchmen at Brecon and Ludlow, and set out eastward. Stafford, the new Earl of Devon, collected six thousand archers in the South-

Western Counties, and set out northward. The King lay at Nottingham with Lord Hastings, Lord Mountjoy, and the Woodvilles. He seems to have had nearly fifteen thousand men in his company; but their spirit was bad. "Sire," said Mountjoy to him in full council of war, "no one wishes your person ill, but it would be well to send away my Lord of Rivers and his children when you have done conferring with them." Edward took this advice. Rivers and John Woodville forthwith retired to Chepstow; Scales joined his sister the Queen at Cambridge.

Meanwhile the Northern rebels were pouring south by way of Doncaster and Derby. Their leaders Coniers and Latimer showed considerable military skill, for by a rapid march on to Leicester they got between the King and Lord Herbert's army. Edward, for once out-generalled, had to follow them southward, but the York-shiremen were some days ahead of him, and on July 25th reached Daventry. On the same day Herbert and Stafford concentrated their forces at Banbury; but on their first meeting the two new earls fell to hard words on a private quarrel, and, although the enemy was so near, Stafford in a moment of pique drew off his six thousand men to Deddington, ten miles away, leaving Pembroke's fourteen thousand Welsh pikemen altogether unprovided with archery.

Next day all the chief actors in the scene were converging on the same spot in central England—Coniers marching from Daventry on to Banbury, Pembroke from Banbury on Daventry, with Stafford following in his rear, while Warwick and Clarence had left London and were moving by St. Albans on Towcester; the

King, following the Yorkshiremen, was somewhere near Northampton.

Coniers and his colleagues, to whom belong all the honours of generalship in this campaign, once more got ahead of their opponents. Moving rapidly on Banbury on the 26th, they found Pembroke's army approaching them on a common named Danesmoor, near Edgecott Park, six miles north of Banbury. The Welsh took up a position covered by a small stream and offered battle, though they were greatly inferior in numbers. The Northerners promptly attacked them, and though one of their three leaders, Henry Neville of Latimer, fell in the first onset, gained a complete victory; "by force of archery they forced the Welsh to descend from the hill into the valley," though Herbert and his brothers did all that brave knights could to save the battle. The King was only a few hours' march away; indeed, his vanguard under Sir Geoffrey Gate and Thomas Clapham actually reached the field, but both were old officers of Warwick, and instead of falling on the rebels' rear, proceeded to join them, and led the final attack on Herbert's position.

Thunderstruck at the deep demoralisation among his troops which this desertion showed, the King fell back on Olney, abandoning Northampton to the rebels. Next day—it was July 27th—the brave Earl of Pembroke and his brother Richard Herbert, both of whom had been taken prisoners, were beheaded in the market-place by Coniers' command without sentence or trial. Their blood lies without doubt on Warwick's head, for though neither he nor Clarence was present, the rebels were obviously acting on his orders, and if

he had instructed them to keep all their captives safe,
they would never have presumed to slay them.   Several
chroniclers indeed say that Warwick and Clarence had
expressly doomed Herbert for death.   This slaughter was
perfectly inexcusable, for Herbert had never descended
to the acts of the Woodvilles; he was an honourable
enemy, and Warwick had actually been reconciled to
him only a year before.[1]  The execution of the Herberts
was not the only token of the fact that the great Earl's
hand was pulling the strings all over England.   His
special aversions, Rivers and John Woodville, were
seized a week later at Chepstow by a band of rioters—
probably retainers from the Despenser estates by the
Severn—and forwarded to Coventry, where they were
put to death early in August.   Even if Pembroke's
execution was the unauthorised work of Coniers and
Fitzhugh, this slaying of the Woodvilles must certainly
have been Warwick's own deed.   Stafford the Earl of
Devon, whose desertion of the Welsh had been the
principal cause of the defeat at Edgecott, fared no better
than the colleague he had betrayed.   He disbanded his
army and fled homeward; but at Bridgewater he was
seized by insurgents, retainers of the late Earl of Devon
whom he had beheaded a year before, and promptly
put to death.

It only remains to relate King Edward's fortunes.
When the news of Edgecott fight reached his army, it
disbanded for the most part, and he was left, with no
great following, at Olney, whither he had fallen back
on July 27th.   Meanwhile Warwick and Clarence,

---

[1] It is fair to say that Herbert was universally disliked ; he was
called the Spoiler of the Church and the Commons.

marching from London on Northampton along the
Roman road, were not far off.  The news of the King's
position reached their army, and George Neville the
Archbishop of York, who was with the vanguard,
resolved on a daring stroke.  Riding up by night with
a great body of horse he surrounded Olney; the King's
sentinels kept bad watch, and at midnight Edward was
roused by the clash of arms at his door.  He found the
streets full of Warwick's men, and the Archbishop waiting in his ante-chamber.  The smooth prelate entered
and requested him to rise and dress himself.  "Then
the King said he would not, for he had not yet had his
rest; but the Archbishop, that false and disloyal priest,
said to him a second time, 'Sire, you must rise and
come to see my brother of Warwick, nor do I think that
you can refuse me.'  So the King, fearing worse might
come to him, rose and rode off to meet his cousin of
Warwick."

The Earl meanwhile had passed on to Northampton,
where he met the Northern rebels on July 29th, and
thanked them for the good service they had done England.  There he dismissed the Kentish levies which had
followed him from London, and moved on to Coventry
escorted by the Yorkshiremen, many of whom must have
been his own tenants.  At Coventry the Archbishop, and
his unwilling companion the King, overtook them.  The
details of the meeting of Warwick and Clarence with
their captive master have not come down to us.  But
apparently Edward repaid the Earl's guile of the past
year by an equally deceptive mask of good humour.
He made no reproaches about the death of his adherents,
signed everything that was required of him, and did not

attempt to escape.    The first batch of privy seals issued
under Warwick's influence are dated from Coventry on
August 2nd.

The great Earl's treacherous plans had been crowned
with complete success.   He had shown that half England
would rise at his word; his enemies were dead; his
master was in his power.   Yet he found that his troubles
were now beginning, instead of reaching their end.    It
was not merely that the whole kingdom had been thrown
into a state of disturbance, and that men had commenced
everywhere to settle old quarrels with the sword—the
Duke of Norfolk, for example, was besieging the Paston's
castle of Caistor, and the Commons of Northumberland
were up in arms demanding the restoration of the Percies
to their heritage.   These troubles might be put down by
the strong arm of Warwick; but the problem of real
difficulty was to arrange a *modus vivendi* with the King.
Edward was no coward or weakling to be frightened
into good behaviour by a rising such as had just occurred.
How could he help resenting with all his passionate
nature the violence of which he had been the victim?
His wife, too, would always be at his side; and though
natural affection was not Elizabeth Woodville's strong
point,[1] still she was far too ambitious and vindictive to
pardon the deaths of her father and brother.   Warwick
knew Edward well enough to realise that for the future
there could never be true confidence between them again,
and that for the rest of his life he must guard his head
well against his master's sword.

But the Earl was proud and self-reliant; he de-

---

[1] As witness her dealings with Richard the Third after he had
murdered her sons.

termined to face the danger and release the King. No other alternative was before him, save, indeed, to slay Edward and proclaim his own son-in-law, Clarence, for King. But the memory of old days spent in Edward's cause was too strong. Clarence, too, though he may have been willing enough to supplant his brother, made no open proposals to extinguish him.

Edward was over a month in his cousin's hands. Part of the time he was kept at Warwick and Coventry, but the last three weeks were spent in the Earl's northern stronghold of Middleham. The few accounts which we have of the time seem to show that the King was all smoothness and fair promises; the Earl and the Archbishop, on the other hand, were careful to make his detention as little like captivity as could be managed. He was allowed free access to every one, and permitted to go hunting three or four miles away from the castle in company with a handful of the Earl's servants. Warwick at the same time gave earnest of his adherence to the Yorkist cause by putting down two Lancastrian risings, the one in favour of the Percies, led by Robin of Holderness, the other raised by his own second-cousin, Sir Humphrey Neville, one of the elder branch, who was taken and beheaded at York.

Before releasing the King, Warwick exacted a few securities from him. The first was a general pardon to himself, Clarence, and all who had been engaged in the rising of Robin of Redesdale. The second was a grant to himself of the chamberlainship of South Wales, and the right to name the governors of Caermarthen and the other South Welsh castles. These offices had been in Herbert's hands, and the Earl had found that they cramped his own power in Glamorganshire and the South Marches. The third was the appointment as Treasurer of Sir John Langstrother, the Prior of the Hospitallers of England; he was evidently chosen as Rivers' successor, because two years before he had been elected to his place as prior in opposition to John Woodville, whom the King had endeavoured to foist on the order. The chancellorship, however, was still left in the hands of Bishop Stillington, against whom no one had a grudge; George Neville did not claim his old preferment.

By October the King was back in London, which he entered in great state, escorted by Montagu, the Archbishop, Richard of Gloucester, and the Earls of Essex and Arundel. "The King himself," writes one of the Pastons that day, "hath good language of my Lords of Clarence, Warwick, and York, saying they be his best friends; but his household have other language, so that what shall hastily fall I can not say." No more, we may add, could any man in England, the King and Warwick included.

# CHAPTER XV

THE peace between Warwick and King Edward lasted for a period even shorter than might have been expected; seven months, from September 1469 to March 1470, was the term for which it was destined to endure. Yet while it did hold firm, all was so smooth outwardly that its rupture came as a thunderclap upon the world. Nothing, indeed, could have looked more promising for lovers of quiet times than the events of the winter of 1469-70. A Parliament ratified all the King's grants of immunity to the insurgents of the last year, and while it sat the King announced a project which promised to bind York and Neville more firmly together than ever. Edward, though now married for six years, had no son; three daughters alone were the issue of his union with Elizabeth Woodville. He now proposed to marry his eldest daughter, and heiress presumptive, to the male heir of the Nevilles, the child George, son of Montagu.[1] To make the boy's rank suitable to his

---

[1] This plan, as Lingard astutely observes, may have two meanings. Either, as we said above, it was a ratification of peace with the Nevilles, or—and this is quite possible—it was intended to draw Montagu apart from his brothers, by giving him a special interest in Edward's prosperity.

o

prospects, Edward created him Duke of Bedford. Montagu had not joined with his brothers in the rising, and had even fought with Robin of Redesdale, so it was all the easier for the King to grant him this crowning honour.

In February Warwick was at Warwick Castle, Montagu in the North, while Clarence and King Edward lay at London. All was quiet enough, when suddenly there came news of troubles in Lincolnshire. Riotous bands, headed by Sir Robert Welles, son of Lord Willoughby and Welles, had come together, sacked the manor of a certain Sir Thomas Burgh, one of Edward's most trusted servants, and were raising the usual seditious cries about the evil government of the realm. At first nothing very dangerous seemed to be on foot. When the King sent for Willoughby, to call him to account for his son's doings, the old peer came readily enough to London to make his excuses, relying on the safe conduct which was sent him. But the riots were now swelling into a regular insurrection, and soon news came that Sir Robert Welles had called out the whole shire-force of Lincoln, mustered fifteen thousand men, and was bidding his troops to shout for King Henry. Edward at once issued commissions of array for raising an overwhelming force against the rebels. Two of the commissions were sent to Warwick and Clarence, who were bidden to collect the men of Warwickshire and Worcestershire. Their orders were dated March 7th, but before they were half carried out, the purpose for which they were issued had already been attained. Edward, taking Lord Willoughby with him as a hostage, had rushed north

with one of these astonishing bursts of energy of which
he was now and again capable. Leaving London on
the 6th, he reached Stamford on March 11th, with the
forces of the home and eastern counties at his back.
On the 12th he met the rebels at Empingham near
Stamford, and when Welles would not bid them disperse,
beheaded his aged father Willoughby in front of his
army. The Lincolnshire men fled in disgraceful rout
before the fire of the King's artillery, casting off their
cassocks with the colours of Welles in such haste that the
fight was known as Lose-coat Field. Sir Robert was
caught and beheaded at Doncaster a few days later, and
the rising was at an end. On Tuesday the 21st the
King reviewed his troops : "It was said that never were
seen in England so many goodly men, and so well
arrayed for a fight; in especial the Duke of Norfolk
was worshipfully accompanied, no lord there so well."
Warwick and Clarence, with a few thousand men from
the shires they had been told to raise, lay that day at
Chesterfield, converging, in accordance with their orders,
on Lincoln.

Suddenly Edward announced to his army that he
had learnt from the dying confession of Sir Robert
Welles that Warwick and Clarence were implicated in
the rising. Though Welles had sometimes used King
Henry's name, it was now said that he had really been
proposing to place Clarence on the throne, and was
acting with Warwick's full approval. Edward added
that he had already sent to the Duke and the Earl,
bidding them come to his presence at once and unaccom-
panied. They had refused to come without a safe
conduct, so he now proclaimed them traitors, but would

grant them their lives if they would appear before him in humble and obeisant wise within a week. The army was at once directed to march on Chesterfield, but when the proclamation reached Warwick and Clarence they did not obey it, and fled for their lives.

This series of events is the most puzzling portion of the whole of Warwick's life. The chroniclers help us very little, and the only two first-hand documents which we possess are official papers drawn up by King Edward. These papers were so widely spread that we meet them repeated word for word and paragraph for paragraph even in the French writers,—with the names, of course, horribly mangled.[1] Edward said that down to the very moment of Welles' capture he had no thought but that Warwick and Clarence were serving him faithfully: it was Welles' confession, and some treasonable papers found on the person of a squire in the Duke of Clarence's livery who was slain in the pursuit, that revealed the plot to him. The second document which the King published was Welles' confession, a rambling effusion which may or may not fully represent the whole story. Why Welles should confess at all we cannot see, unless he expected to save his life thereby ; and if he expected to save his life he would, of course, insert in his tale whatever names the King chose. Welles' narrative relates that all Lincolnshire was afraid that the King would visit it with vengeance for joining Robin of Redesdale last year. Excitement already prevailed, when there came to him, about February 2nd, Sir John Clare, a chaplain of the Duke of Clarence's, who asked him if Lincolnshire would

---

[1] *E.g.* Waurin makes Ranby Howe, the muster-place of the insurgents, into Tabihorch, and Lancashire into Lantreghier.

be ready to rise supposing there was another trouble this year, but bade him make no stir till the Duke should send him word. Without waiting, according to his own tale, for any further communication, Welles raised all Lincolnshire, making proclamation in the King's name as well as that of the Duke of Clarence. Some days after the riots began there came to him a squire in the Duke's livery, who told him that he had provoked the King, and that great multitudes of the Commons must needs die unless they bestirred themselves. So this squire—Welles could not give his surname but only knew that he was called Walter—took over the guiding of the host till he was slain at Stamford. Moreover, one John Wright came to Lincoln, bearing a ring as token, which he said belonged to the Earl of Warwick, with a message of comfort to say that the Earl had sworn to take such part as Lincolnshire should take. "And I understand that they intended to make great risings, and as far as ever I could understand, to the intent to make the Duke of Clarence King, and so it was largely noised in our host." According to his story, Welles had never seen either Warwick or Clarence himself, and had no definite knowledge of their purpose. He only understood that the purpose was to crown Clarence; all his information came from Clare and the anonymous squire.

This is a curious tale, and suggests many doubts. If Warwick wished to act again the comedy of last year, why should he send to a county where he had no influence, to a staunch Lancastrian family (Welles' grandfather fell in Henry's cause at Towton, and his father was the Willoughby who tried to kidnap Warwick

in 1460) in order to provoke a rising?  And if he had
planned a rising in Lincoln, why did he make no attempt
to support it by calling out his own Midland and South
Welsh retainers, or raising Yorkshire or Kent, where he
could command the whole county?  That the Earl was
capable of treasonable double-dealing he had shown
clearly enough in 1469.  But was he capable of such
insane bad management as the arrangements for Welles'
insurrection show?  Last year his own relatives and
retainers worked the plan, and it was most accurately
timed and most successfully executed.  Why should he
now make such a bungle?

It is, moreover, to be observed that while Welles
puts everything down to Clarence in his confession,
Warkworth and other chroniclers say that he bade his
men shout for King Henry, and all his connections were
certainly Lancastrian.  Is it possible that he was trying
to put the guilt off his own shoulders, and to make a
bid for his life, acting on Edward's hints, when he
implicated Warwick and Clarence in his guilt?

It is certainly quite in keeping with Edward's character to suppose that, finding himself at the head of a
loyal and victorious army, it suddenly occurred to him
that his position could be utilised to fall on Warwick
and Clarence and take his revenge for the deaths of
Pembroke and Rivers.

Whether this was so or not, the Duke and the Earl
were most certainly caught unprepared when Edward
marched on Chesterfield.  They left a message that they
would come to the King if he would give them a safe
conduct, and fled to Manchester.  Edward threw his
army between them and York, where they could have

raised men in abundance, and the fugitives, after vainly
trying to interest Lord Stanley in their cause, doubled
back on the Midlands.    With a few hundred men in
their train they got to Warwick, but apparently there
was no time to make a stand even there.  . The King had
sent commissions of array out all over England to trusty
hands, and forces under staunch Yorkists were closing
in towards the Midlands on every side.    Edward calculated on having an enormous army in the field by April;
he himself was coming south with quite twenty thousand
victorious troops, and he had called out the whole of
the levies of Shropshire, Hereford, Gloucester, Stafford,
Wiltshire, Devon, Dorset, and Somerset.    When he heard
that. Warwick was moving south, he sent to Salisbury to
order quarters and provisions for forty thousand men,
who would be concentrated there if the Earl tried to
reach the Montacute lands in that quarter.

So unprepared was the Earl for the assault that,
packing up his valuables in Warwick Castle, and taking
with him his wife and his two daughters, he fled for the
South Coast without waiting to be surrounded by his
enemies.    He quite outstripped the King, who had barely
reached Salisbury when he himself was at Exeter.    There
the Duke and Earl seized a few ships, which they sent
round to Dartmouth ; more vessels were obtained in the
latter place, for the whole seafaring population of England favoured the Earl.    When Edward drew near,
Warwick and his son-in-law went on board their hastily-
extemporised fleet and put to sea.    They ran along the
South Coast as far as Southampton, where they made an
attempt to seize a part of the royal navy, including the
great ship called the *Trinity*, which had lain there since

Scales' abortive expedition in 1469.  But Scales and Howard occupied the town with a great Hampshire levy ; the Earl's attack failed, and three of his ships with their crews fell into the enemy's hands.  Tiptoft Earl of Worcester, "the great butcher of England," tried the captured men, and a squire named Clapham and nineteen more were hung and then impaled by him.  This atrocious punishment sent a shock of horror through England, and Tiptoft's name is still remembered rather for this abomination than for all the learning and accomplishments which made him Caxton's idol.

Warwick made for Calais, where his friend Wenlock was in charge, expecting free admittance.  But the King had sent Galliard de Duras and other officers across to watch the governor, and Wenlock, who was somewhat of a time-server, dared not show his heart.  When Warwick appeared in the roads he refused him entry, and shot off some harmless cannon toward the ships.  At the same time he sent the Earl a secret message that "he would give him a fair account of Calais upon the first opportunity, if he would betake himself to France and wait."  While Warwick lay off Calais his daughter, Clarence's wife, was delivered of a son.  Wenlock sent out for her use two flagons of wine, but would not give her a safe conduct to land—"a great severity for a servant to use towards his lord," remarks Commines.

Repulsed from Calais, though we hear that the majority of the garrison and inhabitants wished to admit them, Warwick and Clarence turned back, and sought refuge in the harbour of Honfleur, where they trusted to get shelter from Louis of France.  On their way between Calais and Honfleur they made

prizes of several ships belonging to the Duke of Burgundy, because they understood that he was arming
against them.   Louis kept away from Warwick for a
time; but he sent his secretary, Du Plessis, to see him,
and his admiral, the Bastard of Bourbon, gave the
fugitives a hearty welcome.   Louis was still at war with
England, and still dreading a descent by King Edward
on the French coast.   He was delighted to learn that he
could now turn Warwick, whose abilities he had learnt
to respect, against his master—anything that would
breed trouble in England would keep his enemy occupied
at home.   The King's first orders to his officers were to
allow Warwick to fit out his ships, give him a supply of
money, and send him off to England as quickly as
possible.   But the narrow seas were too well watched.
Charles the Bold, irritated at Warwick's capture of his
merchantmen, had collected a great fleet of seventy sail,
which swept the Channel and watched the mouth of
the Seine.

The enforced delay in Warwick's departure allowed
time for a new idea to ripen in the French King's restless
brain.   Warwick had now broken hopelessly with King
Edward; they could never trust each other again.   Why
therefore should not the Earl reconcile himself to the
cause of Lancaster?   No sooner was the idea formed
than Louis proceeded to send for Queen Margaret out
of her refuge in the duchy of Bar, and to lay his plan
before her and the Earl, when they all met at Angers
in the middle of July.

The scheme was at first sight revolting to both parties.
There was so much blood and trouble between them
that neither could stomach the proposal.   If Margaret

could bring herself to forget that Warwick had twice driven her out of England, and had led her husband in ignominy to the Tower, she could not pardon the man who, in his moment of wrath, had stigmatised herself as an adulteress and her son as a bastard.[1] Warwick, on the other hand, if he could forgive the plot against his own life which the Queen had hatched in 1459, could not bear to think of meeting the woman who had sent his gray-haired father to the scaffold in cold blood on the day after Wakefield. King Louis asked each party to forget their whole past careers, and sacrifice their dearest hatreds to the exigencies of the moment.

If Warwick and Queen Margaret had been left to themselves, it is most improbable that they would ever have come to an agreement. But between them Louis went busily to and fro, for his unscrupulous mind was perfectly unable to conceive that passion or sentiment could override an obvious political necessity. Gradually the two parties were brought to state their objections to the King's scheme, the first step towards the commencement of negotiations. Warwick was the first to yield; the Queen took far longer to persuade. The Earl, she said, had been the cause of all the trouble that had come on herself, her husband, and her son. She could not pardon him. Moreover, his pardon would lose her more friends than he could bring to her. Warwick's answer was straightforward. He owned all the harm he had done to her and hers. But the offence, he said, had come first from her who had plotted evil against him which he had never deserved. What he

---

[1] Foreign writers record that Warwick used this language to the legate Coppini in 1460.

had done had been done solely in his own defence. But now the new King had broken faith with him, and he was bound to him no longer. If Margaret would forgive him, he would be true to her henceforth; and for that the King of France would be his surety. Louis gave his word, praying the Queen to pardon the Earl, to whom, he said, he was more beholden than to any other man living.[1]

The Queen so pressed, and urged beside by the counsellors of her father King Réné, agreed to pardon Warwick. Louis then broached the second point in his scheme. The new alliance, he urged, should be sealed by a marriage; the Prince of Wales was now seventeen and the Lady Anne, Warwick's younger daughter, sixteen. What match could be fairer or more hopeful?

But to this the Queen would not listen. She could find a better match for her son, she said; and she showed them a letter lately come from Edward offering him the hand of the young Princess Elizabeth.[2] Louis, however, was quietly persistent, and in the end the Queen yielded this point also. On August 4th she met Warwick in the Church of St. Mary at Angers, and there they were reconciled; the Earl swearing on a fragment of the true cross that he would cleave to King Henry's quarrel, the Queen engaging to treat the Earl as her

---

[1] All this comes from the invaluable "Manner of the dealing of the Earl of Warwick at Angiers," printed in the *Chronicle of the White Rose*.

[2] This is a not impossible tale. Edward, fearing Warwick's alliance to the Queen, might hope to separate them by offering Margaret's son the ultimate succession to the throne. For he himself having no male heir, the crown would go with his eldest daughter Elizabeth.

true and faithful subject, and never to make him any reproach for deeds gone by. The Earl placed his daughter in the Queen's hands, saying that the marriage should take place only when he had won back England for King Henry, and then departed for the coast to make preparations for getting his fleet to sea.

One person alone was much vexed at the success of Louis' scheme. The Duke of Clarence had no wish to see his father-in-law reconciled to the house of Lancaster, for he had been speculating on the notion that if Warwick drove out Edward he himself would become King. But wandering exiles must take their fortune as it comes, and Clarence had to be contented with Queen Margaret's promise that his name should be inserted in the succession after that of her son, when she and her husband came to their own again. The Prince was a healthy promising lad, and the prospect offered was hopelessly remote; Clarence began to grow discontented, and to regret that he had ever placed himself under Warwick's guidance. At this juncture his brother sent him a message from England, through a lady attending on the Duchess, praying him not to wreck the fortunes of his own family by adhering to the house of Lancaster, and bidding him remember the hereditary hatred that lay between them. Edward offered his brother a full pardon. Clarence replied by promising to come over to the King so soon as he and Warwick should reach England. Of all these negotiations Warwick suspected not a word.

Edward was so overjoyed by his brother's engagement to wreck the Earl's invasion, that he laughed at Charles of Burgundy for squandering money in keeping a fleet at sea to intercept Warwick, and declared that what he most wished was to see his adversary safely landed on English soil, to be dealt with by himself.

He had his wish soon enough. In September the equinoctial gales caught the Burgundian fleet and blew it to the four winds, some of the vessels being driven as far as Scotland and Denmark. This left the coast clear for Warwick, who had long been waiting to put to sea. The Earl had already taken his precautions to make his task easy. A proclamation, signed by himself and Clarence, had been scattered all over England by willing hands. It said that the exiles were returning "to set right and justice to their places, and to reduce and redeem for ever the realm from its thraldom;" but no mention was made either of Edward or Henry in it, a curious fact which seems to point out that the Lancastrian alliance was not to be avowed till the last moment. But more useful than many proclamations was the message which the Earl sent into the North Country; he prayed his kinsman Fitzhugh to stir up Yorkshire and draw the King northward, as he had done before, when he and Coniers worked the rebellion of Robin of Redesdale.

Fitzhugh had no difficulty in rousing the Neville tenants about Middleham; and Edward, as Warwick expected, no sooner heard of this insurrection than he hurried to put it down, taking with him his brother Richard of Gloucester, Scales, Hastings, Say, and many more of his most trusted barons, with a good part of the army that was disposable to resist a landing on the South Coast. Near York he was to be met by Montagu, who had adhered to him for the past year in spite of

his brother's rebellion.   But the King had paid
Montagu badly for his loyalty.   He had taken from
him the Percy lands in Northumberland, and restored
them to the young heir of that ancient house, compen-
sating, as he thought, the dispossessed Neville by
making him a marquis, and handing him over some of
Warwick's confiscated northern estates.   Montagu complained in secret that "he had been given a marquisate,
and a pie's nest to maintain it withal," and was far
from being so contented as the King supposed.

On September 25th Warwick landed unopposed at
Dartmouth.   In his company was not only Clarence but
several of the great Lancastrian lords who had been
living in exile — Jasper of Pembroke, Oxford, and
many more.   They brought with them about two
thousand men, of whom half were French archers lent
by Louis.   The moment that the invaders landed,
Warwick and Clarence declared themselves, by putting
forth a proclamation in favour of King Henry.   Devon
and Somerset had always been Lancastrian strongholds, and the old retainers of the Beauforts and of
Exeter came in by hundreds to meet their exiled lords.
In a few days Warwick had ten thousand men, and
could march on London ; the King was at Doncaster,
and his lieutenants in the South could make no stand
without him.   A little later Warwick's own Midland
and Wiltshire tenants joined him, the Earl of Shrewsbury
raised the Severn valley in his aid, and all Western
England was in his hands.

Meanwhile King Edward, who had up to this
moment mismanaged his affairs most hopelessly, moved
south by Doncaster and Lincoln, with Montagu and

many other lords in his train.   On October 6th he lay
in a fortified manor near Nottingham with his bodyguard, while his army occupied all the villages round
about.   There, early in the morning, while he still lay
in bed, Alexander Carlisle, the chief of his minstrels,
and Master Lee, his chaplain, came running into his
chamber, to tell him there was treachery in his camp.
Montagu and other lords were riding down the ranks of
his army crying, "God save King Henry!"   The
men were cheering and shouting for Warwick and
Lancaster, and no one was showing any signs of striking
a blow for the cause of York.

Edward rose in haste, drew up his bodyguard to
defend the approach of the manor where he lay, and
sent scouts to know the truth of the report.   They met
Montagu marching against them, and fled back to say
that the rumour was all too true.   Then Edward with
his brother Gloucester, Hastings his chamberlain, Say,
and Scales, and their immediate following, took horse
and fled.   They reached Lynn about eight hundred
strong, seized some merchantmen and two Dutch
carvels which lay in the harbour, and set sail for the
lands of Burgundy.   Buffeted by storms and chased by
Hanseatic pirates, they ran their ships ashore near
Alkmaar, and sought refuge with Louis of Gruthuyse,
Governor of Holland.   King, lords, and archers alike
had escaped with nothing but what they bore on their
backs; Edward himself could only pay the master of
the ship that carried him by giving him the rich gown
lined with martens' fur that he had worn in his flight.

# CHAPTER XVI

THE expulsion of King Edward had been marvellously sudden. Within eleven days after his landing at Dartmouth Warwick was master of all England. Not a blow had been struck for the exiled King. From Calais to Berwick every man mounted the Red Rose or the Ragged Staff with real or simulated manifestations of joy. On October 6th the Earl reached London, which opened its gates with its accustomed readiness. It had only delayed its surrender in fear of a riotous band of Kentishmen, whom Sir Geoffrey Gate had gathered in the Earl's name. They had wrought such mischief in Southwark that the Londoners refused to let them in, and waited for the arrival of Warwick himself before they would formally acknowledge King Henry. Meanwhile all the partisans of York had either fled from the city or taken sanctuary. Queen Elizabeth sought refuge in the precincts of Westminster, where she was soon after delivered of a son, the first male child that had been born to King Edward.

Riding through the city Warwick came to the Tower, and found King Henry in his keeper's hands, "not worshipfully arrayed as a prince, and not so cleanly kept as

should beseem his state." The Earl led him forth from
the fortress,—whither he had himself conducted him, a
prisoner in bonds, five years before,—arrayed him in
royal robes, and brought him in state to St. Paul's, the
Lord Mayor and Sheriffs, with all the Common Council,
walking before him, "while all the people to right and
left rejoiced with clapping of hands, and cried 'God
save King Henry!'" Then the King, after returning
thanks for his deliverance in the Cathedral, rode down
Cheapside and took up his residence in the palace of the
Bishop of London.

Henry was much broken and enfeebled by his captivity. "He sat on his throne as limp and helpless as
a sack of wool," says one unfriendly chronicler. "He
was a mere shadow and pretence, and what was done in
his name was done without his will and knowledge."
All that remained unbroken in him was his piety and
his imperturbable long-suffering patience. But his
weakness only made him the more fit for Warwick's
purpose. His deliverance took place on the 6th, and on
October 9th we find him beginning to sign a long series
of documents which reconstituted the government of the
realm. It was made clear from the first that Warwick
and his friends were to have charge of the King rather
than the Lancastrian peers. In the first batch of
appointments Warwick became the King's Lieutenant,
and resumed his old posts of Captain of Calais and
Admiral. George Neville was restored to the Chancellorship, and Sir John Langstrother, Prior of the
Hospitallers, received again the Treasury, which
Warwick had bestowed on him in 1469. The Duke of
Clarence was made Lieutenant of Ireland, a post he had

P

enjoyed under his bröther till his exile in 1470. Among the Lancastrians, Oxford was made Constable, and Pembroke joint-Lieutenant under Warwick. The rest received back their confiscated lands, but got no official preferment.

Oxford's first exercise of his power as Constable was to try Tiptoft Earl of Worcester, one of the few of King Edward's adherents whom no one could pardon. Oxford had to avenge on him his father and brother, whom the Earl had sentenced to be drawn and quartered in 1462, while Warwick remembered his adherents impaled in the previous April. The Butcher of England got no mercy, as might be expected, and was beheaded on October 18th.

A few days before summonses had been sent out in the King's name for a Parliament to meet on November 26th, for Warwick was eager to set himself right with the nation at the earliest opportunity. Every care was taken to show that the new rule was to be one of tolerance and amnesty. The whole of the surviving peers who had sat in Edward's last Parliament were invited to present themselves to meet King Henry—however bitter their Yorkist partizanship had been—save six only, and of these four had fled over-sea —Gloucester, Scales, Hastings, and Say.

The Parliament met and was greeted by George Neville the Chancellor with a sermon adapted to the times, on the text from Jeremiah, "Turn, O ye backsliding children." The proceedings of the session are lost, but we know that they were mainly formal, confirming the King's appointments to offices, ratifying the agreement made between Queen Margaret and

Clarence, that the latter should be declared heir to
the throne failing issue to the Prince of Wales, and
reversing the attainder of Somerset and Exeter and the
other Lancastrian lords, who were thus able to take
their seats in the Upper House.

The most important political event of the restoration,
however, was the conclusion of the treaty with France,
which Warwick had had so close to his heart ever since
the first abortive negotiations in 1464.   An embassy,
headed by the Bishop of Bayeux, titular Patriarch of
Jerusalem, appeared in London when Warwick's power
was firmly established, and a peace for twelve years and
treaty of alliance was duly concluded.   Its most important feature was that it bound England to take the
French King's side in the struggle with Burgundy.
When he heard that Edward had been expelled and
could no longer aid Charles the Bold, Louis had at once
attacked the towns on the Somme, and taken Amiens
and several other important places.   Next spring his
contest with the Duke would begin in earnest, and he
was overjoyed to know that the English power would
be used for his aid, by one who had a strong personal
dislike to the Burgundian.   Warwick at once took steps
to strengthen the garrison of Calais, which was at this
time entirely surrounded by the Duke's territory, and
began to make preparations for a campaign in the next
spring.

It is rather difficult to gauge with accuracy the feeling with which England received the restoration of King
Henry.   The nation, however, seems on the whole to
have accepted the new government with great equanimity if with no very marked enthusiasm.   The Lancas-

trians were of course contented, though they would
have preferred to have won back their position by their
own arms. Of the Yorkists it was supposed that most
of the important sections held by the Earl and not
by King Edward. This was certainly the case, as later
events showed, with the Commons in most parts of the
country, and notably in Yorkshire and Kent, which
had up to this time been so strongly attached to the
cause of York. There were, however, classes in which
the restoration was not so well received. It was disliked by such of the Yorkist nobility as were not
Nevilles. The Duke of Norfolk and all the Bourchier
clan—Essex, the Archbishop, Cromwell, and Berners—
had not been displeased when Warwick chastened the
Queen's relatives, but had not wished to see Edward
entirely deposed. Other peers, such as Grey Earl of
Kent, and the Earl of Arundel, had committed themselves even more deeply to Edward's side, by allying
themselves by marriage with the Woodvilles. It was
gall and bitterness to all those heads of great houses to
have to seek for pardon and favour from their late
enemies. What, for example, must have been Norfolk's
feelings when he was compelled, as the Paston records
describe, to sue as humbly to the Lancastrian Earl of
Oxford as his own dependents had been wont to sue to
himself !

Another quarter where the restoration was taken ill,
was to be found among the merchants of London. The
late King had been a great spender of money, and was
at the moment of his exile deep in the books of many
wealthy purveyors of the luxuries in which he delighted.
All these debts had now become hopeless, and the

unfortunate creditors were sulky and depressed. Moreover, Edward's courteous and affable manners and
comely person had won him favour in the eyes of the
Londoners in whose midst he habitually dwelt, and
still more so, unless tradition errs, in the eyes of their
wives. Few persons in the city, except declared Lancastrians, looked upon the new government with any
approach to enthusiasm.

There was one individual, too, whose feelings as to
the new government were likely to be of no mean importance. George of Clarence, though he had followed
Warwick to London and taken a prominent part in all
the incidents of the restoration, was profoundly dissatis-
fied with his position. Even when he had been made Lieutenant of Ireland—an office which he chose to discharge
by deputy—and presented with many scores of manors,
he was in no wise conciliated. He was farther from the
throne as the Prince of Wales' ultimate heir than he had
been in the days of his own brother's reign. Had the
chance been given him, it seems likely that he would
have betrayed Warwick and joined King Edward after
his return to England. But events had marched too
rapidly, and he had found no opportunity to strike a
blow for York. During the winter of 1470-71, however,
he put himself once more in communication with his
brother. The correspondence was carried on through
their sisters—the Duchess of Exeter on the English side
of the Channel and the Duchess of Burgundy over-sea.
By this means Clarence renewed his promises of help to
Edward, and swore to join him, with every man that he
could raise, the moment that he set foot again in England. Meanwhile Warwick had no suspicion of his son-

in-law's treachery. He trusted him to the uttermost, heaped favours upon him, and even got his name joined with his own and Pembroke's as Lieutenants for King Henry in all the realm of England.

For five months the Earl's reign was undisturbed. There was no one in the country who dared dispute his will. Queen Margaret, whose presence would have been his greatest difficulty, had not yet crossed the seas. Her delay was strange. Perhaps she still dreaded putting herself in the hands of her old enemy; perhaps the King of France detained her till Warwick should have made his power in England too firm to be troubled by her intrigues. But the Earl himself actually desired her presence. He several times invited her to hasten her arrival, and at last sent over Langstrother, the Treasurer of England, to urge his suit and escort Margaret and her son across the Channel. It was not till March that she could be induced to move; and by March the time was overdue.

Meanwhile King Edward had received but a lukewarm reception at the Court of Burgundy. Duke Charles, saddled with his French war, would have preferred to keep at peace with England. His sympathies were divided between Lancaster and York. If his wife was Edward's sister, he himself had Lancastrian blood in his veins, and had long maintained Somerset, Exeter, and other Lancastrian exiles at his Court. But he was driven into taking a decided line in favour of Edward by the fact that Warwick, his personal enemy, was supreme in the counsels of England. If the Earl allied himself to Louis of France, it became absolutely necessary for Duke Charles to lend his support to his exiled brother-

in-law, with the object of upsetting Warwick's domination.

Edward himself had found again his ancient restless
energy in the day of adversity.  He knew that in the
last autumn he could have made a good defence if it
had not been for Montagu's sudden treachery, and was
determined not to consider his cause lost till it had been
fairly tried by the arbitrament of the sword.  He was
in full communication with England, and had learnt that
many more beside Clarence were eager to see him land.
The adventure would be perilous, for he would have to
fight not only, as of old, the Lancastrian party, but the
vast masses of the Commons whose trust had always
been in the great Earl.  But peril seems to have been
rather an incentive than a deterrent to Edward, when
the reckless mood was on him.  He took the aid that
Charles of Burgundy promised, though it was given in
secret and with a grudging heart.  After a final interview with the Duke at Aire, he moved off in February
to Flushing, where a few ships had been collected for him
in the haven among the marshes of Walcheren.  About
fifteen hundred English refugees accompanied him, including his brother of Gloucester and Lords Hastings,
Say, and Scales.  The Duke had hired for him three
hundred German hand-gun men, and presented him with
fifty thousand florins in gold.  With such slender resources
the exiled King did not scruple to attempt the reconquest
of his kingdom.  On March 11th he and his men set sail.
They were convoyed across the German Ocean by a fleet
of fourteen armed Hanseatic vessels, which the Duke
had sent for their protection.  Yet the moment that
Charles heard they were safely departed, he published,

for Warwick's benefit, a proclamation warning any of
his subjects against aiding or abetting Edward of York
in any enterprise against the realm of England.

However secretly Edward's preparations were concerted, they had not entirely escaped his enemy's
notice.  Warwick had made dispositions for resisting a
landing to the best of his ability.  A fleet stationed at
Calais, under the Bastard of Fauconbridge, watched the
straits and protected the Kentish coast.  The Earl himself lay at London to overawe the discontented and
guard King Henry.  Oxford held command in the
Eastern Counties — the most dangerous district, for
Norfolk and the Bourchiers were rightly suspected of
keeping up communication with Edward.  In the North
Montagu and the Earl of Northumberland were in charge
from Hull to Berwick with divided authority.

As Warwick had expected, the invaders aimed at
landing in East Anglia.  On March 12th Edward and
his fleet lay off Cromer.  He sent two knights ashore to
rouse the country ere he himself set foot on land.  But
in a few hours the messengers returned.  They bade him
hoist sail again, for Oxford was keeping strict watch over
all those parts, and Edward's friends were all in prison
or bound over to good behaviour.  On receiving this
disappointing intelligence, Edward determined on one of
those bold strokes which were so often his salvation.  If
the friendly districts were so well watched, it was likely
that the counties where Warwick's interest was supreme
would be less carefully secured.  The King bade his
pilot steer north and make for the Humber mouth, though
Yorkshire was known to be devoted to the great Earl.

That night a gale from the south swept over the

Wash and scattered Edward's ships far and wide. On
March 15th it abated, and the vessels came to land at
various points on the coast of Holderness. The King
and Hastings, with five hundred men, disembarked at
Ravenspur—a good omen, for this was the same spot at
which Henry of Bolingbroke had commenced his victorious march on London in 1399. The other ships landed
their men at neighbouring points on the coast, and by
the next morning all Edward's two thousand men were
safely concentrated. Their reception by the country-
side was most discouraging. The people deserted their
villages and drew together in great bands, as if minded
to oppose the invaders. Indeed, they only needed
leaders to induce them to take the offensive; but no
man of mark chanced to be in Holderness. Montagu
lay in the West-Riding and Northumberland in the
North. A squire named Delamere, and a priest named
Westerdale, the only leaders whom the men of Holderness could find, contented themselves with following
the King at a distance, and with sending news of his
approach to York.

A less resolute adventurer than Edward Plantagenet
would probably have taken to his ships again when he
found neither help nor sympathy in Yorkshire. But
Edward was resolved to play out his game; the sight of
the hostile country-side only made him determine to eke
out the lion's hide with the fox's skin. Calling to mind
the stratagem which Henry of Bolingbroke had practised
in that same land seventy-two years ago, he sent
messengers everywhere to announce that he came in
arms not to dispossess King Henry, but only to claim
his ancestral duchy of York. When he passed through

towns and villages he bade his men shout for King Henry, and he himself mounted the Lancastrian badge of the ostrich feathers. In these borrowed plumes he came before the walls of York, still unmolested, but without having drawn a man to his banners. Hull, the largest town that he had approached, had resolutely closed its gates against him.

The fate of Edward's enterprise was settled before the gates of York on the morning of March 18th. He found the walls manned by the citizens in arms; but they parleyed instead of firing upon him, and when he declared that he came in peace, aspiring only to his father's dignity and possessions, he himself with sixteen persons only in his train was admitted within the gate. Then upon the cross of the high altar in the Minster he swore "that he never would again take upon himself to be King of England, nor would have done before that time, but for the exciting and stirring of the Earl of Warwick," "and thereto before all the people he cried, 'King Harry! King Harry and Prince Edward!'" Satisfied by these protestations, the men of York admitted the invaders within their walls. Edward, however, only stayed for twelve hours in York, and next morning he marched on Tadcaster.

This day was almost as critical as the last. It was five days since the landing at Ravenspur, and the news had now had time to spread. If Montagu and Northumberland were bent on loyal service to King Henry, they must now be close at hand. But the star of York was in the ascendant. Northumberland remembered at this moment rather his ancient enmity for the Nevilles than his grandfather's loyalty to Lancaster. He gathered

troops indeed, but he made no attempt to march south
or to intercept the invaders.   It is probable that he was
actually in treasonable communication with Edward, as
the Lancastrian chroniclers declare.    Montagu, on the
other hand, collected two or three thousand men and
threw himself into Pontefract, to guard the Great North
Road.    But Edward, instead of approaching Pontefract,
moved his army on to cross-roads, which enabled him
to perform a flank march round his adversary; he
slept that evening at Sendal Castle, the spot where his
father had spent the night before the disastrous battle
of Wakefield.   How Montagu came to let Edward get
past him is one of the problems whose explanation will
never be forthcoming.   It may have been that his scouts
lost sight of the enemy and missed the line of his flank
march.    It may equally well have been that Montagu
overvalued the King's army, which was really no larger
than his own, and would not fight till he should be
joined by his colleague Northumberland.    Some contemporary writers assert that the Marquis, remembering
his old favour with the King, was loath that his hand
should be the one to crush his former master.    Others
say that it was no scruple of ancient loyalty that moved
Montagu, but that he had actually determined to desert
his brother and join Edward's party.    But his later
behaviour renders this most unlikely.

Montagu's fatal inaction was the salvation of Edward.
At Sendal he received the first encouragement which he
had met since his landing.   He was there in the midst
of the estates of the duchy of York, and a considerable
body of men joined him from among his ancestral
retainers.   Encouraged by this accession, he pushed on

rapidly southward, and by marches of some twenty miles a day reached Doncaster on the 21st and Nottingham on the 23rd. On the way recruits began to flock in, and at Nottingham a compact body of six hundred men-at-arms, under Sir James Harrington and Sir William Parr, swelled the Yorkist ranks. Then Edward, for the first time since his landing, paused for a moment to take stock of the position of his friends and his enemies.

Meanwhile the news of his march had run like wildfire all over England, and in every quarter men were arming for his aid or his destruction. Warwick had hoped at first that Montagu and Northumberland would stay the invader, but when he heard that Edward had slipped past, he saw that he himself must take the field. Accordingly he left London on the 22nd, and rode hastily to Warwick to call out his Midland retainers. The guard of the city and the person of King Henry was left to his brother the Archbishop. Simultaneously Somerset departed to levy troops in the South-West, and Clarence set forth to raise Gloucestershire and Wiltshire. Oxford had already taken the field, and on the 22nd lay at Lynn with four thousand men, the force that the not very numerous Lancastrians of Norfolk, Suffolk, and Cambridge could put in arms. From thence he directed his march on Newark, hoping to fall on Edward's flank somewhere near Nottingham.

At that very moment the invader had thrown off the mask he had hitherto worn. Finding himself well received and strongly reinforced, he laid aside his pretence of asking only for the duchy of York, and had himself proclaimed as King. But his position was perilous still : Warwick was gathering head in his front ;

Montagu was following cautiously in his rear; Oxford was about to assail his flank. The enemies must be kept apart at all hazards; so Edward, neglecting the others for the moment, turned fiercely on Oxford. He marched rapidly on Newark with some five or six thousand men. This decision and show of force frightened the Earl, who, though joined by the Duke of Exeter and Lord Bardolph, felt himself too weak to fight. When the vanguard of the Yorkists appeared, he hastily left Newark and fell back on to Stamford in much disorder.

Having thus cleared his flank, Edward turned back on Nottingham and then made for Leicester. Here he was joined by the Yorkists of the East Midlands in great numbers; of the retainers of Lord Hastings alone no less than three thousand came to him in one body.

Warwick, who lay only two short marches from the invader, was straining every nerve to get together an army. His missives ran east and west to call in all the knights of the Midlands who had ever mounted the Ragged Staff or the Red Rose. One of these letters was found in 1889, among other treasures, in the lumber room of Belvoir Castle. It was addressed to Henry Vernon, a great Derbyshire landholder. The first part, written in a secretary's hand, runs as follows:

Right Trusty and Wellbeloved—I grete you well, and desire and heartily pray you that, inasmuch as yonder man Edward, the King our soverain lord's great enemy, rebel, and traitor, is now arrived in the north parts of this land, and coming fast on south, accompanied with Flemings, Easterlings, and Danes, not exceeding the number of two thousand persons, nor the country as he cometh not falling to him, ye will therefore, incontinent and forthwith after the sight hereof,

dispose you to make toward me to Coventry with as many
people defensibly arranged as ye can readily make, and that
ye be with me in all haste possible, as my veray singular heart
is in you, and as I may do thing [*sic*] to your weal or worship
hereafter. And may God keep you.—Written at Warwick
on March 25th."

Then in the Earl's own hand was written the post-
script, appealing to Vernon's personal friendship:
"Henry, I pray you ffayle me not now, as ever I may
do for you."

Sad to say, this urgent appeal, wellnigh the only
autograph of the great Earl that we possess, seems to
have failed in its purpose. Vernon preferred to watch
the game, and as late as April 2nd had made no preparation to take arms for either side.

On March 28th Warwick with six thousand men
advanced to Coventry, a strongly-fortified town facing
Edward's line of advance. On the same day his adversary, whose forces must now have amounted to nearly
ten thousand, marched southward from Leicester. Next
morning Warwick and the King were in sight of each
other, and a battle was expected. But the Earl was
determined to wait for his reinforcements before fighting. He calculated that Montagu must soon arrive from
the north, Oxford from the east, Clarence from the
south-west. Accordingly he shut himself up in Coventry,
and refused to risk an engagement. Edward, whose
movements all through this campaign evince the most
consummate generalship, promptly marched past his
enemy and seized Warwick, where he made his headquarters. He then placed his army across the high road
from Coventry to London, cutting off the Earl's direct

communication with the capital, and waited. Like the
Earl he was expecting his reinforcements.

The first force that drew near was Clarence's levy
from the south-west. With seven thousand men in his
ranks the Duke reached Burford on April 2nd. Next
day he marched for Banbury. On the 4th Warwick
received the hideous news that his son-in-law had
mounted the White Rose and joined King Edward. The
treason had been long meditated, and was carried out
with perfect deliberation and great success. A few miles
beyond Banbury Clarence's array found itself facing that
of the Yorkists. Clarence bade his men shout for King
Edward, and fall into the ranks of the army that confronted
them. Betrayed by their leader, the men made no
resistance, and allowed themselves to be enrolled in the
Yorkist army.

Clarence, for very shame we must suppose, offered to
obtain terms for his father-in-law. "He sent to Coventry,"
says a Yorkist chronicler, "offering certain good and
profitable conditions to the Earl, if he would accept
them. But the Earl, whether he despaired of any dur-
able continuance of good accord betwixt the King and
himself, or else willing to maintain the great oaths,
pacts, and promises sworn to Queen Margaret, or else
because he thought he should still have the upperhand
of the King, or else led by certain persons with him, as
the Earl of Oxford, who bore great malice against the
King, would not suffer any manner of appointment, were
it reasonable or unreasonable." He drove Clarence's
messengers away, "crying that he thanked God he was
himself and not that traitor Duke."

Although Oxford had joined him with four thousand

men, and Montagu was approaching, Warwick still felt himself not strong enough to accept battle when Edward and Clarence drew out their army before the gates of Coventry on the morning of April 5th. He then saw them fall into column of march, and retire along the London road. Edward, having now some eighteen thousand men at his back, thought himself strong enough to strike at the capital, where his friends had been busily astir in his behalf for the last fortnight. Leaving a strong rear - guard behind, with orders to detain Warwick at all hazards, he hurried his main body along the Watling Street, and in five days covered the seventy-five miles which separated him from London.

Meanwhile Warwick had been joined by Montagu as well as by Oxford, and also received news that Somerset, with seven or eight thousand men more, was only fifty miles away. This put him in good spirits, for he counted on London holding out for a few days, and on the men of Kent rallying to his standard when he approached the Thames. He wrote in haste to his brother the Archbishop, who was guarding King Henry, that if he would maintain the city but forty-eight hours, they would crush the invading army between them. Then he left Coventry and hurried after the King, who for the next five days was always twenty miles in front of him.

But all was confusion in London. The Archbishop was not a man of war, and no soldier of repute was at his side. The Lancastrian party in the city had never been strong, and the Yorkists were now organising an insurrection. There were more than two thousand of them in the sanctuaries at Westminster and elsewhere, of whom three hundred were knights and squires. All were prepared to rise at the first signal. When news came that Edward had reached St. Albans, the Archbishop mounted King Henry on horseback and rode with him about London, adjuring the citizens to be true to him and arm in the good cause. But the sight of the frail shadow of a king, with bowed back and lack-lustre eyes, passing before them, was not likely to stir the people to enthusiasm. Only six or seven hundred armed men mustered in St. Paul's Churchyard beneath the royal banner.[1]

Such a force was obviously unequal to defending a disaffected city. Next day, when the army of Edward appeared before the walls, Urswick the Recorder of London, and certain aldermen with him, dismissed the guard at Aldersgate and let Edward in, no man withstanding them. The Archbishop of York and King Henry took refuge in the Bishop of London's palace; they were seized and sent to the Tower. George Neville obtained his pardon so easily that many accused him of treason. It seems quite possible that, when he found at the last moment that he could not raise the Londoners, he sent secretly to Edward and asked for pardon, promising to make no resistance.

The capture of London rendered King Edward's position comparatively secure. He had now the base of operations which he had up to this moment lacked, and had established himself in the midst of a population

---

[1] The *Arrival of King Edward* says "only six or seven thousand" in the printed text. This must be a scribe's blunder, being not a small number but a large one; and Waurin, who copies the *Arrival* verbatim, has "600 or 700."

favourable to the Yorkist cause.   Next day he received
a great accession of strength.   Bourchier Earl of Essex,
his brother Archbishop Bourchier, Lord Berners, and
many other consistent partisans of York, joined him
with seven thousand men levied in the Eastern Counties.
His army was now so strong that he might face any
force which Warwick could bring up, unless the Earl
should wait for the levies of the extreme North and West
to join him.

On Maundy Thursday London had fallen; on Good
Friday the King lay in London; on Saturday afternoon
he moved out again with his army greatly strengthened
and refreshed, and marched north to meet the pursuing
enemy.   Warwick, much retarded on his way by the
rear-guard which the King had left to detain him and
by the necessity of waiting for Somerset's force, had
reached Dunstable on the Friday, only to learn in the
evening that London was lost and his brother and King
Henry captured.   He pushed on, however, and swerv-
ing from the Watling Street at St. Albans threw himself eastward, with the intention, we cannot doubt, of
cutting Edward's communication with the Eastern Midlands, where York was strong, by placing himself across
the line of the Ermine Street.   On Saturday evening his
army encamped on a rising ground near Monken Hadley
Church, overlooking the little town of Barnet which lay
below him in the hollow.   The whole force lay down in
order of battle, ranged behind a line of hedges; in front
of them was the heathy plateau, four hundred feet above
the sea, which slopes down into the plain of Middlesex.

An hour or two after Warwick's footsore troops had
taken post for the night, and long after the dusk had

fallen, the alarm was raised that the Yorkists were at hand. On hearing of the Earl's approach the King had marched out of London with every man that he could raise. His vanguard beat Warwick's scouts out of the town of Barnet, and chased them back on to the main position. Having found the enemy, Edward pushed on through Barnet, climbed the slope, and ranged his men in the dark facing the hedges behind which the Earl's army lay,

much nearer than he had supposed, for he took not his ground so even in the front as he should have done, if he might better have seen them. And there they kept them still without any manner of noise or language. Both sides had guns and ordinance, but the Earl, meaning to have greatly annoyed the King, shot guns almost all the night. But it fortuned that they always overshot the King's host, and hurt them little or nought, for the King lay much nearer to them than they deemed. But the King suffered no guns to be shot on his side, or else right few, which was of great advantage to him, for thereby the Earl should have found the ground that he lay in, and levelled guns thereat.

So, with the cannon booming all night above them, the two hosts lay down in their armour to spend that miserable Easter even. Next day it was obvious that a decisive battle must occur; for the King, whose interest it was to fight at once, before Warwick could draw in his reinforcements from Kent and from the North and West, had placed himself so close to the Earl that there was no possibility of the Lancastrian host withdrawing without being observed. The morrow would settle, once for all, if the name of Richard Neville or that of Edward Plantagenet was to be all-powerful in England.

# CHAPTER XVII

## BARNET

THE Easter morning dawned dim and gray; a dense fog had rolled up from the valley, and the two hosts could see no more of each other than on the previous night. Only the dull sound of unseen multitudes told each that the other was still before them in position.

Of the two armies each, so far as we can judge, must have numbered some twenty-five thousand men. It is impossible in the conflict of evidence to say which was the stronger, but there cannot have been any great difference in force.[1] Each had drawn itself up in the normal order of a medieval army, with a central

---

[1] The Yorkist author of the *Arrival of King Edward* says that his patron had only nine thousand men. But we can account for many more. Edward landed with two thousand; at least six hundred joined at Nottingham, at least three thousand at Leicester; Clarence brought seven thousand, Essex and the other Bourchiers seven thousand more. This makes nineteen thousand six hundred, and many more must have joined in small parties. On the other side Warwick had at Coventry six thousand men; Oxford met him with four thousand, Montagu with three thousand, Somerset with seven thousand, and he too must have drawn in many small, unrecorded reinforcements. The Yorkists called his army thirty thousand strong—probably overstating it by a few thousands. Their own must have been much the same.

main-battle, the van and rear ranged to its right
and left, and a small reserve held back behind the centre.
Both sides, too, had dismounted nearly every man,
according to the universal practice of the English in the
fifteenth century.   Even Warwick himself,—whose wont
it had been to lead his first line to the charge, and then
to mount and place himself at the head of the reserve,
ready to deliver the final blow,—on this one occasion sent
his horse to the rear and fought on foot all day.   He
wished to show his men that this was no common battle,
but that he was risking life as well as lands and name
and power in their company.

   In the Earl's army Montagu and Oxford, with their
men from the North and East, held the right wing;
Somerset with his West-Country archery and billmen
formed the centre; Warwick himself with his own
Midland retainers had the left wing; with him was his
old enemy Exeter,—his unwilling partner in the famous
procession of 1457, his adversary at sea in the spring of
1460.   Here and all down the line the old Lancastrians
and the partisans of Warwick were intermixed; the
Cresset of the Hollands stood hard by the Ragged
Staff; the Dun Bull of Montagu and the Radiant Star
of the De Veres were side by side.   We cannot doubt
that many a look was cast askance at new friends who
had so long been old foes, and that the suspicion of
possible treachery must have been present in every
breast.

   Edward's army was drawn up in a similar order.
Richard of Gloucester commanded the right wing; he
was but eighteen, but his brother had already learnt to
trust much to his zeal and energy.   The King himself

headed Clarence's men in the centre; he was determined
to keep his shifty brother at his side, lest he might re-
pent at the eleventh hour of his treachery to his father-
in-law. Hastings led the rear-battle on the left.

The armies were too close to each other to allow of
manœuvring; the men rose from the muddy ground on
which they had lain all night, and dressed their line
where they stood. But the night had led King Edward
astray; he had drawn up his host so as to overlap the
Earl's extreme left, while he opposed nothing to his extreme right. Gloucester in the one army and Montagu
and Oxford in the other had each the power of out-
flanking and turning the wing opposed to them. The
first glimpse of sunlight would have revealed these facts to
both armies had the day been fair; but in the dense fog
neither party had perceived as yet its advantage or its
danger. It was not till the lines met that they made
out each other's strength and position.

Between four and five o'clock, in the first gray of the
dawning, the two hosts felt their way towards each other;
each side could at last descry the long line of bills and
bows opposed to it, stretching right and left till it was
lost in the mist. For a time the archers and the bom-
bards of the two parties played their part; then the two
lines rolled closer, and met from end to end all along
Gladsmore Heath. The first shock was more favourable
to Warwick than to the King. At the east end of the
line, indeed, the Earl himself was outflanked by Gloucester,
forced to throw back his wing, and compelled to yield
ground towards his centre. But at the other end of the
line the Yorkists suffered a far worse disaster; Montagu
and Oxford not only turned Hastings' flank, but rolled

up his line, broke it, and chased it right over the heath,
and down toward Barnet town.  Many of the routed
troops fled as far as London ere they stopped, spreading
everywhere the news that the King was slain and the
cause of York undone.  But the defeat of Edward's left
wing had not all the effect that might have been expected.  Owing to the fog it was unnoticed by the
victorious right, and even by the centre, where the King
and Clarence were now hard at work with Somerset,
and gaining rather than losing ground.  No panic spread
down the line "for no man was in anything discouraged,
because, saving a few that stood nearest to them, no man
wist of the rout: also the other party by the same flight
and chase were never the greatlier encouraged."  Moreover, the victorious troops threw away their chance;
instead of turning to aid his hard-pressed comrades,
Oxford pursued recklessly, cutting down the flying
enemy for a mile, even into the streets of Barnet.  Con-
sequently he and his men lost themselves in the fog;
many were scattered; the rest collected themselves
slowly, and felt their way back towards the field, guiding themselves by the din that sounded down from the
hillside.  Montagu appears not to have gone so far in
pursuit; he must have retained part of his wing with
him, and would seem to have used it to strengthen his
brother's hard-pressed troops on the left.

But meanwhile King Edward himself was gaining
ground in the centre; his own column, as the Yorkist
chronicler delights to record, "beat and bare down all
that stood in his way, and then turned to range, first on
that hand and then on the other hand, and in length so
beat and bare them down that nothing might stand in

the sight of him and of the well-assured fellowship that attended truly upon him." Somerset, in short, was giving way; in a short time the Lancastrian centre would be broken.

At this moment, an hour after the fight had begun, Oxford and his victorious followers came once more upon the scene. Lost in the fog, they appeared, not where they might have been expected, on Edward's rear, but upon the left rear of their own centre. They must have made a vast detour in the darkness.

Now came the fatal moment of the day. Oxford's men, whose banners and armour bore the Radiant Star of the De Veres, were mistaken by their comrades for a flanking column of Yorkists. In the mist their badge had been taken for the Sun with Rays, which was King Edward's cognisance. When they came close to their friends they received a sharp volley of arrows, and were attacked by Warwick's last reserves. This mistake had the most cruel results. The old and the new Lancastrians had not been without suspicions of each other. Assailed by his own friends, Oxford thought that some one—like Grey de Ruthyn at Northampton—had betrayed the cause. Raising the cry of treason, he and all his men fled northward from the field.[1]

The fatal cry ran down the labouring lines of Warwick's army and wrecked the whole array. The old Lancastrians made up their minds that Warwick—or at least his brother the Marquis, King Edward's ancient favourite

[1] Compare this with an incident at Waterloo. Ziethen's Prussian corps, coming upon the field to the left rear of the English line, took the brigade of the Prince of Saxe-Weimar for French owing to a similarity in uniform, attacked them, and slew many ere the mistake was discovered.

—must have followed the example of the perjured Clarence. Many turned their arms against the Nevilles,[1] and the unfortunate Montagu was slain by his own allies in the midst of the battle. Many more fled without striking another blow; among these was Somerset, who had up to this moment fought manfully against King Edward in the centre.

Warwick's wing still held its ground, but at last the Earl saw that all was lost. His brother was slain; Exeter had been struck down at his side; Somerset and Oxford were in flight. He began to draw back toward the line of thickets and hedges which had lain behind his army. But there the fate met him that had befallen so many of his enemies, at St. Albans and Northampton, at Towton and Hexham. His heavy armour made rapid flight impossible; and in the edge of Wrotham Wood he was surrounded by the pursuing enemy, wounded, beaten down, and slain.

The plunderers stripped the fallen; but King Edward's first desire was to know if the Earl was dead. The field was carefully searched, and the corpses of Warwick and Montagu were soon found. Both were carried to London, where they were laid on the pavement of St. Paul's, stripped to the breast, and exposed three days to the public gaze, "to the intent that the people should not be abused by feigned tales, else the rumour should have been sowed about that the Earl was yet alive."

---

[1] There seems no valid reason for accepting Warkworth's theory that Montagu was actually deserting to King Edward. But there is every sign that the Lancastrians imagined that he was doing so. If he had wished to betray his brother, he could have done it much better at an earlier hour in the battle.

After lying three days on the stones, the bodies were given over to George Neville the Archbishop, who had them both borne to Bisham, and buried in the abbey, hard by the tombs of their father Salisbury and their ancestors the Earls of the house of Montacute. All alike were swept away, together with the roof that covered them, by the Vandalism of the Edwardian reformers, and not a trace remains of the sepulchre of the two unquiet brothers.

Thus ended Richard Neville in the forty-fourth year of his age, slain by the sword in the sixteenth year since he had first taken it up at the Battle of St. Albans. Fortune, who had so often been his friend, had at last deserted him; for no reasonable prevision could have foreseen the series of chances which ended in the disaster of Barnet. Montagu's irresolution and Clarence's treachery were not the only things that had worked against him. If the winds had not been adverse, Queen Margaret, who had been lying on the Norman coast since the first week in March, would have been in London long before Edward arrived, and could have secured the city with the three thousand men under Wenlock, Langstrother, and John Beaufort whom her fleet carried. But for five weeks the wind blew from the north and made the voyage impossible; on Good Friday only did it turn and allow the Queen to sail. It chanced that the first ship, which came to land in Portsmouth harbour the very morning of Barnet, carried among others the Countess of Warwick; at the same moment that she was setting her foot on shore her husband was striking his last blows on Gladsmore Heath. Nor was it only from France that aid was coming; there were reinforcements gathering in the North, and the Kentishmen were only waiting for a leader. Within a few days after Warwick's death the Bastard of Fauconbridge had mustered seventeen thousand men at Canterbury in King Henry's name. If Warwick could have avoided fighting, he might have doubled his army in a week, and offered the Yorkists battle under far more favourable conditions. The wrecks of the party were strong enough to face the enemy on almost equal terms at Tewkesbury, even when their head was gone. The stroke of military genius which made King Edward compel the Earl to fight, by placing his army so close that no retreat was possible from the position of Barnet, was the proximate cause of Warwick's ruin; but in all the rest of the campaign it was fortune rather than skill which fought against the Earl. His adversary played his dangerous game with courage and success; but if only ordinary luck had ruled, Edward must have failed; the odds against him were too many.

But fortune interposed and Warwick fell. For England's sake perhaps it was well that it should be so. If he had succeeded, and Edward had been driven once more from the land, we may be sure that the Wars of the Roses would have dragged on for many another year; the house of York had too many heirs and too many followers to allow of its dispossession without a long time of further trouble. The cause of Lancaster, on the other hand, was bound up in a single life; when Prince Edward fell in the Bloody Meadow, as he fled from the field of Tewkesbury, the struggle was ended perforce, for no one survived to claim his rights. Henry of Richmond, whom an unexpected chance ultimately placed on the throne, was neither in law nor in fact the real heir of the house of Lancaster. On the other hand, Warwick's success would have led, so far as we can judge, first to a continuance of civil war, then, if he had ultimately been successful in rooting out the Yorkists, to a protracted political struggle between the house of Neville and the old Lancastrian party headed by the Beauforts and probably aided by the Queen; for it is doubtful how far the marriage of Prince Edward and Anne Neville would ever have served to reconcile two such enemies as the Earl and Margaret of Anjou. If Warwick had held his own, and his abilities and his popularity combined to make it likely, his victory would have meant the domination of a family group—a form of government which no nation has endured for long. At the best, the history of the last thirty years of the fifteenth century in England would have been a tale resembling that of the days when the house of Douglas struggled with the crown of Scotland, or the Guises with the rulers of France.

Yet for Warwick as a ruler there would have been much to be said. To a king of the type of Henry the Sixth the Earl would have made a perfect minister and vicegerent, if only he could have been placed in the position without a preliminary course of bloodshed and civil war. The misfortune for England was that his lot was cast not with Henry the Sixth, but with strong-willed, hot-headed, selfish Edward the Fourth.

The two prominent features in Warwick's character which made him a leader of men, were not those which might have been expected in a man born and reared in his position. The first was an inordinate love of the activity of business; the second was a courtesy and affability which made him the friend of all men save the one class he could not brook—the "made lords," the parvenu nobility which Edward the Fourth delighted to foster.

Of these characteristics it is impossible to exaggerate the strength of the first. Warwick's ambition took the shape of a devouring love of work of all kinds. Prominent though he was as a soldier, his activity in war was only one side of his passionate desire to manage well and thoroughly everything that came to his hand. He never could cease for a moment to be busy; from the first moment when he entered into official harness in 1455 down to the day of his death, he seems hardly to have rested for a moment. The energy of his soul took him into every employment—general, admiral, governor, judge, councillor, ambassador, as the exigencies of the moment demanded; he was always moving, always busy, and never at leisure. When the details of his life are studied, the most striking point is to find how seldom he was at home, how constantly away at public service. His castles and manors saw comparatively little of him. It was not at Warwick or Amesbury, at Caerphilly or Middleham that he was habitually to be found, but in London, or Calais, or York, or on the Scotch Border. It was not that he neglected his vassals and retainers— the loyalty with which they rallied to him on every occasion is sufficient evidence to the contrary—but he preferred to be a great minister and official, not merely a great baron and feudal chief.

In this sense, then, it is most deceptive to call Warwick the Last of the Barons. Vast though his strength might be as the greatest landholder in England, it was as a statesman and administrator that he left his mark on

the age. He should be thought of as the forerunner of
Wolsey rather than as the successor of Robert of
Belesme, or the Bohuns and Bigods. That the world
remembers him as a turbulent noble is a misfortune.
Such a view is only drawn from a hasty survey of the
last three or four years of his life, when under desperate
provocation he was driven to use for personal ends the
vast feudal power that lay ready to his hand. If he
had died in 1468, he would be remembered in history as
an able soldier and statesman, who with singular perseverance and consistency devoted his life to consolidating
England under the house of York.

After his restless activity, Warwick's most prominent
characteristic was his geniality. No statesman was ever
so consistently popular with the mass of the nation,
through all the alternations of good and evil fortune.
This popularity the Earl owed to his unswerving courtesy
and affability; "he ever had the good voice of the people,
because he gave them fair words, showing himself easy
and familiar," says the chronicler. Wherever he was
well known he was well liked. His own Yorkshire and
Midland vassals, who knew him as their feudal lord,
the seamen who had served under him as admiral, the
Kentishmen who saw so much of him while he was captain of Calais, were all his unswerving followers down to
the day of his death. The Earl's boundless generosity, the
open house which he kept for all who had any claim on
him, the zeal with which he pushed the fortunes of his
dependents, will only partially explain his popularity.
As much must be ascribed to his genial personality as to
the trouble which he took to court the people. His
whole career was possible because the majority of the

nation not only trusted and respected but honestly
liked him.    This it was which explains the "king-
making" of his later years.    Men grew so accustomed to
follow his lead that they would even acquiesce when he
transferred his allegiance from King Edward to King
Henry.  It was not because he was the greatest landholder of England that he was able to dispose of the
crown at his good will; but because, after fifteen years of
public life, he had so commended himself to the majority
of the nation that they were ready to follow his guidance
even when he broke with all his earlier associations.

But Warwick was something more than active, genial,
and popular; nothing less than first-rate abilities would
have sufficed to carry him through his career.   On the
whole, it was as a statesman that he was most fitted to
shine.   His power of managing men was extraordinary;
even King Louis of France, the hardest and most un-
emotional of men, seems to have been amenable to his
influence.   He was as successful with men in the
mass as with individuals; he could sway a parliament or
an army with equal ease to his will.   How far he sur-
passed the majority of his contemporaries in political
prescience is shown by the fact that, in spite of Yorkist
traditions, he saw clearly that England must give up
her ancient claims on France, and continually worked to
reconcile the two countries.

In war Warwick was a commander of ability; good
for all ordinary emergencies where courage and a
cool head would carry him through, but not attaining
the heights of military genius displayed by his pupil
Edward.   His battles were fought in the old English
style of Edward the Third and Henry the Fifth,

by lines of archery flanked by clumps of billmen and
dismounted knights.  He is found employing both
cannon and hand-gun men, but made no decisive or
novel use of either, except in the case of his siege-
artillery in the campaign of 1464.  Nor did he
employ cavalry to any great extent; his men dismounted to fight like their grandfathers at Agincourt,
although the power of horsemen had again revindicated
itself on the Continent.  The Earl was a cool and capable
commander; he was not one of the hot-headed feudal
chiefs who strove to lead every charge.  It was his wont
to conduct his first line to the attack and then to retire
and take command of the reserve, with which he
delivered his final attack in person.  This caution led
some contemporary critics, especially Burgundians who
contrasted his conduct with the headlong valour of
Charles the Rash, to throw doubts on his personal
courage.  The sneer was ridiculous.  The man who was
first into the High Street at St. Albans, who fought
through the ten hours of Towton, and won a name by
his victories at sea in an age when sea-fights were carried
on by desperate hand-to-hand attempts to board, might
afford to laugh at any such criticism.  If he fell at
Barnet "somewhat flying," as the Yorkist chronicler
declares, he was surely right in endeavouring to save
himself for another field; he knew that one lost battle
would not wreck his cause, while his own life was the
sole pledge of the union between the Lancastrian party
and the majority of the nation.

Brave, courteous, liberal, active, and able, a generous
lord to his followers, an untiring servant to the com-
monweal, Warwick had all that was needed to attract the

homage of his contemporaries: they called him, as the
Kentish ballad-monger sang, "a very noble knight, the
flower of manhood." But it is only fair to record that
he bore in his character the fatal marks of the two sins
which distinguished the English nobles of his time.
Occasionally he was reckless in bloodshedding. Once
in his life he descended to the use of a long and deliberate course of treason and treachery.

In the first-named sin Warwick had less to reproach
himself with than most of his contemporaries. He never
authorised a massacre, or broke open a sanctuary, or
entrapped men by false pretences in order to put them
to death. In battle, too, he always bid his men to spare
the Commons. Moreover, some of his crimes of bloodshed are easily to be palliated: Mundeford and the other
captains whom he beheaded at Calais had broken their
oath of loyalty to him; the Bastard of Exeter, whom
he executed at York, had been the prime agent in
the murder of his father. The only wholly unpardonable
act of the Earl was his slaying of the Woodvilles and
Herberts in 1469. They had been his bitter enemies,
it is true; but to avenge political rivalries with the axe,
without any legal form of trial, was unworthy of the
high reputation which Warwick had up to that moment
enjoyed. It increases rather than lessens the sum of his
guilt to say that he did not publicly order their death,
but allowed them to be executed by rebels whom he had
roused and might as easily have quieted.

But far worse, in a moral aspect, than the slaying of
the Woodvilles and Herberts, was the course of treachery
and deceit that had preceded it. That the Earl had been
wantonly insulted by his thankless master in a way that

R

would have driven even one of milder mood to desperation, we have stated elsewhere. An ideally loyal man
might have borne the King's ingratitude in silent dignity,
and foresworn the Court for ever: a hot-headed man
might have burst out at once into open rebellion; but
Warwick did neither. When his first gust of wrath had
passed, he set himself to seek revenge by secret treachery.
He returned to the Court, was superficially reconciled to
his enemies, and bore himself as if he had forgotten
his wrongs. Yet all the while he was organising an
armed rising to sweep the Woodvilles and Herberts
away, and to coerce the King into subjection to his will.
The plan was as unwise as it was unworthy. Although
Warwick's treason was for the moment entirely successful,
it made any confidence between himself and his master
impossible for the future. At the earliest opportunity
Edward revenged himself on Warwick with the same
weapons that had been used against himself, and drove
the Earl into exile.

There is nothing in Warwick's subsequent reconciliation with the Lancastrians which need call up our moral
indignation. It was the line of conduct which forced
him into that connection that was evil, not the connection itself. There is no need to reproach him for chang-
ing his allegiance; no other course was possible to
him in the circumstances. The King had cast him off,
not he the King. When he transferred his loyalty to
the house of Lancaster, he never swerved again. All the
offers which Edward made to him after his return in
1471 were treated with contempt. Warwick was not
the man to sell himself to the highest bidder.

If then Warwick was once in his life driven into

treachery and bloodthirsty revenge, we must set against his crime his fifteen long years of honest and consistent service to the cause he had made his own, and remember how dire was the provocation which drove him to betray it. Counting his evil deeds of 1469-70 at their worst, he will still compare not unfavourably with any other of the leading Englishmen of his time. Even in that demoralised age his sturdy figure stands out in not un-attractive colours. Born in a happier generation, his industry and perseverance, his courage and courtesy, his liberal hand and generous heart, might have made him not only the idol of his followers, but the bulwark of the commonwealth. Cast into the godless times of the Wars of the Roses, he was doomed to spend in the cause of a faction the abilities that were meant to benefit a whole nation; the selfishness, the cruelty, the political immorality of the age, left their mark on his character; his long and honourable career was at last stained by treason, and his roll of successes terminated by a crushing defeat. Even after his death his misfortune has not ended. Popular history has given him a scanty record merely as the Kingmaker or the Last of the Barons, as a selfish intriguer or a turbulent feudal chief; and for four hundred and ten years he has lacked even the doubtful honour of a biography.

THE END

*Printed by* R. & R. CLARK, *Edinburgh.*

*ENGLISH MEN OF ACTION—continued.*

---

**Warren Hastings.** By Sir ALFRED LYALL.

The *Daily News* says:—"May be pronounced without hesitation as the final and decisive verdict of history on the conduct and career of Hastings."

**Peterborough.** By Mr. W. STEBBING.

The *Saturday Review* says:—"An excellent piece of work . . . an interesting and satisfactory biography."

**Captain Cook.** By Mr. WALTER BESANT.

The *Scottish Leader* says:—"It is simply the best and most readable account of the great navigator yet published."

**Sir Henry Havelock.** By Mr. ARCHIBALD FORBES.

The *Speaker* says:—"There is no lack of good writing in this book, and the narrative is sympathetic as well as spirited."

**Clive.** By Colonel Sir CHARLES WILSON.

The *Times* says:—"Sir Charles Wilson, whose literary skill is unquestionable, does ample justice to a great and congenial theme."

**Sir Charles Napier.** By Colonel Sir WILLIAM BUTLER.

The *Daily News* says:—"The 'English Men of Action' series contains no volume more fascinating, both in matter and in style, than Sir William Butler's biography of Sir Charles Napier."

**Drake.** By Mr. JULIAN CORBETT.

**Warwick, the Kingmaker.** By Mr. C. W. OMAN.

---

*And the undermentioned are in the Press or in preparation :—*

**Montrose.** By Mr. MOWBRAY MORRIS.

**Marlborough.** By Colonel Sir WILLIAM BUTLER.

**Rodney.** By Mr. DAVID HANNAY.

**Sir John Moore.** By Colonel MAURICE.

---

MACMILLAN AND CO., LONDON.

# English Men of Letters.

## Edited by JOHN MORLEY.

Crown 8vo.  2s. 6d. each.  Cheap Edition.  1s. 6d. ; sewed, 1s.

JOHNSON.  By LESLIE STEPHEN.
SCOTT.  By R. H. HUTTON.
GIBBON.  By J. COTTER MORISON.
HUME.  By T. H. HUXLEY.
GOLDSMITH.  By WILLIAM BLACK.
SHELLEY.  By J. A. SYMONDS.
DEFOE.  By W. MINTO.
BURNS.  By Principal SHAIRP.
SPENSER.  By the DEAN OF ST. PAUL'S.
THACKERAY.  By ANTHONY TROLLOPE.
MILTON.  By MARK PATTISON.
BURKE.  By JOHN MORLEY.
HAWTHORNE.  By HENRY JAMES.
SOUTHEY.  By Professor DOWDEN.
BUNYAN.  By J. A. FROUDE. .
CHAUCER.  By Professor A. W. WARD.
COWPER.  By GOLDWIN SMITH.
POPE.  By LESLIE STEPHEN.
BYRON.  By Professor NICHOL.
DRYDEN.  By G. SAINTSBURY.
LOCKE.  By Professor FOWLER.
WORDSWORTH.  By F. W. H. MYERS.
LANDOR.  By SIDNEY COLVIN.
DE QUINCEY.  By Professor MASSON.
CHARLES LAMB.  By Rev. ALFRED AINGER.
BENTLEY.  By Professor JEBB.
DICKENS.  By A. W. WARD.
GRAY.  By EDMUND GOSSE.
SWIFT.  By LESLIE STEPHEN.
STERNE.  By H. D. TRAILL.
MACAULAY.  By J. COTTER MORISON.
FIELDING.  By AUSTIN DOBSON.
SHERIDAN.  By Mrs. OLIPHANT.
ADDISON.  By W. J. COURTHOPE.
BACON.  By the DEAN OF ST. PAUL'S.
COLERIDGE.  By H. D. TRAILL.
SIR PHILIP SIDNEY.  By J. A. SYMONDS.
KEATS.  By SIDNEY COLVIN.

*\* *Other volumes to follow.*

MACMILLAN AND CO., LONDON.

# TWELVE ENGLISH STATESMEN.

Crown 8vo. 2s. 6d. each.

---

**WILLIAM THE CONQUEROR.** By Edward A. Freeman,
D.C.L., LL.D.                                                    [*Ready.*

**HENRY II.** By Mrs. J. R. Green.                              [*Ready.*

**EDWARD I.** By F. York Powell.

**HENRY VII.** By James Gairdner.                              [*Ready.*

**CARDINAL WOLSEY.** By Professor M. Creighton, M.A.,
D.C.L., LL.D.                                                    [*Ready.*

**ELIZABETH.** By E. S. Beesley.

**OLIVER CROMWELL.** By Frederic Harrison.                      [*Ready.*

**WILLIAM III.** By H. D. Traill.                              [*Ready.*

**WALPOLE.** By John Morley.                                   [*Ready.*

**CHATHAM.** By John Morley.

**PITT.** By John Morley.

**PEEL.** By J. R. Thursfield.                                 [*Shortly.*

---

# MR. JOHN MORLEY'S COLLECTED WORKS.

A New Edition.  In Eleven Volumes.

Globe 8vo.  Price 5s. each.

| | | | | |
|---|---|---|---|---|
| Voltaire | . . . . 1 Vol. | On Compromise | . . | 1 Vol. |
| Rousseau | . . . . 2 Vols. | Miscellanies | . . . | 3 Vols. |
| Diderot and the En- | | Burke | . . . . . . | 1 Vol. |
| cyclopædists | . 2 Vols. | Studies in Literature | | 1 Vol. |

---

Aphorisms. By John Morley. Globe 8vo. 2s. 6d.

---

MACMILLAN AND CO., LONDON.

# Catalogue of Books

PUBLISHED BY

# MACMILLAN AND CO.

BEDFORD STREET, COVENT GARDEN, LONDON

## January, 1891.

ABBOT (Francis).—SCIENTIFIC THEISM. Crown 8vo. 7s. 6d.

—— THE WAY OUT OF AGNOSTICISM; or, The Philosophy of Free Religion. Cr. 8vo. 4s. 6d.

ABBOTT (Rev. E. A.)—A SHAKESPEARIAN GRAMMAR. Extra fcp. 8vo. 6s.

—— CAMBRIDGE SERMONS. 8vo. 6s.

—— OXFORD SERMONS. 8vo. 7s. 6d.

—— FRANCIS BACON: AN ACCOUNT OF HIS LIFE AND WORKS. 8vo. 14s.

—— BIBLE LESSONS. Crown 8vo. 4s. 6d.

ABBOTT (Rev. E. A.) and RUSHBROOKE (W. G.)—THE COMMON TRADITION OF THE SYNOPTIC GOSPELS, IN THE TEXT OF THE REVISED VERSION. Crown 8vo. 3s. 6d.

ACLAND (Sir H. W.).—THE ARMY MEDICAL SCHOOL. Address at Netley Hospital. 1s.

ACTS OF THE APOSTLES. The Greek Text of Bp. Westcott and Dr. Hort. With Notes by T. E. PAGE, M.A. Fcp. 8vo. 4s. 6d.

ADAMS (Sir F. O.) and CUNNINGHAM (C.)—THE SWISS CONFEDERATION. 8vo. 14s.

ADDISON. By W. J. COURTHOPE. Crown 8vo. 1s. 6d.; sewed, 1s.

ADDISON, SELECTIONS FROM. Chosen and Edited by J. R. GREEN. 18mo. 4s. 6d.

AESCHINES.—IN CTESIPHONTA. Edited, with Notes and Indices, by the Rev. T. GWATKIN, M.A., and E. S. SHUCKBURGH, M.A. Fcp. 8vo. 5s.

ÆSCHYLUS.—PERSÆ. Edited by A. O. PRICKARD, M.A. Fcp. 8vo. 2s. 6d.

—— EUMENIDES. With Notes and Introduction, by BERNARD DRAKE, M.A. 8vo. 5s.

—— PROMETHEUS VINCTUS. With Introduction, Notes, and Vocabulary, by Rev. H. M. STEPHENSON, M.A. 18mo. 1s. 6d.

—— THE "SEVEN AGAINST THEBES." With Introduction, Commentary, and Translation, by A. W. VERRALL, Litt.D. 8vo. 7s. 6d.

—— THE "SEVEN AGAINST THEBES." With Introduction and Notes, by A. W. VERRALL and M. A. BAYFIELD. Fcp. 8vo. 2s. 6d.

—— AGAMEMNON. With Introduction, Commentary, and Translation, by A. W. VERRALL, Litt.D. 8vo. 12s.

—— THE SUPPLICES. Text, Introduction, Notes, Commentary, and Translation, by Prof. T. G. TUCKER. 8vo. 10s. 6d.

ÆSOP—CALDECOTT.—SOME OF ÆSOP'S FABLES, with Modern Instances, shown in Designs by RANDOLPH CALDECOTT. 4to. 5s.

AGASSIZ (LOUIS): HIS LIFE AND CORRESPONDENCE. Edited by ELIZABETH CARY AGASSIZ. 2 vols. Crown 8vo. 18s.

AINGER (Rev. Alfred)—SERMONS PREACHED IN THE TEMPLE CHURCH. Extra fcp. 8vo. 6s.

—— CHARLES LAMB. Globe 8vo. (Library Edition). 5s.—Crn. 8vo. 1s. 6d.; swd. 1s.

AIRY (Sir G. B.).—TREATISE ON THE ALGEBRAICAL AND NUMERICAL THEORY OF ERRORS OF OBSERVATION AND THE COMBINATION OF OBSERVATIONS. Crown 8vo. 6s. 6d.

—— POPULAR ASTRONOMY. With Illustrations. Fcp. 8vo. 4s. 6d.

—— AN ELEMENTARY TREATISE ON PARTIAL DIFFERENTIAL EQUATIONS. Crown 8vo. 5s. 6d.

—— ON SOUND AND ATMOSPHERIC VIBRATIONS. With the Mathematical Elements of Music. 2nd Edition. Crown 8vo. 9s.

—— GRAVITATION. An Elementary Explanation of the Principal Perturbations in the Solar System. 2nd Edition. Crown 8vo. 7s. 6d.

AITKEN (Mary Carlyle).—SCOTTISH SONG. A Selection of the Choicest Lyrics of Scotland. 18mo. 4s. 6d.

AITKEN (Sir W.)—THE GROWTH OF THE RECRUIT AND YOUNG SOLDIER. With a view to the selection of "Growing Lads" for the Army, and a Regulated System of Training for Recruits. Crown 8vo. 8s. 6d.

ALBEMARLE (Earl of).—FIFTY YEARS OF MY LIFE. 3rd Edition, revised. Crown 8vo. 7s. 6d.

ALDIS (Mary Steadman).—THE GREAT GIANT ARITHMOS. A MOST ELEMENTARY ARITHMETIC. Illustrated. Globe 8vo. 2s. 6d.

ALDRICH (T. Bailey). — THE SISTERS' TRAGEDY, AND OTHER POEMS. Fcp. 8vo.

ALEXANDER (C. F.).—THE SUNDAY BOOK OF POETRY FOR THE YOUNG. 18mo. 4s. 6d.

ALEXANDER (T.) and THOMSON (A.).—ELEMENTARY APPLIED MECHANICS. Part II. Transverse Stress; upwards of 150 Diagrams, and 200 Examples carefully worked out. Crown 8vo. 10s. 6d.

ALLBUTT (Dr. T. Clifford).—On the Use of the Ophthalmoscope. 8vo. 15s.

ALLEN (Grant).—On the Colours of Flowers, as Illustrated in the British Flora. With Illustrations. Crown 8vo. 3s. 6d.

ALLINGHAM (William).—The Ballad Book. 18mo. 4s. 6d.

AMIEL (Henri Frederic).—The Journal Intime. Translated by Mrs. Humphry Ward. 2nd Edition. Crown 8vo. 6s.

AN ANCIENT CITY, AND OTHER POEMS. Extra fcp. 8vo. 6s.

AN AUTHOR'S LOVE. Being the Unpublished Letters of Prosper Mérimée's "Inconnue." 2 vols. Ex. cr. 8vo. 12s.

ANDERSON (A.).—Ballads and Sonnets. Crown 8vo. 5s.

ANDERSON (Dr. McCall).—Lectures on Clinical Medicine. Illustrated. 8vo. 10s. 6d.

ANDERSON (L.).—Linear Perspective and Model Drawing. Royal 8vo. 2s.

ANDOCIDES.—De Mysteriis. Edited by W. J. Hickie, M.A. Fcp. 8vo. 2s. 6d.

ANDREWS (Dr. Thomas): The Scientific Papers of the late. With a Memoir by Profs. Tait and Crum Brown. 8vo. 18s.

ANGLO-SAXON LAW : Essays on. Med. 8vo. 18s.

APPLETON (T. G.).—A Nile Journal. Illustrated by Eugene Benson. Crown 8vo. 6s.

ARATUS.—The Skies and Weather Forecasts of Aratus. Translated by E. Poste, M.A. Crown 8vo. 3s. 6d.

ARIOSTO.—Paladin and Saracen. Stories from Ariosto. By H. C. Hollway-Calthrop. Illustrated. Crown 8vo. 6s.

ARISTOPHANES.—The Birds. Translated into English Verse, with Introduction, Notes, and Appendices. By Prof. B. H. Kennedy, D.D. Crown 8vo. 6s.

—— Help Notes for the Use of Students. Crown 8vo. 1s. 6d.

ARISTOTLE ON FALLACIES; or, The Sophistici Elenchi. With Translation and Notes by E. Poste, M.A. 8vo. 8s. 6d.

ARISTOTLE.—The First Book of the Metaphysics of Aristotle. Translated into English Prose, with marginal Analysis and Summary of each Chapter. By a Cambridge Graduate. 8vo. 5s.

—— The Politics. Translated with an Analysis and Critical Notes by J. E. C. Welldon, M.A. 2nd Edition. 10s. 6d.

—— The Rhetoric. By the same Translator. Crown 8vo. 7s. 6d.

ARMY PRELIMINARY EXAMINATION, Specimens of Papers set at the, 1882-89. With Answers to the Mathematical Questions. Crown 8vo. 3s. 6d.

ARNAULD, ANGELIQUE. By Frances Martin. Crown 8vo. 4s. 6d.

ARNOLD (Matthew).—The Complete Poetical Works. New Edition. 3 vols. Crown 8vo. 7s. 6d. each.—Vol. I. Early Poems, Narrative Poems, and Sonnets. —Vol. II. Lyric and Elegiac Poems.—Vol. III. Dramatic and Later Poems.

—— Complete Poetical Works. 1 vol. With Portrait. Crown 8vo. 7s. 6d.

—— Essays in Criticism. 6th Edition. Crown 8vo. 9s.

—— Essays in Criticism. Second Series. With an Introductory Note by Lord Coleridge. Crown 8vo. 7s. 6d.

—— Isaiah XL.—LXVI. With the Shorter Prophecies Allied to it. With Notes. Crown 8vo. 5s.

—— Isaiah of Jerusalem. In the Authorised English Version, with Introduction, Corrections, and Notes. Crown 8vo. 4s. 6d.

—— A Bible-Reading for Schools. The Great Prophecy of Israel's Restoration (Isaiah xl.-lxvi.) Arranged and Edited for Young Learners. 4th Edition. 18mo. 1s.

—— Higher Schools and Universities in Germany. Crown 8vo. 6s.

—— Selected Poems. 18mo. 4s. 6d.

—— Poems of Wordsworth. Chosen and Edited by Matthew Arnold. With Portrait. 18mo. 4s. 6d.

    Large Paper Edition. 9s.

—— Poetry of Byron. Chosen and arranged by Matthew Arnold. With Vignette. 18mo. 4s. 6d.

    Large Paper Edition. 9s.

—— Discourses in America. Cr. 8vo. 4s. 6d.

—— Johnson's Lives of the Poets, The Six Chief Lives from. With Macaulay's "Life of Johnson." With Preface and Notes by Matthew Arnold. Crown 8vo. 4s. 6d.

—— Edmund Burke's Letters, Tracts and Speeches on Irish Affairs. Edited by Matthew Arnold. Crown 8vo. 6s.

—— Reports on Elementary Schools, 1852-82. Edited by the Right Hon. Sir Francis Sandford, K.C.B. Cr. 8vo. 3s. 6d.

ARNOLD (T.)—The Second Punic War. By the late Thomas Arnold, D.D. Edited by William T. Arnold, M.A. With Eight Maps. Crown 8vo. 5s.

ARNOLD (W. T.).—The Roman System of Provincial Administration. Crn. 8vo. 6s.

ARRIAN.—Selections. Edited by J. Bond, M.A., and A. S. Walpole, M.A. 18mo. 1s. 6d.

ART AT HOME SERIES. Edited by W. J. Loftie, B.A.

    Music in the House. By John Hullah. Fourth Edition. Crown 8vo. 2s. 6d.

    The Dining-Room. By Mrs. Loftie. With Illustrations. 2nd Edition. Crown 8vo. 2s. 6d.

    The Bedroom and Boudoir. By Lady Barker. Crown 8vo. 2s. 6d.

    Amateur Theatricals. By Walter H. Pollock and Lady Pollock. Illustrated by Kate Greenaway. Crown 8vo. 2s. 6d.

ART AT HOME SERIES—*continued.*

NEEDLEWORK. By ELIZABETH GLAISTER. Illustrated. Crown 8vo. 2s. 6d.

THE LIBRARY. By ANDREW LANG, with a Chapter on English Illustrated Books, by AUSTIN DOBSON. Crown 8vo. 3s. 6d.

ARTEVELDE. JAMES AND PHILIP VAN ARTEVELDE. By W. J. ASHLEY. Crown 8vo. 6s.

ATKINSON (J. B.).—AN ART TOUR TO NORTHERN CAPITALS OF EUROPE. 8vo. 12s.

ATTIC ORATORS, SELECTIONS FROM THE. Antiphon, Andocides, Lysias, Isocrates, and Isaeus. Edited, with Notes, by Prof. R. C. JEBB, Litt.D. 2nd Edition. Fcp. 8vo. 5s.

ATTWELL (H.)—A BOOK OF GOLDEN THOUGHTS. 18mo. 4s. 6d.

AULUS GELLIUS (STORIES FROM). Edited by Rev. G. H. NALL, M.A. 18mo. 1s. 6d.

AUSTIN (Alfred).—POETICAL WORKS. New Collected Edit. In 6 vols. Cr. 8vo. 5s. each. Monthly Vols. from December, 1890:

  Vol. I. THE TOWER OF BABEL.
  Vol. II. SAVONAROLA, etc.
  Vol. III. SATIRES, etc.
  Vol. IV. PRINCE LUCIFER.
  Vol. V. THE HUMAN TRAGEDY
  Vol. VI. LYRICAL POEMS.

—— SAVONAROLA: A TRAGEDY. Crown 8vo. 7s.

—— SOLILOQUIES IN SONG. Crown 8vo. 6s.

—— AT THE GATE OF THE CONVENT; AND OTHER POEMS. Crown 8vo. 6s.

—— PRINCE LUCIFER. Crown 8vo. 6s.

—— MADONNA'S CHILD. Crown 4to. 3s. 6d.

—— ROME OR DEATH. Crown 4to. 9s.

—— THE GOLDEN AGE. Crown 8vo. 5s.

—— THE SEASON. Crown 8vo. 5s.

—— LOVE'S WIDOWHOOD: AND OTHER POEMS. Crown 8vo. 6s.

—— THE HUMAN TRAGEDY. Cr. 8vo. 7s. 6d.

—— ENGLISH LYRICS. Crown 8vo. 3s. 6d.

AUTENRIETH (Dr. G.).—AN HOMERIC DICTIONARY. Translated from the German, by R. P. KEEP, Ph.D. Crown 8vo. 6s.

AWDRY (Frances).—THE STORY OF A FELLOW SOLDIER. (A Life of Bishop Patteson for the Young.) With a Preface by CHARLOTTE M. YONGE. Globe 8vo. 2s. 6d.

BABRIUS. With Introductory Dissertations, Critical Notes, Commentary, and Lexicon, by W. G. RUTHERFORD, LL.D. 8vo. 12s. 6d.

"BACCHANTE." THE CRUISE OF H.M.S. "BACCHANTE," 1879-1882. Compiled from the private Journals, Letters and Note-books of PRINCE ALBERT VICTOR and PRINCE GEORGE OF WALES. By the Rev. Canon DALTON. 2 vols. Medium 8vo. 52s. 6d.

BACON. By the Very Rev. Dean CHURCH. Globe 8vo. 5s.; Cm. 8vo. 1s. 6d.; swd., 1s.

BACON'S ESSAYS AND COLOURS OF GOOD AND EVIL. With Notes and Glossarial Index, by W. ALDIS WRIGHT, M.A. With Vignette. 18mo. 4s. 6d.

BACON'S ESSAYS. Edited by Prof. F. G. SELBY, M.A. Globe 8vo. 3s.; sewed, 2s. 6d.

BACON (FRANCIS): ACCOUNT OF HIS LIFE AND WORKS. By E. A. ABBOTT. 8vo. 14s.

BAINES (Rev. Edward).—SERMONS. With a Preface and Memoir, by ALFRED BARRY, D.D., late Bishop of Sydney. Cra. 8vo. 6s.

BAKER (Sir Samuel White).—ISMAILIA. A Narrative of the Expedition to Central Africa for the Suppression of the Slave Trade, organised by ISMAIL, Khedive of Egypt. Crown 8vo. 6s.

—— THE NILE TRIBUTARIES OF ABYSSINIA, AND THE SWORD HUNTERS OF THE HAMRAN ARABS. Crown 8vo. 6s.

—— THE ALBERT N'YANZA GREAT BASIN OF THE NILE AND EXPLORATION OF THE NILE SOURCES. Crown 8vo. 6s.

—— CYPRUS AS I SAW IT IN 1879. 8vo. 12s. 6d.

—— CAST UP BY THE SEA: OR, THE ADVENTURES OF NED GRAY. With Illustrations by HUARD. Crown 8vo. 6s..

—— THE EGYPTIAN QUESTION, Letters to the *Times* and the *Pall Mall Gazette*. 8vo. 2s.

—— TRUE TALES FOR MY GRANDSONS. Illustrated by W. J. HENNESSY. Cr. 8vo. 3s. 6d.

—— WILD BEASTS AND THEIR WAYS: REMINISCENCES OF EUROPE, ASIA, AFRICA, AND AMERICA. Illustrated. 2 vols. 8vo. 1l. 12s.

BALCH (Elizabeth). — GLIMPSES OF OLD ENGLISH HOMES. Illustrated. Gl. 4to. 14s.

BALDWIN (Prof. J. M.)—HANDBOOK OF PSYCHOLOGY: SENSES AND INTELLECT. 2nd Edition. 8vo. 12s. 6d.

BALFOUR (The Right Hon. A. J.)—A DEFENCE OF PHILOSOPHIC DOUBT. Being an Essay on the Foundations of Belief. 8vo. 12s.

BALFOUR (Prof. F. M.).—ELASMOBRANCH FISHES. With Plates. 8vo. 21s.

—— COMPARATIVE EMBRYOLOGY. With Illustrations. 2 vols. 2nd Edition. 8vo.—Vol. I. 18s.—Vol. II. 21s.

—— THE COLLECTED WORKS. Memorial Edition. Edited by M. FOSTER, F.R.S., and ADAM SEDGWICK, M.A. 4 vols. 8vo. 6l. 6s.

  Vols. I. and IV. Special Memoirs. May be had separately. Price 73s. 6d. net.

BALL (Sir R. S.).—EXPERIMENTAL MECHANICS. Illustrated. New Edit. Cr. 8vo. 6s.

BALL (W. Platt).—ARE THE EFFECTS OF USE AND DISUSE INHERITED? An Examination of the View held by Spencer and Darwin. Crown 8vo. 3s. 6d.

BALL (W. W. R.).—THE STUDENT'S GUIDE TO THE BAR. 5th Edition, revised. Crown 8vo. 2s. 6d.

—— A SHORT ACCOUNT OF THE HISTORY OF MATHEMATICS. Crown 8vo. 10s. 6d.

BALLIOL COLLEGE. PSALMS AND HYMNS FOR BALLIOL COLLEGE. 18mo. 2s. 6d.

BARKER (Lady).—FIRST LESSONS IN THE PRINCIPLES OF COOKING. 3rd Ed. 18mo. 1s.

—— A YEAR'S HOUSEKEEPING IN SOUTH AFRICA. Illustrated. Crown 8vo. 3s. 6d.

—— STATION LIFE IN NEW ZEALAND. Crown 8vo. 3s. 6d.

BARKER (Lady).—LETTERS TO GUY. Crn. 8vo. 5s.

—— THE BED ROOM AND BOUDOIR. With numerous Illustrations. Crown 8vo. 2s. 6d.

BARNES. LIFE OF WILLIAM BARNES, POET AND PHILOLOGIST. By his Daughter, LUCY BAXTER ("Leader Scott"). Cr. 8vo. 7s. 6d.

BARRY (Bishop).—FIRST WORDS IN AUSTRALIA: Sermons. Crown 8vo. 5s.

BARTHOLOMEW (J. G.).—ELEMENTARY SCHOOL ATLAS. 4to. 1s.

—— LIBRARY REFERENCE ATLAS OF THE WORLD. With Index to 100,000 places. Folio. 2l. 12s. 6d. net.

—— PHYSICAL AND POLITICAL SCHOOL ATLAS. With 80 maps. 4to. 7s. 6d.; half mor. 10s. 6d.

BARWELL (Richard, F.R.C.S.).—THE CAUSES AND TREATMENT OF LATERAL CURVATURE OF THE SPINE. Crown 8vo. 5s.

—— ON ANEURISM, ESPECIALLY OF THE THORAX AND ROOT OF THE NECK. 3s. 6d.

BASTIAN (H. Charlton).—THE BEGINNINGS OF LIFE. 2 vols. Crown 8vo. 28s.

—— EVOLUTION AND THE ORIGIN OF LIFE. Crown 8vo. 6s. 6d.

—— ON PARALYSIS FROM BRAIN DISEASE IN ITS COMMON FORMS. Crown 8vo. 10s. 6d.

BATHER (Archdeacon).—ON SOME MINISTERIAL DUTIES, CATECHIZING, PREACHING, &c. Edited, with a Preface, by C. J. VAUGHAN, D.D. Fcp. 8vo. 4s. 6d.

BATH (Marquis of).—OBSERVATIONS ON BULGARIAN AFFAIRS. Crown 8vo. 3s. 6d.

BEASLEY (R. D.). — AN ELEMENTARY TREATISE ON PLANE TRIGONOMETRY. With numerous Examples. 9th Ed. Cr. 8vo. 3s. 6d.

BEAUMARCHAIS. LE BARBIER DE SÉVILLE, ou LE PRÉCAUTION INUTILE. Comedie en Quatre Actes. Edited by L. P. BLOUET, B.A., Univ. Gallic. Fcp. 8vo. 3s. 6d.

BECKER (B. H.).—DISTURBED IRELAND. Letters written during 1880-81. Crn. 8vo. 6s.

BEESLY (Mrs.).—STORIES FROM THE HISTORY OF ROME. Fcp. 8vo. 2s. 6d.

BEHAGHEL.—THE GERMAN LANGUAGE. Translated by EMIL TRECHMANN, B.A., Ph.D. Globe 8vo.

BELCHER (Rev. H.).—SHORT EXERCISES IN LATIN PROSE COMPOSITION, AND EXAMINATION PAPERS IN LATIN GRAMMAR; WITH A CHAPTER ON ANALYSIS OF SENTENCES. 18mo. 1s. 6d.

   KEY (for Teachers only). 3s. 6d.

—— SHORT EXERCISES IN LATIN PROSE COMPOSITION. Part II. On the Syntax of Sentences. With an Appendix. 18mo. 2s.

   KEY (for Teachers only). 18mo. 3s.

BENHAM (Rev. W.).—A COMPANION TO THE LECTIONARY. Crown 8vo. 4s. 6d.

BENTLEY. By Professor JEBB. Crown 8vo. 1s. 6d.; sewed, 1s.

BERLIOZ (Hector): AUTOBIOGRAPHY OF. Transl. by RACHEL and ELEANOR HOLMES. 2 vols. Crown 8vo. 21s.

BERNARD (M.).—FOUR LECTURES ON SUBJECTS CONNECTED WITH DIPLOMACY. 8vo. 9s.

BERNARD (St.) THE LIFE AND TIMES OF ST. BERNARD, ABBOT OF CLAIRVAUX. By J. C. MORISON, M.A. Crown 8vo. 6s.

BERNERS (J.).—FIRST LESSONS ON HEALTH. 18mo. 1s.

BESANT (Walter).—CAPTAIN COOK. With Portrait. Crown 8vo. 2s. 6d.

BETHUNE-BAKER (J. F.).—THE INFLUENCE OF CHRISTIANITY ON WAR. 8vo. 5s.

—— THE STERNNESS OF CHRIST'S TEACHING, AND ITS RELATION TO THE LAW OF FORGIVENESS. Crown 8vo. 2s. 6d.

BETSY LEE: A FO'C'S'LE YARN. Extra fcp. 8vo. 3s. 6d.

BETTANY (G. T.).—FIRST LESSONS IN PRACTICAL BOTANY. 18mo. 1s.

BIGELOW (M. M.).—HISTORY OF PROCEDURE IN ENGLAND FROM THE NORMAN CONQUEST. The Norman Period, 1066-1204. 8vo. 16s.

BIKÉLAS (D.).—LOUKIS LARAS; or, THE REMINISCENCES OF A CHIOTE MERCHANT DURING THE GREEK WAR OF INDEPENDENCE. Translated by J. GENNADIUS, Greek Minister in London. Crown 8vo. 7s. 6d.

BINNIE (the late Rev. William).—SERMONS. Crown 8vo. 6s.

BIRKBECK (William Lloyd).—HISTORICAL SKETCH OF THE DISTRIBUTION OF LAND IN ENGLAND. Crown 8vo. 4s. 6d.

BIRKS (Thomas Rawson, M.A.).—FIRST PRINCIPLES OF MORAL SCIENCE; OR, FIRST COURSE OF LECTURES DELIVERED IN THE UNIVERSITY OF CAMBRIDGE. Cr. 8vo. 8s.

—— MODERN UTILITARIANISM; or, THE SYSTEMS OF PALEY, BENTHAM, AND MILL EXAMINED AND COMPARED. Crn. 8vo. 6s. 6d.

—— THE DIFFICULTIES OF BELIEF IN CONNECTION WITH THE CREATION AND THE FALL, REDEMPTION AND JUDGMENT. 2nd Edition. Crown 8vo. 5s.

—— COMMENTARY ON THE BOOK OF ISAIAH, CRITICAL, HISTORICAL, AND PROPHETICAL; INCLUDING A REVISED ENGLISH TRANSLATION. 2nd Edition. 8vo. 12s. 6d.

—— THE NEW TESTAMENT. Essay on the Right Estimation of MS. Evidence in the Text of the New Testament. Cr. 8vo. 3s. 6d.

—— SUPERNATURAL REVELATION; OR, FIRST PRINCIPLES OF MORAL THEOLOGY. 8vo. 8s.

—— MODERN PHYSICAL FATALISM, AND THE DOCTRINE OF EVOLUTION. Including an Examination of Mr. Herbert Spencer's "First Principles." Crown 8vo. 6s.

—— JUSTIFICATION AND IMPUTED RIGHTEOUSNESS. Being a Review of Ten Sermons on the Nature and Effects of Faith by JAMES THOMAS O'BRIEN, D.D., late Bishop of Ossory, Ferns, and Leighlin. Cr. 8vo. 6s.

BJÖRNSON (B.). — SYNNÖVE SOLBAKKEN. Translated by JULIE SUTTER. Cr. 8vo. 6s.

BLACK (William).—THE STRANGE ADVENTURES OF A PHAETON. Illustrated. Cr. 8vo. 6s.

—— A PRINCESS OF THULE. Crown 8vo. 6s.

—— THE MAID OF KILLEENA, AND OTHER TALES. Crown 8vo. 6s.

—— MADCAP VIOLET. Crown 8vo. 6s.

BLACK (Wm.).—GREEN PASTURES AND PICCADILLY. Crown 8vo. 6s.

—— MACLEOD OF DARE. With Illustrations by eminent Artists. Crown 8vo. 6s.

—— WHITE WINGS: A YACHTING ROMANCE. Crown 8vo. 6s.

—— THE BEAUTIFUL WRETCH: THE FOUR MACNICOLS: THE PUPIL OF AURELIUS. Crown 8vo. 6s.

—— SHANDON BELLS. Crown 8vo. 6s.

—— YOLANDE. Crown 8vo. 6s.

—— JUDITH SHAKESPEARE. Crown 8vo. 6s.

—— GOLDSMITH. Cr. 8vo. 1s. 6d.; sewed, 1s.

—— THE WISE WOMEN OF INVERNESS: A TALE. AND OTHER MISCELLANIES. Cr. 8vo. 6s.

—— WHITE HEATHER. Crown 8vo. 6s.

—— SABINA ZEMBRA. Crown 8vo. 6s.

BLACKBURNE. LIFE OF THE RIGHT HON. FRANCIS BLACKBURNE, late Lord Chancellor of Ireland, by his son, EDWARD BLACK-BURNE. With Portrait. 8vo. 12s.

BLACKIE (Prof. John Stuart.).—GREEK AND ENGLISH DIALOGUES FOR USE IN SCHOOLS AND COLLEGES. 3rd Edition. Fcp. 8vo. 2s. 6d.

—— HORÆ HELLENICÆ. 8vo. 12s.

—— THE WISE MEN OF GREECE: IN A SERIES OF DRAMATIC DIALOGUES. Cr. 8vo. 9s.

—— GOETHE'S FAUST. Translated into English Verse. 2nd Edition. Crown 8vo. 9s.

—— LAY SERMONS. Crown 8vo. 6s.

—— MESSIS VITÆ: Gleanings of Song from a Happy Life. Crown 8vo. 4s. 6d.

—— WHAT DOES HISTORY TEACH? Two Edinburgh Lectures. Globe 8vo. 2s. 6d.

BLAKE (J. F.)—ASTRONOMICAL MYTHS. With Illustrations. Crown 8vo. 9s.

BLAKE. LIFE OF WILLIAM BLAKE. With Selections from his Poems and other Writings. Illustrated from Blake's own Works. By ALEXANDER GILCHRIST. New and Enlarged Edition. 2 vols. cloth gilt. Medium 8vo. 2l. 2s.

BLAKISTON (J. R.).—THE TEACHER: HINTS ON SCHOOL MANAGEMENT. Cr. 8vo. 2s. 6d.

BLANFORD (H. F.).—THE RUDIMENTS OF PHYSICAL GEOGRAPHY FOR THE USE OF INDIAN SCHOOLS. 12th Edition. Illustrated. Globe 8vo. 2s. 6d.

—— A PRACTICAL GUIDE TO THE CLIMATES AND WEATHER OF INDIA, CEYLON AND BURMA, AND THE STORMS OF INDIAN SEAS. 8vo. 12s. 6d.

—— ELEMENTARY GEOGRAPHY OF INDIA, BURMA, AND CEYLON. Illustrated. Globe 8vo. 2s. 6d.

BLANFORD (W. T.).—GEOLOGY AND ZOOLOGY OF ABYSSINIA. 8vo. 21s.

BLYTH (A. Wynter).—A MANUAL OF PUBLIC HEALTH. 8vo. 17s. net.

BÖHM-BAWERK (Prof.).—CAPITAL AND INTEREST. Translated by W. SMART, M.A. 8vo. 14s.

BOLDREWOOD (Rolf).—ROBBERY UNDER ARMS: A STORY OF LIFE AND ADVENTURE IN THE BUSH AND IN THE GOLDFIELDS OF AUSTRALIA. Crown 8vo. 3s. 6d.

—— THE MINER'S RIGHT. Crn. 8vo. 3s. 6d.

—— THE SQUATTER'S DREAM. Cr. 8vo. 3s. 6d.

—— A COLONIAL REFORMER. 3 vols. Cr. 8vo. 31s. 6d.

BOLEYN (ANNE): A Chapter of English History, 1527-1536. By PAUL FRIEDMANN. 2 vols. 8vo. 28s.

BONAR (James).—MALTHUS AND HIS WORK. 8vo. 12s. 6d.

BOOK OF GOLDEN DEEDS OF ALL TIMES AND ALL LANDS. By CHARLOTTE M. YONGE. 18mo. 4s. 6d. Edition for Schools. Globe 8vo. 2s. Abridged Edition. 18mo. 1s.

BOOLE (George).—A TREATISE ON THE CALCULUS OF FINITE DIFFERENCES. Edited by J. F. MOULTON. 3rd Edition. Cr. 8vo. 10s. 6d.

—— THE MATHEMATICAL ANALYSIS OF LOGIC. 8vo. Sewed, 5s.

BOTTOMLEY (J. T.). — FOUR-FIGURE MATHEMATICAL TABLES. Comprising Logarithmic and Trigonometrical Tables, and Tables of Squares, Square Roots and Reciprocals, 8vo. 2s. 6d.

BOUGHTON (G. H.) and ABBEY (E. A.).—SKETCHING RAMBLES IN HOLLAND. With Illustrations. Fcp. 4to. 21s.

BOWEN (H. Courthope).—FIRST LESSONS IN FRENCH. 18mo. 1s.

BOWER (Prof. F. O.).—A COURSE OF PRACTICAL INSTRUCTION IN BOTANY. Cr. 8vo. 10s. 6d.

BRADSHAW (J. G.).—A COURSE OF EASY ARITHMETICAL EXAMPLES FOR BEGINNERS. Globe 8vo. 2s. With Answers. 2s. 6d.

BRAIN. A JOURNAL OF NEUROLOGY. Edited for the Neurological Society of London, by A. DE WATTEVILLE. Published Quarterly. 8vo. 3s. 6d. (Part I. in January, 1878.) Yearly Vols. I. to XII. 8vo, cloth. 15s. each. [Cloth covers for binding, 1s. each.]

BREYMANN (Prof. H.).—A FRENCH GRAMMAR BASED ON PHILOLOGICAL PRINCIPLES. 3rd Edition. Extra fcp. 8vo. 4s. 6d.

—— FIRST FRENCH EXERCISE BOOK. 2nd Edition. Extra fcp. 8vo. 4s. 6d.

—— SECOND FRENCH EXERCISE BOOK. Extra fcp. 8vo. 2s. 6d.

BRIDGES (John A.).—IDYLLS OF A LOST VILLAGE. Crown 8vo. 7s. 6d.

BRIGHT (John).—SPEECHES ON QUESTIONS OF PUBLIC POLICY. Edited by the late Prof. THOROLD ROGERS. 2nd Edition. 2 vols. 8vo. 25s. With Portrait. Author's Popular Edition. Extra fcp. 8vo. 3s. 6d.

—— PUBLIC ADDRESSES. Edited by J. E. T. ROGERS. 8vo. 14s.

BRIGHT (H. A.)—THE ENGLISH FLOWER GARDEN. Crown 8vo. 3s. 6d.

BRIMLEY (George).—ESSAYS. Globe 8vo. 5s.

BRODIE (Sir Benjamin).—IDEAL CHEMISTRY. Crown 8vo. 2s.

BROOKE, Sir Jas., The Raja of Sarawak (Life of). By Gertrude L. Jacob. 2 vols. 8vo. 25s.

BROOKE (Stopford A.).—Primer of English Literature. 18mo. 1s.
— Large Paper Edition. 8vo. 7s. 6d.
—— Riquet of the Tuft : A Love Drama. Extra crown 8vo. 6s.
—— Poems. Globe 8vo. 6s.
—— Milton. Fcp. 8vo. 1s. 6d.
— Large Paper Edition. 8vo. 21s. net.
—— Poems of Shelley. Edited by Stopford A. Brooke, M.A. With Vignette. 18mo. 4s. 6d.
— Large Paper Edition. 12s. 6d.
—— Dove Cottage, Wordsworth's Home, from 1800—1808. Globe 8vo. 1s.
—— Early English Literature. 2 vols. 8vo. [Vol. I. in the Press.

BROOKS (Rev. Phillips).—The Candle of the Lord, and other Sermons. Cr 8vo. 6s.
—— Sermons Preached in English Churches. Crown 8vo. 6s.
—— Twenty Sermons. Crown 8vo. 6s.
—— Tolerance. Crown 8vo. 2s. 6d.

BROOKSMITH (J.)—Arithmetic in Theory and Practice. Crown 8vo. 4s. 6d.
—— Key to Arithmetic in Theory and Practice. Crown 8vo. 10s. 6d.

BROOKSMITH (J. and E. J.).—Arithmetic for Beginners. Globe 8vo. 1s. 6d.

BROOKSMITH (E. J.).—Woolwich Mathematical Papers, for Admission in the Royal Military Academy for the years 1880—1888. Edited by E. J. Brooksmith, B.A. Crown 8vo. 6s.
—— Sandhurst Mathematical Papers, for Admission into the Royal Military College, 1881—89. Edited by E. J. Brooksmith, B.A. Crown 8vo. 3s. 6d.

BROWN (J. Allen).—Palæolithic Man in North-West Middlesex. 8vo. 7s. 6d.

BROWN (T. E.).—The Manx Witch: and other Poems. Crown 8vo. 7s. 6d.

BROWNE (J. H. Balfour).—Water Supply. Crown 8vo. 2s. 6d.

BROWNE (Sir Thomas).—Religio Medici ; Letter to a Friend, &c., and Christian Morals. Edited by W. A. Greenhill, M.D. With Portrait. 18mo. 4s. 6d.

BRUNTON (Dr. T. Lauder).—A Text-Book of Pharmacology, Therapeutics, and Materia Medica. 3rd Edition. Medium 8vo. 21s.
—— Disorders of Digestion : their Consequences and Treatment. 8vo. 10s. 6d.
—— Pharmacology and Therapeutics ; or, Medicine Past and Present. Cr. 8vo. 6s.
—— Tables of Materia Medica : A Companion to the Materia Medica Museum. 8vo. 5s.
—— The Bible and Science. With Illustrations. Crown 8vo. 10s. 6d.
—— Croonian Lectures on the Connection between Chemical Constitution and Physiological Action. Being an Introduction to Modern Therapeutics. 8vo.

BRYANS (Clement).—Latin Prose Exercises Based upon Caesar's "Gallic War." With a Classification of Caesar's Phrases, and Grammatical Notes on Caesar's Chief Usages. Pott 8vo. 2s. 6d.
— Key (for Teachers only). 4s. 6d.

BRYCE (James, M.P., D.C.L.).—The Holy Roman Empire. 8th Edition. Crown 8vo. 7s. 6d.—Library Edition. 8vo. 14s.
—— Transcaucasia and Ararat. 3rd Edition. Crown 8vo. 9s.
—— The American Commonwealth. 2nd Edition. 2 vols. Extra Crown 8vo. 25s.

BUCHHEIM (Dr.).—Deutsche Lyrik. 18mo. 4s. 6d.
—— Deutsche Balladen und Romanzen. 18mo. [In the Press.

BUCKLAND (Anna).—Our National Institutions. 18mo. 1s.

BUCKLEY (Arabella).—History of England for Beginners. With Coloured Maps and Chronological and Genealogical Tables. Globe 8vo. 3s.

BUCKNILL (Dr.).—The Care of the Insane. Crown 8vo. 3s. 6d.

BUCKTON (G. B.).—Monograph of the British Cicada, or Tettigidæ. In 8 parts, Quarterly. Part I. January, 1890. 8vo.—I. II. III. and IV. ready. 8s. each net.—Vol. I. 8vo. 33s. 6d. net.

BUMBLEBEE BOGO'S BUDGET. By a Retired Judge. Illustrations by Alice Havers. Crown 8vo. 2s. 6d.

BUNYAN (John).—The Pilgrim's Progress from this World to that which is to Come. 18mo. 4s. 6d.

BUNYAN. By J. A. Froude. Crown 8vo. 1s. 6d.; sewed, 1s.

BURGON (Dean).—Poems. Ex. fcp.8vo. 4s.6d.

BURKE (Edmund).—Letters, Tracts, and Speeches on Irish Affairs. Edited by Matthew Arnold, with Preface. Cr. 8vo. 6s.

BURKE. By John Morley. Globe 8vo. 5s. Crown 8vo. 1s. 6d.; sewed, 1s.
—— Reflections on the French Revolution. Ed. by F. G. Selby. Gl. 8vo. 5s.

BURN (Robert).—Roman Literature in Relation to Roman Art. With Illustrations. Extra Crown 8vo. 14s.

BURNETT (F. Hodgson).—"Haworth's." Globe 8vo. 2s.
—— Louisiana : and That Lass o' Lowrie's. Two Stories. Illustrated. Cr. 8vo. 3s. 6d. Cheap Edition. Globe 8vo. 2s.

BURNS, The Complete Works of. Edited by Alexander Smith. Globe 8vo. 3s. 6d.
—— The Poetical Works. With a Biographical Memoir by Alexander Smith. In 2 vols. fcp. 8vo. 10s.

BURNS. By Principal Shairp. Crown 8vo. 1s. 6d.; sewed, 1s.

BURY (J. B.).—A History of the Later Roman Empire from Arcadius to Irene, A.D. 390—800. 2 vols. 8vo. 32s.
—— Pindar : Nemean Odes. 8vo. 12s.

BUTCHER (Prof. S. H.).—Demosthenes. Fcp. 8vo. 1s. 6d.

BUTLER (Archer).—SERMONS, DOCTRINAL AND PRACTICAL. 11th Edition. 8vo. 8s.
—— SECOND SERIES OF SERMONS. 8vo. 7s.
—— LETTERS ON ROMANISM. 8vo. 10s. 6d.

BUTLER (George).—SERMONS PREACHED IN CHELTENHAM COLLEGE CHAPEL. 8vo. 7s. 6d.

BUTLER (Col. Sir W.).—GENERAL GORDON. With Portrait. Crown 8vo. 2s. 6d.
—— SIR CHARLES NAPIER. With Portrait. Crown 8vo. 2s. 6d.

BUTLER'S HUDIBRAS. Edited by ALFRED MILNES. Fcp. 8vo. Part I. 3s. 6d. Part II. and III. 4s. 6d.

BYRON.—POETRY OF BYRON, chosen and arranged by MATTHEW ARNOLD. 18mo. 4s. 6d.
Large Paper Edition. Crown 8vo. 9s.

BYRON. By Prof. NICHOL. Crown 8vo. 1s. 6d.; sewed, 1s.

CAESAR.—THE HELVETIAN WAR. Selected from Book I. of The Gallic War, with Notes, Vocabulary, and Exercises, by W. WELCH and C. G. DUFFIELD. 18mo. 1s. 6d.
—— THE INVASION OF BRITAIN. Being Selections from Books IV. and V. of the Gallic War. With Notes, Vocabulary, and Exercises, by W. WELCH, M.A., and C. G. DUFFIELD, M.A. 18mo. 1s. 6d.
—— SCENES FROM THE FIFTH AND SIXTH BOOKS OF THE GALLIC WAR. Selected and Ed. by C. COLBECK, M.A. 18mo. 1s. 6d.
—— THE GALLIC WAR. Edited by the Rev. J. BOND, M.A., and Rev. A. S. WALPOLE, M.A. Fcp. 8vo. 4s. 6d.
—— THE GALLIC WAR. Book I. Edited, with Notes and Vocabulary by Rev. A. S. WALPOLE, M.A. 18mo. 1s. 6d.
—— THE GALLIC WAR.—Books II. and III. Edited by W. G. RUTHERFORD, LL.D. 18mo. 1s. 6d.
—— THE GALLIC WAR.—Book IV. Edited, with Introduction, Notes, and Vocabulary, by CLEMENT BRYANS, M.A. 18mo. 1s. 6d.
—— THE GALLIC WAR.—Book V. Edited with Notes and Vocabulary, by C. COLBECK, M.A. 18mo. 1s. 6d.
—— THE GALLIC WAR.—Book VI. By the same Editor. With Notes and Vocabulary. 18mo. 1s. 6d.
—— THE GALLIC WAR—Book VII. Edited by the Rev. J. BOND, M.A., and Rev. A. S. WALPOLE, M.A. With Notes and Vocabulary. 18mo. 1s. 6d.

CAIRNES (Prof. J. E.).—POLITICAL ESSAYS. 8vo. 10s. 6d.
—— SOME LEADING PRINCIPLES OF POLITICAL ECONOMY NEWLY EXPOUNDED. 8vo. 14s.
—— THE SLAVE POWER. 8vo. 10s. 6d.
—— THE CHARACTER AND LOGICAL METHOD OF POLITICAL ECONOMY. Crown 8vo. 6s.

CALDERON.—SELECT PLAYS OF CALDERON. Edited by NORMAN MACCOLL, M.A. Crown 8vo. 14s.

CALDERWOOD (Prof.)—HANDBOOK OF MORAL PHILOSOPHY. Crown 8vo. 6s.
—— THE RELATIONS OF MIND AND BRAIN. 2nd Edition. 8vo. 12s.

CALDERWOOD (Prof.).—THE PARABLES OF OUR LORD. Crown 8vo. 6s.
—— THE RELATIONS OF SCIENCE AND RELIGION. Crown 8vo. 5s.
—— ON TEACHING. 4th Edition. Extra fcp. 8vo. 2s. 6d.

CALVERT (A.).—SCHOOL-READINGS IN THE GREEK TESTAMENT. With Notes and Vocabulary, by A. CALVERT. Fcp. 8vo. 2s. 6d.

CAMBRIDGE. COOPER'S LE KEUX'S MEMORIALS OF CAMBRIDGE. Illustrated with 90 Woodcuts in the Text, 154 Plates on Steel and Copper by LE KEUX, STORER, &c., including 20 Etchings by R. FARREN. 3 vols. 4to, half levant morocco. 10l. 10s.

CAMBRIDGE SENATE-HOUSE PROBLEMS AND RIDERS, WITH SOLUTIONS:
1848—51. RIDERS. By JAMESON. 8vo. 7s. 6d.
1875. PROBLEMS AND RIDERS. Edited by Prof. A. G. GREENHILL. Cr. 8vo. 8s. 6d.
1878. SOLUTIONS BY THE MATHEMATICAL MODERATORS AND EXAMINERS. Edited by J. W. L. GLAISHER, M.A. 8vo. 12s.

CAMEOS FROM ENGLISH HISTORY. By the Author of "The Heir of Redclyffe." Extra fcp. 8vo. 5s. each volume.
Vol. I. Rollo to Edward II. II. The Wars in France. III. The Wars of the Roses. IV. Reformation Times. V. England and Spain. VI. Forty Years of Stuart Rule (1603—43). VII. The Rebellion and Restoration (1642-78).

CAMERON (V. L.).—OUR FUTURE HIGHWAY TO INDIA. 2 vols. Crown 8vo. 21s.

CAMPBELL (Dr. John M'Leod).—THE NATURE OF THE ATONEMENT. 6th Edition. Crown 8vo. 6s.
—— REMINISCENCES AND REFLECTIONS. Ed., with an Introductory Narrative, by his Son, DONALD CAMPBELL, M.A. Cr. 8vo. 7s. 6d.
—— RESPONSIBILITY FOR THE GIFT OF ETERNAL LIFE. Compiled from Sermons preached at Row, in the years 1829—31. Cr. 8vo. 5s.
—— THOUGHTS ON REVELATION. 2nd Edit. Crown 8vo. 5s.

CAMPBELL (J. F.).—MY CIRCULAR NOTES. Cheaper issue. Crown 8vo. 6s.

CAMPBELL (Lord George).—LOG-LETTERS FROM THE "CHALLENGER." Crown 8vo. 6s.

CAMPBELL (Prof. Lewis).—SOPHOCLES. Fcp. 8vo. 1s. 6d.

CANDLER (H.).—HELP TO ARITHMETIC. 2nd Edition. Globe 8vo. 2s. 6d.

CANTERBURY (His Grace Edward White, Archbishop of).—BOY-LIFE: ITS TRIAL, ITS STRENGTH, ITS FULNESS. Sundays in Wellington College, 1859—73. 4th Edition. Crown 8vo. 6s.
—— THE SEVEN GIFTS. Addressed to the Diocese of Canterbury in his Primary Visitation. 2nd Edition. Crown 8vo. 6s.
—— CHRIST AND HIS TIMES. Addressed to the Diocese of Canterbury in his Second Visitation. Crown 8vo. 6s.

CAPES (Rev. W. W.).—LIVY. Fcp. 8vo. 1s. 6d.

CARLES (W. R.).—LIFE IN COREA. 8vo. 12s. 6d.

CARLYLE (Thomas).—REMINISCENCES. Ed. by CHARLES ELIOT NORTON. 2 vols. Crown 8vo. 12s.

—— EARLY LETTERS OF THOMAS CARLYLE. Edited by C. E. NORTON. 2 vols. 1814—26. Crown 8vo. 18s.

—— LETTERS OF THOMAS CARLYLE. Edited by C. E. NORTON. 2 vols. 1826—36. Crown 8vo. 18s.

—— GOETHE AND CARLYLE, CORRESPONDENCE BETWEEN. Edited by C. E. NORTON. Crown 8vo. 9s.

CARMARTHEN (Marchioness of). — A LOVER OF THE BEAUTIFUL. Crn. 8vo. 6s.

CARNOT—THURSTON.—REFLECTIONS ON THE MOTIVE POWER OF HEAT, AND ON MACHINES FITTED TO DEVELOP THAT POWER. From the French of N. L. S. CARNOT. Edited by R. H. THURSTON, LL.D. Crown 8vo. 7s. 6d.

CARPENTER (Bishop W. Boyd).—TRUTH IN TALE. Addresses, chiefly to Children. Cr. 8vo. 4s. 6d.

—— THE PERMANENT ELEMENTS OF RELIGION: Bampton Lectures, 1887. 8vo. 14s.

CARR (J. Comyns).—PAPERS ON ART. Cr. 8vo. 8s. 6d.

CARROLL (Lewis).—ALICE'S ADVENTURES IN WONDERLAND. With 42 Illustrations by TENNIEL. Crown 8vo. 6s. net.

People's Edition. With all the original Illustrations. Crown 8vo. 2s. 6d. net.

A GERMAN TRANSLATION OF THE SAME. Crown 8vo, gilt. 6s. net.

A FRENCH TRANSLATION OF THE SAME. Crown 8vo, gilt. 6s. net.

AN ITALIAN TRANSLATION OF THE SAME. Crown 8vo, gilt. 6s. net.

—— ALICE'S ADVENTURES UNDER-GROUND. Being a Facsimile of the Original MS. Book, afterwards developed into "Alice's Adventures in Wonderland." With 27 Illustrations by the Author. Crown 8vo. 4s. net.

—— THROUGH THE LOOKING-GLASS AND WHAT ALICE FOUND THERE. With 50 Illustrations by TENNIEL. Cr. 8vo, gilt. 6s. net.

People's Edition. With all the original Illustrations. Crown 8vo. 2s. 6d. net.

People's Edition of "Alice's Adventures in Wonderland," and "Through the Looking-Glass." 1 vol. Crown 8vo. 4s. 6d. net.

—— THE GAME OF LOGIC. Cr. 8vo. 3s. net.

—— RHYME? AND REASON? With 65 Illustrations by ARTHUR B. FROST, and 9 by HENRY HOLIDAY. Crown 8vo. 6s. net.

—— A TANGLED TALE. Reprinted from the "Monthly Packet." With 6 Illustrations by ARTHUR B. FROST. Crn. 8vo. 4s. 6d. net.

—— SYLVIE AND BRUNO. With 46 Illustrations by HARRY FURNISS. Cr. 8vo. 7s 6d. net.

—— THE NURSERY "ALICE." Twenty Coloured Enlargements from TENNIEL'S Illustrations to "Alice's Adventures in Wonderland," with Text adapted to Nursery Readers. 4to. 4s. net.

CARROLL (Lewis).—THE HUNTING OF THE SNARK, AN AGONY IN EIGHT FITS. With 9 Illustrations by HENRY HOLIDAY. Crown 8vo. 4s. 6d. net.

CARSTARES (WM.): A Character and Career of the Revolutionary Epoch (1649—1715). By R. H. STORY. 8vo. 12s.

CARTER (R. Brudenell, F.C.S.).—A PRACTICAL TREATISE ON DISEASES OF THE EYE. 8vo. 16s.

CARTER (R. Brudenell).—EYESIGHT, GOOD AND BAD. Cr. 8vo. 6s.

—— MODERN OPERATIONS FOR CATARACT. 8vo. 6s.

CASSEL (Dr. D.).—MANUAL OF JEWISH HISTORY AND LITERATURE. Translated by Mrs. HENRY LUCAS. Fcp. 8vo. 2s. 6d.

CATULLUS.—SELECT POEMS. Edited by F. P. SIMPSON, B.A. Fcp. 8vo. 3s. 6d.

CAUCASUS: NOTES ON THE. By "Wanderer." 8vo. 9s.

CAUTLEY (G. S.).—A CENTURY OF EMBLEMS. With Illustrations by the Lady MARIAN ALFORD. Small 4to. 10s. 6d.

CAZENOVE (J. Gibson).—CONCERNING THE BEING AND ATTRIBUTES OF GOD. 8vo. 5s.

CHALMERS (J. B.).—GRAPHICAL DETERMINATION OF FORCES IN ENGINEERING STRUCTURES. 8vo. 24s.

CHALMERS (M.D.).—LOCAL GOVERNMENT. Crown 8vo. 3s. 6d.

CHASSERESSE (D.).—SPORTING SKETCHES. Illustrated. Crown 8vo. 3s. 6d.

CHATTERTON: A BIOGRAPHICAL STUDY. By Sir DANIEL WILSON, LL.D. Crown 8vo. 6s. 6d.

CHAUCER. By Prof. A. W. WARD. Crown 8vo. 1s. 6d.; sewed, 1s.

CHERRY (Prof. R. R.).—LECTURES ON THE GROWTH OF CRIMINAL LAW IN ANCIENT COMMUNITIES. 8vo. 5s. net.

CHEYNE (C. H. H.).—AN ELEMENTARY TREATISE ON THE PLANETARY THEORY. Crown 8vo. 7s. 6d.

CHEYNE (T. K.).—THE BOOK OF ISAIAH CHRONOLOGICALLY ARRANGED. Crown 8vo. 7s. 6d.

CHILDREN'S GARLAND FROM THE BEST POETS. Selected and arranged by COVENTRY PATMORE. 18mo. 4s. 6d.

Globe Readings Edition for Schools. 2s.

CHOICE NOTES ON THE FOUR GOSPELS, drawn from Old and New Sources. Crown 8vo. 4 vols. 4s. 6d. each. (St. Matthew and St. Mark in 1 vol. 9s.)

CHRISTIE (J.).—CHOLERA EPIDEMICS IN EAST AFRICA. 8vo. 15s.

CHRISTIE (J. R.).—ELEMENTARY TEST QUESTIONS IN PURE AND MIXED MATHEMATICS. Crown 8vo. 8s. 6d.

CHRISTMAS CAROL, A. Printed in Colours, with Illuminated Borders from MSS. of the Fourteenth and Fifteenth Centuries. 4to. 21s.

CHRISTY CAREW. By the Author of "Hogan, M.P." Globe 8vo. 2s.

CHURCH (Very Rev. R. W.).—THE SACRED POETRY OF EARLY RELIGIONS. 2nd Edition. 18mo. 1s.

—— ST. ANSELM. Globe 8vo. 5s.

—— HUMAN LIFE AND ITS CONDITIONS. Cr. 8vo. 6s.

—— THE GIFTS OF CIVILISATION, and other Sermons and Lectures. Crown 8vo. 7s. 6d.

—— DISCIPLINE OF THE CHRISTIAN CHARACTER, and other Sermons. Crown 8vo. 4s. 6d.

—— ADVENT SERMONS. 1885. Cr. 8vo. 4s. 6d.

—— MISCELLANEOUS WRITINGS. Collected Edition. 5 vols. Globe 8vo. 5s. each. Vol. I. MISCELLANEOUS ESSAYS. II DANTE: AND OTHER ESSAYS. III. ST. ANSELM. IV. SPENSER. V. BACON.

—— SPENSER. Globe 8vo. Library Edition. 5s.—Crown 8vo. 1s. 6d.; sewed, 1s.

—— BACON. Globe 8vo. Library Edition. 5s.—Crown 8vo, 1s. 6d.; sewed, 1s.

—— THE OXFORD MOVEMENT. 8vo.

CHURCH (Rev. A. J.).—LATIN VERSION OF SELECTIONS FROM TENNYSON. By Prof. CONINGTON, Prof. SEELEY, Dr. HESSEY, T. E. KEBBEL, &c. Edited by A. J. CHURCH, M.A. Extra fcp. 8vo. 6s.

—— HENRY V. With Portrait. Cr. 8vo. 2s. 6d.

—— STORIES FROM THE BIBLE. Illustrated. Crown 8vo. 5s.

CHURCH (A. J.) and BRODRIBB (W. J.).— TACITUS. Fcp. 8vo. 1s. 6d.

CICERO. THE LIFE AND LETTERS OF MARCUS TULLIUS CICERO. By the Rev. G. E. JEANS, M.A. 2nd Edit. Cr. 8vo. 10s. 6d.

—— THE ACADEMICA. The Text revised and explained by J. S. REID, M.L. 8vo. 15s.

—— THE ACADEMICS. Translated by J. S. REID, M.L. 8vo. 5s. 6d.

—— DE AMICITIA. Edited by E. S. SHUCKBURGH, M.A. With Notes, Vocabulary, and Biographical Index. 18mo. 1s. 6d.

—— DE SENECTUTE. Edited, with Notes, Vocabulary, and Biographical Index, by E. S. SHUCKBURGH, M.A. 18mo. 1s. 6d.

—— SELECT LETTERS. Edited by Rev. G. E. JEANS, M.A. 18mo. 1s. 6d.

—— SELECT LETTERS. Edit. by Prof. R. Y. TYRRELL, M.A. Fcp. 8vo.

—— THE SECOND PHILIPPIC ORATION. Edited by Prof. JOHN E. B. MAYOR. New Edition, revised. Fcp. 8vo. 3s. 6d.

—— THE SECOND PHILIPPIC. Translated, with Historical Introduction and Notes, by E. S. SHUCKBURGH. Crown 8vo. 3s. 6d.

—— PRO PUBLIO SESTIO. Edited by Rev. H. A. HOLDEN, M.A., LL.D. Fcp. 8vo. 3s. 6d.

—— THE CATILINE ORATIONS. Edited by Prof. A. S. WILKINS, Litt.D. New Edition. Fcp. 8vo. 2s. 6d.

—— PRO LEGE MANILIA. Edited by Prof. A. S. WILKINS, Litt.D. Fcp. 8vo. 2s. 6d.

—— PRO ROSCIO AMERINO. Edited by E. H. DONKIN, M.A. Fcp. 8vo. 2s. 6d.

—— STORIES OF ROMAN HISTORY. With Notes, Vocabulary, and Exercises by G. E. JEANS, M.A., and A. V. JONES. 18mo. 1s. 6d.

CLARK. MEMORIALS FROM JOURNALS AND LETTERS OF SAMUEL CLARK, M.A. Edited by his Wife. Crown 8vo. 7s. 6d.

CLARK (L.) and SADLER (H.).—THE STAR GUIDE. Roy. 8vo. 5s.

CLARKE (C. B.).—A GEOGRAPHICAL READER AND COMPANION TO THE ATLAS. Cr. 8vo. 2s.

—— A CLASS-BOOK OF GEOGRAPHY. With 18 Coloured Maps. Fcp. 8vo. 3s. 6d.; swd., 3s.

—— SPECULATIONS FROM POLITICAL ECONOMY. Crown 8vo. 3s. 6d.

CLASSICAL WRITERS. Edited by JOHN RICHARD GREEN. Fcp. 8vo. 1s. 6d. each.

EURIPIDES. By Prof. MAHAFFY.

MILTON. By the Rev. STOPFORD A. BROOKE.

LIVY. By the Rev. W. W. CAPES, M.A.

VERGIL. By Prof. NETTLESHIP, M.A.

SOPHOCLES. By Prof. L. CAMPBELL, M.A.

DEMOSTHENES. By Prof. BUTCHER, M.A.

TACITUS. By CHURCH and BRODRIBB.

CLAUSIUS (R.).—THE MECHANICAL THEORY OF HEAT. Translated by WALTER R. BROWNE. Crown 8vo. 10s. 6d.

CLERGYMAN'S SELF-EXAMINATION CONCERNING THE APOSTLES' CREED. Extra fcp. 8vo. 1s. 6d.

CLIFFORD (Prof. W. K.).—ELEMENTS OF DYNAMIC. An Introduction to the Study of Motion and Rest in Solid and Fluid Bodies. Crown 8vo. Part I. Kinematic. Books I.— III. 7s. 6d. Book IV. and Appendix, 6s.

—— LECTURES AND ESSAYS. Ed. by LESLIE STEPHEN and Sir F. POLLOCK. Cr. 8vo. 8s. 6d.

—— SEEING AND THINKING. With Diagrams. Crown 8vo. 3s. 6d.

—— MATHEMATICAL PAPERS. Edited by R. TUCKER. With an Introduction by H. J. STEPHEN SMITH, M.A. 8vo. 30s.

CLIFFORD (Mrs. W. K.).—ANYHOW STORIES. With Illustrations by DOROTHY TENNANT. Crown 8vo. 1s. 6d.; paper covers, 1s.

CLIVE. By Col. Sir CHARLES WILSON. With Portrait. Crown 8vo. 2s. 6d.

CLOUGH (A. H.).—POEMS. New Edition. Crown 8vo. 7s. 6d.

—— PROSE REMAINS. With a Selection from his Letters, and a Memoir by his Wife. Crown 8vo. 7s. 6d.

COAL: ITS HISTORY AND ITS USES. By Profs. GREEN, MIALL, THORPE, RÜCKER, and MARSHALL. 8vo. 12s. 6d.

COBDEN (Richard).—SPEECHES ON QUESTIONS OF PUBLIC POLICY. Ed. by J. BRIGHT and J. E. THOROLD ROGERS. Gl. 8vo. 3s. 6d.

COCKSHOTT (A.) and WALTERS (F. B.). —A TREATISE ON GEOMETRICAL CONICS. Crown 8vo. 5s.

COHEN (Dr. Julius B.).—THE OWENS COLLEGE COURSE OF PRACTICAL ORGANIC CHEMISTRY. Fcp. 8vo. 2s. 6d.

COLBECK (C.).—FRENCH READINGS FROM ROMAN HISTORY. Selected from various Authors, with Notes. 18mo. 4s. 6d.

COLENSO (Bp.).—THE COMMUNION SERVICE FROM THE BOOK OF COMMON PRAYER, WITH SELECT READINGS FROM THE WRITINGS OF THE REV. F. D. MAURICE. Edited by the late BISHOP COLENSO. 6th Ed. 16mo. 2s. 6d.

COLERIDGE.—THE POETICAL AND DRAMATIC WORKS OF SAMUEL TAYLOR COLERIDGE. 4 vols. Fcp. 8vo. 31s. 6d.

Also an Edition on Large Paper, 2l. 12s. 6d.

COLERIDGE. By H. D. TRAILL. Crown 8vo. 1s. 6d. ; sewed, 1s.

COLLECTS OF THE CHURCH OF ENGLAND. With a Coloured Floral Design to each Collect. Crown 8vo. 12s.

COLLIER (John).—A PRIMER OF ART. 18mo. 1s.

COLQUHOUN.—RHYMES AND CHIMES. By F. S. COLQUHOUN (née F. S. FULLER MAITLAND). Extra fcp. 8vo. 2s. 6d.

COLSON (F. H.).—FIRST GREEK READER. Stories and Legends. With Notes, Vocabulary, and Exercises. Globe 8vo. 3s.

COLVIN (S.).—LANDOR. Crown 8vo. 1s. 6d. ; sewed, 1s.

—— SELECTIONS FROM THE WRITINGS OF W. S. LANDOR. 18mo. 4s. 6d.

—— KEATS. Crown 8vo. 1s. 6d. ; sewed, 1s.

COMBE. LIFE OF GEORGE COMBE. By CHARLES GIBBON. 2 vols. 8vo. 32s.

—— EDUCATION : ITS PRINCIPLES AND PRACTICE AS DEVELOPED BY GEORGE COMBE. Edited by WILLIAM JOLLY. 8vo. 15s.

CONGREVE (Rev. John).—HIGH HOPES AND PLEADINGS FOR A REASONABLE FAITH, NOBLER THOUGHTS, LARGER CHARITY. Crown 8vo. 5s.

CONSTABLE (Samuel).—GEOMETRICAL EXERCISES FOR BEGINNERS. Cr. 8vo. 3s. 6d.

CONWAY (Hugh).—A FAMILY AFFAIR. Globe 8vo. 2s.

—— LIVING OR DEAD. Globe 8vo. 2s.

COOK (CAPTAIN). By WALTER BESANT. With Portrait. Crown 8vo. 2s. 6d.

COOK (E. T.).—A POPULAR HANDBOOK TO THE NATIONAL GALLERY. Including, by special permission, Notes collected from the Works of Mr. RUSKIN. 3rd Edition. Crown 8vo, half morocco. 14s.

Also an Edition on Large Paper, limited to 250 copies. 2 vols. 8vo.

COOKE (Josiah P., jun.).—PRINCIPLES OF CHEMICAL PHILOSOPHY. New Ed. 8vo. 16s.

—— RELIGION AND CHEMISTRY. Crown 8vo. 7s. 6d.

—— ELEMENTS OF CHEMICAL PHYSICS. 4th Edition. Royal 8vo. 21s.

COOKERY. MIDDLE CLASS BOOK. Compiled for the Manchester School of Cookery. Fcp. 8vo. 1s. 6d.

CO-OPERATION IN THE UNITED STATES : HISTORY OF. Edited by H. B. ADAMS. 8vo. 15s.

COPE (E. D.).—THE ORIGIN OF THE FITTEST. Essays on Evolution. 8vo. 12s. 6d.

COPE (E. M.).—AN INTRODUCTION TO ARISTOTLE'S RHETORIC. 8vo. 14s.

CORBETT (Julian).—THE FALL OF ASGARD : A Tale of St. Olaf's Day. 2 vols. 12s.

—— FOR GOD AND GOLD. Crown 8vo. 6s.

—— KOPHETUA THE THIRTEENTH. 2 vols. Globe 8vo. 12s.

—— MONK. With Portrait. Cr. 8vo. 2s. 6d.

—— DRAKE. With Portrait. Cr. 8vo.

CORE (T. H.).—QUESTIONS ON BALFOUR STEWART'S "LESSONS IN ELEMENTARY PHYSICS." Fcp. 8vo. 2s.

CORFIELD (Dr. W. H.).—THE TREATMENT AND UTILISATION OF SEWAGE. 3rd Edition, Revised by the Author, and by LOUIS C. PARKES, M.D. 8vo. 16s.

CORNAZ (S.).—NOS ENFANTS ET LEURS AMIS. Edited by EDITH HARVEY. Globe 8vo. 1s. 6d.

CORNELL UNIVERSITY STUDIES IN CLASSICAL PHILOLOGY. Edited by I. FLAGG, W. G. HALE, and B. I. WHEELER. I. The *CUM*-Constructions : their History and Functions. Part I. Critical. 1s. 8d. net. Part II. Constructive. By W. G. HALE. 3s. 4d. net. II. Analogy and the Scope of its Application in Language. By B. I. WHEELER. 1s. 3d. net.

CORNEILLE.—LE CID. Ed. by G. EUGÈNE FASNACHT. 18mo. 1s.

COSSA.—GUIDE TO THE STUDY OF POLITICAL ECONOMY. From the Italian of Dr. LUIGI COSSA. Crown 8vo. 4s. 6d.

COTTERILL (Prof. James H.).—APPLIED MECHANICS : An Introduction to the Theory of Structures and Machines. 2nd Edition. Med. 8vo. 18s.

COTTERILL (Prof. J. H.) and SLADE (J. H.).— LESSONS IN APPLIED MECHANICS. Fcp. 8vo.

COTTON (Bishop).—SERMONS PREACHED TO ENGLISH CONGREGATIONS IN INDIA. Crown 8vo. 7s. 6d.

COTTON and PAYNE.—COLONIES AND DEPENDENCIES. Part I. INDIA. By J. S. COTTON. Part II. THE COLONIES. By E. J. PAYNE. Crown 8vo. 3s. 6d.

COUES (Elliott).—KEY TO NORTH AMERICAN BIRDS. Illustrated. 8vo. 2l. 2s.

—— HANDBOOK OF FIELD AND GENERAL ORNITHOLOGY. Illustrated. 8vo. 10s. net.

COURTHOPE (W. J.).—ADDISON. Crown 8vo. 1s. 6d. ; sewed, 1s.

COWPER.—COWPER'S POETICAL WORKS. Edited by Rev. W. BENHAM. Globe 8vo. 3s. 6d.

—— THE TASK : An Epistle to Joseph Hill, Esq. ; TIROCINIUM, or a Review of the Schools ; and the HISTORY OF JOHN GILPIN. Edited by WILLIAM BENHAM Globe 8vo. 1s.

—— LETTERS OF WILLIAM COWPER. Edited by the Rev. W. BENHAM. 18mo. 4s. 6d.

—— SELECTIONS FROM COWPER'S POEMS. Introduction by Mrs. OLIPHANT. 18mo. 4s. 6d.

COWPER. By GOLDWIN SMITH. Crown 8vo. 1s. 6d. ; sewed, 1s.

COX (G. V.).—Recollections of Oxford. 2nd Edition. Crown 8vo. 6s.

CRAIK (Mrs.).—Olive. Illustrated. Crown 8vo. 3s. 6d.

—— The Ogilvies. Illustrated. Crown 8vo. 3s. 6d.—Cheap Edition. Globe 8vo. 2s.

—— Agatha's Husband. Illustrated. Crown 8vo. 3s.6d.—Cheap Edition. Globe 8vo. 2s.

—— The Head of the Family. Illustrated. Crown 8vo. 3s. 6d.

—— Two Marriages. Crown 8vo. 3s. 6d.—Globe 8vo. 2s.

—— The Laurel Bush. Crown 8vo. 3s. 6d.

—— My Mother and I. Illustrated. Crown 8vo. 3s. 6d.

—— Miss Tommy: A Mediæval Romance. Illustrated. Crown 8vo. 3s. 6d.

—— King Arthur: Not a Love Story. Crown 8vo. 3s. 6d.

—— Poems. New and Enlarged Edition. Extra fcp. 8vo. 6s.

—— Children's Poetry. Ex. fcp. 8vo. 4s. 6d.

—— Songs of our Youth. Small 4to. 6s.

—— Concerning Men: and other Papers. Crown 8vo. 4s. 6d.

—— About Money: and other Things. Crown 8vo. 6s.

—— Sermons out of Church. Cr. 8vo. 6s.

—— An Unknown Country. Illustrated by F. Noel Paton. Royal 8vo. 7s. 6d.

—— Alice Learmont: A Fairy Tale. With Illustrations. 4s. 6d.

—— An Unsentimental Journey through Cornwall. Illustrated. 4to. 12s. 6d.

—— Our Year: A Child's Book in Prose and Verse. Illustrated. 2s. 6d.

—— Little Sunshine's Holiday. Globe 8vo. 2s. 6d.

—— The Adventures of a Brownie. Illustrated by Mrs. Allingham. 4s. 6d.

—— The Little Lame Prince and his Travelling Cloak. A Parable for Old and Young. With 24 Illustrations by J. McL. Ralston. Crown 8vo. 4s. 6d.

—— The Fairy Book: The Best Popular Fairy Stories. Selected and rendered anew. With a Vignette by Sir Noel Paton. 18mo. 4s. 6d.

CRAIK (Henry).—The State in its Relation to Education. Crown 8vo. 3s. 6d.

CRANE (Lucy).—Lectures on Art and the Formation of Taste. Cr. 8vo. 6s.

CRANE (Walter).—The Sirens Three. A Poem. Written and Illustrated by Walter Crane. Royal 8vo. 10s. 6d.

CRAVEN (Mrs. Dacre).—A Guide to District Nurses. Crown 8vo. 2s. 6d.

CRAWFORD (F. Marion).—Mr. Isaacs: A Tale of Modern India. Cr. 8vo. 3s. 6d.

—— Doctor Claudius: A True Story. Crown 8vo. 3s. 6d.

—— A Roman Singer. Crown 8vo. 3s. 6d.

—— Zoroaster. Crown 8vo. 3s. 6d.

CRAWFORD (F. Marion).—A Tale of a Lonely Parish. Crown 8vo. 3s. 6d.

—— Marzio's Crucifix. Crown 8vo. 3s. 6d.

—— Paul Patoff. Crown 8vo. 3s. 6d.

—— With the Immortals. Cr. 8vo. 3s. 6d.

—— Greifenstein. Crown 8vo. 3s. 6d.

—— Sant' Ilario. Crown 8vo. 3s. 6d.

—— A Cigarette Maker's Romance. 2 vols. Globe 8vo. 12s.

CREIGHTON (M.).—Rome. 18mo. 1s.

—— Cardinal Wolsey. Crown 8vo. 2s. 6d.

CROMWELL (OLIVER). By Frederic Harrison. Crown 8vo. 2s. 6d.

CROSS (Rev. J. A.).—Bible Readings Selected from the Pentateuch and the Book of Joshua. 2nd Ed. Globe 8vo. 2s. 6d.

CROSSLEY (E.), GLEDHILL (J.), and WILSON (J. M.).—A Handbook of Double Stars. 8vo. 21s.

—— Corrections to the Handbook of Double Stars. 8vo. 1s.

CUMMING (Linnæus).—Electricity. An Introduction to the Theory of Electricity. With numerous Examples. Cr. 8vo. 8s. 6d.

CUNNINGHAM (Sir H. S.).—The Cœruleans: A Vacation Idyll. Cr. 8vo. 3s. 6d.

—— The Heriots. Crown 8vo. 3s. 6d.

—— Wheat and Tares. Crn. 8vo. 3s. 6d.

CUNNINGHAM (Rev. W.).—The Epistle of St. Barnabas. A Dissertation, including a Discussion of its Date and Authorship. Together with the Greek Text, the Latin Version, and a New English Translation and Commentary. Crown 8vo. 7s. 6d.

—— Christian Civilisation, with Special Reference to India. Crown 8vo. 5s.

—— The Churches of Asia: A Methodical Sketch of the Second Century. Crown 8vo. 6s.

CUNNINGHAM (Rev. John). — The Growth of the Church in its Organisation and Institutions. Being the Croall Lectures for 1886. 8vo. 9s.

CUNYNGHAME (Gen. Sir A. T.).—My Command in South Africa, 1874–78. 8vo. 12s. 6d.

CURTEIS (Rev. G. H.).—Dissent in its Relation to the Church of England. Bampton Lectures for 1871. Cr. 8vo. 7s. 6d.

—— The Scientific Obstacles to Christian Belief. The Boyle Lectures, 1884. Cr. 8vo. 6s.

CUTHBERTSON (Francis). — Euclidian Geometry. Extra fcp. 8vo. 4s. 6d.

DAGONET THE JESTER. Cr. 8vo. 4s. 6d.

DAHN (Felix).—Felicitas. Translated by M. A. C. E. Crown 8vo. 4s. 6d.

"DAILY NEWS."—Correspondence of the War between Russia and Turkey, 1877. To the Fall of Kars. Cr. 8vo. 6s.

—— Correspondence of the Russo-Turkish War. From the Fall of Kars to the Conclusion of Peace. Crown 8vo. 6s.

DALE (A. W. W.).—The Synod of Elvira, and Christian Life in the Fourth Century. Crown 8vo. 10s. 6d.

**DALTON** (Rev. T.).—RULES AND EXAMPLES IN ARITHMETIC. New Edition. 18mo. 2s. 6d.

—— RULES AND EXAMPLES IN ALGEBRA. Part I. New Edit. 18mo. 2s. Part II. 2s.6d. KEY TO ALGEBRA. Part I. Crn. 8vo. 7s.6d.

**DAMIEN** (Father): A JOURNEY FROM CASH-MERE TO HIS HOME IN HAWAII. By EDWARD CLIFFORD. Portrait. Crown 8vo. 2s. 6d.

**DAMPIER.** By W. CLARK RUSSELL. With Portrait. Crown 8vo. 2s. 6d.

**DANIELL** (Alfred).—A TEXT-BOOK OF THE PRINCIPLES OF PHYSICS. With Illustrations. 2nd Edition. Medium 8vo. 21s.

**DANTE.**—THE PURGATORY OF DANTE ALI-GHIERI. Edited, with Translations and Notes, by A. J. BUTLER. Cr. 8vo. 12s.6d.

—— THE PARADISO OF DANTE. Edited, with a Prose Translation and Notes, by A. J. BUTLER. Crown 8vo. 12s. 6d.

—— DE MONARCHIA. Translated by F. J. CHURCH. 8vo. 4s. 6d.

—— DANTE: AND OTHER ESSAYS. By the DEAN OF ST. PAUL's. Globe 8vo. 5s.

—— READINGS ON THE PURGATORIO OF DANTE. Chiefly based on the Commentary of Benvenuto Da Imola. By the Hon. W. W. VERNON, M.A. With an Introduction by the Very Rev. the DEAN OF ST. PAUL's. 2 vols. Crown 8vo. 24s.

**DARWIN** (CHAS.): MEMORIAL NOTICES, reprinted from *Nature*. By T. H. HUXLEY, G. F. ROMANES, ARCHIBALD GEIKIE, and W. T. THISELTON DYER. With a Portrait. Crown 8vo. 2s. 6d.

**DAVIES** (Rev. J. Llewellyn).—THE GOSPEL AND MODERN LIFE. 2nd Edition, to which is added MORALITY ACCORDING TO THE SA-CRAMENT OF THE LORD's SUPPER. Extra fcp. 8vo. 6s.

—— WARNINGS AGAINST SUPERSTITION. Ex. fcp. 8vo. 2s. 6d.

—— THE CHRISTIAN CALLING. Ex.fcp.8vo. 6s.

—— THE EPISTLES OF ST. PAUL TO THE EPHESIANS, THE COLOSSIANS, AND PHILE-MON. With Introductions and Notes. 2nd Edition. 8vo. 7s. 6d.

—— SOCIAL QUESTIONS FROM THE POINT OF VIEW OF CHRISTIAN THEOLOGY. 2nd Ed. Crown 8vo. 6s.

**DAVIES** (J. Ll.) and **VAUGHAN** (D. J.).—THE REPUBLIC OF PLATO. Translated into English. 18mo. 4s. 6d.

**DAWKINS** (Prof. W. Boyd).—EARLY MAN IN BRITAIN AND HIS PLACE IN THE TER-TIARY PERIOD. Medium 8vo. 25s.

**DAWSON** (Sir J. W.).—ACADIAN GEOLOGY, THE GEOLOGICAL STRUCTURE, ORGANIC REMAINS, AND MINERAL RESOURCES OF NOVA SCOTIA, NEW BRUNSWICK, AND PRINCE EDWARD ISLAND. 3rd Ed. 8vo. 21s.

**DAWSON** (James).—AUSTRALIAN ABORI-GINES. Small 4to. 14s.

**DAY** (Rev. Lal Behari).—BENGAL PEASANT LIFE. Crown 8vo. 6s.

—— FOLK TALES OF BENGAL. Cr. 8vo. 4s. 6d.

**DAY** (R. E.).—ELECTRIC LIGHT ARITHMETIC. Pott 8vo. 2s.

**DAY** (H. G.).—PROPERTIES OF CONIC SEC-TIONS PROVED GEOMETRICALLY. Crown 8vo. 3s. 6d.

**DAYS WITH SIR ROGER DE COVER-LEY.** From the *Spectator*. With Illustra-tions by HUGH THOMSON. Fcp. 4to. 6s.

**DEÁK** (FRANCIS): HUNGARIAN STATES-MAN. A Memoir. 8vo. 12s. 6d.

**DEFOE** (Daniel). — THE ADVENTURES OF ROBINSON CRUSOE. Ed. by HENRY KINGS-LEY. Globe 8vo. 3s. 6d.

*Golden Treasury Series Edition.* Edited by J. W. CLARK, M.A. 18mo. 4s. 6d.

**DEFOE.** By W. MINTO. Crown 8vo. 1s. 6d. ; sewed, 1s.

**DELAMOTTE** (Prof. P. H.).—A BEGINNER's DRAWING-BOOK. Progressively arranged. With Plates. 3rd Edit. Crn. 8vo. 3s. 6d.

**DE MAISTRE.**—LA JEUNE SIBÉRIENNE ET LE LÉPREUX DE LA CITÉ D'AOSTE. Edited, with Notes and Vocabulary, by S. BARLET, B.Sc. Globe 8vo. 1s. 6d.

**DEMOCRACY: AN AMERICAN NOVEL.** Crown 8vo. 4s. 6d.

**DE MORGAN** (Mary).—THE NECKLACE OF PRINCESS FIORIMONDE, AND OTHER STORIES. Illustrated by WALTER CRANE. Extra fcp. 8vo. 3s. 6d. Also a Large Paper Edition, with the Illustrations on India Paper. 100 copies only printed.

**DEMOSTHENES.**—ADVERSUS LEPTINEM. Edited by Rev. J. R. KING, M.A. Fcp. 8vo. 2s. 6d.

—— THE ORATION ON THE CROWN. Edited by B. DRAKE, M.A. 7th Edition. Fcp. 8vo. 3s. 6d.

—— THE FIRST PHILIPPIC. Edited by Rev. T. GWATKIN, M.A. Fcp. 8vo. 2s. 6d.

**DEMOSTHENES.** By Prof. S. H. BUT-CHER, M.A. Fcp. 8vo. 1s. 6d.

**DE QUINCEY.** By Prof. MASSON. Crown 8vo. 1s. 6d. : sewed, 1s.

**DEUTSCHE LYRIK.** THE GOLDEN TREA-SURY OF THE BEST GERMAN LYRICAL POEMS. Selected and arranged by Dr. BUCHHEIM. 18mo. 4s. 6d.

**DEUTSCHE BALLADEN.**—THE GOLDEN TREASURY OF THE BEST GERMAN BALLADS. Selected and arranged by the same Editor. 18mo. [*In the Press.*

**DE VERE** (Aubrey).—ESSAYS CHIEFLY ON POETRY. 2 vols. Globe 8vo. 12s.

—— ESSAYS, CHIEFLY LITERARY AND ETHI-CAL. Globe 8vo. 6s.

**DE WINT.**—MEMOIR OF PETER DE WINT. By WALTER ARMSTRONG, B.A. Oxon. Illus-trated by 24 Photogravures from the Artist's pictures. Super-Royal 4to. 31s. 6d.

**DICEY** (Prof. A. V.).—LECTURES INTRODUC-TORY TO THE STUDY OF THE LAW OF THE CONSTITUTION. 3rd Edition. 8vo. 12s. 6d.

—— LETTERS ON UNIONIST DELUSIONS. Crown 8vo. 2s. 6d.

—— THE PRIVY COUNCIL. Crown 8vo. 3s. 6d.

DICKENS (Charles). — THE POSTHUMOUS PAPERS OF THE PICKWICK CLUB. With Notes and numerous Illustrations. Edited by CHARLES DICKENS the younger. 2 vols. Extra crown 8vo. 21s.

DICKENS. By A. W. WARD. Crown 8vo. 1s. 6d.; sewed, 1s.

DICKSON (R.) and EDMOND (J. P.). — ANNALS OF SCOTTISH PRINTING, FROM THE INTRODUCTION OF THE ART IN 1507 TO THE BEGINNING OF THE SEVENTEENTH CENTURY. Dutch hand-made paper. Demy 4to, buckram, 2l. 2s. net. — Royal 4to, 2 vols. half Japanese vellum, 4l. 4s. net.

DIDEROT AND THE ENCYCLOPÆDISTS. By JOHN MORLEY. 2 vols. Globe 8vo. 10s.

DIGGLE (Rev. J. W.). — GODLINESS AND MANLINESS. A Miscellany of Brief Papers touching the Relation of Religion to Life. Crown 8vo. 6s.

DILETTANTI SOCIETY'S PUBLICATIONS. — ANTIQUITIES OF IONIA. Vols. I. II. and III. 2l. 2s. each, or 3l. 5s. the set, net. Vol. IV., folio, half mor., 3l. 13s. 6d. net. — PENROSE (Francis C.). An Investigation of the Principles of Athenian Architecture. Illustrated by numerous engravings. New Edition. Enlarged. Folio. 7l. 7s. net. — SPECIMENS OF ANCIENT SCULPTURE: EGYPTIAN, ETRUSCAN, GREEK, AND ROMAN. Selected from different Collections in Great Britain by the Society of Dilettanti. Vol. II. Folio. 5l. 5s. net.

DILKE (Sir C. W.). — GREATER BRITAIN. A RECORD OF TRAVEL IN ENGLISH-SPEAKING COUNTRIES DURING 1866-67. (America, Australia, India.) 9th Edition. Crown 8vo. 6s. — PROBLEMS OF GREATER BRITAIN. Maps. 4th Edition. Extra crown 8vo. 12s. 6d.

DILLWYN (E. A.). — JILL. Crown 8vo. 6s. — JILL AND JACK. 2 vols. Globe 8vo. 12s.

DOBSON (Austin). — FIELDING. Crown 8vo. 1s. 6d.; sewed, 1s.

DODGSON (C. L.). — EUCLID. Books I. and II. With Words substituted for the Algebraical Symbols used in the first edition. 4th Edition. Crown 8vo. 2s. — EUCLID AND HIS MODERN RIVALS. 2nd Edition. Cr. 8vo. 6s. — SUPPLEMENT TO FIRST EDITION OF "EUCLID AND HIS MODERN RIVALS." Cr. 8vo. Sewed, 1s. — CURIOSA MATHEMATICA. Part I. A New Theory of Parallels. 3rd Ed. Cr. 8vo. 2s.

DONALDSON (Prof. James). — THE APOSTOLICAL FATHERS. A CRITICAL ACCOUNT OF THEIR GENUINE WRITINGS, AND OF THEIR DOCTRINES. 2nd Ed. Cr. 8vo. 7s. 6d.

DONISTHORPE (Wordsworth). — INDIVIDUALISM: A SYSTEM OF POLITICS. 8vo. 14s.

DOWDEN (Prof. E.). — SHAKSPERE. 18mo. 1s. — SOUTHEY. Crown 8vo. 1s. 6d.; sewed, 1s.

DOYLE (J. A.). — HISTORY OF AMERICA. With Maps. 18mo. 4s. 6d.

DOYLE (Sir F. H.). — THE RETURN OF THE GUARDS: AND OTHER POEMS. Cr. 8vo. 7s. 6d.

DRAKE. By JULIAN CORBETT. With Portrait. Crown 8vo.

DREW (W. H.). — A GEOMETRICAL TREATISE ON CONIC SECTIONS. 8th Ed. Cr. 8vo. 5s.

DRUMMOND (Prof. James). — INTRODUCTION TO THE STUDY OF THEOLOGY. Crown 8vo. 5s.

DRYDEN: ESSAYS OF. Edited by Prof. C. D. YONGE. Fcp. 8vo. 2s. 6d. — POETICAL WORKS. Edited, with Memoir, Revised Text, and Notes, by W. D. CHRISTIE, C.B. Globe 8vo. 3s. 6d. [Globe Edition.

DRYDEN. By G. SAINTSBURY. Crown 8vo. 1s. 6d.; sewed, 1s.

DU CANE (Col. Sir E. F.). — THE PUNISHMENT AND PREVENTION OF CRIME. Crown 8vo. 3s. 6d.

DUFF (Right Hon. Sir M. E. Grant). — NOTES OF AN INDIAN JOURNEY. 8vo. 10s. 6d. — MISCELLANIES, POLITICAL AND LITERARY. 8vo. 10s. 6d.

DUMAS. — LES DEMOISELLES DE ST. CYR. Comédie par ALEXANDRE DUMAS. Edited by VICTOR OGER. 18mo. 1s. 6d.

DÜNTZER (H.). — LIFE OF GOETHE. Translated by T. W. LYSTER. With Illustrations. 2 vols. Crown 8vo. 21s. — LIFE OF SCHILLER. Translated by P. E. PINKERTON. Illustrations. Cr. 8vo. 10s. 6d.

DUPUIS (Prof. N. F.). — ELEMENTARY SYNTHETIC GEOMETRY OF THE POINT, LINE, AND CIRCLE IN THE PLANE. Gl. 8vo. 4s. 6d.

DYER (J. M.). — EXERCISES IN ANALYTICAL GEOMETRY. Crown 8vo. 4s. 6d.

DYNAMICS, SYLLABUS OF ELEMENTARY. Part I. LINEAR DYNAMICS. With an Appendix on the Meanings of the Symbols in Physical Equations. Prepared by the Association for the Improvement of Geometrical Teaching. 4to. 1s.

EADIE (Prof. John). — THE ENGLISH BIBLE: AN EXTERNAL AND CRITICAL HISTORY OF THE VARIOUS ENGLISH TRANSLATIONS OF SCRIPTURE. 2 vols. 8vo. 28s. — ST. PAUL'S EPISTLES TO THE THESSALONIANS, COMMENTARY ON THE GREEK TEXT. 8vo. 12s. — LIFE OF JOHN EADIE, D.D., LL.D. By JAMES BROWN, D.D. 2nd Ed. Cr. 8vo. 7s. 6d.

EAGLES (T. H.). — CONSTRUCTIVE GEOMETRY OF PLANE CURVES. Crown 8vo. 12s.

EASTLAKE (Lady). — FELLOWSHIP: LETTERS ADDRESSED TO MY SISTER-MOURNERS. Cr. 8vo. 2s. 6d.

EBERS (Dr. George). — THE BURGOMASTER'S WIFE. Translated by CLARA BELL. Crown 8vo. 4s. 6d. — ONLY A WORD. Translated by CLARA BELL. Crown 8vo. 4s. 6d.

ECCE HOMO. A SURVEY OF THE LIFE AND WORK OF JESUS CHRIST. 20th Ed. Cr. 8vo. 6s.

ECONOMICS, THE QUARTERLY JOURNAL OF. Vol. II. Parts II. III. IV. 2s. 6d. each; Vol. III. 4 parts, 2s. 6d. each; Vol. IV. 4 parts, 2s. 6d. each. Vol. V. Part I. 2s. 6d. net.

EDGAR (J. H.) and PRITCHARD (G. S.).—
Note-Book on Practical Solid or De-
scriptive Geometry, containing Pro-
blems with help for Solution. 4th
Edition, Enlarged. By Arthur G. Meeze.
Globe 8vo. 4s. 6d.

EDWARDS (Joseph). — An Elementary
Treatise on the Differential Calculus. Crown 8vo. 10s. 6d.

EDWARDS-MOSS (Sir J. E.).—A Season in
Sutherland. Crown 8vo. 1s. 6d.

EGYPT. Recensement Général de
L'Egypt. Tome Premier. 4to. 2l. 2s. net.

EICKE (K. M.).—First Lessons in Latin.
Extra fcp. 8vo. 2s.

EIMER (G. H. T.).—Organic Evolution
as the Result of the Inheritance of
Acquired Characters according to the
Laws of Organic Growth. Translated by
J. T. Cunningham, M.A. 8vo. 12s. 6d.

ELDERTON (W. A.).—Maps and Map
Drawing. Pott 8vo. 1s.

ELLERTON (Rev. John).—The Holiest
Manhood, and its Lessons for Busy
Lives. Crown 8vo. 6s.

ELLIOT (Hon. A.).—The State and the
Church. Crown 8vo. 3s. 6d.

ELLIOTT. Life of Henry Venn Elliott,
of Brighton. By Josiah Bateman, M.A.
3rd Edition. Extra fcp. 8vo. 6s.

ELLIS (A. J.).—Practical Hints on the
Quantitative Pronunciation of Latin.
Extra fcp. 8vo. 4s. 6d.

ELLIS (Tristram).—Sketching from Nature. Illustr. by H. Stacy Marks, R.A.
and the Author. 2nd Edition. Cr. 8vo. 3s. 6d.

EMERSON.—The Life of Ralph Waldo
Emerson. By J. L. Cabot. 2 vols. Crown
8vo. 18s.

—— The Collected Works of Ralph
Waldo Emerson. 6 vols. (1) Miscellanies.
With an Introductory Essay by John Mor-
ley. (2) Essays. (3) Poems. (4) English
Traits; and Representative Men. (5)
Conduct of Life; and Society and So-
litude. (6) Letters; and Social Aims,
&c. Globe 8vo. 5s. each.

ENGLAND (E. B.).—Exercises in Latin
Syntax and Idiom. Arranged with refer-
ence to Roby's School Latin Grammar.
Crown 8vo. 2s. 6d.
    Key. Crown 8vo. 2s. 6d.

ENGLISH CITIZEN, THE.—A Series of
Short Books on his Rights and Responsibili-
ties. Edited by Henry Craik, C.B. Crown
8vo. 3s. 6d. each.
    Central Government. By H. D. Traill,
    D.C.L.
    The Electorate and the Legislature.
    By Spencer Walpole.
    The Poor Law. By the Rev. T. W. Fowle.
    The National Budget; The National
    Debt; Taxes and Rates. By A. J.
    Wilson.

ENGLISH CITIZEN, THE—continued.
    The State in Relation to Labour. By
    W. Stanley Jevons, LL.D., F.R.S.
    The State and the Church. By the Hon.
    Arthur Elliott, M.P.
    Foreign Relations. By Spencer Wal-
    pole.
    The State in its Relation to Trade.
    By Sir T. H. Farrer, Bart.
    Local Government. By M. D. Chalmers.
    The State in its Relation to Educa-
    tion. By Henry Craik, C.B.
    The Land Laws. By Sir F. Pollock,
    Bart. 2nd Edition.
    Colonies and Dependencies.
        Part I. India. By J. S. Cotton, M.A.
            II. The Colonies. By E. J. Payne.
    Justice and Police. By F. W. Maitland.
    The Punishment and Prevention of
    Crime. By Colonel Sir Edmund du Cane.
    The National Defences. By Colonel
    Maurice, R.A. [In the Press.

ENGLISH HISTORY, READINGS IN.—
Selected and Edited by John Richard
Green. 3 Parts. Fcp. 8vo. 1s. 6d. each.
Part I. Hengist to Cressy. II. Cressy to
Cromwell. III. Cromwell to Balaklava.

ENGLISH ILLUSTRATED MAGAZINE,
THE.—Profusely Illustrated. Published
Monthly. Number I. October, 1883. 6d.
Vol. I. 1884. 7s. 6d. Vols. II.—VII. Super
royal 8vo, extra cloth, coloured edges. 8s.
each. [Cloth Covers for binding Volumes,
1s. 6d. each.]

—— Proof Impressions of Engravings originally
published in The English Illustrated Magazine. 1884. In Portfolio 4to. 21s.

ENGLISH MEN OF ACTION.—Crown
8vo. With Portraits. 2s. 6d. each.
    The following Volumes are Ready:
    General Gordon. By Col. Sir W. Butler.
    Henry V. By the Rev. A. J. Church.
    Livingstone. By Thomas Hughes.
    Lord Lawrence. By Sir Richard Temple.
    Wellington. By George Hooper.
    Dampier. By W. Clark Russell.
    Monk. By Julian Corbett.
    Strafford. By H. D. Traill.
    Warren Hastings. By Sir Alfred Lyall.
    Peterborough. By W. Stebbing.
    Captain Cook. By Walter Besant.
    Sir Henry Havelock. By A. Forbes.
    Clive. By Colonel Sir Charles Wilson.
    Sir Charles Napier. By Col. Sir Wm.
    Butler.
    Drake. By Julian Corbett.

    The undermentioned are in the Press or in
    Preparation:
    Warwick, the King-Maker. By C. W.
    Oman.

    Montrose. By Mowbray Morris.

ENGLISH MEN OF ACTION—contd.

*In preparation.*

MARLBOROUGH. By Col. Sir WM. BUTLER.
RODNEY. By DAVID HANNAY.
SIR JOHN MOORE. By Colonel MAURICE.

ENGLISH MEN OF LETTERS.—Edited by JOHN MORLEY. Crown 8vo. 2s. 6d. each. Cheap Edition. 1s. 6d.; sewed, 1s.

JOHNSON. By LESLIE STEPHEN.
SCOTT. By R. H. HUTTON.
GIBBON. By J. COTTER MORISON.
HUME. By T. H. HUXLEY.
GOLDSMITH. By WILLIAM BLACK.
SHELLEY. By J. A. SYMONDS.
DEFOE. By W. MINTO.
BURNS. By Principal SHAIRP.
SPENSER. By the DEAN OF ST. PAUL's.
THACKERAY. By ANTHONY TROLLOPE.
MILTON. By MARK PATTISON.
BURKE. By JOHN MORLEY.
HAWTHORNE. By HENRY JAMES.
SOUTHEY. By Prof. DOWDEN.
BUNYAN. By J. A. FROUDE.
CHAUCER. By Prof. A. W. WARD.
COWPER. By GOLDWIN SMITH.
POPE. By LESLIE STEPHEN.
BYRON. By Prof. NICHOL.
DRYDEN. By G. SAINTSBURY.
LOCKE. By Prof. FOWLER.
WORDSWORTH. By F. W. H. MYERS.
LANDOR. By SIDNEY COLVIN.
DE QUINCEY. By Prof. MASSON.
CHARLES LAMB. By Rev. ALFRED AINGER.
BENTLEY. By Prof. JEBB.
DICKENS. By A. W. WARD.
GRAY. By EDMUND GOSSE.
SWIFT. By LESLIE STEPHEN.
STERNE. By H. D. TRAILL.
MACAULAY. By J. COTTER MORISON.
FIELDING. By AUSTIN DOBSON.
SHERIDAN. By Mrs OLIPHANT.
ADDISON. By W. J. COURTHOPE.
BACON. By the DEAN OF ST. PAUL's.
COLERIDGE. By H. D. TRAILL.
SIR PHILIP SIDNEY. By J. A. SYMONDS.
KEATS. By SIDNEY COLVIN.

ENGLISH POETS. Selections, with Critical Introductions by various Writers, and a General Introduction by MATTHEW ARNOLD. Edited by T. H. WARD, M.A. 2nd Edition. 4 vols. Crown 8vo. 7s. 6d. each.
  Vol. I. CHAUCER TO DONNE. II. BEN JONSON TO DRYDEN. III. ADDISON TO BLAKE. IV. WORDSWORTH TO ROSSETTI.

ENGLISH STATESMEN (TWELVE). Crown 8vo. 2s. 6d. each.
  WILLIAM THE CONQUEROR. By EDWARD A. FREEMAN, D.C.L., LL.D. [*Ready.*

ENGLISH STATESMEN—*continued.*

HENRY II. By Mrs. J. R. GREEN. [*Ready.*
EDWARD I. By F. YORK POWELL.
HENRY VII. By JAMES GAIRDNER. [*Ready.*
CARDINAL WOLSEY. By Prof. M. CREIGHTON. [*Ready.*
ELIZABETH. By E. S. BEESLY.
OLIVER CROMWELL. By FREDERIC HARRISON. [*Ready.*
WILLIAM III. By H. D. TRAILL. [*Ready.*
WALPOLE. By JOHN MORLEY. [*Ready.*
CHATHAM. By JOHN MORLEY.
PITT. By JOHN MORLEY.
PEEL. By J. R. THURSFIELD.

ESSEX FIELD CLUB MEMOIRS. Vol. I. REPORT ON THE EAST ANGLIAN EARTHQUAKE OF 22ND APRIL, 1884. By RAPHAEL MELDOLA, F.R.S., and WILLIAM WHITE, F.E.S. Maps and Illustrations. 8vo. 3s. 6d.

ETON COLLEGE, HISTORY OF, 1440—1884. By H. C. MAXWELL LYTE, C.B. Illustrations. 2nd Edition. Med. 8vo. 21s.

EURIPIDES.—MEDEA. Edited by A. W. VERRALL, Litt.D. 8vo. 7s. 6d.

—— IPHIGENEIA IN AULIS. Edited, with Introduction, Notes, and Commentary, by E. B. ENGLAND, M.A. 8vo.

—— HIPPOLYTUS. Edited by J. P. MAHAFFY, M.A., and J. B. BURY. Fcp. 8vo. 2s. 6d.

—— HECUBA. Edit. by Rev. J. BOND, M.A., and A. S. WALPOLE, M.A. 18mo. 1s. 6d.

—— IPHIGENIA IN TAURIS. Edited by E. B. ENGLAND, M.A. Fcp. 8vo. 3s.

—— MEDEA. Edited by A. W. VERRALL, Litt.D. Fcp. 8vo. 2s. 6d.

—— MEDEA. Edited by A. W. VERRALL, Litt.D., and Rev. M. A. BAYFIELD, M.A. 18mo. 1s. 6d.

—— ION. Edited by Rev. M. A. BAYFIELD, M.A. Fcp. 8vo. 2s. 6d.

—— ION. Translated by Rev. M. A. BAYFIELD, M.A. Crown 8vo. 2s. net. With Music, 4to. 4s. 6d. net.

—— ALCESTIS. Edited by Rev. M. A. BAYFIELD, M.A. 18mo. 1s. 6d.

EURIPIDES. By Prof. MAHAFFY. Fcp. 8vo. 1s. 6d.

EUROPEAN HISTORY, NARRATED IN A SERIES OF HISTORICAL SELECTIONS FROM THE BEST AUTHORITIES. Edited and arranged by E. M. SEWELL and C. M. YONGE. 2 vols. 3rd Edition. Crown 8vo. 6s. each.

EUTROPIUS. Adapted for the Use of Beginners. With Notes, Exercises, and Vocabularies. By W. WELCH, M.A., and C. G. DUFFIELD, M.A. 18mo. 1s. 6d.

EVANS (Sebastian).—BROTHER FABIAN's MANUSCRIPT, AND OTHER POEMS. Fcp. 8vo, cloth. 6s.

—— IN THE STUDIO: A DECADE OF POEMS. Extra fcp. 8vo. 5s.

EVERETT (Prof. J. D.).—UNITS AND PHYSICAL CONSTANTS. 2nd Ed. Globe 8vo. 5s.

FAIRFAX. LIFE OF ROBERT FAIRFAX OF STEETON, Vice-Admiral, Alderman, and Member for York, A.D. 1666—1725. By CLEMENTS R. MARKHAM, C.B. 8vo. 12s. 6d.

FAITH AND CONDUCT: An Essay on Verifiable Religion. Crown 8vo. 7s. 6d.

FARRAR (Archdeacon).—The Fall of Man, and other Sermons. 5th Ed. Cr. 8vo. 6s.

—— The Witness of History to Christ. Being the Hulsean Lectures for 1870. 7th Edition. Crown 8vo. 5s.

—— Seekers after God. The Lives of Seneca, Epictetus, and Marcus Aurelius. 12th Edition. Crown 8vo. 6s.

—— The Silence and Voices of God. University and other Sermons. 7th Ed. Cr. 8vo. 6s.

—— In the Days of thy Youth. Sermons on Practical Subjects, preached at Marlborough College. 9th Edition. Cr. 8vo. 9s.

—— Eternal Hope. Five Sermons, preached in Westminster Abbey. 28th Thousand. Crown 8vo. 6s.

—— Saintly Workers. Five Lenten Lectures. 3rd Edition. Crown 8vo. 6s.

—— Ephphatha; or, The Amelioration of the World. Sermons preached at Westminster Abbey. Crown 8vo. 6s.

—— Mercy and Judgment. A few Last Words on Christian Eschatology. 2nd Ed. Crown 8vo. 10s. 6d.

—— The Messages of the Books. Being Discourses and Notes on the Books of the New Testament. 8vo. 14s.

—— Sermons and Addresses delivered in America. Crown 8vo. 7s. 6d.

—— The History of Interpretation. Being the Bampton Lectures, 1885. 8vo. 16s.

FARREN (Robert).—The Granta and the Cam, from Byron's Pool to Ely. Thirty-six Etchings. Large Imperial 4to, cloth gilt. 52s. 6d. net.

A few Copies, Proofs, Large Paper, of which but 50 were printed, half morocco. 8l. 8s. net.

—— Cambridge and its Neighbourhood. A Series of Etchings. With an Introduction by John Willis Clark, M.A. Imp. 4to. 52s. 6d. net.—Proofs, half mor., 7l. 7s. net.

—— A Round of Melodies. A Series of Etched Designs. Oblong folio, half morocco. 52s. 6d. net.

—— The Birds of Aristophanes. 13s. net. Proofs. 47s. net.

—— Cathedral Cities: Ely and Norwich. With Introduction by E.A. Freeman, D.C.L. Col. 4to. 3l. 3s. net.

Proofs on Japanese paper. 6l. 6s. net.

—— Peterborough. With the Abbeys of Crowland and Thorney. With Introduction by Edmund Venables, M.A. Col. 4to. 2l. 2s. net. Proofs, folio, 5l. 5s. net.

The Edition is limited to 125 Small Paper and 45 Large.

—— The Eumenides of Æschylus. As performed by Members of the University at the Theatre Royal, Cambridge. Oblong 4to. Small size, 10s. 6d. net. Large size, India Proofs, 21s. net. On Whatman paper, 27s. net.

—— The Oedipus Tyrannus of Sophocles. As performed at Cambridge. Oblong 4to. Prints, 10s. 6d. net. Proofs, 21s. net.

FARRER (Sir T. H.).—The State in its Relation to Trade. Crown 8vo. 3s. 6d.

FASNACHT (G. Eugène).—The Organic Method of Studying Languages. I. French. Extra fcp. 8vo. 3s. 6d.

—— A Synthetic French Grammar for Schools. Crown 8vo. 3s. 6d.

FAWCETT (Rt. Hon. Henry).—Manual of Political Economy. 7th Edition, revised. Crown 8vo. 12s.

—— An Explanatory Digest of Professor Fawcett's Manual of Political Economy. By Cyril A. Waters. Cr. 8vo. 2s. 6d.

—— Speeches on some Current Political Questions. 8vo. 10s. 6d.

—— Free Trade and Protection. 6th Edition. Crown 8vo. 3s. 6d.

FAWCETT (Mrs. H.).—Political Economy for Beginners, with Questions. 7th Edition. 18mo. 2s. 6d.

—— Some Eminent Women of Our Times. Short Biographical Sketches. Cr. 8vo. 2s. 6d.

FAWCETT (Rt. Hon. Henry and Mrs. H.).—Essays and Lectures on Political and Social Subjects. 8vo. 10s. 6d.

FAY (Amy.).—Music-Study in Germany. With a Preface by Sir George Grove, D.C.L. Crown 8vo. 4s. 6d.

FEARNLEY (W.).—A Manual of Elementary Practical Histology. Cr. 8vo. 7s. 6d.

FEARON (D. R.).—School Inspection. 6th Edition. Crown 8vo. 2s. 6d.

FERREL (Prof. W.).—A Popular Treatise on the Winds. 8vo. 18s.

FERRERS (Rev. N. M.).—A Treatise on Trilinear Co-ordinates, the Method of Reciprocal Polars, and the Theory of Projections. 4th Ed. Cr. 8vo. 6s. 6d.

—— Spherical Harmonics and Subjects connected with them. Crown 8vo. 7s. 6d.

FESSENDEN (C.).—Physics for Public Schools. Globe 8vo.

FIELDING. By Austin Dobson. Crown 8vo. 1s. 6d.; sewed, 1s.

FINCK (Henry T.).—Romantic Love and Personal Beauty. 2 vols. Cr. 8vo. 18s.

FIRST LESSONS IN BUSINESS MATTERS. By A Banker's Daughter. 2nd Edition. 18mo. 1s.

FISHER (Rev. Osmond).—Physics of the Earth's Crust. 2nd Edition. 8vo. 12s.

FISKE (John).—Outlines of Cosmic Philosophy, based on the Doctrine of Evolution. 2 vols. 8vo. 25s.

—— Darwinism, and other Essays. Crown 8vo. 7s. 6d.

—— Man's Destiny Viewed in the Light of his Origin. Crown 8vo. 3s. 6d.

—— American Political Ideas Viewed from the Stand-point of Universal History. Crown 8vo. 4s.

—— The Critical Period in American History, 1783–89. Ex. Cr. 8vo. 10s. 6d.

FISKE (John).—THE BEGINNINGS OF NEW ENGLAND; OR, THE PURITAN THEOCRACY IN ITS RELATIONS TO CIVIL AND RELIGIOUS LIBERTY. Crown 8vo. 7s. 6d.

—— CIVIL GOVERNMENT IN THE UNITED STATES CONSIDERED WITH SOME REFERENCE TO ITS ORIGIN. Crown 8vo. 6s. 6d.

FISON (L.) and HOWITT (A. W.).—KAMILAROI AND KURNAI GROUP. Group-Marriage and Relationship and Marriage by Elopement, drawn chiefly from the usage of the Australian Aborigines, also the Kurnai Tribe, their Customs in Peace and War. With an Introduction by LEWIS H. MORGAN, LL.D. 8vo. 15s.

FITCH (J. G.).—NOTES ON AMERICAN SCHOOLS AND TRAINING COLLEGES. Reprinted by permission from the Report of the English Education Department for 1888—89. Globe 8vo. 2s. 6d.

FITZGERALD (Edward): LETTERS AND LITERARY REMAINS OF. Ed. by W. ALDIS WRIGHT, M.A. 3 vols. Crown 8vo. 31s. 6d.

—— THE RUBÁIYAT OF OMAR KHÁYYÁM. Extra Crown 8vo. 10s. 6d.

FITZ GERALD (Caroline).—VENETIA VICTRIX, AND OTHER POEMS. Ex. fcp. 8vo. 3s. 6d.

FLEAY (Rev. F. G.).—A SHAKESPEARE MANUAL. Extra fcp. 8vo. 4s. 6d.

FLEISCHER (Dr. Emil).—A SYSTEM OF VOLUMETRIC ANALYSIS. Translated by M. M. PATTISON MUIR, F.R.S.E. Cr. 8vo. 7s. 6d.

FLEMING (George).—A NILE NOVEL. Gl. 8vo. 2s.

—— MIRAGE. A Novel. Globe 8vo. 2s.

—— THE HEAD OF MEDUSA. Globe 8vo. 2s.

—— VESTIGIA. Globe 8vo. 2s.

FLITTERS, TATTERS, AND THE COUNSELLOR; WEEDS; AND OTHER SKETCHES. By the Author of "Hogan, M.P." Globe 8vo. 2s.

FLORIAN'S FABLES. Selected and Edited by Rev. CHARLES YELD, M.A. Illustrated. Globe 8vo. 2s. 6d.

FLOWER (Prof. W. H.).—AN INTRODUCTION TO THE OSTEOLOGY OF THE MAMMALIA. With numerous Illustrations. 3rd Edition, revised with the assistance of HANS GADOW, Ph.D., M.A. Crown 8vo. 10s. 6d.

FLÜCKIGER (F. A.) and HANBURY (D.). —PHARMACOGRAPHIA. A History of the principal Drugs of Vegetable Origin met with in Great Britain and India. 2nd Edition, revised. 8vo. 21s.

FO'C'SLE YARNS, including "Betsy Lee," and other Poems. Crown 8vo. 7s. 6d.

FORBES (Archibald).—SOUVENIRS OF SOME CONTINENTS. Crown 8vo. 6s.

—— SIR HENRY HAVELOCK. With Portrait. Crown 8vo. 2s. 6d.

FORBES (Edward): MEMOIR OF. By GEORGE WILSON, M.D., and ARCHIBALD GEIKIE, F.R.S., &c. Demy 8vo. 14s.

FORBES (Rev. Granville).—THE VOICE OF GOD IN THE PSALMS. Crown 8vo. 6s. 6d.

FORBES (George).—THE TRANSIT OF VENUS. Crown 8vo. 3s. 6d.

FORSYTH (A. R.).—A TREATISE ON DIFFERENTIAL EQUATIONS. Demy 8vo. 14s.

FOSTER (Prof. Michael).—A TEXT-BOOK OF PHYSIOLOGY. Illustrated. 5th Edition. 3 Parts. 8vo. Part I., Book I. Blood—The Tissues of Movement, the Vascular Mechanism. 10s. 6d.—Part II., Book II. The Tissues of Chemical Action, with their Respective Mechanisms—Nutrition. 10s. 6d. Part III., Book III. The Central Nervous System. 7s. 6d.—Book IV. The Tissues and Mechanisms of Reproduction.

—— PRIMER OF PHYSIOLOGY. 18mo. 1s.

FOSTER (Prof. Michael) and BALFOUR (F. M.) (the late).—THE ELEMENTS OF EMBRYOLOGY. Edited by ADAM SEDGWICK, M.A., and WALTER HEAPE. Illustrated. 3rd Ed., revised and enlarged. Cr. 8vo. 10s. 6d.

FOSTER (Michael) and LANGLEY (J. N.). —A COURSE OF ELEMENTARY PRACTICAL PHYSIOLOGY AND HISTOLOGY. 6th Edition, enlarged. Crown 8vo. 7s. 6d.

FOTHERGILL (Dr. J. Milner).—THE PRACTITIONER'S HANDBOOK OF TREATMENT; OR, THE PRINCIPLES OF THERAPEUTICS. 3rd Edition, enlarged. 8vo. 16s.

—— THE ANTAGONISM OF THERAPEUTIC AGENTS, AND WHAT IT TEACHES. Cr. 8vo. 6s.

—— FOOD FOR THE INVALID, THE CONVALESCENT, THE DYSPEPTIC, AND THE GOUTY. 2nd Edition. Crown 8vo. 3s. 6d.

FOWLE (Rev. T. W.).—THE POOR LAW. New Ed. with Appendix. Cr. 8vo. 3s. 6d.

—— A NEW ANALOGY BETWEEN REVEALED RELIGION AND THE COURSE AND CONSTITUTION OF NATURE. Crown 8vo. 6s.

FOWLER (Rev. Thomas).—LOCKE. Crown 8vo. 1s. 6d.; sewed, 1s.

—— PROGRESSIVE MORALITY: AN ESSAY IN ETHICS. Crown 8vo. 5s.

FOWLER (W. W.).—TALES OF THE BIRDS. Illustrated. Crown 8vo. 3s. 6d.

—— A YEAR WITH THE BIRDS. Illustrated. Crown 8vo. 3s. 6d.

FOX (Dr. Wilson).—ON THE ARTIFICIAL PRODUCTION OF TUBERCLE IN THE LOWER ANIMALS. With Plates. 4to. 5s. 6d.

—— ON THE TREATMENT OF HYPERPYREXIA, AS ILLUSTRATED IN ACUTE ARTICULAR RHEUMATISM BY MEANS OF THE EXTERNAL APPLICATION OF COLD. 8vo. 2s. 6d.

FRAMJI (Dosabhai).—HISTORY OF THE PARSIS: INCLUDING THEIR MANNERS, CUSTOMS, RELIGION, AND PRESENT POSITION. With Illustrations. 2 vols. Medium 8vo. 36s.

FRANKLAND (Prof. Percy).—A HANDBOOK OF AGRICULTURAL CHEMICAL ANALYSIS. Founded upon "Leitfaden für die Agricultur-Chemische Analyse," von Dr. F. KROCKER. Crown 8vo. 7s. 6d.

FRASER — HUGHES. — JAMES FRASER, SECOND BISHOP OF MANCHESTER: A Memoir. By T. HUGHES. Crown 8vo. 6s.

2

FRASER.—SERMONS. By the Right Rev. JAMES FRASER, D.D., Second Bishop of Manchester. Edited by Rev. JOHN W. DIGGLE. 2 vols. Crown 8vo. 6s. each.

FRASER-TYTLER. — SONGS IN MINOR KEYS. By C. C. FRASER-TYTLER (Mrs. EDWARD LIDDELL). 2nd Ed. 18mo. 6s.

FRATERNITY: A Romance. 2 vols. Cr. 8vo. 21s.

FRAZER (J. G.).—THE GOLDEN BOUGH : A Study in Comparative Religion. 2 vols. 8vo. 28s.

FREDERICK (Mrs.).—HINTS TO HOUSE-WIVES ON SEVERAL POINTS, PARTICULARLY ON THE PREPARATION OF ECONOMICAL AND TASTEFUL DISHES. Crown 8vo. 1s.

FREEMAN (Prof. E. A.)—HISTORY OF THE CATHEDRAL CHURCH OF WELLS. Crown 8vo. 3s. 6d.

—— OLD ENGLISH HISTORY. With 5 Col. Maps. 9th Edition, revised. Extra fcp. 8vo. 6s.

—— HISTORICAL ESSAYS. First Series. 4th Edition. 8vo. 10s. 6d.

—— HISTORICAL ESSAYS. Second Series. 3rd Edition. With Additional Essays. 8vo. 10s. 6d.

—— —— Third Series. 8vo. 12s.

—— THE GROWTH OF THE ENGLISH CONSTI-TUTION FROM THE EARLIEST TIMES. 5th Edition. Crown 8vo. 5s.

—— GENERAL SKETCH OF EUROPEAN HIS-TORY. With Maps, &c. 18mo. 3s. 6d.

—— EUROPE. 18mo. 1s. [Literature Primers.

—— COMPARATIVE POLITICS. Lectures at the Royal Institution. To which is added "The Unity of History." 8vo. 14s.

—— HISTORICAL AND ARCHITECTURAL SKETCHES: CHIEFLY ITALIAN. Illustrated by the Author. Crown 8vo. 10s. 6d.

—— SUBJECT AND NEIGHBOUR LANDS OF VENICE. Illustrated. Crown 8vo. 10s. 6d.

—— ENGLISH TOWNS AND DISTRICTS. A Series of Addresses and Essays. 8vo. 14s.

—— THE OFFICE OF THE HISTORICAL PRO-FESSOR. Inaugural Lecture at Oxford. Crown 8vo. 2s.

—— DISESTABLISHMENT AND DISENDOW-MENT. WHAT ARE THEY? 4th Edition. Crown 8vo. 1s.

—— GREATER GREECE AND GREATER BRI-TAIN: GEORGE WASHINGTON THE EX-PANDER OF ENGLAND. With an Appendix on IMPERIAL FEDERATION. Cr. 8vo. 3s. 6d.

—— THE METHODS OF HISTORICAL STUDY. Eight Lectures at Oxford. 8vo. 10s. 6d.

—— THE CHIEF PERIODS OF EUROPEAN HIS-TORY. Six Lectures read in the University of Oxford, with an Essay on GREEK CITIES UNDER ROMAN RULE. 8vo. 10s. 6d.

—— FOUR OXFORD LECTURES, 1887. FIFTY YEARS OF EUROPEAN HISTORY—TEUTONIC CONQUEST IN GAUL AND BRITAIN. 8vo. 5s.

—— WILLIAM THE CONQUEROR. Crown 8vo. 2s. 6d.          [Twelve English Statesmen.

FRENCH COURSE.—See p. 40.

FRENCH READINGS FROM ROMAN HISTORY. Selected from various Authors. With Notes by C. COLBECK. 18mo. 4s. 6d.

FRIEDMANN (Paul).—ANNE BOLEYN. A Chapter of English History, 1527—36. 2 vols. 8vo. 28s.

FROST (Percival).—AN ELEMENTARY TREA-TISE ON CURVE TRACING. 8vo. 12s.

—— THE FIRST THREE SECTIONS OF NEW-TON'S PRINCIPIA. 4th Edition. 8vo. 12s.

—— SOLID GEOMETRY. 3rd Edition. 8vo. 16s.

—— HINTS FOR THE SOLUTION OF PROBLEMS IN THE THIRD EDITION OF SOLID GEOME-TRY. 8vo. 8s. 6d.

FROUDE (J. A.).—BUNYAN. Crown 8vo. 1s. 6d. ; sewed, 1s.

FURNIVALL (F. J.).—LE MORTE ARTHUR. Edited from the Harleian MS. 2252, in the British Museum. Fcp. 8vo. 7s. 6d.

FYFFE (C. A.).—GREECE. 18mo. 1s.

GAIRDNER (Jas.).—HENRY VII. Crown 8vo. 2s. 6d.

GALTON (Francis). — METEOROGRAPHICA; OR, METHODS OF MAPPING THE WEATHER. 4to. 9s.

—— ENGLISH MEN OF SCIENCE : THEIR NA-TURE AND NURTURE. 8vo. 8s. 6d.

—— INQUIRIES INTO HUMAN FACULTY AND ITS DEVELOPMENT. 8vo. 16s.

—— RECORD OF FAMILY FACULTIES. Con-sisting of Tabular Forms and Directions for Entering Data. 4to. 2s. 6d.

—— LIFE HISTORY ALBUM : Being a Personal Note-book, combining the chief advantages of a Diary, Photograph Album, a Register of Height, Weight, and other Anthropometrical Observations, and a Record of Illnesses. 4to. 3s. 6d.—Or, with Cards of Wools for Testing Colour Vision. 4s. 6d.

—— NATURAL INHERITANCE. 8vo. 9s.

GAMGEE (Prof. Arthur).—A TEXT-BOOK OF THE PHYSIOLOGICAL CHEMISTRY OF THE ANIMAL BODY, including an account of the Chemical Changes occurring in Disease. Vol. I. Med. 8vo. 18s.

GANGUILLET (E.) and KUTTER (W. R.).—A GENERAL FORMULA FOR THE UNIFORM FLOW OF WATER IN RIVERS AND OTHER CHANNELS. Translated by RUDOLPH HERING and JOHN C. TRAUTWINE, Jun. 8vo. 17s.

GARDNER (Percy).—SAMOS AND SAMIAN COINS. An Essay. 8vo. 7s. 6d.

GARNETT (R.).—IDYLLS AND EPIGRAMS. Chiefly from the Greek Anthology. Fcp. 8vo. 2s. 6d.

GASKOIN (Mrs. Herman). — CHILDREN'S TREASURY OF BIBLE STORIES. 18mo. 1s. each.—Part I. Old Testament; II. New Testa-ment; III. Three Apostles.

GEDDES (Prof. William D.).—THE PROBLEM OF THE HOMERIC POEMS. 8vo. 14s.

—— FLOSCULI GRÆCI BOREALES, SIVE AN-THOLOGIA GRÆCA ABERDONENSIS CON-TEXUIT GULIELMUS D. GEDDES. Cr. 8vo. 6s.

GEDDES (Prof. Wm. D.).—THE PHAEDO OF PLATO. Edited, with Introduction and Notes. 2nd Edition. 8vo. 8s. 6d.

GEIKIE (Archibald).—PRIMER OF PHYSICAL GEOGRAPHY. With Illustrations. 18mo. 1s.
—— PRIMER OF GEOLOGY. Illust. 18mo. 1s.
—— ELEMENTARY LESSONS IN PHYSICAL GEOGRAPHY. With Illustrations. Fcp. 8vo. 4s. 6d.—QUESTIONS ON THE SAME. 1s. 6d.
—— OUTLINES OF FIELD GEOLOGY. With numerous Illustrations. Crown 8vo. 3s. 6d.
—— TEXT-BOOK OF GEOLOGY. Illustrated. 2nd Edition. 7th Thousand. Med. 8vo. 28s.
—— CLASS-BOOK OF GEOLOGY. Illustrated. 2nd Edition. Crown 8vo. 4s. 6d.
—— GEOLOGICAL SKETCHES AT HOME AND ABROAD. With Illustrations. 8vo. 10s. 6d.
—— THE SCENERY OF SCOTLAND. Viewed in connection with its Physical Geology. 2nd Edition. Crown 8vo. 12s. 6d.
—— THE TEACHING OF GEOGRAPHY. A Practical Handbook for the use of Teachers. Globe 8vo. 2s.
—— GEOGRAPHY OF THE BRITISH ISLES. 18mo. 1s.

GEOMETRY, SYLLABUS OF PLANE. Corresponding to Euclid I.—VI. Prepared by the Association for the Improvement of Geometrical Teaching. New Edition. Crown 8vo. 1s.

GEOMETRY, SYLLABUS OF MODERN PLANE. Association for the Improvement of Geometrical Teaching. Crown 8vo, sewed. 1s.

GIBBON. By J. C. MORISON. Crown 8vo. 1s. 6d. ; sewed, 1s.

GILES (P.). — MANUAL OF GREEK AND LATIN PHILOLOGY. Cr. 8vo. [In the Press.

GILMAN (N. P.). — PROFIT-SHARING BETWEEN EMPLOYER AND EMPLOYÉ. A Study in the Evolution of the Wages System. Crown 8vo. 7s. 6d.

GILMORE (Rev. John).—STORM WARRIORS; OR, LIFEBOAT WORK ON THE GOODWIN SANDS. Crown 8vo. 3s. 6d.

GLADSTONE (Rt. Hon. W. E.).—HOMERIC SYNCHRONISM. An Inquiry into the Time and Place of Homer. Crown 8vo. 6s.
—— PRIMER OF HOMER. 18mo. 1s.
—— LANDMARKS OF HOMERIC STUDY, TOGETHER WITH AN ESSAY ON THE POINTS OF CONTACT BETWEEN THE ASSYRIAN TABLETS AND THE HOMERIC TEXT. Cr. 8vo. 2s. 6d.

GLADSTONE (J. H.).—SPELLING REFORM FROM AN EDUCATIONAL POINT OF VIEW. 3rd Edition. Crown 8vo. 1s. 6d.

GLADSTONE (J. H.) and TRIBE (A.).—THE CHEMISTRY OF THE SECONDARY BATTERIES OF PLANTÉ AND FAURE. Crown 8vo. 2s. 6d.

GLAISTER (Elizabeth). — NEEDLEWORK. Crown 8vo. 2s. 6d.

GLOBE EDITIONS. Gl. 8vo. 3s. 6d. each.
THE COMPLETE WORKS OF WILLIAM SHAKESPEARE. Edited by W. G. CLARK and W. ALDIS WRIGHT.

GLOBE EDITIONS—continued.
MORTE D'ARTHUR. Sir Thomas Malory's Book of King Arthur and of his Noble Knights of the Round Table. The Edition of Caxton; revised for modern use. By Sir E. STRACHEY, Bart.
THE POETICAL WORKS OF SIR WALTER SCOTT. With Essay by Prof. PALGRAVE.
THE POETICAL WORKS AND LETTERS OF ROBERT BURNS. Edited, with Life and Glossarial Index, by ALEXANDER SMITH.
THE ADVENTURES OF ROBINSON CRUSOE. With Introduction by HENRY KINGSLEY.
GOLDSMITH'S MISCELLANEOUS WORKS. Edited by Prof. MASSON.
POPE'S POETICAL WORKS. Edited, with Memoir and Notes, by Prof. WARD.
SPENSER'S COMPLETE WORKS. Edited by R. MORRIS. Memoir by J. W. HALES.
DRYDEN'S POETICAL WORKS. A revised Text and Notes. By W. D. CHRISTIE.
COWPER'S POETICAL WORKS. Edited by the Rev. W. BENHAM, B.D.
VIRGIL'S WORKS. Rendered into English by JAMES LONSDALE and S. LEE.
HORACE'S WORKS. Rendered into English by JAMES LONSDALE and S. LEE.
MILTON'S POETICAL WORKS. Edited, with Introduction, &c., by Prof. MASSON.

GLOBE READERS, THE.—A New Series of Reading Books for Standards I.—VI Selected, arranged, and Edited by A. F MURISON, sometime English Master at Aberdeen Grammar School. With Original Illustrations. Globe 8vo.

| Primer I. | ... | ... | (48 pp.) | 3d. |
| Primer II. | ... | ... | (48 pp.) | 3d. |
| Book I. | ... | ... | (96 pp.) | 6d. |
| Book II. | ... | ... | (136 pp.) | 9d. |
| Book III. | ... | ... | (232 pp.) | 1s. |
| Book IV. | ... | ... | (328 pp.) | 1s. 9d. |
| Book V. | ... | ... | (416 pp.) | 2s. |
| Book VI. | ... | ... | (448 pp.) | 2s. 6d. |

GLOBE READERS, THE SHORTER.—A New Series of Reading Books for Standards I.—VI. Edited by A. F. MURISON, Gl. 8vo.

| Primer I. | ... | ... | (48 pp.) | 3d. |
| Primer II. | ... | ... | (48 pp.) | 3d. |
| Standard I. | ... | ... | (90 pp.) | 6d. |
| Standard II. | ... | ... | (124 pp.) | 9d. |
| Standard III. | ... | ... | (178 pp.) | 1s. |
| Standard IV. | ... | ... | (182 pp.) | 1s. |
| Standard V. | ... | ... | (216 pp.) | 1s. 3d. |
| Standard VI. | ... | ... | (228 pp.) | 1s. 6d. |

*⁎* This Series has been abridged from the "Globe Readers" to meet the demand for smaller reading books.

GLOBE READINGS FROM STANDARD AUTHORS. Globe 8vo.
COWPER'S TASK: An Epistle to Joseph Hill, Esq.; TIROCINIUM, or a Review of the Schools; and the HISTORY OF JOHN GILPIN. Edited, with Notes, by Rev. WILLIAM BENHAM, B.D. 1s.
GOLDSMITH'S VICAR OF WAKEFIELD. With a Memoir of Goldsmith by Prof. MASSON. 1s.

GLOBE READINGS—*continued*.

LAMB'S (CHARLES) TALES FROM SHAK-SPEARE. Edited, with Preface, by Rev. ALFRED AINGER, M.A. 2s.

SCOTT'S (SIR WALTER) LAY OF THE LAST MINSTREL : and the LADY OF THE LAKE. Edited by Prof. F. T. PALGRAVE. 1s.

MARMION ; and THE LORD OF THE ISLES. By the same Editor. 1s.

THE CHILDREN'S GARLAND FROM THE BEST POETS. Selected and arranged by COVEN-TRY PATMORE. 2s.

A BOOK OF GOLDEN DEEDS OF ALL TIMES AND ALL COUNTRIES. Gathered and narrated anew by CHARLOTTE M. YONGE. 2s.

GODFRAY (Hugh).— AN ELEMENTARY TREATISE ON LUNAR THEORY. 2nd Edition. Crown 8vo. 5s. 6d.

—— A TREATISE ON ASTRONOMY, FOR THE USE OF COLLEGES AND SCHOOLS. 8vo. 12s. 6d.

GOETHE—CARLYLE.—CORRESPONDENCE BETWEEN GOETHE AND CARLYLE. Edited by C. E. NORTON. Crown 8vo. 9s.

GOETHE'S LIFE. By Prof. HEINRICH DÜNTZER. Translated by T. W. LYSTER. 2 vols. Crown 8vo. 21s.

GOETHE.—FAUST. Translated into English Verse by JOHN STUART BLACKIE. 2nd Edition. Crown 8vo. 9s.

—— —— Part I. Edited, with Introduction and Notes; followed by an Appendix on Part II., by JANE LEE. 18mo. 4s. 6d.

—— REYNARD THE FOX. Trans. into English Verse by A. D. AINSLIE. Crn. 8vo. 7s. 6d.

—— GÖTZ VON BERLICHINGEN. Edited by H. A. BULL, M.A. 18mo. 2s.

GOLDEN TREASURY SERIES. — Uniformly printed in 18mo, with Vignette Titles by Sir J. E. MILLAIS, Sir NOEL PATON, T. WOOLNER, W. HOLMAN HUNT, ARTHUR HUGHES, &c. Engraved on Steel. Bound in extra cloth. 4s. 6d. each.

THE GOLDEN TREASURY OF THE BEST SONGS AND LYRICAL POEMS IN THE ENGLISH LANGUAGE. Selected and arranged, with Notes, by Prof. F. T. PALGRAVE.

THE CHILDREN'S GARLAND FROM THE BEST POETS. Selected by COVENTRY PATMORE.

THE BOOK OF PRAISE. From the best English Hymn Writers. Selected by ROUN-DELL, EARL OF SELBORNE.

THE FAIRY BOOK: THE BEST POPULAR FAIRY STORIES. Selected by the Author of "John Halifax, Gentleman."

THE BALLAD BOOK. A Selection of the Choicest British Ballads. Edited by WILLIAM ALLINGHAM.

THE JEST BOOK. The Choicest Anecdotes and Sayings. Arranged by MARK LEMON.

BACON'S ESSAYS AND COLOURS OF GOOD AND EVIL. With Notes and Glossarial Index by W. ALDIS WRIGHT, M.A.

THE PILGRIM'S PROGRESS FROM THIS WORLD TO THAT WHICH IS TO COME. By JOHN BUNYAN.

GOLDEN TREASURY SERIES—*contd.*

THE SUNDAY BOOK OF POETRY FOR THE YOUNG. Selected by C. F. ALEXANDER.

A BOOK OF GOLDEN DEEDS OF ALL TIMES AND ALL COUNTRIES. By the Author of "The Heir of Redclyffe."

THE ADVENTURES OF ROBINSON CRUSOE. Edited by J. W. CLARK, M.A.

THE REPUBLIC OF PLATO. Translated by J. LL. DAVIES, M.A., and D. J. VAUGHAN.

THE SONG BOOK. Words and Tunes Selected and arranged by JOHN HULLAH.

LA LYRE FRANÇAISE. Selected and arranged, with Notes, by G. MASSON.

TOM BROWN'S SCHOOL DAYS. By AN OLD BOY.

A BOOK OF WORTHIES. By the Author of "The Heir of Redclyffe."

GUESSES AT TRUTH. By TWO BROTHERS.

THE CAVALIER AND HIS LADY. Selections from the Works of the First Duke and Duchess of Newcastle. With an Introductory Essay by EDWARD JENKINS.

SCOTTISH SONG. Compiled by MARY CAR-LYLE AITKEN.

DEUTSCHE LYRIK. The Golden Treasury of the best German Lyrical Poems. Selected by Dr. BUCHHEIM.

CHRYSOMELA. A Selection from the Lyrical Poems of Robert Herrick. By Prof. F. T. PALGRAVE.

POEMS OF PLACES—ENGLAND AND WALES. Edited by H. W. LONGFELLOW. 2 vols.

SELECTED POEMS OF MATTHEW ARNOLD.

THE STORY OF THE CHRISTIANS AND MOORS IN SPAIN. By CHARLOTTE M. YONGE.

LAMB'S TALES FROM SHAKSPEARE. Edited by Rev. ALFRED AINGER, M.A.

SHAKESPEARE'S SONGS AND SONNETS. Ed. with Notes, by Prof. F. T. PALGRAVE.

POEMS OF WORDSWORTH. Chosen and Edited by MATTHEW ARNOLD.

Large Paper Edition. 9s.

POEMS OF SHELLEY. Ed. by S. A. BROOKE.

Large Paper Edition. 12s. 6d.

THE ESSAYS OF JOSEPH ADDISON. Chosen and Edited by JOHN RICHARD GREEN.

POETRY OF BYRON. Chosen and arranged by MATTHEW ARNOLD.

Large Paper Edition. 9s.

SIR THOMAS BROWNE'S RELIGIO MEDICI; LETTER TO A FRIEND, &c., AND CHRISTIAN MORALS. Ed. by W. A. GREENHILL, M.D.

THE SPEECHES AND TABLE-TALK OF THE PROPHET MOHAMMAD. Translated by STANLEY LANE-POOLE.

SELECTIONS FROM WALTER SAVAGE LAN-DOR. Edited by SIDNEY COLVIN.

SELECTIONS FROM COWPER'S POEMS. With an Introduction by Mrs. OLIPHANT.

LETTERS OF WILLIAM COWPER. Edited, With Introduction, by Rev. W. BENHAM.

THE POETICAL WORKS OF JOHN KEATS. Edited by Prof. F. T. PALGRAVE.

GOLDEN TREASURY SERIES—contd.

LYRICAL POEMS OF LORD TENNYSON. Selected and Annotated by Prof. FRANCIS T. PALGRAVE.
— Large Paper Edition. 9s.

IN MEMORIAM. By LORD TENNYSON, Poet Laureate.
— Large Paper Edition. 9s.

THE TRIAL AND DEATH OF SOCRATES. Being the Euthyphron, Apology, Crito, and Phaedo of Plato. Translated by F. J. CHURCH.

A BOOK OF GOLDEN THOUGHTS. By HENRY ATTWELL.

PLATO.—PHAEDRUS, LYSIS, AND PROTAGORAS. A New Translation, by J. WRIGHT.

THEOCRITUS, BION, AND MOSCHUS. Rendered into English Prose by ANDREW LANG. Large Paper Edition. 9s.

BALLADS, LYRICS, AND SONNETS. From the Works of HENRY W. LONGFELLOW.

DEUTSCHE BALLADEN UND ROMANZEN. The Golden Treasury of the Best German Ballads and Romances. Selected and arranged by Dr. BUCHHEIM. [In the Press.

GOLDEN TREASURY PSALTER. THE STUDENT'S EDITION. Being an Edition with briefer Notes of "The Psalms Chronologically Arranged by Four Friends." 18mo. 3s. 6d.

GOLDSMITH. By WILLIAM BLACK. Crown 8vo. 1s. 6d.; sewed, 1s.

GOLDSMITH. — MISCELLANEOUS WORKS. With Biographical Essay by Prof. MASSON. Globe 8vo. 3s. 6d.

—— ESSAYS OF OLIVER GOLDSMITH. Edited by C. D. YONGE, M.A. Fcp. 8vo. 2s. 6d.

—— THE TRAVELLER AND THE DESERTED VILLAGE. With Notes by J. W. HALES, M.A. Crown 8vo. 6d.

—— THE TRAVELLER AND THE DESERTED VILLAGE. Edited, with Introduction and Notes, by Prof. A. BARRETT, M.A. Gl. 8vo. 1s. 9d.; sewed, 1s. 6d. THE TRAVELLER (separately), 1s. 3d.; sewed, 1s.

—— THE VICAR OF WAKEFIELD. With a Memoir of Goldsmith by Prof. MASSON. Globe 8vo. 1s.

—— THE VICAR OF WAKEFIELD. With 182 Illustrations by HUGH THOMSON, and Preface by AUSTIN DOBSON. Crown 8vo. 6s.
Also with uncut edges, paper label. 6s.
Edition de Luxe. Super roy. 8vo. 30s. net.

GONE TO TEXAS. LETTERS FROM OUR BOYS. Edited, with Preface, by THOMAS HUGHES, Q.C. Crown 8vo. 4s. 6d.

GOODALE (G. L.).—PHYSIOLOGICAL BOTANY. Part I. OUTLINES OF THE HISTORY OF PHÆNOGAMOUS PLANTS; II. VEGETABLE PHYSIOLOGY. 6th Edition. 8vo. 10s. 6d.

GOODWIN (Prof. W. W.).—SYNTAX OF THE GREEK MOODS AND TENSES. 8vo. 14s.

—— A GREEK GRAMMAR. Crown 8vo. 6s.

—— A SCHOOL GREEK GRAMMAR. Crown 8vo. 3s. 6d.

GORDON (General). A SKETCH. By REGINALD H. BARNES. Crown 8vo. 1s.

GORDON (General).—LETTERS OF GENERAL C. G. GORDON TO HIS SISTER, M. A. GORDON. 4th Edition. Crown 8vo. 3s. 6d.

GORDON. By Colonel Sir WILLIAM BUTLER. With Portrait. Crown 8vo. 1s. 6d.

GORDON (Lady Duff). — LAST LETTERS FROM EGYPT, TO WHICH ARE ADDED LETTERS FROM THE CAPE. 2nd Edition. Cr. 8vo. 9s.

GOSCHEN (Rt. Hon. George J.).—REPORTS AND SPEECHES ON LOCAL TAXATION. 8vo. 5s.

GOSSE (E.).—GRAY. Cr. 8vo. 1s. 6d.; swd., 1s.

—— A HISTORY OF EIGHTEENTH CENTURY LITERATURE (1660—1780). Cr. 8vo. 7s. 6d.

GOW (Dr. James).—A COMPANION TO SCHOOL CLASSICS. Illustrated. 2nd Ed. Cr. 8vo. 6s.

GOYEN (P.).—HIGHER ARITHMETIC AND ELEMENTARY MENSURATION, for the Senior Classes of Schools and Candidates preparing for Public Examinations. Globe 8vo. 5s.

GRAHAM (David).—KING JAMES I. An Historical Tragedy. Globe 8vo. 7s.

GRAHAM (John W.).—NEÆRA: A TALE OF ANCIENT ROME. Crown 8vo. 6s.

GRAHAM (R. H.)—GEOMETRY OF POSITION. Illustrated. Crown 8vo.

GRAND'HOMME. — CUTTING OUT AND DRESSMAKING. From the French of Mdlle. E. GRAND'HOMME. 18mo. 1s.

GRAY (Prof. Andrew).—THE THEORY AND PRACTICE OF ABSOLUTE MEASUREMENTS IN ELECTRICITY AND MAGNETISM. 2 vols. Crown 8vo. Vol. I. 12s. 6d.

—— ABSOLUTE MEASUREMENTS IN ELECTRICITY AND MAGNETISM. 2nd Edition, revised. Fcp. 8vo. 5s. 6d.

GRAY (Prof. Asa).—STRUCTURAL BOTANY; OR, ORGANOGRAPHY ON THE BASIS OF MORPHOLOGY. 8vo. 10s. 6d.

—— THE SCIENTIFIC PAPERS OF ASA GRAY. Selected by CHARLES S. SARGENT. 2 vols. 8vo. 21s.

GRAY (Thomas).—Edited by EDMUND GOSSE. In 4 vols. Globe 8vo. 20s.—Vol. I. POEMS, JOURNALS, AND ESSAYS.—II. LETTERS.—III. LETTERS.—IV. NOTES ON ARISTOPHANES; AND PLATO.

GRAY. By EDMUND GOSSE. Crown 8vo. 1s. 6d.; sewed, 1s.

GREAVES (John).—A TREATISE ON ELEMENTARY STATICS. 2nd Ed. Cr. 8vo. 6s. 6d.

—— STATICS FOR BEGINNERS. Gl. 8vo. 3s. 6d.

GREEK ELEGIAC POETS. FROM CALLINUS TO CALLIMACHUS. Selected and Edited by Rev. H. KYNASTON. 18mo. 1s. 6d.

GREEK TESTAMENT. THE NEW TESTAMENT IN THE ORIGINAL GREEK. The Text revised by Bishop WESTCOTT, D.D., and Prof. F. J. A. HORT, D.D., 2 vols. Crn. 8vo. 10s. 6d. each.—Vol. I. Text; II. Introduction and Appendix.

THE NEW TESTAMENT IN THE ORIGINAL GREEK, FOR SCHOOLS. The Text Revised by Bishop WESTCOTT, D.D., and F. J. A. HORT, D.D. 12mo. cloth. 4s. 6d.—18mo. roan, red edges. 5s. 6d.; morocco, 6s. 6d.

**GREEK TESTAMENT**—*continued.*

SCHOOL READINGS IN THE GREEK TESTAMENT. Being the Outlines of the Life of our Lord as given by St. Mark, with additions from the Text of the other Evangelists. Edited, with Notes and Vocabulary, by A. CALVERT, M.A. Fcp. 8vo. 2s. 6d.

THE GREEK TESTAMENT AND THE ENGLISH VERSION, A COMPANION TO. By PHILIP SCHAFF, D.D. Crown 8vo. 12s.

THE GOSPEL ACCORDING TO ST. MATTHEW. Greek Text as Revised by Bishop WESTCOTT and Dr. HORT. With Introduction and Notes by Rev. A. SLOMAN, M.A. Fcp. 8vo. 2s. 6d.

THE GOSPEL ACCORDING TO ST. LUKE. The Greek Text as revised by Bp. WESTCOTT and Dr. HORT. With Introduction and Notes by Rev. J. BOND, M.A. Fcp. 8vo. 2s. 6d.

THE ACTS OF THE APOSTLES. Being the Greek Text as Revised by Bishop WESTCOTT and Dr. HORT. With Explanatory Notes by T. E. PAGE, M.A. Fcp.8vo. 3s.6d.

GREEN (John Richard).—A SHORT HISTORY OF THE ENGLISH PEOPLE. With Coloured Maps, Genealogical Tables, and Chronological Annals. New Edition, thoroughly revised. Cr. 8vo. 8s. 6d. 150th Thousand. Also the same in Four Parts. With the corresponding portion of Mr. Tait's "Analysis." 3s. each. Part I. 607—1265. II. 1204—1553. III. 1540—1689. IV. 1660—1873.

—— HISTORY OF THE ENGLISH PEOPLE. In 4 vols. 8vo.—Vol. I. With 8 Coloured Maps. 16s.—II. 16s.—III. With 4 Maps. 16s.—IV. With Maps and Index. 16s.

—— THE MAKING OF ENGLAND. With Maps. 8vo. 16s.

—— THE CONQUEST OF ENGLAND. With Maps and Portrait. 8vo. 18s.

—— READINGS IN ENGLISH HISTORY. In 3 Parts. Fcp. 8vo. 1s. 6d. each.

—— ESSAYS OF JOSEPH ADDISON. 18mo. 4s. 6d.

GREEN (J. R.) and GREEN (Alice S.).— A SHORT GEOGRAPHY OF THE BRITISH ISLANDS. With 28 Maps. Fcp. 8vo. 3s. 6d.

GREEN (Mrs. J. R.).—HENRY II. Crown 8vo. 2s. 6d.

GREEN (W. S.).—AMONG THE SELKIRK GLACIERS. Crown 8vo. 7s. 6d.

GREENHILL (Prof. A. G.).—DIFFERENTIAL AND INTEGRAL CALCULUS. Cr. 8vo. 7s. 6d.

GREENWOOD (Jessy E.). — THE MOON MAIDEN: AND OTHER STORIES. Crown 8vo. 3s. 6d.

GREENWOOD (J. G.).—THE ELEMENTS OF GREEK GRAMMAR. Crown 8vo. 5s. 6d.

GRIFFITHS (W. H.).—LESSONS ON PRESCRIPTIONS AND THE ART OF PRESCRIBING. New Edition. 18mo. 3s. 6d.

GRIMM'S FAIRY TALES. A Selection from the Household Stories. Translated from the German by LUCY CRANE, and done into Pictures by WALTER CRANE. Crown 8vo. 6s.

GRIMM.—KINDER-UND-HAUSMÄRCHEN. Selected and Edited, with Notes and Vocabulary, by G. E. FASNACHT. Gl. 8vo. 2s. 6d.

GROVE (Sir George).—A DICTIONARY OF MUSIC AND MUSICIANS, A.D. 1450—1889. Edited by Sir GEORGE GROVE, D.C.L. In 4 vols. 8vo. 21s. each. With Illustrations in Music Type and Woodcut.—Also published in Parts. Parts I.—XIV., XIX.—XXII. 3s. 6d. each; XV. XVI. 7s.; XVII. XVIII. 7s.; XXIII.—XXV., Appendix, Edited by J. A. FULLER MAITLAND, M.A. 9s. [Cloth cases for binding the volumes, 1s. each.]

—— A COMPLETE INDEX TO THE ABOVE. By Mrs. E. WODEHOUSE. 8vo. 7s. 6d.

—— PRIMER OF GEOGRAPHY. Maps. 18mo. 1s.

GUEST (M. J.).—LECTURES ON THE HISTORY OF ENGLAND. Crown 8vo. 6s.

GUEST (Dr. E.).—ORIGINES CELTICÆ (A Fragment) and other Contributions to the History of Britain. Maps. 2 vols. 8vo. 32s.

GUIDE TO THE UNPROTECTED, In Every-day Matters relating to Property and Income. 5th Ed. Extra fcp. 8vo. 3s. 6d.

GUILLEMIN (Amédée).—THE FORCES OF NATURE. A Popular Introduction to the Study of Physical Phenomena. 455 Woodcuts. Royal 8vo. 21s.

—— THE APPLICATIONS OF PHYSICAL FORCES. With Coloured Plates and Illustrations. Royal 8vo. 21s.

—— ELECTRICITY AND MAGNETISM. A Popular Treatise. Translated and Edited, with Additions and Notes, by Prof. SYLVANUS P. THOMPSON. Royal 8vo. [In the Press.

GUIZOT.—GREAT CHRISTIANS OF FRANCE. ST. LOUIS AND CALVIN. Crown 8vo. 6s.

GUNTON (George).—WEALTH AND PROGRESS. Crown 8vo. 6s.

HADLEY (Prof. James).—ESSAYS, PHILOLOGICAL AND CRITICAL. 8vo. 14s.

HADLEY-ALLEN.—A GREEK GRAMMAR FOR SCHOOLS AND COLLEGES. By Prof. JAMES HADLEY. Revised and in part Rewritten by Prof. FREDERIC DE FOREST ALLEN. Crown 8vo. 6s.

HAILSTONE (H.).—NOVAE ARUNDINES; OR, NEW MARSH MELODIES. Fcp. 8vo. 3s. 6d.

HALES (Prof. J. W.).—LONGER ENGLISH POEMS, with Notes, Philological and Explanatory, and an Introduction on the Teaching of English. 12th Edition. Extra fcp. 8vo. 4s. 6d.

HALL (H. S.) and KNIGHT (S. R.).—ELEMENTARY ALGEBRA FOR SCHOOLS. 6th Ed. revised. Gl. 8vo. 3s. 6d. With Answers, 4s. 6d.

—— KEY TO ELEMENTARY ALGEBRA. Crown 8vo. 8s. 6d.

—— ALGEBRAICAL EXERCISES AND EXAMINATION PAPERS to accompany "Elementary Algebra." 2nd Edition. Globe 8vo. 2s. 6d.

—— HIGHER ALGEBRA. A Sequel to "Elementary Algebra for Schools." 3rd Edition. Crown 8vo. 7s. 6d.

HALL (H. S.) and KNIGHT (S. R.).—Solutions of the Examples in "Higher Algebra." Crown 8vo. 10s. 6d.

—— Arithmetical Exercises and Examination Papers. Globe 8vo. 2s. 6d.

HALL (H. S.) and STEVENS (F. H.).—A Text-Book of Euclid's Elements. Globe 8vo. Book I. 1s.; I. II. 1s. 6d.; I.—IV. 3s.; III. and IV. 2s.; V. VI. and XI. 2s. 6d.; I.—VI. and XI. 4s. 6d.; XI. 1s.

HALLWARD (R. F.).—Flowers of Paradise. Music, Verse, Design, Illustration. Royal 4to. 6s.

HALSTED (G. B.).—The Elements of Geometry. 8vo. 12s. 6d.

HAMERTON (P. G.).—The Intellectual Life. 4th Edition. Crown 8vo. 10s. 6d.

—— Etching and Etchers. 3rd Edition, revised. With 48 Plates. Colombier 8vo.

—— Thoughts about Art. New Edition. Crown 8vo. 8s. 6d.

—— Human Intercourse. 4th Edition. Crown 8vo. 8s. 6d.

—— French and English: A Comparison. Crown 8vo. 10s. 6d.

HAMILTON (John).—On Truth and Error. Crown 8vo. 5s.

—— Arthur's Seat; or, The Church of the Banned. Crown 8vo. 6s.

—— Above and Around: Thoughts on God and Man. 12mo. 2s. 6d.

HAMILTON (Prof. D. J.).—On the Pathology of Bronchitis, Catarrhal Pneumonia, Tubercle, and Allied Lesions of the Human Lung. 8vo. 8s. 6d.

—— A Text-Book of Pathology, Systematic and Practical. Illustrated. Vol. I. 8vo. 25s.

HANBURY (Daniel).—Science Papers, chiefly Pharmacological and Botanical. Medium 8vo. 14s.

HANDEL. Life of George Frederick Handel. By W. S. Rockstro. Crown 8vo. 10s. 6d.

HARDWICK (Ven. Archdeacon).—Christ and other Masters. 6th Edition. Crown 8vo. 10s. 6d.

—— A History of the Christian Church. Middle Age. 6th Edition. Edit. by Bishop Stubbs. Crown 8vo. 10s. 6d.

—— A History of the Christian Church during the Reformation. 9th Edition. Revised by Bishop Stubbs. Cr. 8vo. 10s. 6d.

HARDY (Arthur Sherburne).—But yet a Woman. A Novel. Crown 8vo. 4s. 6d.

—— The Wind of Destiny. 2 vols. Globe 8vo. 12s.

HARDY (H. J.).—A Latin Reader for the Lower Forms in Schools. Globe 8vo. 2s. 6d.

HARDY (Thomas).—The Woodlanders. Crown 8vo. 3s. 6d.

—— Wessex Tales: Strange, Lively, and Commonplace. Crown 8vo. 3s. 6d.

HARE (Julius Charles).—The Mission of the Comforter. New Edition. Edited by Prof. E. H. Plumptre. Crown 8vo. 7s. 6d.

—— The Victory of Faith. Edited by Prof. Plumptre, with Introductory Notices by the late Prof. Maurice and by the late Dean Stanley. Crown 8vo. 6s. 6d.

—— Guesses at Truth. By Two Brothers, Augustus William Hare and Julius Charles Hare. With a Memoir and Two Portraits. 18mo. 4s. 6d.

HARMONIA. By the Author of "Estelle Russell." 3 vols. Crown 8vo. 31s. 6d.

HARPER (Father Thomas).—The Metaphysics of the School. In 5 vols. Vols. I. and II. 8vo. 18s. each; Vol. III., Part I. 12s.

HARRIS (Rev. G. C.).—Sermons. With a Memoir by Charlotte M. Yonge, and Portrait. Extra fcp. 8vo. 6s.

HARRISON (Frederic).—The Choice of Books. Globe 8vo. 6s.

Large Paper Edition. Printed on handmade paper. 15s.

—— Oliver Cromwell. Crown 8vo. 2s. 6d.

HARRISON (Miss Jane) and VERRALL (Mrs.).—Mythology and Monuments of Ancient Athens. Illustrated. Cr. 8vo. 16s.

HARTE (Bret).—Cressy: A Novel. Crown 8vo. 3s. 6d.

—— The Heritage of Dedlow Marsh: and other Tales. Crown 8vo. 3s. 6d.

HARTLEY (Prof. W. Noel).—A Course of Quantitative Analysis for Students. Globe 8vo. 5s.

HARWOOD (George).—Disestablishment; or, A Defence of the Principle of a National Church. 8vo. 12s.

—— The Coming Democracy. Cr. 8vo. 6s.

—— From Within. Crown 8vo. 6s.

HASTINGS (Warren). By Sir Alfred Lyall. With Portrait. Crown 8vo. 2s. 6d.

HAUFF.—Die Karavane. Edited, with Notes and Vocabulary, by Herman Hager, Ph. D. Globe 8vo. 3s.

HAVELOCK (SIR HENRY). By Archibald Forbes. Portrait. Crn. 8vo. 2s. 6d.

HAWTHORNE. By Henry James. Crn. 8vo. 1s. 6d.; sewed, 1s.

HAYWARD (R. B.).—The Elements of Solid Geometry. Globe 8vo. 3s.

HEARD (Rev. W. A.).—A Second Greek Exercise Book. Globe 8vo. 2s. 6d.

HEINE. Selections from the Reisebilder and other Prose Works. Edited by C. Colbeck, M.A. 18mo. 2s. 6d.

HELLENIC STUDIES, THE JOURNAL OF.—8vo. Vol. I. With Plates of Illustrations. 30s.—Vol. II. 30s. With Plates of Illustrations. Or in 2 Parts, 15s. each.—Vol. III. 2 Parts. With Plates of Illustrations. 15s. each.—Vol. IV. 2 Parts. With Plates. Part I. 15s. Part II. 21s. Or complete, 30s.—Vol. V. With Plates. 30s.—Vol. VI. With Plates. Part I. 15s. Part II. 15s. Or complete, 30s.—Vol. VII. Part I. 15s. Part II. 15s. Or complete, 30s.—Vol. VIII. Part I. 15s. Part II. 15s.—Vol. IX. 2 Parts. 15s. each.—Vol. X. 30s.—Vol. XI. Pt. I. 15s. net.

The Journal will be sold at a reduced price to Libraries wishing to subscribe, but official application must in each case be made to the Council. Information on this point, and upon the conditions of Membership, may be obtained on application to the Hon. Sec., Mr. George Macmillan, 29, Bedford Street, Covent Garden.

HELPS (Sir A.).—ESSAYS WRITTEN IN THE INTERVALS OF BUSINESS. Edited by F. J. ROWE, M.A., and W. T. WEBB, M.A. Globe 8vo. 1s. 9d.; sewed, 1s. 6d.

HENRY II. By Mrs. J. R. GREEN. Crown 8vo. 2s. 6d.

HENRY V. By the Rev. A. J. CHURCH. With Portrait. Crown 8vo. 2s. 6d.

HENRY VII. By J. GAIRDNER. Cr. 8vo. 2s. 6d.

HENSLOW (Rev. G.).—THE THEORY OF EVOLUTION OF LIVING THINGS, AND THE APPLICATION OF THE PRINCIPLES OF EVOLUTION TO RELIGION. Crown 8vo. 6s.

HERODOTUS.—THE HISTORY. Translated into English, with Notes and Indices, by G. C. MACAULAY, M.A. 2 vols. Cr. 8vo. 18s.
—— BOOKS I.—III. Edited by A. H. SAYCE, M.A. 8vo. 16s.
—— BOOK III. Edited by G. C. MACAULAY, M.A. Fcp. 8vo. 2s. 6d.
—— BOOK VI. Edit. by Prof. J. STRACHAN, M.A. Fcp. 8vo.
—— BOOK VII. Edited by Mrs. MONTAGU BUTLER. Fcp. 8vo.
—— SELECTIONS FROM BOOKS VII. and VIII. THE EXPEDITION OF XERXES. Edited by A. H. COOKE, M.A. 18mo. 1s. 6d.

HERRICK. — CHRYSOMELA. A Selection from the Lyrical Poems of ROBERT HERRICK. Arranged, with Notes, by Prof. F. T. PALGRAVE. 18mo. 4s. 6d.

HERTEL (Dr.).—OVERPRESSURE IN HIGH SCHOOLS IN DENMARK. With Introduction by Sir J. CRICHTON-BROWNE. Cr. 8vo. 3s. 6d.

HERVEY (Rt. Rev. Lord Arthur).—THE GENEALOGIES OF OUR LORD AND SAVIOUR JESUS CHRIST. 8vo. 10s. 6d.

HICKS (W. M.).—ELEMENTARY DYNAMICS OF PARTICLES AND SOLIDS. Cr. 8vo. 6s. 6d.

HILL (Florence D.).—CHILDREN OF THE STATE. Ed. by FANNY FOWKE. Cr. 8vo. 6s.

HILL (Octavia).—OUR COMMON LAND, AND OTHER ESSAYS. Extra fcp. 8vo. 3s. 6d.
——HOMES OF THE LONDON POOR. Sewed. Crown 8vo. 1s.

HIORNS (Arthur H.).—PRACTICAL METALLURGY AND ASSAYING. A Text-Book for the use of Teachers, Students, and Assayers. With Illustrations. Globe 8vo. 6s.
—— A TEXT-BOOK OF ELEMENTARY METALLURGY FOR THE USE OF STUDENTS. Gl. 8vo. 4s.
—— IRON AND STEEL MANUFACTURE. A Text-Book for Beginners. Illustr. Gl. 8vo. 3s. 6d.
—— MIXED METALS AND METALLIC ALLOYS. Globe 8vo.

HISTORICAL COURSE FOR SCHOOLS. Ed. by EDW. A. FREEMAN, D.C.L. 18mo.
Vol. I. GENERAL SKETCH OF EUROPEAN HISTORY. By E. A. FREEMAN. With Maps, &c. 3s. 6d.
    II. HISTORY OF ENGLAND. By EDITH THOMPSON. Coloured Maps. 2s. 6d.
    III. HISTORY OF SCOTLAND. By MARGARET MACARTHUR. 2s.
    IV. HISTORY OF ITALY. By the Rev. W. HUNT, M.A. With Coloured Maps. 3s. 6d.
    V. HISTORY OF GERMANY. By JAMES SIME, M.A. 3s.
    VI. HISTORY OF AMERICA. By J. A. DOYLE. With Maps. 4s. 6d.
    VII. HISTORY OF EUROPEAN COLONIES. By E. J. PAYNE, M.A. Maps. 4s. 6d.
    VIII. HISTORY OF FRANCE. By CHARLOTTE M. YONGE. Maps. 3s. 6d.

HOBART. — ESSAYS AND MISCELLANEOUS WRITINGS OF VERE HENRY, LORD HOBART. With a Biographical Sketch. Edited by MARY, LADY HOBART. 2 vols. 8vo. 25s.

HOBDAY (E.). — VILLA GARDENING. A Handbook for Amateur and Practical Gardeners. Extra crown 8vo. 6s.

HODGSON (F.).—MYTHOLOGY FOR LATIN VERSIFICATION. 6th Edition. Revised by F. C. HODGSON, M.A. 18mo. 3s.

HODGSON. — MEMOIR OF REV. FRANCIS HODGSON, B.D., SCHOLAR, POET, AND DIVINE. By his Son, the Rev. JAMES T. HODGSON, M.A. 2 vols. Crown 8vo. 18s.

HÖFFDING (Prof.).—OUTLINES OF PSYCHOLOGY. Translated by M. E. LOWNDES. Crown 8vo.                    [In the Press.

HOFMANN (Prof. A. W.).—THE LIFE WORK OF LIEBIG IN EXPERIMENTAL AND PHILOSOPHIC CHEMISTRY. 8vo. 5s.

HOGAN, M.P. Globe 8vo. 2s.

HOLE (Rev. C.).—GENEALOGICAL STEMMA OF THE KINGS OF ENGLAND AND FRANCE. On a Sheet. 1s.
—— A BRIEF BIOGRAPHICAL DICTIONARY. 2nd Edition. 18mo. 4s. 6d.

HOLLAND (Prof. T. E.).—THE TREATY RELATIONS OF RUSSIA AND TURKEY, FROM 1774 TO 1853. Crown 8vo. 2s.

HOLMES (O. W., Jun.).—THE COMMON LAW. 8vo. 12s.

HOMER.—THE ODYSSEY OF HOMER DONE INTO ENGLISH PROSE. By S. H. BUTCHER, M.A., and A. LANG, M.A. 7th Edition. Crown 8vo. 6s.

HOMER.—ODYSSEY. Book I. Edited with Notes and Vocabulary, by Rev. J. BOND, M.A., and Rev. A. S. WALPOLE, M.A. 18mo. 1s. 6d.

—— ODYSSEY. Book IX. Edited by JOHN E. B. MAYOR, M.A. Fcp. 8vo. 2s. 6d.

—— ODYSSEY. THE TRIUMPH OF ODYSSEUS. Books XXI.—XXIV. Edited by S. G. HAMILTON, B.A. Fcp. 8vo. 2s. 6d.

—— THE ODYSSEY OF HOMER. Books I.—XII. Translated into English Verse by the EARL OF CARNARVON. Crown 8vo. 7s. 6d.

—— THE ILIAD. Edited, with English Notes and Introduction, by WALTER LEAF, Litt.D. 2 vols. 8vo. 14s. each.—Vol. I. Bks. I.—XII; Vol. II. Bks. XIII.—XXIV.

—— ILIAD. THE STORY OF ACHILLES. Edited by J. H. PRATT, M.A., and WALTER LEAF, Litt.D. Fcap. 8vo. 5s.

—— ILIAD. Book I. Edited by Rev. J. BOND, M.A., and Rev. A. S. WALPOLE, M.A. With Notes and Vocabulary. 18mo. 1s. 6d.

—— ILIAD. Book XVIII. THE ARMS OF ACHILLES. Edited by Rev. S. R. JAMES, M.A., with Notes and Vocabulary. 18mo. 1s. 6d.

—— ILIAD. Translated into English Prose. By ANDREW LANG, WALTER LEAF, and ERNEST MYERS. Crown 8vo. 12s. 6d.

—— PRIMER OF HOMER. By Rt. Hon. W. E. GLADSTONE, M.P. 18mo. 1s.

HON. MISS FERRARD, THE. By the Author of "Hogan, M.P." Globe 8vo. 2s.

HOOKER (Sir J. D.)—THE STUDENT'S FLORA OF THE BRITISH ISLANDS. 3rd Edition. Globe 8vo. 10s. 6d.

—— PRIMER OF BOTANY. 18mo. 1s.

HOOKER (Sir Joseph D.) and BALL (J.)—JOURNAL OF A TOUR IN MAROCCO AND THE GREAT ATLAS. 8vo. 21s.

HOOLE (C. H.)—THE CLASSICAL ELEMENT IN THE NEW TESTAMENT. Considered as a Proof of its Genuineness, with an Appendix on the Oldest Authorities used in the Formation of the Canon. 8vo. 10s. 6d.

HOOPER (G.).—WELLINGTON. With Portrait. Crown 8vo. 2s. 6d.

HOOPER (W. H.) and PHILLIPS (W. C.).—A MANUAL OF MARKS ON POTTERY AND PORCELAIN. 16mo. 4s. 6d.

HOPE (Frances J.).—NOTES AND THOUGHTS ON GARDENS AND WOODLANDS. Cr. 8vo. 6s.

HOPKINS (Ellice).—AUTUMN SWALLOWS: A Book of Lyrics. Extra fcp. 8vo. 6s.

HOPPUS (Mary).—A GREAT TREASON: A Story of the War of Independence. 2 vols. Crown 8vo. 9s.

HORACE.—THE WORKS OF HORACE RENDERED INTO ENGLISH PROSE. By J. LONSDALE and S. LEE. Globe 8vo. 3s. 6d.

—— STUDIES, LITERARY AND HISTORICAL, IN THE ODES OF HORACE. By A. W. VERRALL, Litt.D. 8vo. 8s. 6d.

—— THE ODES OF HORACE IN A METRICAL PARAPHRASE. By R. M. HOVENDEN, B.A. Extra fcap. 8vo. 4s. 6d.

HORACE.—LIFE AND CHARACTER: AN EPITOME OF HIS SATIRES AND EPISTLES. By R. M. HOVENDEN, B.A. Ext. fcp. 8vo. 4s. 6d.

—— WORD FOR WORD FROM HORACE: The Odes Literally Versified. By W. T. THORNTON, C.B. Crown 8vo. 7s. 6d.

—— ODES. Books I. II. III. and IV. Edited by T. E. PAGE, M.A. With Vocabularies. 18mo. 1s. 6d. each.

—— ODES. Books I.—IV. and CARMEN SECULARE. Edited by T. E. PAGE, M.A. Fcap. 8vo. 5s.; or separately, 2s. each.

—— THE SATIRES. Edited by ARTHUR PALMER, M.A. Fcap. 8vo. 5s.

—— THE EPISTLES AND ARS POETICA. Edited by A. S. WILKINS, Litt.D. Fcp. 8vo. 5s.

—— SELECTIONS FROM THE EPISTLES AND SATIRES. Edited by Rev. W. J. F. V. BAKER, B.A. 18mo. 1s. 6d.

—— SELECT EPODES AND ARS POETICA. Edited by Rev. H. A. DALTON, M.A. 18mo. 1s. 6d.

HORT.—TWO DISSERTATIONS. I. On MONOΓΕΝΗΣ ΘΕΟΣ in Scripture and Tradition. II. On the "Constantinopolitan" Creed and other Eastern Creeds of the Fourth Century. By FENTON JOHN ANTHONY HORT, D.D. 8vo. 7s. 6d.

HORTON (Hon. S. Dana).—THE SILVER POUND AND ENGLAND'S MONETARY POLICY SINCE THE RESTORATION. With a History of the Guinea. 8vo. 14s.

HOWELL (George).—THE CONFLICTS OF CAPITAL AND LABOUR. 2nd Edition. Crown 8vo. 7s. 6d.

HOWES (Prof. G. B.).—AN ATLAS OF PRACTICAL ELEMENTARY BIOLOGY. With a Preface by Prof. HUXLEY. 4to. 14s.

HOWSON (Very Rev. J. S.).—BEFORE THE TABLE: An INQUIRY, HISTORICAL AND THEOLOGICAL, INTO THE MEANING OF THE CONSECRATION RUBRIC IN THE COMMUNION SERVICE OF THE CHURCH OF ENGLAND. 8vo. 7s. 6d.

HOZIER (Lieut.-Colonel H. M.).—THE SEVEN WEEKS' WAR. 3rd Edition. Crown 8vo. 6s.

—— THE INVASIONS OF ENGLAND. 2 vols. 8vo. 28s.

HÜBNER (Baron von).—A RAMBLE ROUND THE WORLD. Crown 8vo. 6s.

HUGHES (Thomas).—ALFRED THE GREAT. Crown 8vo. 6s.

—— TOM BROWN'S SCHOOL DAYS. By An OLD BOY. Illustrated Edition. Crown 8vo. 6s.—Golden Treasury Edition. 4s. 6d.—Uniform Edition. 3s. 6d.—People's Edition. 2s.—People's Sixpenny Edition, Illustrated. Med. 4to. 6d.—Uniform with Sixpenny Kingsley. Medium 8vo. 6d.

—— TOM BROWN AT OXFORD. Crown 8vo. 6s.—Uniform Edition. 3s. 6d.

—— MEMOIR OF DANIEL MACMILLAN. With Portrait. Cr. 8vo. 4s. 6d.—Popular Edition. Sewed. Crown 8vo. 1s.

—— RUGBY, TENNESSEE. Crown 8vo. 4s. 6d.

—— GONE TO TEXAS. Edited by THOMAS HUGHES, Q.C. Crown 8vo. 4s. 6d.

HUGHES (T.).—The Scouring of the White Horse, and the Ashen Faggot. Uniform Edition. 3s. 6d.

—— James Fraser, Second Bishop of Manchester. A Memoir, 1818—85. Cr. 8vo. 6s.

—— Livingstone. With Portrait and Map. Cr. 8vo. 2s. 6d. [English Men of Action.

HULL (E.).—A Treatise on Ornamental and Building Stones of Great Britain and Foreign Countries. 8vo. 12s.

HULLAH (John).—The Song Book. Words and Tunes from the best Poets and Musicians. With Vignette. 18mo. 4s. 6d.

—— Music in the House. 4th Edition. Crown 8vo. 2s. 6d.

HULLAH (M. E.).—Hannah Tarne. A Story for Girls. Globe 8vo. 2s. 6d.

HUME. By Thomas H. Huxley. Crown 8vo. 1s. 6d.; sewed, 1s.

HUMPHRY (Prof. G. M.).—The Human Skeleton (including the Joints). With 260 Illustrations drawn from Nature. Med. 8vo. 14s.

—— The Human Foot and the Human Hand. With Illustrations. Fcp. 8vo. 4s. 6d.

—— Observations in Myology. 8vo. 6s.

—— Old Age. The Results of Information received respecting nearly nine hundred persons who had attained the age of eighty years, including seventy-four centenarians. Crown 8vo. 4s. 6d.

HUNT (Rev. W.).—History of Italy. Maps. 3rd Edition. 18mo. 3s. 6d.

HUNT (W.).—Talks about Art. With a Letter from Sir J. E. Millais, Bart., R.A. Crown 8vo. 3s. 6d.

HUSS (Hermann).—A System of Oral Instruction in German. Crown 8vo. 5s.

HUTTON (R. H.).—Essays on some of the Modern Guides of English Thought in Matters of Faith. Globe 8vo. 6s.

—— Scott. Crown 8vo. 1s. 6d.; sewed, 1s.

—— Essays. 2 vols. Globe 8vo. 6s. each. —Vol. I. Literary Essays; II. Theological Essays.

HUXLEY (Thomas Henry).—Lessons in Elementary Physiology. With numerous Illustrations. New Edit. Fcp. 8vo. 4s. 6d.

—— Lay Sermons, Addresses, and Reviews. 9th Edition. 8vo. 7s. 6d.

—— Essays selected from Lay Sermons, Addresses, and Reviews. 3rd Edition. Crown 8vo. 1s.

—— Critiques and Addresses. 8vo. 10s. 6d.

—— Physiography. An Introduction to the Study of Nature. 13th Ed. Cr.8vo. 6s.

—— American Addresses, with a Lecture on the Study of Biology. 8vo. 6s. 6d.

—— Science and Culture, and other Essays. 8vo. 10s. 6d.

—— Introductory Primer. 18mo. 1s.

—— Hume. Crown 8vo. 1s. 6d.; sewed, 1s.

HUXLEY'S PHYSIOLOGY, Questions on, for Schools. By T. Alcock, M.D. 5th Edition. 18mo. 1s. 6d.

HUXLEY (T. H.) and MARTIN (H. N.).— A Course of Practical Instruction in Elementary Biology. New Edition, Revised and Extended by Prof. G. B. Howes and D. H Scott, M.A., Ph.D. With Preface by T. H. Huxley, F.R.S. Cr. 8vo. 10s. 6d.

IBBETSON (W. J.).— An Elementary Treatise on the Mathematical Theory of Perfectly Elastic Solids. 8vo. 21s.

ILLINGWORTH (Rev. J. R.).—Sermons Preached in a College Chapel. Cr.8vo. 5s.

IMITATIO CHRISTI, Libri IV. Printed in Borders after Holbein, Dürer, and other old Masters, containing Dances of Death, Acts of Mercy, Emblems, &c. Cr. 8vo. 7s.6d.

INDIAN TEXT-BOOKS.—Primer of English Grammar. By R. Morris, LL.D. 18mo. 1s.; sewed, 10d.

Primer of Astronomy. By J. N. Lockyer. 18mo. 1s.; sewed, 10d.

Easy Selections from Modern English Literature. For the use of the Middle Classes in Indian Schools. With Notes. By Sir Roper Lethbridge. Cr.8vo. 1s.6d.

Selections from Modern English Literature. For the use of the Higher Classes in Indian Schools. By Sir Roper Lethbridge, M.A. Crown 8vo. 3s. 6d.

Series of Six English Reading Books for Indian Children. By P.C. Sircar. Revised by Sir Roper Lethbridge. Cr. 8vo. Book I. 4d.; Nagari Characters, 5d.; Persian Characters, 5d.; Book II. 6d.; Book III. 8d.; Book IV. 1s.; Book V. 1s. 2d.; Book VI. 1s. 3d.

High School Reader. By Eric Robertson. Crown 8vo. 2s.

A Geographical Reader and Companion to the Atlas. By C. B. Clarke, F.R.S. Crown 8vo. 2s.

A Class-Book of Geography. By the same. Fcap. 8vo. 3s. 6d.; sewed, 3s.

The World's History. Compiled under direction of Sir Roper Lethbridge. Crown 8vo. 1s.

Easy Introduction to the History of India. By Sir Roper Lethbridge. Crown 8vo. 1s. 6d.

History of England. Compiled under direction of Sir Roper Lethbridge. Crown 8vo. 1s. 6d.

Easy Introduction to the History and Geography of Bengal. By Sir Roper Lethbridge. Crown 8vo. 1s. 6d.

Arithmetic. With Answers. By Barnard Smith. 18mo. 2s.

Algebra. By I. Todhunter. 18mo, sewed. 2s. 3d.

Euclid. First Four Books. With Notes, &c. By I. Todhunter. 18mo. 2s.

Elementary Mensuration and Land Surveying. By the same Author. 18mo. 2s.

Euclid. Books I.—IV. By H. S. Hall and F. H. Stevens. Gl. 8vo. 3s.; sewed, 2s.6d.

Physical Geography. By H. F. Blanford. Crown 8vo. 2s. 6d.

Elementary Geometry and Conic Sections. By J. M. Wilson. Ex. fcp. 8vo. 6s.

INGRAM (T. Dunbar).—A HISTORY OF THE LEGISLATIVE UNION OF GREAT BRITAIN AND IRELAND. 8vo. 10s. 6d.

—— TWO CHAPTERS OF IRISH HISTORY: I. The Irish Parliament of James II.; II. The Alleged Violation of the Treaty of Limerick. 8vo. 6s.

IONIA.—ANTIQUITIES OF IONIA. Folio. Vols. I. II. and III. 2l. 2s. each, or 5l. 5s. the set.—Vol. IV. 3l. 13s. 6d.

IRVING (Joseph).—ANNALS OF OUR TIME. A Diurnal of Events, Social and Political, Home and Foreign. From the Accession of Queen Victoria to Jubilee Day, being the First Fifty Years of Her Majesty's Reign. In 2 vols. 8vo.—Vol. I. June 20th, 1837, to February 28th, 1871. Vol. II. February 24th, 1871, to June 24th, 1887. 18s. each. The Second Volume may also be had in Three Parts: Part I. February 24th, 1871, to March 19th, 1874, 4s. 6d. Part II. March 20th, 1874, to July 22nd, 1878, 4s. 6d. Part III. July 23rd, 1878, to June 24th, 1887, 9s.

IRVING (Washington).—OLD CHRISTMAS. From the Sketch Book. With upwards of 100 Illustrations by RANDOLPH CALDECOTT. Cloth elegant, gilt edges. Crown 8vo. 6s.

Also with uncut edges, paper label. 6s.

*People's Edition.* Medium 4to. 6d.

—— BRACEBRIDGE HALL. With 120 Illustrations by RANDOLPH CALDECOTT. Cloth elegant, gilt edges. Crown 8vo. 6s.

Also with uncut edges, paper label. 6d.

*People's Edition.* Medium 4to. 6d.

—— OLD CHRISTMAS AND BRACEBRIDGE HALL. Illustrations by RANDOLPH CALDECOTT. *Edition de Luxe.* Royal 8vo. 21s.

ISMAY'S CHILDREN. By the Author of "Hogan, M.P." Globe 8vo. 2s.

JACK AND THE BEAN-STALK. English Hexameters by the Honourable HALLAM TENNYSON. With 40 Illustrations by RANDOLPH CALDECOTT. Fcp. 4to. 3s. 6d.

JACKSON (Rev. Blomfield).—FIRST STEPS TO GREEK PROSE COMPOSITION. 12th Edit. 18mo. 1s. 6d.

KEY (supplied to Teachers only). 3s. 6d.

—— SECOND STEPS TO GREEK PROSE COMPOSITION. 18mo, 2s. 6d.

KEY (supplied to Teachers only). 3s. 6d.

JACKSON (Helen).—RAMONA: A Story. Globe 8vo. 2s.

JACOB (Rev. J. A.).—BUILDING IN SILENCE, AND OTHER SERMONS. Extra fcp. 8vo. 6s.

JAMES (Henry).—THE EUROPEANS: A Novel. Crown 8vo. 6s.

—— DAISY MILLER, AND OTHER STORIES. Crown 8vo. 6s.—Globe 8vo. 2s.

—— THE AMERICAN. Crown 8vo. 6s.

—— RODERICK HUDSON. Crown 8vo. 6s.— Globe 8vo. 2s.

—— THE MADONNA OF THE FUTURE, AND OTHER TALES. Crown 8vo. 6s. — Globe 8vo. 2s.

—— WASHINGTON SQUARE: THE PENSION BEAUREPAS. Cra. 8vo. 6s.—Globe 8vo. 2s.

JAMES (Henry). — THE PORTRAIT OF A LADY. Crown 8vo. 6s.

—— STORIES REVIVED. In Two Series. Crown 8vo. 6s. each.

—— THE BOSTONIANS. Crown 8vo. 6s.

—— NOVELS AND TALES. Pocket Edition. 18mo. 14 vols. 2s. each volume: THE PORTRAIT OF A LADY. 3 vols.—RODERICK HUDSON. 2 vols.—THE AMERICAN. 2 vols. —WASHINGTON SQUARE. 1 vol.—THE EUROPEANS. 1 vol.—CONFIDENCE. 1 vol. —THE SIEGE OF LONDON; MADAME DE MAUVES. 1 vol.—AN INTERNATIONAL EPISODE; THE PENSION BEAUREPAS; THE POINT OF VIEW. 1 vol.—DAISY MILLER, A STUDY; FOUR MEETINGS; LONGSTAFF'S MARRIAGE; BENVOLIO. 1 vol.—THE MADONNA OF THE FUTURE; A BUNDLE OF LETTERS; THE DIARY OF A MAN OF FIFTY; EUGENE PICKERING. 1 vol.

—— HAWTHORNE. Cr. 8vo. 1s. 6d.; swd. 1s.

—— FRENCH POETS AND NOVELISTS. New Edition. Crown 8vo. 4s. 6d.

—— TALES OF THREE CITIES. Cr. 8vo. 4s. 6d.

—— PORTRAITS OF PLACES. Cr. 8vo. 7s. 6d.

—— THE PRINCESS CASAMASSIMA. Crown 8vo. 6s.—Globe 8vo. 2s.

—— PARTIAL PORTRAITS. Crown 8vo. 6s.

—— THE REVERBERATOR. Crown 8vo. 6s.

—— THE ASPERN PAPERS; LOUISA PALLANT; THE MODERN WARNING. Crn. 8vo. 3s. 6d.

—— A LONDON LIFE. Crown 8vo. 3s. 6d.

—— THE TRAGIC MUSE. 3 vols. Crown 8vo. 31s. 6d.

JAMES (Rev. Herbert). — THE COUNTRY CLERGYMAN AND HIS WORK. Cr. 8vo. 6s.

JAMES (Right Hon. Sir William Milbourne). —THE BRITISH IN INDIA. 8vo. 12s. 6d.

JAMES (Wm.).—THE PRINCIPLES OF PSYCHOLOGY. 2 vols. 8vo. 25s. net.

JARDINE (Rev. Robert).—THE ELEMENTS OF THE PSYCHOLOGY OF COGNITION. Third Edition. Crown 8vo. 6s. 6d.

JEANS (Rev. G. E.).—HAILEYBURY CHAPEL, AND OTHER SERMONS. Fcp. 8vo. 3s. 6d.

—— THE LIFE AND LETTERS OF MARCUS TULLIUS CICERO. Being a Translation of the Letters included in Mr. Watson's Selection. Crown 8vo. 10s. 6d.

JEBB (Prof. R. C.).—THE ATTIC ORATORS, FROM ANTIPHON TO ISAEOS. 2 vols. 8vo. 25s.

—— THE ATTIC ORATORS. Selections from Antiphon, Andocides, Lysias, Isocrates, and Isaeos. Ed. with Notes. 2nd Ed. Fcp.8vo. 6s.

—— MODERN GREECE. Two Lectures. Crown 8vo. 5s.

—— PRIMER OF GREEK LITERATURE. 18mo. 1s.

—— BENTLEY. Crown 8vo. 1s. 6d.; sewed, 1s.

JELLETT (Rev. Dr.).—THE ELDER SON, AND OTHER SERMONS. Crown 8vo. 6s.

—— THE EFFICACY OF PRAYER. 3rd Edition. Crown 8vo. 5s.

JENNINGS (A. C.).—CHRONOLOGICAL TABLES OF ANCIENT HISTORY. With Index. 8vo. 5s.

JENNINGS (A. C.) and LOWE (W. H.).—
THE PSALMS, WITH INTRODUCTIONS AND
CRITICAL NOTES. 2 vols. 2nd Edition.
Crown 8vo. 10s. 6d. each.

JEVONS (W. Stanley).—THE PRINCIPLES OF
SCIENCE: A TREATISE ON LOGIC AND
SCIENTIFIC METHOD. Crown 8vo. 12s. 6d.

—— ELEMENTARY LESSONS IN LOGIC: DE-
DUCTIVE AND INDUCTIVE. 18mo. 3s. 6d.

—— PRIMER OF LOGIC. 18mo. 1s.

—— THE THEORY OF POLITICAL ECONOMY.
3rd Edition. 8vo. 10s. 6d.

—— PRIMER OF POLITICAL ECONOMY. 18mo. 1s.

—— STUDIES IN DEDUCTIVE LOGIC. 2nd
Edition. Crown 8vo. 6s.

—— INVESTIGATIONS IN CURRENCY AND FI-
NANCE. Edited, with an Introduction, by
H. S. FOXWELL, M.A. Illustrated by 20
Diagrams. 8vo. 21s.

—— METHODS OF SOCIAL REFORM. 8vo. 10s. 6d.

—— THE STATE IN RELATION TO LABOUR.
Crown 8vo. 3s. 6d.

—— LETTERS AND JOURNAL. Edited by His
Wife. 8vo. 14s.

—— PURE LOGIC, AND OTHER MINOR WORKS.
Edited by R. ADAMSON, M.A., and HAR-
RIET A. JEVONS. With a Preface by Prof.
ADAMSON. 8vo. 10s. 6d.

JEX-BLAKE (Dr. Sophia).—THE CARE OF
INFANTS: A Manual for Mothers and
Nurses. 18mo. 1s.

JOHNSON (W. E.).—A TREATISE ON TRIGO-
NOMETRY. Crown 8vo. 8s. 6d.

JOHNSON (Prof. W. Woolsey).—CURVE
TRACING IN CARTESIAN CO-ORDINATES.
Crown 8vo. 4s. 6d.

—— A TREATISE ON ORDINARY AND DIFFER-
ENTIAL EQUATIONS. Crown 8vo. 15s.

—— AN ELEMENTARY TREATISE ON THE IN-
TEGRAL CALCULUS. Crown 8vo. 9s.

JOHNSON'S LIVES OF THE POETS.
The Six Chief Lives, with Macaulay's "Life
of Johnson." Edited by MATTHEW ARNOLD.
Crown 8vo. 4s. 6d.

JOHNSON. By LESLIE STEPHEN. Crown
8vo. 1s. 6d.; sewed, 1s.

JONES (D. E.).—EXAMPLES IN PHYSICS.
Containing 1000 Problems, with Answers
and numerous solved Examples. Fcp. 8vo.
3s. 6d.

—— SOUND, LIGHT, AND HEAT. An Elementary Text-Book. Fcp. 8vo.

JONES (F.).—THE OWENS COLLEGE JUNIOR
COURSE OF PRACTICAL CHEMISTRY. With
Preface by Sir HENRY E. ROSCOE. New
Edition. 18mo. 2s. 6d.

—— QUESTIONS ON CHEMISTRY. A Series of
Problems and Exercises in Inorganic and
Organic Chemistry. 18mo. 3s.

JONES (Rev. C. A.) and CHEYNE (C. H.).
—ALGEBRAICAL EXERCISES. Progressively
arranged. 18mo. 2s. 6d.

—— SOLUTIONS OF SOME OF THE EXAMPLES
IN THE ALGEBRAICAL EXERCISES OF MESSRS.
JONES AND CHEYNE. By the Rev. W.
FAILES. Crown 8vo. 7s. 6d.

JUVENAL. THIRTEEN SATIRES OF JUVE-
NAL. With a Commentary by Prof. J. E. B.
MAYOR, M.A. 4th Edition. Vol. I. Crown
8vo. 10s. 6d.—Vol. II. Crown 8vo. 10s. 6d.

SUPPLEMENT to Third Edition, containing
the Principal Changes made in the Fourth
Edition. 5s.

—— THIRTEEN SATIRES. Edited, for the Use
of Schools, with Notes, Introduction, and
Appendices, by E. G. HARDY, M.A. Fcp.
8vo. 5s.

—— SELECT SATIRES. Edited by Prof. JOHN
E. B. MAYOR. Satires X. and XI. 3s. 6d.—
Satires XII. and XVI. Fcp. 8vo. 4s. 6d.

—— THIRTEEN SATIRES. Translated into
English after the Text of J. E. B. MAYOR
by ALEX. LEEPER, M.A. Cr. 8vo. 3s. 6d.

KANT.—KANT'S CRITICAL PHILOSOPHY FOR
ENGLISH READERS. By JOHN P. MAHAFFY,
D.D., and JOHN H. BERNARD, B.D. New
Edition. 2 vols. Crown 8vo. Vol. I. THE
KRITIK OF PURE REASON EXPLAINED AND
DEFENDED. 7s. 6d.—Vol. II. THE "PRO-
LEGOMENA." Translated, with Notes and
Appendices. 6s.

KANT—MAX MÜLLER.—CRITIQUE OF
PURE REASON BY IMMANUEL KANT. Translated by F. MAX MÜLLER. With Introduction by LUDWIG NOIRÉ. 2 vols. 8vo.
16s. each.—Sold separately.. Vol. I. HIS-
TORICAL INTRODUCTION, by LUDWIG NOIRÉ,
etc., etc.; Vol. II. CRITIQUE OF PURE
REASON.

KAVANAGH (Rt. Hon. A. McMurrough):
A Biography compiled by his Cousin, SARAH
L. STEELE, from papers chiefly unpublished.
With Portrait. 8vo.

KAY (Rev. W.).—A COMMENTARY ON ST.
PAUL'S TWO EPISTLES TO THE CORINTHIANS.
Greek Text, with Commentary. 8vo. 9s.

KEARY (Annie).—JANET'S HOME. Globe
8vo. 2s.

—— CLEMENCY FRANKLYN. Globe 8vo. 2s.

—— OLDBURY. Globe 8vo. 2s.

—— A YORK AND A LANCASTER ROSE. Crn.
8vo. 3s. 6d.

—— CASTLE DALY: THE STORY OF AN IRISH
HOME THIRTY YEARS AGO. Cr. 8vo. 3s. 6d.

—— A DOUBTING HEART. Crown 8vo. 6s.

—— NATIONS AROUND. Crown 8vo. 4s. 6d.

KEARY (Eliza).—THE MAGIC VALLEY; OR,
PATIENT ANTOINE. With Illustrations by
"E.V.B." Globe 8vo. 4s. 6d.

KEARY (A. and E.).—THE HEROES OF
ASGARD. Tales from Scandinavian Mythology. Globe 8vo. 2s. 6d.

KEATS.—THE POETICAL WORKS OF JOHN
KEATS. With Notes, by Prof. F. T. PAL-
GRAVE. 18mo. 4s. 6d.

KEATS. By SIDNEY COLVIN. Crown 8vo.
1s. 6d.; sewed, 1s.

—— LETTERS OF KEATS. Edited by SIDNEY
COLVIN. Globe 8vo.

KELLAND (P.) and TAIT (P. G.).—INTRO-
DUCTION TO QUATERNIONS, WITH NUMEROUS
EXAMPLES. 2nd Edition. Cr. 8vo. 7s. 6d.

KELLOGG (Rev. S. H.).—THE LIGHT OF ASIA AND THE LIGHT OF THE WORLD. Cr. 8vo. 7s. 6d.

KEMPE (A. B.).—HOW TO DRAW A STRAIGHT LINE. A Lecture on Linkages. Cr. 8vo. 1s.6d.

KENNEDY (Prof. Alex. W. B.).—THE MECHANICS OF MACHINERY. With Illustrations. Crown 8vo. 12s. 6d.

KERNEL AND THE HUSK (THE): LETTERS ON SPIRITUAL CHRISTIANITY. By the Author of "Philochristus." Crown 8vo. 5s.

KEYNES (J. N.).—STUDIES AND EXERCISES IN FORMAL LOGIC. 2nd Ed. Cr. 8vo. 10s.6d.

—— THE SCOPE AND METHOD OF POLITICAL ECONOMY. 2nd Edition. Crown 8vo.

KIEPERT (H.).—MANUAL OF ANCIENT GEOGRAPHY. Crown 8vo. 5s.

KILLEN (W. D.).—ECCLESIASTICAL HISTORY OF IRELAND, FROM THE EARLIEST DATE TO THE PRESENT TIME. 2 vols. 8vo. 25s.

KINGSLEY (Charles).—NOVELS AND POEMS. Eversley Edition. 13 vols. Gl. 8vo. 5s. each.
WESTWARD HO! 2 vols.—TWO YEARS AGO. 2 vols.—HYPATIA. 2 vols.—YEAST. 1 vol.—ALTON LOCKE. 2 vols.—HEREWARD THE WAKE. 2 vols.—POEMS. 2 vols.

—— Complete Edition OF THE WORKS OF CHARLES KINGSLEY. Cr. 8vo. 3s. 6d. each.
WESTWARD HO! With a Portrait.
HYPATIA.
YEAST.
ALTON LOCKE.
TWO YEARS AGO.
HEREWARD THE WAKE.
POEMS.
THE HEROES; OR, GREEK FAIRY TALES FOR MY CHILDREN.
THE WATER BABIES: A FAIRY TALE FOR A LAND-BABY.
MADAM HOW AND LADY WHY; OR, FIRST LESSONS IN EARTH-LORE FOR CHILDREN.
AT LAST: A CHRISTMAS IN THE WEST INDIES.
PROSE IDYLLS.
PLAYS AND PURITANS.
THE ROMAN AND THE TEUTON. With Preface by Professor MAX MÜLLER.
SANITARY AND SOCIAL LECTURES.
HISTORICAL LECTURES AND ESSAYS.
SCIENTIFIC LECTURES AND ESSAYS.
LITERARY AND GENERAL LECTURES.
THE HERMITS.
GLAUCUS; OR, THE WONDERS OF THE SEA-SHORE. With Coloured Illustrations.
VILLAGE AND TOWN AND COUNTRY SERMONS.
THE WATER OF LIFE, AND OTHER SERMONS.
SERMONS ON NATIONAL SUBJECTS, AND THE KING OF THE EARTH.
SERMONS FOR THE TIMES.

KINGSLEY (Charles)—continued.
GOOD NEWS OF GOD.
THE GOSPEL OF THE PENTATEUCH, AND DAVID.
DISCIPLINE, AND OTHER SERMONS.
WESTMINSTER SERMONS.
ALL SAINTS' DAY, AND OTHER SERMONS.

KINGSLEY (C.).—A Sixpenny Edition OF CHARLES KINGSLEY'S NOVELS. Med. 8vo. 6d. each.
WESTWARD HO!—HYPATIA.—YEAST.—ALTON LOCKE.—TWO YEARS AGO.—HEREWARD THE WAKE.

—— THE WATER BABIES: A FAIRY TALE FOR A LAND BABY. New Edition, with a Hundred New Pictures by LINLEY SAMBOURNE; engraved by J. SWAIN. Fcp. 4to. 12s. 6d.

—— HEALTH AND EDUCATION. Cr. 8vo. 6s.

—— POEMS. Pocket Edition. 18mo. 1s. 6d.

—— SELECTIONS FROM SOME OF THE WRITINGS OF CHARLES KINGSLEY. Crown 8vo. 6s.

—— OUT OF THE DEEP: WORDS FOR THE SORROWFUL. From the Writings of CHARLES KINGSLEY. Extra fcp. 8vo. 3s. 6d.

—— DAILY THOUGHTS. Selected from the Writings of CHARLES KINGSLEY. By His WIFE. Crown 8vo. 6s.

—— THE HEROES; OR, GREEK FAIRY TALES FOR MY CHILDREN. Extra cloth, gilt edges. Presentation Edition. Crown 8vo. 7s. 6d.

—— GLAUCUS; OR, THE WONDERS OF THE SEA SHORE. With Coloured Illustrations, extra cloth, gilt edges. Presentation Edition. Crown 8vo. 7s. 6d.

—— FROM DEATH TO LIFE. Fragments of Teaching to a Village Congregation. With Letters on the "Life after Death." Edited by His WIFE. Fcp. 8vo. 2s. 6d.

—— CHARLES KINGSLEY: HIS LETTERS, AND MEMORIES OF HIS LIFE. Edited by His WIFE. 2 vols. Crown 8vo. 12s.—Cheap Edition, 6s.

—— TRUE WORDS FOR BRAVE MEN. Crown 8vo. 2s. 6d.

KINGSLEY (Henry).—TALES OF OLD TRAVEL. Crown 8vo. 3s. 6d.

KIPLING (Rudyard).—PLAIN TALES FROM THE HILLS. Crown 8vo. 6s.

KITCHENER (F. E.).—GEOMETRICAL NOTE-BOOK. Containing Easy Problems in Geometrical Drawing, preparatory to the Study of Geometry. 4to. 2s.

KLEIN (Dr. E.).—MICRO-ORGANISMS AND DISEASE. An Introduction into the Study of Specific Micro-Organisms. With 121 Engravings. 3rd Edition. Crown 8vo. 6s.

—— THE BACTERIA IN ASIATIC CHOLERA. Crown 8vo. 5s.

KNOX (A.).—DIFFERENTIAL CALCULUS FOR BEGINNERS. Fcp. 8vo. 3s. 6d.

KTESIAS.—THE FRAGMENTS OF THE PERSIKA OF KTESIAS. Edited, with Introduction and Notes, by J. GILMORE, M.A. 8vo. 8s.6d.

KUENEN (Prof. A.).—AN HISTORICO-CRITICAL INQUIRY INTO THE ORIGIN AND COMPOSITION OF THE HEXATEUCH (PENTATEUCH AND BOOK OF JOSHUA). Translated by PHILIP H. WICKSTEED, M.A. 8vo. 14s.

KYNASTON (Herbert, D.D.).—SERMONS PREACHED IN THE COLLEGE CHAPEL, CHELTENHAM. Crown 8vo. 6s.

—— PROGRESSIVE EXERCISES IN THE COMPOSITION OF GREEK IAMBIC VERSE. Extra fcp. 8vo. 5s.
KEY (supplied to Teachers only). 4s. 6d.

—— EXEMPLARIA CHELTONIENSIA. Sive quae discipulis sals Carmina identidem Latine reddenda proposuit ipse reddidit ex cathedra dictavit HERBERT KYNASTON, M.A. Extra fcp. 8vo. 5s.

LABBERTON (R. H.).—NEW HISTORICAL ATLAS AND GENERAL HISTORY. 4to. 15s.

LAFARGUE (Philip).—THE NEW JUDGMENT OF PARIS : A Novel. 2 vols. Gl. 8vo. 12s.

LA FONTAINE'S FABLES. A Selection, with Introduction, Notes, and Vocabulary, by L. M. MORIARTY, B.A. Illustrations by RANDOLPH CALDECOTT. Globe 8vo. 2s. 6d.

LAMB.—COLLECTED WORKS. Edited, with Introduction and Notes, by the Rev. ALFRED AINGER, M.A. Globe 8vo. 5s. each volume.
I. ESSAYS OF ELIA.—II. PLAYS, POEMS, AND MISCELLANEOUS ESSAYS.—III. MRS. LEICESTER'S SCHOOL ; THE ADVENTURES OF ULYSSES; AND OTHER ESSAYS.—IV. TALES FROM SHAKSPEARE.—V. and VI. LETTERS. Newly arranged, with additions.

—— THE LIFE OF CHARLES LAMB. By Rev. ALFRED AINGER, M.A. Uniform with above. Globe 8vo. 5s.

TALES FROM SHAKSPEARE. 18mo. 4s. 6d.
Globe Readings Edition. For Schools. Globe 8vo. 2s.

LAMB. By Rev. ALFRED AINGER, M.A. Crown 8vo. 1s. 6d. ; sewed, 1s.

LANCIANI (Prof. R.).—ANCIENT ROME IN THE LIGHT OF RECENT DISCOVERIES. 4to. 24s.

LAND OF DARKNESS (THE). Along with some further Chapters in the Experiences of The Little Pilgrim. By the Author of " A Little Pilgrim in the Unseen." Crown 8vo. 5s.

LANDAUER (J.).—BLOWPIPE ANALYSIS. Authorised English Edition by JAMES TAYLOR and WM. E. KAY. Ext. fcp. 8vo. 4s. 6d.

LANDOR.—SELECTIONS FROM THE WRITINGS OF WALTER SAVAGE LANDOR. Arranged and Edited by SIDNEY COLVIN. 18mo. 4s. 6d.

LANDOR. By SIDNEY COLVIN. Crown 8vo, 1s. 6d. ; sewed, 1s.

LANE-POOLE.—SELECTIONS FROM THE SPEECHES AND TABLE-TALK OF MOHAMMAD. By S. LANE-POOLE. 18mo. 4s. 6d.

LANG (Andrew).—THE LIBRARY. With a Chapter on Modern Illustrated Books, by AUSTIN DOBSON. Crown 8vo. 3s. 6d.

LANG (Prof. Arnold).—TEXT-BOOK OF COMPARATIVE ANATOMY. Translated by H. M. BERNARD, M.A., F.Z.S., and MATILDA BERNARD. With Preface by Professor E. HAECKEL. 2 vols. Illustrated. 8vo

LANKESTER (Prof. E. Ray).—THE ADVANCEMENT OF SCIENCE : OCCASIONAL ESSAYS AND ADDRESSES. 8vo. 10s. 6d.

—— COMPARATIVE LONGEVITY IN MAN AND THE LOWER ANIMALS. Crn. 8vo. 4s. 6d.

LASLETT (Thomas).—TIMBER AND TIMBER TREES, NATIVE AND FOREIGN. Cr. 8vo. 8s. 6d.

LATIN ACCIDENCE AND EXERCISES ARRANGED FOR BEGINNERS. By WILLIAM WELCH, M.A., and C. G. DUFFIELD, M.A. 18mo. 1s. 6d.

LAWRENCE (LORD). By Sir RICHARD TEMPLE. With Portrait. Crown 8vo. 2s. 6d.

LEAHY (Sergeant).—THE ART OF SWIMMING IN THE ETON STYLE. With Preface by Mrs. OLIPHANT. Crown 8vo. 2s.

LECTURES ON ART. By REGD. STUART POOLE, Professor W. B. RICHMOND, E. J. POYNTER, R.A., J. T. MICKLETHWAITE, and WILLIAM MORRIS. Crown 8vo. 4s. 6d.

LEE (Margaret).—FAITHFUL AND UNFAITHFUL. Crown 8vo. 3s. 6d.

LEGGE (Alfred O.).—THE GROWTH OF THE TEMPORAL POWER OF THE PAPACY. Crown 8vo. 8s. 6d.

LEMON.—THE JEST BOOK. The Choicest Anecdotes and Sayings. Selected by MARK LEMON. 18mo. 4s. 6d.

LEPROSY INVESTIGATION COMMITTEE, JOURNAL OF THE. Ed. by P. S. ABRAHAM, M.A. No. 1. Aug. 1890. 2s. 6d. net.

LETHBRIDGE (Sir Roper). — A SHORT MANUAL OF THE HISTORY OF INDIA. With Maps. Crown 8vo. 5s.
For other Works by this Author, see Indian Text-Books Series, p. 26.

LEVY (Amy).—REUBEN SACHS : A SKETCH. Crown 8vo. 3s. 6d.

LEWIS (Richard).—HISTORY OF THE LIFE-BOAT AND ITS WORK. Crown 8vo. 5s.

LIECHTENSTEIN (Princess Marie).—HOLLAND HOUSE. With Steel Engravings, Woodcuts, and nearly 40 Illustrations by the Woodburytype Permanent Process. 2 vols. Medium 4to. Half mor., elegant. 4l. 4s.

LIGHTFOOT (The Right Rev. Bishop)—ST. PAUL'S EPISTLE TO THE GALATIANS. A Revised Text, with Introduction, Notes, and Dissertations. 10th Edition. 8vo. 12s.

—— ST. PAUL'S EPISTLE TO THE PHILIPPIANS. A Revised Text, with Introduction, Notes and Dissertations. 9th Edition. 8vo. 12s.

—— ST. PAUL'S EPISTLES TO THE COLOSSIANS AND TO PHILEMON. A Revised Text, with Introductions, etc. 9th Edition. 8vo. 12s.

—— THE APOSTOLIC FATHERS. Part I. ST. CLEMENT OF ROME. A Revised Text, with Introductions, Notes, Dissertations, and Translations. 2 vols. 8vo. 32s.

—— THE APOSTOLIC FATHERS. Part II. ST. IGNATIUS to ST. POLYCARP. Revised Texts, with Introductions, Notes, Dissertations, and Translations. 3 vols. 2nd Ed. Demy 8vo. 48s.

—— APOSTOLIC FATHERS. Abridged Edition. With Short Introductions, Greek Text, and English Translation. 8vo.

LIGHTFOOT (Bishop).—Essays on the Work entitled "Supernatural Religion." 8vo. 10s. 6d.

—— A Charge delivered to the Clergy of the Diocese of Durham, Nov. 25th, 1886. Demy 8vo. 2s.

—— Leaders in the Northern Church. Crown 8vo. 6s.

—— Ordination Addresses and Counsels to Clergy. Crown 8vo. 6s.

—— Cambridge Sermons. Crown 8vo. 6s.

—— St. Paul's Sermons. Crown 8vo.

LIGHTWOOD (J. M.)—The Nature of Positive Law. 8vo. 12s. 6d.

LINDSAY (Dr. J. A.).—The Climatic Treatment of Consumption. Cr. 8vo. 5s.

LITTLE PILGRIM IN THE UNSEEN. 24th Thousand. Crown 8vo. 2s. 6d.

LIVINGSTONE. By Thomas Hughes. With Portrait and Map. Crown 8vo. 2s. 6d.

LIVY. By Rev. W. W. Capes. Fcp. 8vo. 1s. 6d.

—— The Hannibalian War. Being part of the 21st and 22nd Books of Livy, adapted for the Use of Beginners. By G. C. Macaulay, M.A. 18mo. 1s. 6d.

—— The Siege of Syracuse. Being part of Books XXIV. and XXV. of Livy. Adapted for the Use of Beginners, with Notes, Exercises, and Vocabulary, by G. Richards, M.A., and A. S. Walpole, M.A. 18mo. 1s. 6d.

—— The Last Two Kings of Macedon. Extracts from the fourth and fifth Decades of Livy. Selected and Edited, with Introduction and Notes, by F. H. Rawlins, M.A. With Maps. Fcp. 8vo. 2s. 6d.

—— Legends of Ancient Rome, from Livy. Adapted and Edited, with Notes, Exercises, and Vocabularies, by H. Wilkinson, M.A. 18mo. 1s. 6d.

—— Book I. Edited, with Notes and Vocabulary, by H. M. Stephenson. 18mo. 1s. 6d.

—— Books II. and III. Edited by H. M. Stephenson, M.A. Fcp. 8vo. 3s. 6d.

—— Book XXI. Adapted from Mr. Capes' Edition. With Notes and Vocabulary by W. W. Capes, M.A., and J. E. Melhuish, M.A. 18mo. 1s. 6d.

—— Book XXII. By the same. 18mo. 1s. 6d.

—— Hannibal's First Campaign in Italy. Books XXI. and XXII. Edited by Rev. W. W. Capes, M.A. Fcp. 8vo. 4s. 6d.

—— Books XXI.—XXV. The Second Punic War. Translated by A. J. Church, M.A., and W. J. Brodribb, M.A. With Maps. Crown 8vo. 7s. 6d.

—— Books XXIII. and XXIV. Edited by G. C. Macaulay. Maps. Fcp. 8vo. 3s. 6d.

LOCK (Rev. J. B.)—Arithmetic for Schools. 4th Edition, revised. Globe 8vo. Complete with Answers, 4s. 6d. Without Answers, 4s. 6d.—Part I., with Answers, 2s. Part II., with Answers, 3s.

—— Key to "Arithmetic for Schools." By the Rev. R. G. Watson. Cr. 8vo. 10s. 6d.

LOCK (Rev. J. B.).—Arithmetic for Beginners. A School Class-Book of Commercial Arithmetic. Globe 8vo. 2s. 6d.

—— Key to "Arithmetic for Beginners." By Rev. R. G. Watson. Crown 8vo. 8s. 6d.

—— A Shilling Book of Arithmetic for Elementary Schools. 18mo. 1s.—With Answers, 1s. 6d.

—— Trigonometry. Globe 8vo. Part I. Elementary Trigonometry. 4s. 6d.—Part II. Higher Trigonometry. 4s. 6d. Complete, 7s. 6d.

—— Key to "Elementary Trigonometry." By H. Carr, B.A. Crown 8vo. 8s. 6d.

—— Trigonometry for Beginners. As far as the Solution of Triangles. Gl. 8vo. 2s. 6d.

—— Key to "Trigonometry for Beginners." Crown 8vo. 6s. 6d.

—— Elementary Statics. Gl. 8vo. 4s. 6d.

—— Dynamics for Beginners. 3rd Edit. Globe 8vo. 4s. 6d.

LOCKE. By Prof. Fowler. Crown 8vo. 1s. 6d.; sewed, 1s.

LOCKYER (J. Norman, F.R.S.).—Elementary Lessons in Astronomy. Illustrations and Diagram. New Edit. 18mo. 5s. 6d.

—— Contributions to Solar Physics. With Illustrations. Royal 8vo. 31s. 6d.

—— Primer of Astronomy. Illustrated. New Edition. 18mo. 1s.

—— Outlines of Physiography: The Movements of the Earth. Crown 8vo. 1s. 6d.

—— The Chemistry of the Sun. 8vo. 14s.

—— The Meteoritic Hypothesis of the Origin of Cosmical Systems. 8vo. 17s. net.

LOCKYER'S ASTRONOMY, Questions on. By J. Forbes-Robertson. 18mo. 1s. 6d.

LOCKYER—SEABROKE.—Star-Gazing Past and Present. By J. Norman Lockyer, F.R.S. Expanded from Shorthand Notes with the assistance of G. M. Seabroke, F.R.A.S. Royal 8vo. 21s.

LODGE (Prof. Oliver J.).—Modern Views of Electricity. Crown 8vo. 6s. 6d.

LOEWY (B.).—Questions and Examples in Experimental Physics, Sound, Light, Heat, Electricity, and Magnetism. Fcp. 8vo. 2s.

—— A Graduated Course of Natural Science, Experimental and Theoretical, for Schools and Colleges. Part I. First Year's Course for Elementary Schools and the Junior Classes of Technical Schools and Colleges. Globe 8vo. 2s.

LOFTIE (Mrs.).—The Dining-Room. With Illustrations. Crown 8vo. 2s. 6d.

LONGFELLOW.—Poems of Places: England and Wales. Edited by H. W Longfellow. 2 vols. 18mo. 9s.

—— Ballads, Lyrics, and Sonnets. From the Poetic Works of Henry Wadsworth Longfellow. 18mo. 4s. 6d.

LONGINUS.—On the Sublime. Translated by H. L. Havell, B.A. With Introduction by Andrew Lang. Crown 8vo. 4s. 6d.

LOWE (W. H.)—The Hebrew Student's Commentary on Zechariah, Hebrew and LXX. 8vo. 10s. 6d.

LOWELL (James Russell). — Complete Poetical Works. 18mo. 4s. 6d.

—— Democracy, and other Addresses. Crown 8vo. 5s.

—— Heartsease and Rue. Crown 8vo. 5s.

—— Political Essays. Ext. cr. 8vo. 7s. 6d.

—— Complete Works. 10 vols. Crn. 8vo. 6s. each. Monthly vols. from October, 1890.

| Vol. | I. Literary Essays, Vol. I. |
|------|------|
| „ | II. „ „ Vol. II. |
| „ | III. „ „ Vol. III. |
| „ | IV. „ „ Vol. IV. |
| „ | V. Political Essays. |
| „ | VI. Literary and Political Addresses. |
| „ | VII. Poetical Works, Vol. I. |
| „ | VIII. „ „ Vol. II. |
| „ | IX. „ „ Vol. III. |
| „ | X. „ „ Vol. IV. |

LUBBOCK (Sir John, Bart.).—The Origin and Metamorphoses of Insects. With Illustrations. Crown 8vo. 3s. 6d.

—— On British Wild Flowers considered in their Relation to Insects. With Illustrations. Crown 8vo. 4s. 6d.

—— Flowers, Fruits, and Leaves. With Illustrations. Crown 8vo. 4s. 6d.

—— Scientific Lectures. With Illustrations. 2nd Edition, revised. 8vo. 8s. 6d.

—— Political and Educational Addresses. 8vo. 8s. 6d.

—— The Pleasures of Life. New Edition. Gl. 8vo. 1s. 6d.; swd., 1s. 60th Thousand. Library Edition. Globe 8vo. 3s. 6d.

Part II. Globe 8vo. 1s. 6d.; sewed, 1s. Library Edition. Globe 8vo. 3s. 6d.

—— Two Parts in one vol. Gl. 8vo. 2s. 6d.

—— Fifty Years of Science: Address to the British Association, 1881. 5th Edition. Crown 8vo. 2s. 6d.

LUCAS (F.).—Sketches of Rural Life. Poems. Globe 8vo. 5s.

LUCIAN.—Extracts from Lucian. Edited, with Introduction, Exercises, Notes, and Vocabulary, by the Rev. J. Bond, M.A., and Rev. A. S. Walpole, M.A. 18mo. 1s. 6d.

LUCRETIUS.—Books I.–III. Edited by J. H. Warburton Lee. Fcp. 8vo. 3s. 6d.

LUPTON (J. H.).—An Introduction to Latin Elegiac Verse Composition. Globe 8vo. 2s. 6d.

—— Latin Rendering of the Exercises in Part II. (xxv.-c.) to Lupton's "Introduction to Latin Elegiac Verse Composition." Globe 8vo. 3s. 6d.

—— An Introduction to Latin Lyric Verse Composition. Gl.8vo. 3s.—Key, 4s. 6d.

LUPTON (Sydney).—Chemical Arithmetic. With 1200 Examples. Fcp. 8vo. 4s. 6d.

—— Numerical Tables and Constants in Elementary Science. Ex. fcp. 8vo. 2s. 6d.

LYALL (Sir Alfred).—Warren Hastings. With Portrait. 2s. 6d.

LYSIAS.—Select Orations. Edited by E. S. Shuckburgh, M.A. Fcp. 8vo. 5s.

LYRE FRANÇAISE (LA). Selected and arranged by G. Masson. 18mo. 4s. 6d.

LYTE (H. C. Maxwell).—Eton College, History of, 1440—1884. With Illustrations. 2nd Edition. 8vo. 21s.

—— The University of Oxford, A History of, from the Earliest Times to the Year 1530. 8vo. 16s.

LYTTON (Rt. Hon. Earl of).—The Ring of Amasis: A Romance. Crown 8vo. 3s. 6d.

MACARTHUR (Margaret). — History of Scotland. 18mo. 2s.

MACAULAY. By J. C. Morison. Crown 8vo. 1s. 6d.; sewed, 1s.

M'CLELLAND (W. J.) and PRESTON (T.). —A Treatise on Spherical Trigonometry. With numerous Examples. Crown 8vo. 8s. 6d.—Or Part I. 4s. 6d.; Part II. 5s.

McCOSH (Rev. Dr. James).—The Method of the Divine Government, Physical and Moral. 8vo. 10s. 6d.

—— The Supernatural in Relation to the Natural. Crown 8vo. 7s. 6d.

—— The Intuitions of the Mind. New Edition. 8vo. 10s. 6d.

—— An Examination of Mr. J. S. Mill's Philosophy. 8vo. 10s. 6d.

—— The Laws of Discursive Thought. A Text-Book of Formal Logic. Crn. 8vo. 5s.

—— Christianity and Positivism. Lectures on Natural Theology and Apologetics. Crown 8vo. 7s. 6d.

—— The Scottish Philosophy, from Hutcheson to Hamilton, Biographical, Expository, Critical. Royal 8vo. 16s.

—— The Emotions. 8vo. 9s.

—— Realistic Philosophy Defended in a Philosophic Series. 2 vols. Vol. I. Expository. Vol. II. Historical and Critical. Crown 8vo. 14s.

—— Psychology. Crown 8vo. I. The Cognitive Powers. 6s. 6d.—II. The Motive Powers. 6s. 6d.

—— First and Fundamental Truths. Being a Treatise on Metaphysics. 8vo. 9s.

MACDONALD (George).—England's Antiphon. Crown 8vo. 4s. 6d.

MACDONELL (John).—The Land Question. 8vo. 10s. 6d.

MACFARLANE (Alexander). — Physical Arithmetic. Crown 8vo. 7s. 6d.

MACGREGOR (James Gordon).—An Elementary Treatise on Kinematics and Dynamics. Crown 8vo. 10s. 6d.

MACKENZIE (Sir Morell).—The Hygiene of the Vocal Organs. 7th Ed. Crn. 8vo. 6s.

MACKIE (Rev. Ellis).—Parallel Passages for Translation into Greek and English. Globe 8vo. 4s. 6d.

MACLAGAN (Dr. T.).—The Germ Theory. 8vo. 10s. 6d.

MACLAREN (Rev. Alexander).—SERMONS PREACHED AT MANCHESTER. 11th Edition. Fcp. 8vo. 4s. 6d.

—— A SECOND SERIES OF SERMONS. 7th Edition. Fcp. 8vo. 4s. 6d.

—— A THIRD SERIES. 6th Edition. Fcp. 8vo. 4s. 6d.

—— WEEK-DAY EVENING ADDRESSES. 4th Edition. Fcp. 8vo. 2s. 6d.

—— THE SECRET OF POWER, AND OTHER SERMONS. Fcp. 8vo. 4s. 6d.

MACLAREN (Arch.).—THE FAIRY FAMILY. A Series of Ballads and Metrical Tales. Crown 8vo, gilt. 5s.

MACLEAN (Surgeon-General W. C.).— DISEASES OF TROPICAL CLIMATES. Crown 8vo. 10s. 6d.

MACLEAR (Rev. Canon).—A CLASS-BOOK OF OLD TESTAMENT HISTORY. With Four Maps. 18mo. 4s. 6d.

—— A CLASS-BOOK OF NEW TESTAMENT HISTORY. Including the connection of the Old and New Testament. 18mo. 5s. 6d.

—— A SHILLING BOOK OF OLD TESTAMENT HISTORY. 18mo. 1s.

—— A SHILLING BOOK OF NEW TESTAMENT HISTORY. 18mo. 1s.

—— A CLASS-BOOK OF THE CATECHISM OF THE CHURCH OF ENGLAND. 18mo. 1s. 6d.

—— A FIRST CLASS-BOOK OF THE CATECHISM OF THE CHURCH OF ENGLAND, WITH SCRIPTURE PROOFS FOR JUNIOR CLASSES AND SCHOOLS. 18mo. 6d.

—— A MANUAL OF INSTRUCTION FOR CONFIRMATION AND FIRST COMMUNION, WITH PRAYERS AND DEVOTIONS. 32mo. 2s.

—— FIRST COMMUNION, WITH PRAYERS AND DEVOTIONS FOR THE NEWLY CONFIRMED. 32mo. 6d.

—— THE ORDER OF CONFIRMATION, WITH PRAYERS AND DEVOTIONS. 32mo. 6d.

—— THE HOUR OF SORROW; OR, THE OFFICE FOR THE BURIAL OF THE DEAD. 32mo. 2s.

—— APOSTLES OF MEDIÆVAL EUROPE. Crn. 8vo. 4s. 6d.

—— AN INTRODUCTION TO THE CREEDS. 18mo. 2s. 6d.

—— AN INTRODUCTION TO THE THIRTY-NINE ARTICLES. 18mo.

M'LENNAN (J. F.).—THE PATRIARCHAL THEORY. Edited and completed by DONALD M'LENNAN, M.A. 8vo. 14s.

—— STUDIES IN ANCIENT HISTORY. Comprising a Reprint of "Primitive Marriage." New Edition. 8vo. 16s.

MACMILLAN (D.). MEMOIR OF DANIEL MACMILLAN. By THOMAS HUGHES, Q.C. Crown 8vo. 4s. 6d.

*Popular Edition.* Crown 8vo, sewed. 1s.

MACMILLAN (Rev. Hugh).—BIBLE TEACHINGS IN NATURE. 15th Ed. Gl. 8vo. 6s.

—— HOLIDAYS ON HIGH LANDS; OR, RAMBLES AND INCIDENTS IN SEARCH OF ALPINE PLANTS. 2nd Edition. Globe 8vo. 6s.

MACMILLAN (Hugh).—THE TRUE VINE; OR, THE ANALOGIES OF OUR LORD'S ALLEGORY. 5th Edition. Globe 8vo. 6s.

—— THE MINISTRY OF NATURE. 8th Edition. Globe 8vo. 6s.

—— THE SABBATH OF THE FIELDS. 6th Edition. Globe 8vo. 6s.

—— THE MARRIAGE IN CANA. Globe 8vo. 6s.

—— TWO WORLDS ARE OURS. 3rd Edition. Globe 8vo. 6s.

—— THE OLIVE LEAF. Globe 8vo. 6s.

—— ROMAN MOSAICS; OR, STUDIES IN ROME AND ITS NEIGHBOURHOOD. Globe 8vo. 6s.

MACMILLAN (M. C.)—FIRST LATIN GRAMMAR. Extra fcp. 8vo. 1s. 6d.

MACMILLAN'S MAGAZINE. Published Monthly. 1s.—Vols. I.—LXII. 7s. 6d. each. [Cloth covers for binding, 1s. each.]

MACMILLAN'S SIX-SHILLING NOVELS. 6s. each vol. Crown 8vo, cloth.

*By the Rev. Charles Kingsley.*

WESTWARD HO!

HYPATIA.

HEREWARD THE WAKE.

TWO YEARS AGO.

YEAST.

ALTON LOCKE. With Portrait.

*By William Black.*

A PRINCESS OF THULE.

STRANGE ADVENTURES OF A PHAETON. Illustrated.

THE MAID OF KILLEENA, AND OTHER TALES.

MADCAP VIOLET.

GREEN PASTURES AND PICCADILLY.

THE BEAUTIFUL WRETCH; THE FOUR MACNICOLS; THE PUPIL OF AURELIUS.

MACLEOD OF DARE. Illustrated.

WHITE WINGS: A YACHTING ROMANCE.

SHANDON BELLS. | YOLANDE.

JUDITH SHAKESPEARE.

THE WISE WOMEN OF INVERNESS, A TALE: AND OTHER MISCELLANIES.

WHITE HEATHER. | SABINA ZEMBRA.

*By Mrs. Craik, Author of "John Halifax Gentleman."*

THE OGILVIES. Illustrated.

THE HEAD OF THE FAMILY. Illustrated.

OLIVE. Illustrated.

AGATHA'S HUSBAND. Illustrated.

MY MOTHER AND I. Illustrated.

MISS TOMMY: A MEDIÆVAL ROMANCE. Illustrated.

KING ARTHUR: NOT A LOVE STORY.

*By J. H. Shorthouse.*

JOHN INGLESANT. | SIR PERCIVAL.

A TEACHER OF THE VIOLIN, AND OTHER TALES.

THE COUNTESS EVE.

3

MACMILLAN'S SIX-SHILLING NO-
VELS—*continued.*

*By Annie Keary.*
A DOUBTING HEART.

*By Henry James.*
THE AMERICAN.
THE EUROPEANS.
DAISY MILLER; AN INTERNATIONAL EPI-
SODE; FOUR MEETINGS.
THE MADONNA OF THE FUTURE, AND
OTHER TALES.
RODERICK HUDSON.
WASHINGTON SQUARE; THE PENSION BEAU-
REPAS; A BUNDLE OF LETTERS.
THE PORTRAIT OF A LADY.
STORIES REVIVED. Two Series. 6s. each.
THE BOSTONIANS.
THE REVERBERATOR.

PLAIN TALES FROM THE HILLS. By RUD-
YARD KIPLING.
REALMAH. By the Author of "Friends in
Council."
OLD SIR DOUGLAS. By the Hon. Mrs.
NORTON.
VIRGIN SOIL. By TOURGENIEF.
THE HARBOUR BAR.
BENGAL PEASANT LIFE. By LAL BEHARI
DAY.
VIDA: STUDY OF A GIRL. By AMY DUNS-
MUIR.
JILL. By E. A. DILLWYN.
NÆRA: A TALE OF ANCIENT ROME. By
J. W. GRAHAM.
THE NEW ANTIGONE: A ROMANCE.
A LOVER OF THE BEAUTIFUL. By the
MARCHIONESS OF CARMARTHEN.
A SOUTH SEA LOVER. By ALFRED ST.
JOHNSTON.

MACMILLAN'S THREE-AND-SIX-
PENNY NOVELS. Crown 8vo. 3s. 6d.

*By Rolf Boldrewood.*
ROBBERY UNDER ARMS: A Story of Life and
Adventure in the Bush and in the Gold-
fields of Australia.
THE MINER'S RIGHT.
THE SQUATTER'S DREAM.

*By Sir H. S. Cunningham.*
THE CŒRULEANS: A VACATION IDYLL
THE HERIOTS.
WHEAT AND TARES.

*By Thomas Hardy.*
THE WOODLANDERS.
WESSEX TALES: STRANGE, LIVELY, AND
COMMONPLACE.

*By Bret Harte.*
CRESSY.
THE HERITAGE OF DEDLOW MARSH, AND
OTHER TALES.

MACMILLAN'S THREE-AND-SIX-
PENNY NOVELS—*continued.*

*By Henry James.*
A LONDON LIFE.
THE ASPERN PAPERS, ETC.

*By Annie Keary.*
CASTLE DALY.
JANET'S HOME.
A YORK AND A LANCASTER ROSE.

*By D. Christie Murray.*
AUNT RACHEL.      |      SCHWARTZ.
THE WEAKER VESSEL.
JOHN VALE'S GUARDIAN.

*By Mrs. Oliphant.*
NEIGHBOURS ON THE GREEN.
JOYCE.
A BELEAGUERED CITY.

FAITHFUL AND UNFAITHFUL. By MAR-
GARET LEE.
REUBEN SACHS. By AMY LEVY.
MISS BRETHERTON. By Mrs. HUMPHRY
WARD.
LOUISIANA, AND THAT LASS O' LOWRIE'S.
By FRANCES HODGSON BURNETT.
THE RING OF AMASIS. By Lord LYTTON.
MAROONED. By W. CLARK RUSSELL.

*Uniform with the above.*

STORM WARRIORS; OR, LIFEBOAT WORK
ON THE GOODWIN SANDS. By the Rev.
JOHN GILMORE.
TALES OF OLD JAPAN. By A. B. MITFORD.
A YEAR WITH THE BIRDS. By W. WARDE
FOWLER. Illustrated by BRYAN HOOK.
TALES OF THE BIRDS. By the same. Illus-
trated by BRYAN HOOK.
LEAVES OF A LIFE. By MONTAGU WIL-
LIAMS, Q.C.
TRUE TALES FOR MY GRANDSONS. By Sir
SAMUEL W. BAKER, F.R.S.
TALES OF OLD TRAVEL. By HENRY
KINGSLEY.

MACMILLAN'S TWO-SHILLING NO-
VELS. Globe 8vo. 2s. each.

*By Mrs. Craik, Author of "John Halifax,
Gentleman."*
TWO MARRIAGES.
AGATHA'S HUSBAND.
THE OGILVIES.

*By Mrs. Oliphant.*
THE CURATE IN CHARGE.
A SON OF THE SOIL.
YOUNG MUSGRAVE.
HE THAT WILL NOT WHEN HE MAY.
A COUNTRY GENTLEMAN.
HESTER.      |      SIR TOM.
THE SECOND SON.
THE WIZARD'S SON.

MACMILLAN'S TWO-SHILLING NO-
VELS—*continued.*

*By the Author of "Hogan, M.P."*
HOGAN, M.P.
THE HONOURABLE MISS FERRARD.
FLITTERS, TATTERS, AND THE COUNSELLOR, WEEDS, AND OTHER SKETCHES.
CHRISTY CAREW.
ISMAY'S CHILDREN.

*By George Fleming.*
A NILE NOVEL. | MIRAGE.
THE HEAD OF MEDUSA. | VESTIGIA.

*By Mrs. Macquoid.*
PATTY.

*By Annie Keary.*
JANET'S HOME. | OLDBURY.
CLEMENCY FRANKLYN.
A YORK AND A LANCASTER ROSE.

*By W. E. Norris.*
MY FRIEND JIM. | CHRIS.

*By Henry James.*
DAISY MILLER; AN INTERNATIONAL EPISODE; FOUR MEETINGS.
RODERICK HUDSON.
THE MADONNA OF THE FUTURE, AND OTHER TALES.
WASHINGTON SQUARE.
PRINCESS CASAMASSIMA.

*By Frances Hodgson Burnett.*
LOUISIANA, AND THAT LASS O' LOWRIE'S. Two Stories.
HAWORTH'S.

*By Hugh Conway.*
A FAMILY AFFAIR. | LIVING OR DEAD.

*By D. Christie Murray.*
AUNT RACHEL.

*By Helen Jackson.*
RAMONA: A STORY.

A SLIP IN THE FENS.

MACMILLAN'S HALF-CROWN SERIES OF JUVENILE BOOKS. Globe 8vo, cloth, extra. 2s. 6d.
OUR YEAR. By the Author of "John Halifax, Gentleman."
LITTLE SUNSHINE'S HOLIDAY. By the Author of "John Halifax, Gentleman."
WHEN I WAS A LITTLE GIRL. By the Author of "St. Olave's."
NINE YEARS OLD. By the Author of "When I was a Little Girl," etc.
A STOREHOUSE OF STORIES. Edited by CHARLOTTE M. YONGE. 2 vols.
AGNES HOPETOUN'S SCHOOLS AND HOLIDAYS. By Mrs. OLIPHANT.

MACMILLAN'S HALF-CROWN SERIES OF JUVENILE BOOKS—*continued.*
THE STORY OF A FELLOW SOLDIER. By FRANCES AWDRY. (A Life of Bishop Patteson for the Young.)
RUTH AND HER FRIENDS: A STORY FOR GIRLS.
THE HEROES OF ASGARD: TALES FROM SCANDINAVIAN MYTHOLOGY. By A. and E. KEARY.
THE RUNAWAY. By the Author of "Mrs. Jerningham's Journal."
WANDERING WILLIE. By the Author of "Conrad the Squirrel."
PANSIE'S FLOUR BIN. Illustrated by ADRIAN STOKES.
MILLY AND OLLY. By Mrs. T. H. WARD. Illustrated by Mrs. ALMA TADEMA.
THE POPULATION OF AN OLD PEAR TREE; OR, STORIES OF INSECT LIFE. From the French of E. VAN BRUYSSEL. Edited by CHARLOTTE M. YONGE. Illustrated.
HANNAH TARNE. By MARY E. HULLAH. Illustrated by W. J. HENNESSY.

*By Mrs. Molesworth. Illustrated by Walter Crane.*
"CARROTS," JUST A LITTLE BOY.
TELL ME A STORY.
THE CUCKOO CLOCK.
A CHRISTMAS CHILD.
ROSY.
THE TAPESTRY ROOM.
GRANDMOTHER DEAR.
HERR BABY.
"US": AN OLD-FASHIONED STORY.
LITTLE MISS PEGGY.
TWO LITTLE WAIFS.
CHRISTMAS-TREE LAND.
FOUR WINDS FARM.
THE RECTORY CHILDREN.

MACMILLAN'S READING BOOKS. Adapted to the English and Scotch Codes.
Primer . . . . . (48 pp.) 18mo, 2d.
Book I. for Standard I. (96 pp.) 18mo, 4d.
Book II. for Standard II. (144 pp.) 18mo, 5d.
Book III. for Standard III. (160 pp.) 18mo, 6d.
Book IV. for Standard IV. (176 pp.) 18mo, 8d.
Book V. for Standard V. (380 pp.) 18mo, 1s.
Book VI. for Standard VI. (430 pp.) Cr.8vo, 2s.

MACMILLAN'S COPY-BOOKS.
*1. Initiatory Exercises and Short Letters.
*2. Words consisting of Short Letters.
*3. Long Letters, with words containing Long Letters. Figures.
*4. Words containing Long Letters.
4A. Practising and Revising Copybook for Nos. 1 to 4.
*5. Capitals, and Short Half-text Words beginning with a Capital.
*6. Half-text Words beginning with a Capital. Figures.
*7. Small-hand and Half-text, with Capitals and Figures.

MACMILLAN'S COPY-BOOKS—*contd.*

*8. Small-hand and Half-text, with Capitals and Figures.
8A. Practising and Revising Copybook for Nos. 5 to 8.
*9. Small-hand Single Head Lines. Figures.
10. Small-hand Single Head Lines. Figures.
*11. Small-hand Double Head Lines. Figures.
12. Commercial and Arithmetical Examples, etc.
12A. Practising and Revising Copybook for Nos. 8 to 12.

The Copybooks may be had in two sizes:
(1) Large Post 4to, 4*d.* each;
(2) Post oblong, 2*d.* each.

The numbers marked * may also be had in Large Post 4to, with GOODMAN'S PATENT SLIDING COPIES. 6*d.* each.

MACMILLAN'S LATIN COURSE. Part I. By A. M. COOK, M.A. 2nd Edition, enlarged. Globe 8vo. 3*s.*
Part II. By the same. Gl. 8vo. 2*s.* 6*d.*

MACMILLAN'S SHORTER LATIN COURSE. By A. M. COOK, M.A. Being an Abridgment of "Macmillan's Latin Course, Part I." Globe 8vo. 1*s.* 6*d.*

MACMILLAN'S LATIN READER. A Latin Reader for the Lower Forms in Schools. By H. J. HARDY. Gl. 8vo. 2*s.* 6*d.*

MACMILLAN'S GREEK COURSE. Edit. by Rev. W. G. RUTHERFORD, M.A. Gl. 8vo.
I. FIRST GREEK GRAMMAR. By the Rev. W. G. RUTHERFORD, M.A. Gl. 8vo. Part I. Accidence, 2*s.*; Part II. Syntax, 2*s.*; or in 1 vol. 3*s.* 6*d.*
II. EASY EXERCISES IN GREEK ACCIDENCE. By H. G. UNDERHILL, M.A. 2*s.*
III. SECOND GREEK EXERCISE BOOK. By Rev. W. A. HEARD, M.A. 2*s.* 6*d.*

MACMILLAN'S GREEK READER. Stories and Legends. A First Greek Reader. With Notes, Vocabulary, and Exercises, by F. H. COLSON, M.A. Globe 8vo. 3*s.*

MACMILLAN'S ELEMENTARY CLASSICS. 18mo. 1*s.* 6*d.* each.

This Series falls into two classes:—
(1) First Reading Books for Beginners, provided not only with *Introductions and Notes*, but with *Vocabularies*, and in some cases with *Exercises* based upon the Text.
(2) Stepping-stones to the study of particular authors, intended for more advanced students, who are beginning to read such authors as Terence, Plato, the Attic Dramatists, and the harder parts of Cicero, Horace, Virgil, and Thucydides.

These are provided with Introductions and Notes, but no *Vocabulary*. The Publishers have been led to provide the more strictly Elementary Books with Vocabularies by the representations of many teachers, who hold that beginners do not understand the use of a Dictionary, and of others who, in the case of middle-class schools where the cost of books is a serious consideration, advocate the Vocabulary system on grounds of economy. It is hoped that the two parts of the Series, fitting into one another, may together fulfil all the requirements of Elementary and Preparatory Schools, and the Lower Forms of Public Schools.

MACMILLAN'S ELEMENTARY CLASSICS—*continued.*

The following Elementary Books, *with Introductions, Notes, and Vocabularies*, and in some cases with *Exercises*, are either ready or in preparation:

LATIN ACCIDENCE AND EXERCISES ARRANGED FOR BEGINNERS. By WILLIAM WELCH, M.A., and C. G. DUFFIELD, M.A.

ÆSCHYLUS.—PROMETHEUS VINCTUS. Edit. by Rev. H. M. STEPHENSON, M.A.

ARRIAN.—SELECTIONS. Edited by JOHN BOND, M.A., and A. S. WALPOLE, M.A.

AULUS GELLIUS, STORIES FROM. By Rev. G. H. NALL, M.A.

CÆSAR. — THE INVASION OF BRITAIN. Being Selections from Books IV. and V. of the "De Bello Gallico." Adapted for Beginners by W. WELCH, and C. G. DUFFIELD.

— THE HELVETIAN WAR. Selected from Book I. of "The Gallic War," arranged for the use of Beginners by W. WELCH, M.A., and C. G. DUFFIELD, M.A.

— THE GALLIC WAR. Scenes from Books V. and VI. Edited by C. COLBECK, M.A.

— THE GALLIC WAR. Book I. Edited by Rev. A. S. WALPOLE, M.A.

— THE GALLIC WAR. Books II. and III. Ed. by Rev. W. G. RUTHERFORD, M.A.

— THE GALLIC WAR. Book IV. Edited by C. BRYANS, M.A.

— THE GALLIC WAR. Books V. and VI. (separately). By the same Editor.

— THE GALLIC WAR. Book VII. Ed. by J. BOND, M.A., and A. S. WALPOLE, M.A.

CICERO.—DE SENECTUTE. Edited by E. S. SHUCKBURGH, M.A.

— DE AMICITIA. Edited by E. S. SHUCKBURGH, M.A.

— STORIES OF ROMAN HISTORY. Edited by Rev. G. E. JEANS, M.A., and A. V. JONES, M.A.

EURIPIDES.—ALCESTIS. By the Rev. M. A. BAYFIELD, M.A.

— HECUBA. Edited by Rev. J. BOND, M.A., and A. S. WALPOLE, M.A.

— MEDEA. Edited by A. W. VERRALL, Litt.D., and Rev. M. A. BAYFIELD, M.A.

EUTROPIUS. Adapted for the use of Beginners by W. WELCH, M.A., and C. G. DUFFIELD, M.A.

HOMER.—ILIAD. Book I. Ed. by Rev. J. BOND, M.A., and A. S. WALPOLE, M.A.

— ILIAD. Book XVIII. THE ARMS OF ACHILLES. Edited by S. R. JAMES, M.A.

— ODYSSEY. Book I. Edited by Rev. J. BOND, M.A., and A. S. WALPOLE, M.A.

HORACE.—ODES. Books I.—IV. Edited by T. E. PAGE, M.A. 1*s.* 6*d.* each.

LIVY. Book I. Edited by H. M. STEPHENSON, M.A.

— THE HANNIBALIAN WAR. Being part of the 21st and 22nd Books of Livy. Adapted for Beginners by G. C. MACAULAY, M.A.

MACMILLAN'S ELEMENTARY CLAS-
SICS—*continued.*

LIVY.—THE SIEGE OF SYRACUSE. Being part of the 24th and 25th Books of Livy. Adapted for Beginners by G. RICHARDS, M.A., and Rev. A. S. WALPOLE, M.A.

— Book XXI. With Notes adapted from Mr. Capes' Edition for Junior Students, by Rev. W. W. CAPES, M.A., and J. E. MELHUISH, M.A.

— Book XXII. By the same Editors.

— LEGENDS OF ANCIENT ROME, FROM LIVY. Adapted for Beginners. With Notes, by H. WILKINSON, M.A.

LUCIAN, EXTRACTS FROM. Edited by J. BOND, M.A., and A. S. WALPOLE, M.A.

NEPOS.—SELECTIONS ILLUSTRATIVE OF GREEK AND ROMAN HISTORY. Edited by G. S. FARNELL, B.A.

OVID.—SELECTIONS. Edited by E. S. SHUCKBURGH, M.A.

— EASY SELECTIONS FROM OVID IN ELE-GIAC VERSE. Arranged for the use of Beginners by H. WILKINSON, M.A.

— STORIES FROM THE METAMORPHOSES. Arranged for the use of Beginners by J. BOND, M.A., and A. S. WALPOLE, M.A.

PHÆDRUS.—SELECT FABLES. Adapted for use of Beginners by Rev. A. S. WAL-POLE, M.A.

THUCYDIDES.—THE RISE OF THE ATHENIAN EMPIRE. Book I. Ch. 89—117 and 128—138. Edited by F. H. COLSON, M.A.

VIRGIL.—GEORGICS. Book I. Edited by T. E. PAGE, M.A.

— GEORGICS. Book II. Edited by Rev. J. H. SKRINE, M.A.

— ÆNEID. Book I. Edited by A. S. WALPOLE, M.A.

— ÆNEID. Book II. Ed. by T. E. PAGE.

— ÆNEID. Book III. Edited by T. E. PAGE, M.A.

— ÆNEID. Book IV. Edit. by Rev. H. M. STEPHENSON, M.A.

— ÆNEID. Book V. Edited by Rev. A. CALVERT, M.A.

— ÆNEID. Book VI. Ed. by T. E. PAGE.

— ÆNEID. Book VII. THE WRATH OF TURNUS. Edited by A. CALVERT, M.A.

— ÆNEID. Book VIII. Edited by Rev. A. CALVERT, M.A.

— ÆNEID. Book IX. Edited by Rev. H. M. STEPHENSON, M.A.

— ÆNEID. Book X. Ed. by S. G. OWEN, M.A.

— SELECTIONS. Edited by E. S. SHUCK-BURGH, M.A.

XENOPHON.—ANABASIS. Edited by W. WELCH, M.A., and C. G. DUFFIELD, M.A.

— — BOOK I., Chaps. i.—viii. Edited by E. A. WELLS, M.A.

— ANABASIS. Book I. Edited by Rev. A. S. WALPOLE, M.A.

— ANABASIS. Book II. Edited by Rev. A. S. WALPOLE, M.A.

MACMILLAN'S ELEMENTARY CLAS-
SICS—*continued.*

XENOPHON. - ANABASIS. Book III. Edit. by Rev. G. H. NALL, M.A.

— ANABASIS. Book IV. Edited by Rev. E. D. STONE, M.A.

— SELECTIONS FROM BOOK IV. OF "THE ANABASIS." Edit. by Rev. E. D. STONE.

— SELECTIONS FROM THE CYROPAEDIA. Edited by Rev. A. H. COOKE, M.A.

The following more advanced books have *Introductions, Notes,* but no *Vocabularies*:

CICERO.—SELECT LETTERS. Edit. by Rev. G. E. JEANS, M.A.

HERODOTUS.—SELECTIONS FROM BOOKS VII. AND VIII. THE EXPEDITION OF XERXES. Edited by A. H. COOKE, M.A.

HORACE.—SELECTIONS FROM THE SATIRES AND EPISTLES. Edited by Rev. W. J. V. BAKER, M.A.

— SELECT EPODES AND ARS POETICA. Edited by H. A. DALTON, M.A.

PLATO.—EUTHYPHRO AND MENEXENUS. Edited by C. E. GRAVES, M.A.

TERENCE.—SCENES FROM THE ANDRIA. Edited by F. W. CORNISH, M.A.

THE GREEK ELEGIAC POETS, FROM CAL-LINUS TO CALLIMACHUS. Selected and Edited by Rev. H. KYNASTON.

THUCYDIDES. Book IV., Chaps. i.—lxi. THE CAPTURE OF SPHACTERIA. Edited by C. E. GRAVES, M.A.

*Other Volumes to follow.*

MACMILLAN'S CLASSICAL SERIES FOR COLLEGES AND SCHOOLS. Fcp. 8vo. Being select portions of Greek and Latin authors, edited, with Introductions and Notes, for the use of Middle and Upper Forms of Schools, or of Candidates for Public Examinations at the Universities and else-where.

ÆSCHINES.—IN CTESIPHONTA. Edited by Rev. T. GWATKIN, M.A., and E. S. SHUCKBURGH, M.A. 5s.

ÆSCHYLUS. — PERSÆ. Edited by A. O. PRICKARD, M.A. With Map. 2s. 6d.

— THE "SEVEN AGAINST THEBES." Edit. by A. W. VERRALL, Litt.D., and M. A. BAYFIELD, M.A. 2s. 6d.

ANDOCIDES.—DE MYSTERIIS. Edited by W. J. HICKIE, M.A. 2s. 6d.

ATTIC ORATORS, SELECTIONS FROM THE. Antiphon, Andocides, Lysias, Isocrates, and Isaeus. Ed. by R. C. JEBB, Litt.D. 5s.

CÆSAR.—THE GALLIC WAR. Edited after Kraner by Rev. J. BOND, M.A., and Rev. A. S. WALPOLE, M.A. With Maps. 4s. 6d.

CATULLUS.—SELECT POEMS. Edited by F. P. SIMPSON, B.A. 3s. 6d. [The Text of this Edition is carefully adapted to School use.]

CICERO.—THE CATILINE ORATIONS. From the German of Karl Halm. Edited by A. S. WILKINS, Litt.D. 2s. 6d.

— PRO LEGE MANILIA. Edited, after Halm, by Prof. A. S. WILKINS, Litt.D. 2s. 6d.

MACMILLAN'S CLASSICAL SERIES—
*continued.*

CICERO.—THE SECOND PHILIPPIC ORATION.
From the German of Karl Halm. Edited,
with Corrections and Additions, by Prof.
J. E. B. MAYOR. 3*s.* 6*d.*

— PRO ROSCIO AMERINO. Edited, after
Halm, by E. H. DONKIN, M.A. 2*s.* 6*d.*

— PRO P. SESTIO. Edited by Rev. H. A.
HOLDEN, M.A. 3*s.* 6*d.*

— SELECT LETTERS. Edited by Prof. R. Y.
TYRRELL, M.A.

DEMOSTHENES.—DE CORONA. Edited by B.
DRAKE, M.A. New and revised edit. 3*s.* 6*d.*

— ADVERSUS LEPTINEM. Edited by Rev.
J. R. KING, M.A. 2*s.* 6*d.*

— THE FIRST PHILIPPIC. Edited, after C.
Rehdantz, by Rev. T. GWATKIN. 2*s.* 6*d.*

EURIPIDES.—HIPPOLYTUS. Edited by Prof.
J. P. MAHAFFY and J. B. BURY. 2*s.* 6*d.*

— MEDEA. Edited by A. W. VERRALL,
Litt.D. 2*s.* 6*d.*

— IPHIGENIA IN TAURIS. Edited by E. B.
ENGLAND, M.A. 3*s.*

— ION. Ed. by M. A. BAYFIELD, M.A. 2*s.*6*d.*

HERODOTUS. Book III. Edited by G. C.
MACAULAY, M.A. 2*s.* 6*d.*

— Book VI. Ed. by Prof. J. STRACHAN, M.A.

— Book VII. Ed. by Mrs. MONTAGU BUTLER.

HOMER.—ILIAD. Books I. IX. XI. XVI.-
XXIV. THE STORY OF ACHILLES. Ed. by
J. H. PRATT, M.A., and W. LEAF, Litt.D. 5*s.*

— ODYSSEY. Book IX. Edited by Prof.
J. E. B. MAYOR, M.A. 2*s.* 6*d.*

— ODYSSEY. Books XXI.—XXIV. THE
TRIUMPH OF ODYSSEUS. Edited by S. G.
HAMILTON, B.A. 2*s.* 6*d.*

HORACE.—THE ODES. Edited by T. E.
PAGE, M.A. 5*s.* (Books I. II. III. and
IV. separately, 2*s.* each.)

— THE SATIRES. Edited by Prof. A.
PALMER, M.A. 5*s.*

— THE EPISTLES AND ARS POETICA. Edit.
by Prof. A. S. WILKINS, Litt.D. 5*s.*

JUVENAL.—THIRTEEN SATIRES. Edited, for
the use of Schools, by E. G. HARDY, M.A.
5*s.* [The Text of this Edition is carefully
adapted to School use.]

— SELECT SATIRES. Edited by Prof. JOHN
E. B. MAYOR. X. and XI. 3*s.* 6*d.* ; XII.—
XVI. 4*s.* 6*d.*

LIVY. Books II. and III. Edited by Rev.
H. M. STEPHENSON, M.A. 3*s.* 6*d.*

— Books XXI. and XXII. Edited by Rev.
W. W. CAPES, M.A. 4*s.* 6*d.*

— Books XXIII. and XXIV. Ed. by G. C.
MACAULAY. With Maps. 3*s.* 6*d.*

— THE LAST TWO KINGS OF MACEDON.
Extracts from the Fourth and Fifth De-
cades of Livy. Selected and Edit. by F. H.
RAWLINS, M.A. With Maps. 2*s.* 6*d.*

LUCRETIUS. Books I.—III. Edited by
J. H. WARBURTON LEE, M.A. 3*s.* 6*d.*

MACMILLAN'S CLASSICAL SERIES—
*continued.*

LYSIAS.—SELECT ORATIONS. Edited by
E. S. SHUCKBURGH, M.A. 5*s.*

MARTIAL.—SELECT EPIGRAMS. Edited by
Rev. H. M. STEPHENSON, M.A. 5*s.*

OVID.—FASTI. Edited by G. H. HALLAM,
M.A. With Maps. 3*s.* 6*d.*

— HEROIDUM EPISTULÆ XIII. Edited by
E. S. SHUCKBURGH, M.A. 3*s.* 6*d.*

— METAMORPHOSES. Books XIII. and XIV.
Edited by C. SIMMONS, M.A. 3*s.* 6*d.*

PLATO.—THE REPUBLIC. Books I.—V.
Edited by T. H. WARREN, M.A. 5*s.*

— LACHES. Edited by M. T. TATHAM,
M.A. 2*s.* 6*d.*

PLAUTUS.—MILES GLORIOSUS. Edited by
Prof. R. Y. TYRRELL, M.A. 3*s.* 6*d.*

— AMPHITRUO. Edited by A. PALMER,
M.A. 3*s.* 6*d.*

— CAPTIVI. Ed. by A. RHYS-SMITH, M.A.

PLINY.—LETTERS. Books I. and II. Edited
by J. COWAN, M.A. 3*s.*

PLINY.—LETTERS. Book III. Edited by Prof.
J. E. B. MAYOR. With Life of Pliny by
G. H. RENDALL. 3*s.* 6*d.*

PLUTARCH. — LIFE OF THEMISTOKLES.
Edited by Rev. H. A. HOLDEN, M.A.,
LL.D. 3*s.* 6*d.*

— LIVES OF GALBA AND OTHO. Edited by
E. G. HARDY, M.A. 5*s.*

POLYBIUS. The History of the Achæan
League as contained in the remains of
Polybius. Edited by W. W. CAPES. 5*s.*

PROPERTIUS.—SELECT POEMS. Edited by
Prof. J. P. POSTGATE, M.A. 5*s.*

SALLUST.—CATILINE AND JUGURTHA. Ed.
by C. MERIVALE, D.D. 3*s.* 6*d.*—Or separately, 2*s.* each.

— BELLUM CATULINÆ. Edited by A. M.
COOK, M.A. 2*s.* 6*d.*

TACITUS.—AGRICOLA AND GERMANIA. Ed
by A. J. CHURCH, M.A., and W. J.
BRODRIBB, M.A. 3*s.* 6*d.*—Or separately,
2*s.* each.

— THE ANNALS. Book VI. By the same
Editors. 2*s.*

— THE HISTORIES. Books I. and II.
Edited by A. D. GODLEY, M.A. 3*s.* 6*d.*

— THE HISTORIES. Books III.—V. By
the same Editor. 3*s.* 6*d.*

TERENCE.—HAUTON TIMORUMENOS. Edit.
by E. S. SHUCKBURGH, M.A. 2*s.* 6*d.*—With
Translation, 3*s.* 6*d.*

— PHORMIO. Ed. by Rev. J. BOND, M.A.,
and Rev. A. S. WALPOLE, M.A. 2*s.* 6*d.*

THUCYDIDES. Book II. Edited by E. C.
MARCHANT, M.A.

— Book IV. Edited by C. E. GRAVES,
M.A. 3*s.* 6*d.*

— Book V. By the same Editor.

— Books VI. and VII. THE SICILIAN EX-
PEDITION. Edited by Rev. P. FROST,
M.A. With Map. 3*s.* 6*d.*

## MACMILLAN'S CLASSICAL SERIES—continued.

VIRGIL.—ÆNEID. Books II. and III. THE NARRATIVE OF ÆNEAS. Edited by E. W. HOWSON, M.A. 2s.

XENOPHON.—HELLENICA. Books I. and II. Edited by H. HAILSTONE, M.A. 2s. 6d.

— CYROPÆDIA. Books VII. and VIII. Ed. by Prof. A. GOODWIN, M.A. 2s. 6d.

— MEMORABILIA SOCRATIS. Edited by A. R. CLUER, B.A. 5s.

— THE ANABASIS. Books I.—IV. Edited by Professors W. W. GOODWIN and J. W. WHITE. Adapted to Goodwin's Greek Grammar. With a Map. 3s. 6d.

— HIERO. Edited by Rev. H. A. HOLDEN, M.A., LL.D. 2s. 6d.

— OECONOMICUS. By the same Editor. With Introduction, Explanatory Notes Critical Appendix, and Lexicon. 5s.

*The following are in preparation:*

DEMOSTHENES.—IN MIDIAM. Edited by Prof. A. S. WILKINS, Litt.D., and HERMAN HAGER, Ph.D.

EURIPIDES.—BACCHAE. Edited by Prof. R. Y. TYRRELL, M.A.

HERODOTUS. Book V. Edited by Prof. J. STRACHAN, M.A.

ISÆOS.—THE ORATIONS. Edited by Prof WM. RIDGEWAY, M.A.

OVID.—METAMORPHOSES. Books I.—III. Edited by C. SIMMONS, M.A.

SALLUST.—JUGURTHA. Edited by A. M COOK, M.A.

TACITUS.—THE ANNALS. Books I. and II Edited by J. S. REID, Litt.D.

*Other Volumes will follow.*

## MACMILLAN'S GEOGRAPHICAL SERIES. Edited by ARCHIBALD GEIKIE, F.R.S., Director-General of the Geologica Survey of the United Kingdom.

THE TEACHING OF GEOGRAPHY. A Practical Handbook for the use of Teachers. Globe 8vo. 9s.

GEOGRAPHY OF THE BRITISH ISLES. By ARCHIBALD GEIKIE, F.R.S. 18mo. 1s.

THE ELEMENTARY SCHOOL ATLAS. 24 Maps in Colours. By JOHN BARTHOLOMEW, F.R.G.S. 4to. 1s.

AN ELEMENTARY CLASS-BOOK OF GENERAL GEOGRAPHY. By HUGH ROBERT MILL, D.Sc. Edin. Illustrated. Cr. 8vo. 3s. 6d.

MAPS AND MAP DRAWING. By W. A. ELDERTON. Pott 8vo. 1s.

GEOGRAPHY OF THE BRITISH COLONIES. By G. M. DAWSON and ALEX. SUTHERLAND.

GEOGRAPHY OF EUROPE. By JAMES SIME, M.A. With Illustrations. Gl. 8vo. 3s.

GEOGRAPHY OF NORTH AMERICA. By Prof. N. S. SHALER.

ELEMENTARY GEOGRAPHY OF INDIA, BURMA, AND CEYLON. By H. F. BLANFORD, F.G.S. Globe 8vo. 2s. 6d.

## MACMILLAN'S SCIENCE CLASS-BOOKS. Fcp. 8vo.

LESSONS IN ELEMENTARY PHYSICS. By Prof. BALFOUR STEWART, F.R.S. New Edition. 4s. 6d. (Questions on, 2s.)

EXAMPLES IN PHYSICS. By Prof. D. E. JONES, B.Sc. 3s. 6d.

QUESTIONS AND EXAMPLES ON EXPERIMENTAL PHYSICS: Sound, Light, Heat, Electricity, and Magnetism. By B. LOEWY, F.R.A.S. Fcp. 8vo. 2s.

A GRADUATED COURSE OF NATURAL SCIENCE FOR ELEMENTARY AND TECHNICAL SCHOOLS AND COLLEGES. Part I. First Year's Course. By the same. Gl. 8vo. 2s.

SOUND, ELEMENTARY LESSONS ON. By Dr. W. H. STONE. 3s. 6d.

ELECTRIC LIGHT ARITHMETIC. By R. E. DAY, M.A. 2s.

A COLLECTION OF EXAMPLES ON HEAT AND ELECTRICITY. By H. H. TURNER. 2s. 6d.

AN ELEMENTARY TREATISE ON STEAM. By Prof. J. PERRY, C.E. 4s. 6d.

ELECTRICITY AND MAGNETISM. By Prof SILVANUS THOMPSON. 4s. 6d.

POPULAR ASTRONOMY. By Sir G. B. AIRY, K.C.B., late Astronomer-Royal. 4s. 6d.

ELEMENTARY LESSONS ON ASTRONOMY. By J. N. LOCKYER, F.R.S. New Edition. 5s. 6d. (Questions on, 1s. 6d.)

LESSONS IN ELEMENTARY CHEMISTRY. By Sir H. ROSCOE, F.R.S. 4s. 6d.—Problems adapted to the same, by Prof. THORPE. With Key. 2s.

OWENS COLLEGE JUNIOR COURSE OF PRACTICAL CHEMISTRY. By F. JONES. With Preface by Sir H. ROSCOE, F.R.S. 2s. 6d.

QUESTIONS ON CHEMISTRY. A Series of Problems and Exercises in Inorganic and Organic Chemistry. By F. JONES. 3s.

OWENS COLLEGE COURSE OF PRACTICAL ORGANIC CHEMISTRY. By JULIUS B. COHEN, Ph.D. With Preface by Sir H. ROSCOE and Prof. SCHORLEMMER. 2s. 6d.

ELEMENTS OF CHEMISTRY. By Prof. IRA REMSEN. 2s. 6d.

EXPERIMENTAL PROOFS OF CHEMICAL THEORY FOR BEGINNERS. By WILLIAM RAMSAY, Ph.D. 2s. 6d.

NUMERICAL TABLES AND CONSTANTS IN ELEMENTARY SCIENCE. By SYDNEY LUPTON, M.A. 2s. 6d.

PHYSICAL GEOGRAPHY, ELEMENTARY LESSONS IN. By ARCHIBALD GEIKIE, F.R.S. 4s. 6d. (Questions on, 1s. 6d.)

ELEMENTARY LESSONS IN PHYSIOLOGY. By T. H. HUXLEY, F.R.S. 4s. 6d. (Questions on, 1s. 6d.)

LESSONS IN ELEMENTARY ANATOMY. By ST. G. MIVART, F.R.S. 6s. 6d.

LESSONS IN ELEMENTARY BOTANY. By Prof. D. OLIVER, F.R.S. 4s. 6d.

DISEASES OF FIELD AND GARDEN CROPS. By W. G. SMITH. 4s. 6d.

LESSONS IN LOGIC, INDUCTIVE AND DEDUCTIVE. By W. S. JEVONS, LL.D. 3s. 6d.

POLITICAL ECONOMY FOR BEGINNERS. By Mrs. FAWCETT. With Questions. 2s. 6d.

**MACMILLAN'S SCIENCE CLASS-BOOKS** *continued.*

THE ECONOMICS OF INDUSTRY. By Prof. A. MARSHALL and M. P. MARSHALL. 2s. 6d.

ELEMENTARY LESSONS IN THE SCIENCE OF AGRICULTURAL PRACTICE. By Prof. H. TANNER. 3s. 6d.

CLASS-BOOK OF GEOGRAPHY. By C. B. CLARKE, F.R.S. 3s. 6d.; sewed, 3s.

SHORT GEOGRAPHY OF THE BRITISH ISLANDS. By J. R. GREEN and ALICE S. GREEN. With Maps. 3s. 6d.

**MACMILLAN'S PROGRESSIVE FRENCH COURSE.** By G. EUGÈNE FASNACHT. Extra fcp. 8vo.

I. FIRST YEAR, CONTAINING EASY LESSONS IN THE REGULAR ACCIDENCE. Thoroughly revised Edition. 1s.

II. SECOND YEAR, CONTAINING AN ELEMENTARY GRAMMAR. With copious Exercises, Notes, and Vocabularies. New Edition, enlarged. 2s.

III. THIRD YEAR, CONTAINING A SYSTEMATIC SYNTAX AND LESSONS IN COMPOSITION. 2s. 6d.

THE TEACHER'S COMPANION TO THE SAME. With copious Notes, Hints for different renderings, Synonyms, Philological Remarks, etc. 1st Year, 4s. 6d. 2nd Year, 4s. 6d. 3rd Year, 4s. 6d.

**MACMILLAN'S PROGRESSIVE FRENCH READERS.** By G. EUGÈNE FASNACHT. Extra fcp. 8vo.

I. FIRST YEAR, CONTAINING TALES, HISTORICAL EXTRACTS, LETTERS, DIALOGUES, FABLES, BALLADS, NURSERY SONGS, etc. With Two Vocabularies: (1) In the Order of Subjects; (2) In Alphabetical Order. 2s. 6d.

II. SECOND YEAR, CONTAINING FICTION IN PROSE AND VERSE, HISTORICAL AND DESCRIPTIVE EXTRACTS, ESSAYS, LETTERS, etc. 2s. 6d.

**MACMILLAN'S FRENCH COMPOSITION.** By G. EUGÈNE FASNACHT. Extra fcp. 8vo.

Part I. ELEMENTARY. 2s. 6d. — Part II. ADVANCED.

THE TEACHER'S COMPANION TO THE SAME. Part I. 4s. 6d.

**MACMILLAN'S FRENCH READINGS FOR CHILDREN.** By G. E. FASNACHT. Illustrated. Globe 8vo.

**MACMILLAN'S PROGRESSIVE GERMAN COURSE.** By G. EUGÈNE FASNACHT. Extra fcp. 8vo.

I. FIRST YEAR, CONTAINING EASY LESSONS ON THE REGULAR ACCIDENCE. 1s. 6d.

II. SECOND YEAR, CONTAINING CONVERSATIONAL LESSONS ON SYSTEMATIC ACCIDENCE AND ELEMENTARY SYNTAX, WITH PHILOLOGICAL ILLUSTRATIONS AND ETYMOLOGICAL VOCABULARY. New Edition, enlarged. 3s. 6d.

THE TEACHER'S COMPANION TO THE SAME. 1st Year, 4s. 6d.; 2nd Year, 4s. 6d.

**MACMILLAN'S PROGRESSIVE GERMAN READERS.** By G. EUGÈNE FASNACHT. Extra fcap. 8vo.

I. FIRST YEAR, CONTAINING AN INTRODUCTION TO THE GERMAN ORDER OF WORDS, WITH COPIOUS EXAMPLES, EXTRACTS FROM GERMAN AUTHORS IN PROSE AND POETRY, NOTES, VOCABULARIES. 2s. 6d.

**MACMILLAN'S GERMAN COMPOSITION.** By G. E. FASNACHT. Extra fcp. 8vo.—Part I. FIRST COURSE: PARALLEL GERMAN-ENGLISH EXTRACTS, PARALLEL ENGLISH-GERMAN SYNTAX. 2s. 6d.

**MACMILLAN'S SERIES OF FOREIGN SCHOOL CLASSICS.** Edited by G. E. FASNACHT. 18mo.

Select works of the best foreign Authors, with suitable Notes and Introductions based on the latest researches of French and German Scholars by practical masters and teachers.

### FRENCH.

CORNEILLE.—LE CID. Edited by G. E. FASNACHT. 1s.

DUMAS.—LES DEMOISELLES DE ST. CYR. Edited by VICTOR OGER. 1s. 6d.

FRENCH READINGS FROM ROMAN HISTORY. Selected from various Authors. Edited by C. COLBECK, M.A. 4s. 6d.

LA FONTAINE'S FABLES. Books I.—VI. Ed. by L. M. MORIARTY. [*In preparation.*

MOLIÈRE.—LES FEMMES SAVANTES. By G. E. FASNACHT. 1s.

— LE MISANTHROPE. By the same. 1s.

— LE MÉDECIN MALGRÉ LUI. By the same. 1s.

— L'AVARE. Edited by L. M. MORIARTY. 1s.

— LE BOURGEOIS GENTILHOMME. By the same. 1s. 6d.

RACINE.—BRITANNICUS. Edited by EUGÈNE PELLISSIER. 2s.

SAND (George).—LA MARE AU DIABLE. Edited by W. E. RUSSELL, M.A. 1s.

SANDEAU (Jules).—MADEMOISELLE DE LA SEIGLIÈRE. Edit. by H. C. STEEL. 1s. 6d.

THIERS'S HISTORY OF THE EGYPTIAN EXPEDITION. Edited by Rev. H. A. BULL, M.A.

VOLTAIRE.—CHARLES XII. Edited by G. E. FASNACHT. 3s. 6d.

### GERMAN.

FREYTAG.—DOKTOR LUTHER. Edited by FRANCIS STORR, M.A. [*In preparation.*

GOETHE.—GÖTZ VON BERLICHINGEN. Edit. by H. A. BULL, M.A. 2s.

— FAUST. Part I. Ed. by Miss J. LEE. 4s. 6d.

HEINE.—SELECTIONS FROM THE REISEBILDER AND OTHER PROSE WORKS. Edit. by C. COLBECK, M.A. 2s. 6d.

LESSING.—MINNA VON BARNHELM. Edited by J. SIME, M.A. [*In preparation.*

SCHILLER.—DIE JUNGFRAU VON ORLEANS. Edited by JOSEPH GOSTWICK. 2s. 6d.

**MACMILLAN'S FOREIGN SCHOOL CLASSICS**—*continued.*

SCHILLER.—WALLENSTEIN. Part I. DAS LAGER. Edited by H. B. COTTERILL, M.A. 2s.

— MARIA STUART. Edited by C. SHELDON, M.A., D.Lit. 2s. 6d.

— WILHELM TELL. Edited by G. E. FASNACHT. 2s. 6d.

— SELECTIONS FROM SCHILLER'S LYRICAL POEMS. Edited by E. J. TURNER, M.A., and E. D. A. MORSHEAD, M.A. 2s. 6d.

UHLAND.—SELECT BALLADS. Adapted as a First Easy Reading Book for Beginners. Edited by G. E. FASNACHT. 1s.

**MACMILLAN'S PRIMARY SERIES OF FRENCH AND GERMAN READING BOOKS.** Edited by G. EUGÈNE FASNACHT. With Illustrations. Globe 8vo.

CORNAZ.—NOS ENFANTS ET LEURS AMIS. Edited by EDITH HARVEY. 1s. 6d.

DE MAISTRE.—LA JEUNE SIBÉRIENNE ET LE LÉPREUX DE LA CITÉ D'AOSTE. Edit. by S. BARLET, B.Sc. 1s. 6d.

FLORIAN.—SELECT FABLES. Edited by CHARLES YELD, M.A. 1s. 6d.

GRIMM.—KINDER- UND HAUSMÄRCHEN. Selected and Edited by G. E. FASNACHT. Illustrated. 2s. 6d.

HAUFF.—DIE KARAVANE. Edited by HERMAN HAGER, Ph.D. With Exercises by G. E. FASNACHT. 3s.

LA FONTAINE.—FABLES. A Selection, by L. M. MORIARTY, M.A. With Illustrations by RANDOLPH CALDECOTT. 2s. 6d.

MOLESWORTH.—FRENCH LIFE IN LETTERS. By Mrs. MOLESWORTH. 1s. 6d.

PERRAULT.—CONTES DE FÉES. Edited by G. E. FASNACHT. 1s. 6d.

SCHMID.—HEINRICH VON EICHENFELS. Ed. by G. E. FASNACHT. 2s. 6d.

**MACNAMARA (C.).**—A HISTORY OF ASIATIC CHOLERA. Crown 8vo. 10s. 6d.

**MACQUOID (K. S.).**—PATTY. Globe 8vo. 2s.

**MADAGASCAR : AN HISTORICAL AND DESCRIPTIVE ACCOUNT OF THE ISLAND AND ITS FORMER DEPENDENCIES.** By Captain S. OLIVER, F.S.A. 2 vols. Med. 8vo. 2l. 12s. 6d.

**MADAME TABBY'S ESTABLISHMENT.** By KARI. Illustrated by L. WAIN. Crown 8vo. 4s. 6d.

**MADOC (Fayr).**—THE STORY OF MELICENT. Crown 8vo. 4s. 6d.

**MAGUIRE (J. F.).**—YOUNG PRINCE MARIGOLD. Illustrated. Globe 8vo. 4s. 6d.

**MAHAFFY (Rev. Prof. J. P.).**—SOCIAL LIFE IN GREECE, FROM HOMER TO MENANDER. 6th Edition. Crown 8vo. 9s.

—— GREEK LIFE AND THOUGHT FROM THE AGE OF ALEXANDER TO THE ROMAN CONQUEST. Crown 8vo. 12s. 6d.

—— RAMBLES AND STUDIES IN GREECE. Illustrated. 3rd Edition. Crn. 8vo. 10s. 6d.

—— A HISTORY OF CLASSICAL GREEK LITERATURE. 2 vols. Crown 8vo. Vol. I. The Poets. With an Appendix on Homer by Prof. SAYCE. 9s.—Vol. II. The Prose Writers. In 2 Parts, 4s. 6d. each

**MAHAFFY (Rev. Prof. J. P.).**—THE GREEK WORLD UNDER ROMAN SWAY, FROM POLYBIUS TO PLUTARCH. Crown 8vo. 10s. 6d.

—— GREEK ANTIQUITIES. Illust. 18mo. 1s.

—— EURIPIDES. 18mo. 1s. 6d.

—— THE DECAY OF MODERN PREACHING: AN ESSAY. Crown 8vo. 3s. 6d.

—— THE PRINCIPLES OF THE ART OF CONVERSATION. 2nd Ed. Crown 8vo. 4s. 6d.

**MAHAFFY (Rev. Prof. J. P.) and ROGERS (J. E.).**—SKETCHES FROM A TOUR THROUGH HOLLAND AND GERMANY. Illustrated by J. E. ROGERS. Extra crown 8vo. 10s. 6d.

**MAHAFFY (Prof. J. P.) and BERNARD (J. H.).**—KANT'S CRITICAL PHILOSOPHY FOR ENGLISH READERS. A new and completed Edition in 2 vols. Crown 8vo.—Vol. I. THE KRITIK OF PURE REASON EXPLAINED AND DEFENDED. 7s. 6d.—Vol. II. THE "PROLEGOMENA." Translated, with Notes and Appendices. 6s.

**MAITLAND (F. W.).**—PLEAS OF THE CROWN FOR THE COUNTY OF GLOUCESTER, A.D. 1221. Edited by F. W. MAITLAND. 8vo. 7s. 6d.

—— JUSTICE AND POLICE. Cr. 8vo. 3s. 6d.

**MALET (Lucas).**—MRS. LORIMER: A SKETCH IN BLACK AND WHITE. Cr. 8vo. 4s. 6d.

**MANCHESTER SCIENCE LECTURES FOR THE PEOPLE.** Eighth Series, 1876—77. With Illustrations. Cr. 8vo. 2s.

**MANSFIELD (C. B.).**—A THEORY OF SALTS. Crown 8vo. 14s.

—— AERIAL NAVIGATION. Cr. 8vo. 10s. 6d.

**MARCUS AURELIUS ANTONINUS.**—BOOK IV. OF THE MEDITATIONS. The Greek Text Revised. With Translation and Commentary, by HASTINGS CROSSLEY, M.A. 8vo. 6s.

**MARKHAM (C. R.).**—LIFE OF ROBERT FAIRFAX, OF STEETON. 8vo. 12s. 6d.

**MARRIOTT (J. A. R.).**—THE MAKERS OF MODERN ITALY: MAZZINI, CAVOUR, GARIBALDI. Three Oxford Lectures. Crown 8vo. 1s. 6d.

**MARSHALL (Prof. Alfred).**—PRINCIPLES OF ECONOMICS. 2 vols. 8vo. Vol. 1. 12s. 6d. net.

**MARSHALL (Prof. A. and Mary P.).**—THE ECONOMICS OF INDUSTRY. Ex.fcp.8vo. 2s.6d.

**MARSHALL (J. M.).**—A TABLE OF IRREGULAR GREEK VERBS. 8vo. 1s.

**MARTEL (Chas.).**—MILITARY ITALY. With Map. 8vo. 12s. 6d.

**MARTIAL.**—SELECT EPIGRAMS FOR ENGLISH READERS. Translated by W. T. WEBB, M.A. Extra fcp. 8vo. 4s. 6d.

—— SELECT EPIGRAMS. Edited by Rev. H. M. STEPHENSON, M.A. Fcp. 8vo. 5s.

**MARTIN (Frances).**—THE POET'S HOUR. Poetry Selected and Arranged for Children. 12mo. 2s. 6d.

—— SPRING-TIME WITH THE POETS. 18mo. 3s. 6d.

—— ANGELIQUE ARNAULD, Abbess of Port Royal. Crown 8vo. 4s. 6d.

MARTIN (Frederick).—The History of Lloyd's, and of Marine Insurance in Great Britain. 8vo. 14s.

MARTINEAU (Harriet). — Biographical Sketches, 1852—75. Crown 8vo. 6s.

MARTINEAU (Dr. James).—Spinoza. 2nd Edition. Crown 8vo. 6s.

MARTINEAU (Miss C. A.).—Easy Lessons on Heat. Globe 8vo. 2s. 6d.

MASSON (Prof. David).—Recent British Philosophy. 3rd Edition. Cr. 8vo. 6s.

—— Drummond of Hawthornden. Crown 8vo. 10s. 6d.

—— Wordsworth, Shelley, Keats, and other Essays. Crown 8vo. 5s.

—— Chatterton: A Story of the Year 1770. Crown 8vo. 5s.

—— Life of Milton. See "Milton."

—— Milton's Poems. See "Milton."

—— De Quincey. Cr. 8vo. 1s. 6d. ; sewed, 1s.

MASSON (Gustave).—A Compendious Dictionary of the French Language (French-English and English-French). Crown 8vo. 6s.

—— La Lyre Française. Selected and arranged, with Notes. Vignette. 18mo. 4s. 6d.

MASSON (Mrs.).—Three Centuries of English Poetry. Being Selections from Chaucer to Herrick. Globe 8vo. 3s. 6d.

MATHEWS.—The Life of Charles J. Mathews. Edited by Charles Dickens. With Portraits. 2 vols. 8vo. 25s.

MATTHEWS (G. F.).—Manual of Logarithms. 8vo. 5s. net.

MATURIN (Rev. W.).—The Blessedness of the Dead in Christ. Cr. 8vo. 7s. 6d.

MAUDSLEY (Dr. Henry).—The Physiology of Mind. Crown 8vo. 10s. 6d.

—— The Pathology of Mind. 8vo. 18s.

—— Body and Mind. Crown 8vo. 6s. 6d.

MAURICE.—Life of Frederick Denison Maurice. By his Son, Frederick Maurice, Two Portraits. 3rd Ed. 2 vols. Demy 8vo. 36s.

Popular Edition (4th Thousand) 2 vols. Crown 8vo. 16s.

MAURICE (Frederick Denison).—The Kingdom of Christ. 3rd Ed. 2 vols. Cr. 8vo. 12s.

—— Lectures on the Apocalypse. 2nd Edition. Crown 8vo. 6s.

—— Social Morality. 3rd Ed. Cr. 8vo. 6s.

—— The Conscience. Lectures on Casuistry. 3rd Edition. Crown 8vo. 4s. 6d.

—— Dialogues on Family Worship. Crown 8vo. 4s. 6d.

—— The Patriarchs and Lawgivers of the Old Testament. 7th Ed. Cr. 8vo. 4s. 6d.

—— The Prophets and Kings of the Old Testament. 5th Edition. Crown 8vo. 6s.

—— The Gospel of the Kingdom of Heaven. 3rd Edition. Crown 8vo. 6s.

—— The Gospel of St. John. 8th Edition. Crown 8vo. 6s.

MAURICE (F. D.).—The Epistles of St. John. 4th Edition. Crown 8vo. 6s.

—— Expository Sermons on the Prayer-Book; and on the Lord's Prayer. New Edition. Crown 8vo. 6s.

—— Theological Essays. 4th Edition. Crn. 8vo. 6s.

—— The Doctrine of Sacrifice deduced from the Scriptures. 2nd Edition. Crown 8vo. 6s.

—— Moral and Metaphysical Philosophy. 4th Edition. 2 vols. 8vo. 16s.

—— The Religions of the World. 6th Edition. Crown 8vo. 4s. 6d.

—— On the Sabbath Day; the Character of the Warrior; and on the Interpretation of History. Fcp. 8vo. 2s. 6d.

—— Learning and Working. Cr. 8vo. 4s. 6d.

—— The Lord's Prayer, the Creed, and the Commandments. 18mo. 1s.

—— Sermons Preached in Country Churches. 2nd Edition. Crown 8vo. 6s.

—— The Friendship of Books, and other Lectures. 3rd Edition. Cr. 8vo. 4s. 6d.

—— The Unity of the New Testament. 2nd Edition. 2 vols. Crown 8vo. 12s.

—— Lessons of Hope. Readings from the Works of F. D. Maurice. Selected by Rev. J. Ll. Davies, M.A. Crown 8vo. 5s.

—— The Communion Service from the Book of Common Prayer, with Select Readings from the Writings of the Rev. F. D. Maurice. Edited by the Right Rev. Bishop Colenso. 16mo. 2s. 6d.

MAXWELL.—Professor Clerk Maxwell, a Life of. By Prof. L. Campbell, M.A., and W. Garnett, M.A. 2nd Edition. Crown 8vo. 7s. 6d.

MAYER (Prof. A. M.).—Sound. A Series of Simple, Entertaining, and Inexpensive Experiments in the Phenomena of Sound. With Illustrations. Crown 8vo. 3s. 6d.

MAYER (Prof. A. M.) and BARNARD (C.)—Light. A Series of Simple, Entertaining, and Useful Experiments in the Phenomena of Light. Illustrated. Crown 8vo. 2s. 6d.

MAYOR (Prof. John E. B.).—A First Greek Reader. New Edition. Fcp. 8vo. 4s. 6d.

—— Autobiography of Matthew Robinson. Fcp. 8vo. 5s.

—— A Bibliographical Clue to Latin Literature. Crown 8vo. 10s. 6d. [See also under "Juvenal."]

MAYOR (Prof. Joseph B.).—Greek for Beginners. Fcp. 8vo. Part I. 1s. 6d.—Parts II. and III. 3s. 6d.—Complete, 4s. 6d.

MAZINI (Linda).—In the Golden Shell. With Illustrations. Globe 8vo. 4s. 6d.

MELBOURNE.—Memoirs of Viscount Melbourne. By W. M. Torrens. With Portrait. 2nd Edition. 2 vols. 8vo. 32s.

MELDOLA (Prof. R.).—The Chemistry of Photography. Crown 8vo. 6s.

MELDOLA (Prof. R.) and WHITE (Wm.).—Report on the East Anglian Earthquake of 22nd April, 1884. 8vo. 3s. 6d.

MELEAGER: FIFTY POEMS OF. Translated by WALTER HEADLAM. Fcp. 4to. 7s. 6d.

MENDENHALL (T. C.).—A CENTURY OF ELECTRICITY. Crown 8vo. 4s. 6d.

MERCIER (Dr. C.).—THE NERVOUS SYSTEM AND THE MIND. 8vo. 12s. 6d.

MERCUR (Prof. J.).—ELEMENTS OF THE ART OF WAR. 8vo. 17s.

MEREDITH (George).—A READING OF EARTH. Extra fcp. 8vo. 5s.

—— POEMS AND LYRICS OF THE JOY OF EARTH. Extra fcp. 8vo. 6s.

—— BALLADS AND POEMS OF TRAGIC LIFE. Crown 8vo. 6s.

MEYER (Ernst von).—HISTORY OF CHEMISTRY. Trans. by G. MacGOWAN, M.A. 8vo.

MIALL.—LIFE OF EDWARD MIALL. By his Son, ARTHUR MIALL. 8vo. 10s. 6d.

MICHELET. — A SUMMARY OF MODERN HISTORY. Translated by M. C. M. SIMPSON. Globe 8vo. 4s. 6d.

MILL (H. R.).—ELEMENTARY CLASS-BOOK OF GENERAL GEOGRAPHY. Cr. 8vo. 3s. 6d.

MILLAR (J.B.).—ELEMENTS OF DESCRIPTIVE GEOMETRY. 2nd Edition. Crown 8vo. 6s.

MILLER (R. Kalley).—THE ROMANCE OF ASTRONOMY. 2nd Ed. Cr. 8vo. 4s. 6d.

MILLIGAN (Rev. Prof. W.).—THE RESURRECTION OF OUR LORD. 2nd Ed. Cr. 8vo. 5s.

—— THE REVELATION OF ST. JOHN. 2nd Edition. Crown 8vo. 7s. 6d.

MILNE (Rev. John J.).—WEEKLY PROBLEM PAPERS. Fcp. 8vo. 4s. 6d.

—— COMPANION TO WEEKLY PROBLEMS. Cr. 8vo. 10s. 6d.

—— SOLUTIONS OF WEEKLY PROBLEM PAPERS. Crown 8vo. 10s. 6d.

MILNE (Rev. J. J.) and DAVIS (R. F.).—GEOMETRICAL CONICS. Part I. THE PARABOLA. Crown 8vo. 2s.

MILTON.—THE LIFE OF JOHN MILTON. By Prof. DAVID MASSON. Vol. I., 21s.; Vol. III., 18s.; Vols. IV. and V., 32s.; Vol. VI., with Portrait, 21s.

—— POETICAL WORKS. Edited, with Introductions and Notes, by Prof. DAVID MASSON, M.A. 3 vols. 8vo. 2l. 2s. (Uniform with the Cambridge Shakespeare.)

—— POETICAL WORKS. Ed. by Prof. MASSON. 3 vols. Fcp. 8vo. 15s.

—— POETICAL WORKS. (Globe Edition.) Ed. by Prof. MASSON. Globe 8vo. 3s. 6d.

—— PARADISE LOST. Books I. and II. Ed., with Introduction and Notes, by Prof. M. MACMILLAN. Globe 8vo. 1s. 9d.; sewed, 1s. 6d. (Or separately, 1s. each sewed.)

—— L'ALLEGRO, IL PENSEROSO, LYCIDAS, ARCADES, SONNETS, ETC. Edited by Prof. WM. BELL, M.A. Gl. 8vo. 1s. 9d.; sewed, 1s.

—— COMUS. Edited by Prof. WM. BELL, M.A. Globe 8vo. 1s. 3d.; sewed, 1s.

—— SAMSON AGONISTES. By H. M. PERCIVAL, M.A. Globe 8vo. 2s.; sewed, 1s. 9d.

MILTON. By MARK PATTISON. Cr. 8vo. 1s. 6d.; sewed, 1s.

MILTON. By Rev. STOPFORD A. BROOKE, M.A. Fcp. 8vo. 1s. 6d.

—— Large Paper Edition. 21s. net.

MINCHIN (Rev. Prof. G. M.).—NATURÆ VERITAS. Fcp. 8vo. 2s. 6d.

MINTO (W.).—THE MEDIATION OF RALPH HARDELOT. 3 vols. Crown 8vo. 31s. 6d.

—— DEFOE. Crown 8vo. 1s. 6d.; sewed, 1s.

MITFORD (A. B.).—TALES OF OLD JAPAN. With Illustrations. Crown 8vo. 3s. 6d.

MIVART (St. George).—LESSONS IN ELEMENTARY ANATOMY. 18mo. 6s. 6d.

MIXTER (Prof. W. G.).—AN ELEMENTARY TEXT-BOOK OF CHEMISTRY. 2nd Edition. Crown 8vo. 7s. 6d.

MIZ MAZE (THE); OR, THE WINKWORTH PUZZLE. A Story in Letters by Nine Authors. Crown 8vo. 4s. 6d.

MOHAMMAD.—THE SPEECHES AND TABLE-TALK OF THE PROPHET. Translated by STANLEY LANE-POOLE. 18mo. 4s. 6d.

MOLESWORTH (Mrs.). Illustrated by WALTER CRANE.

HERR BABY. Globe 8vo. 2s. 6d.

GRANDMOTHER DEAR. Globe 8vo. 2s. 6d.

THE TAPESTRY ROOM. Globe 8vo. 2s. 6d.

A CHRISTMAS CHILD. Globe 8vo. 2s. 6d.

ROSY. Globe 8vo. 2s. 6d.

TWO LITTLE WAIFS. Globe 8vo. 2s. 6d.

CHRISTMAS TREE LAND. Gl. 8vo. 2s. 6d.

"US": AN OLD-FASHIONED STORY. Globe 8vo. 2s. 6d.

"CARROTS," JUST A LITTLE BOY. Globe 8vo. 2s. 6d.

TELL ME A STORY. Globe 8vo. 2s. 6d.

THE CUCKOO CLOCK. Globe 8vo. 2s. 6d.

FOUR WINDS FARM. Globe 8vo. 2s. 6d.

LITTLE MISS PEGGY. Globe 8vo. 2s. 6d.

THE RECTORY CHILDREN. Gl. 8vo. 2s. 6d.

A CHRISTMAS POSY. Crown 8vo. 4s. 6d.

THE CHILDREN OF THE CASTLE. Crown 8vo. 4s. 6d.

SUMMER STORIES. Crown 8vo. 4s. 6d.

FOUR GHOST STORIES. Crown 8vo. 6s.

FRENCH LIFE IN LETTERS. With Notes on Idioms, etc. Globe 8vo. 1s. 6d.

MOLIÈRE.—LE MALADE IMAGINAIRE. Edit. by F. TARVER, M.A. Fcp. 8vo. 2s. 6d.

—— LES FEMMES SAVANTES. Edited by G. E. FASNACHT. 18mo. 1s.

—— LE MÉDECIN MALGRÉ LUI. By the same Editor. 18mo. 1s.

—— LE MISANTHROPE. By the same Editor. 18mo. 1s.

—— L'AVARE. Edited by L. M. MORIARTY, M.A. 18mo. 1s.

—— LE BOURGEOIS GENTILHOMME. By the same Editor. 18mo. 1s. 6d.

MOLLOY (Rev. G.).—GLEANINGS IN SCIENCE: A SERIES OF POPULAR LECTURES ON SCIENTIFIC SUBJECTS. 8vo. 7s. 6d.

MONAHAN (James H.).—THE METHOD OF LAW. Crown 8vo. 6s.

MONK. By JULIAN CORBETT. With Portrait. Crown 8vo. 2s. 6d.

MONTELIUS—WOODS.—THE CIVILISATION OF SWEDEN IN HEATHEN TIMES. By Prof. OSCAR MONTELIUS. Translated by Rev. F. H. WOODS, B.D. With Illustrations. 8vo. 14s.

MOORE (Prof. C. H.).—THE DEVELOPMENT AND CHARACTER OF GOTHIC ARCHITECTURE. Illustrated. Medium 8vo. 18s.

MOORHOUSE (Rt. Rev. Bishop).—JACOB: THREE SERMONS. Extra fcp. 8vo. 3s. 6d.

MORISON (J. C.).—THE LIFE AND TIMES OF SAINT BERNARD. 4th Edition. Crown 8vo. 6s

—— GIBBON. Cr. 8vo. 1s. 6d. ; sewed, 1s.

—— MACAULAY. Cr. 8vo. 1s. 6d. ; sewed, 1s.

MORISON (Jeanie).—THE PURPOSE OF THE AGES. Crown 8vo. 9s.

MORLEY (John).—WORKS. Collected Edit. In 11 vols. Globe 8vo. 5s. each.

VOLTAIRE. 1 vol.—ROUSSEAU. 2 vols.—DIDEROT AND THE ENCYCLOPÆDISTS. 2 vols.—ON COMPROMISE. 1 vol.—MISCELLANIES. 3 vols.—BURKE. 1 vol.—STUDIES IN LITERATURE. 1 vol.

—— BURKE. Crown 8vo. 1s. 6d. ; sewed, 1s.

—— WALPOLE. Crown 8vo. 2s. 6d.

—— APHORISMS. An Address before the Philosophical Society of Edinburgh. Globe 8vo. 1s. 6d.

MORRIS (Rev. Richard, LL.D.).—HISTORICAL OUTLINES OF ENGLISH ACCIDENCE. Fcp. 8vo. 6s.

—— ELEMENTARY LESSONS IN HISTORICAL ENGLISH GRAMMAR. 18mo. 2s. 6d.

—— PRIMER OF ENGLISH GRAMMAR. 18mo, cloth. 1s.

MORRIS (R.) and BOWEN (H. C.).—ENGLISH GRAMMAR EXERCISES. 18mo. 1s.

MORRIS (R.) and KELLNER (L.).—HISTORICAL OUTLINES OF ENGLISH SYNTAX. Extra fcp. 8vo.

MORTE D'ARTHUR. THE EDITION OF CAXTON REVISED FOR MODERN USE. By Sir EDWARD STRACHEY. Gl. 8vo. 3s. 6d.

MOULTON (Louise Chandler).—SWALLOW-FLIGHTS. Extra fcp. 8vo. 4s. 6d.

—— IN THE GARDEN OF DREAMS: LYRICS AND SONNETS. Crown 8vo. 6s.

MUDIE (C. E.).—STRAY LEAVES: POEMS. 4th Edition. Extra fcp. 8vo. 3s. 6d.

MUIR (T.).—THE THEORY OF DETERMINANTS IN THE HISTORICAL ORDER OF ITS DEVELOPMENT. Part I. DETERMINANTS IN GENERAL. Leibnitz (1693) to Cayley (1841). 8vo. 10s. 6d.

MUIR (M. M. Pattison).—PRACTICAL CHEMISTRY FOR MEDICAL STUDENTS. Fcp. 8vo. 1s. 6d.

MUIR (M. M. P.) and WILSON (D. M.).—THE ELEMENTS OF THERMAL CHEMISTRY. 8vo. 12s. 6d.

MÜLLER—THOMPSON.—THE FERTILISATION OF FLOWERS. By Prof. HERMANN MÜLLER. Translated by D'ARCY W. THOMPSON. With a Preface by CHARLES DARWIN, F.R.S. Medium 8vo. 21s.

MULLINGER (J. B.).—CAMBRIDGE CHARACTERISTICS IN THE SEVENTEENTH CENTURY. Crown 8vo. 4s. 6d.

MURPHY (J. J.).—HABIT AND INTELLIGENCE. 2nd Ed. Illustrated. 8vo. 16s.

MURRAY (E. C. Grenville).—ROUND ABOUT FRANCE. Crown 8vo. 7s. 6d.

MURRAY (D. Christie).—AUNT RACHEL. Crown 8vo. 3s. 6d.

—— SCHWARTZ. Crown 8vo. 3s. 6d.

—— THE WEAKER VESSEL. Cr. 8vo. 3s. 6d.

—— JOHN VALE'S GUARDIAN. Cr. 8vo. 3s. 6d.

MUSIC.—A DICTIONARY OF MUSIC AND MUSICIANS, A.D. 1450—1889. Edited by Sir GEORGE GROVE, D.C.L. In 4 vols. 8vo. 21s. each.—Parts I.—XIV., XIX.—XXII. 3s. 6d. each.—Parts XV. XVI. 7s.—Parts XVII. XVIII. 7s.—Parts XXIII.—XXV. APPENDIX. Edited by J. A. FULLER MAITLAND, M.A. 9s. [Cloth cases for binding, 1s. each.]

—— A COMPLETE INDEX TO THE ABOVE. By Mrs. E. WODEHOUSE. 8vo. 7s. 6d.

MYERS (F. W. H.).—THE RENEWAL OF YOUTH, AND OTHER POEMS. Crown 8vo. 7s. 6d.

—— ST. PAUL : A POEM. Ex. fcp. 8vo. 2s. 6d.

—— WORDSWORTH. Crown 8vo. 1s. 6d. ; sewed, 1s.

—— ESSAYS. 2 vols.—I. Classical. II. Modern. Crown 8vo. 4s. 6d. each.

MYERS (E.).—THE PURITANS : A POEM. Extra fcap. 8vo. 2s. 6d.

—— PINDAR'S ODES. Translated, with Introduction and Notes. Crown 8vo. 5s.

—— POEMS. Extra fcp. 8vo. 4s. 6d.

—— THE DEFENCE OF ROME, AND OTHER POEMS. Extra fcp. 8vo. 5s.

—— THE JUDGMENT OF PROMETHEUS, AND OTHER POEMS. Extra fcap. 8vo. 3s. 6d.

MYLNE (The Rt. Rev. Bishop).—SERMONS PREACHED IN ST. THOMAS'S CATHEDRAL, BOMBAY. Crown 8vo. 6s.

NADAL (E. S.).—ESSAYS AT HOME AND ELSEWHERE. Crown 8vo. 6s.

NAPIER (SIR CHARLES). By Col. Sir W. BUTLER. With Portrait. Cr. 8vo. 2s. 6d.

NAPOLEON I., HISTORY OF. By P. LANFREY. 4 vols. Crown 8vo. 30s.

NATURAL RELIGION. By the Author of "Ecce Homo." 3rd Ed. Ext. fcap. 8vo. 6s.

NATURE: A WEEKLY ILLUSTRATED JOUR-
NAL OF SCIENCE. Published every Thursday.
Price 6d. Monthly Parts, 2s. and 2s. 6d.;
Current Half-yearly vols., 15s. each. Vols.
I.—XLI. [Cases for binding vols., 1s. 6d.
each.]

NATURE PORTRAITS. A Series of Portraits of Scientific Worthies engraved by
JEENS and others in Portfolio. India Proofs,
5s. each. [Portfolio separately, 6s. net.]

NATURE SERIES. Crown 8vo:

THE ORIGIN AND METAMORPHOSES OF
INSECTS. By Sir JOHN LUBBOCK, M.P.,
F.R.S. With Illustrations. 3s. 6d.

THE TRANSIT OF VENUS. By Prof. G.
FORBES. With Illustrations. 3s. 6d.

POLARISATION OF LIGHT. By W. SPOTTIS-
WOODE, LL.D. Illustrated. 3s. 6d.

ON BRITISH WILD FLOWERS CONSIDERED
IN RELATION TO INSECTS. By Sir JOHN
LUBBOCK, M.P., F.R.S. Illustrated. 4s. 6d.

FLOWERS, FRUITS, AND LEAVES. By Sir
JOHN LUBBOCK. Illustrated. 4s. 6d.

HOW TO DRAW A STRAIGHT LINE: A LEC-
TURE ON LINKAGES. By A. B. KEMPE,
B.A. Illustrated. 1s. 6d.

LIGHT: A SERIES OF SIMPLE, ENTERTAIN-
ING, AND USEFUL EXPERIMENTS. By A. M.
MAYER and C. BARNARD. Illustrated.
2s. 6d.

SOUND: A SERIES OF SIMPLE, ENTERTAIN-
ING, AND INEXPENSIVE EXPERIMENTS.
By A. M. MAYER. 3s. 6d.

SEEING AND THINKING. By Prof. W. K.
CLIFFORD, F.R.S. Diagrams. 3s. 6d.

CHARLES DARWIN. Memorial Notices re-
printed from "Nature." By THOMAS H.
HUXLEY, F.R.S., G. J. ROMANES, F.R.S.,
ARCHIBALD GEIKIE, F.R.S., and W. T.
DYER, F.R.S. 2s. 6d.

ON THE COLOURS OF FLOWERS. By GRANT
ALLEN. Illustrated. 3s. 6d.

THE CHEMISTRY OF THE SECONDARY BAT-
TERIES OF PLANTÉ AND FAURE. By J.
H. GLADSTONE and A. TRIBE. 2s. 6d.

A CENTURY OF ELECTRICITY. By T. C.
MENDENHALL. 4s. 6d.

ON LIGHT, The Burnett Lectures. By Sir
GEORGE GABRIEL STOKES, M.P., P.R.S.
Three Courses: I. On the Nature of Light.
II. On Light as a Means of Investiga-
tion. III. On Beneficial Effects of Light.
7s. 6d.

THE SCIENTIFIC EVIDENCES OF ORGANIC
EVOLUTION. By GEORGE J. ROMANES,
M.A., LL.D. 2s. 6d.

POPULAR LECTURES AND ADDRESSES. By
Sir WM. THOMSON. In 3 vols. Vol. I.
Constitution of Matter. Illustrated. 6s.
Vol. II. Navigation.

THE CHEMISTRY OF PHOTOGRAPHY. By Prof.
R. MELDOLA, F.R.S. Illustrated. 6s.

MODERN VIEWS OF ELECTRICITY. By Prof.
O. J. LODGE, LL.D. Illustrated. 6s. 6d.

TIMBER AND SOME OF ITS DISEASES. By
Prof. H. M. WARD, M.A. Illustrated. 6s.

NATURE SERIES—continued.

ARE THE EFFECTS OF USE AND DISUSE IN-
HERITED? An Examination of the View
held by Spencer and Darwin. By W.
PLATT BALL. 3s. 6d.

NEPOS. SELECTIONS ILLUSTRATIVE OF
GREEK AND ROMAN HISTORY FROM COR-
NELIUS NEPOS. Edited by G. S. FARNELL,
M.A. 18mo. 1s. 6d.

NETTLESHIP.—VIRGIL. By Prof. NETTLE-
SHIP, M.A. Fcap. 8vo. 1s. 6d.

NEW ANTIGONE, THE: A ROMANCE.
Crown 8vo. 6s.

NEWCASTLE (Duke and Duchess of).—
THE CAVALIER AND HIS LADY. Selections
from the Works of the First Duke and
Duchess of Newcastle. With an Introductory Essay by E. JENKINS. 18mo. 4s. 6d.

NEWCOMB (Prof. Simon).—POPULAR AS-
TRONOMY. With 112 Engravings and Maps
of the Stars. 2nd Edition. 8vo. 18s.

NEWMAN (F. W.).—MATHEMATICAL
TRACTS. Part I. 8vo. 5s.—Part II. 4s.

—— ELLIPTIC INTEGRALS. 8vo. 9s.

NEWTON (Sir C. T.).—ESSAYS ON ART AND
ARCHÆOLOGY. 8vo. 12s. 6d.

NEWTON'S PRINCIPIA. Edited by Prof.
Sir W. THOMSON and Prof. BLACKBURN.
4to. 31s. 6d.

—— FIRST BOOK. Sections I. II. III. With
Notes, Illustrations, and Problems. By
P. FROST, M.A. 3rd Edition. 8vo. 12s.

NICHOL (Prof. John).—PRIMER OF ENGLISH
COMPOSITION. 18mo. 1s.

—— BYRON. Crown 8vo. 1s. 6d.; sewed, 1s.

NICHOL (Prof. John) and M'CORMICK
(W. S.).—QUESTIONS AND EXERCISES IN
ENGLISH COMPOSITION. 18mo. 1s.

NINE YEARS OLD. By the Author of
"St. Olave's." Illustrated by FRÖLICH. New
Edition. Globe 8vo. 2s. 6d.

NIXON (J. E.).—PARALLEL EXTRACTS. Arranged for Translation into English and
Latin, with Notes on Idioms. Part I. Historical and Epistolary. 2nd Edition. Crown
8vo. 3s. 6d.

—— PROSE EXTRACTS. Arranged for Translation into English and Latin, with General
and Special Prefaces on Style and Idiom.
I. Oratorical. II. Historical. III. Philosophical. IV. Anecdotes and Letters. 2nd
Edition, enlarged to 280 pages. Crown
8vo. 4s. 6d.—SELECTIONS FROM THE SAME.
Globe 8vo. 3s.

NOEL (Lady Augusta).—WANDERING WILLIE.
Globe 8vo. 2s. 6d.

—— HITHERSEA MERE. 3 vols. Cr. 8vo. 31s. 6d.

NORDENSKIÖLD.—VOYAGE OF THE
"VEGA" ROUND ASIA AND EUROPE. By
Baron A. E. VON NORDENSKIÖLD. Translated by ALEXANDER LESLIE. 400 Illustrations, Maps, etc. 2 vols. Medium 8vo. 45s.

Popular Edition. With Portrait, Maps
and Illustrations. Crown 8vo. 6s.

NORDENSKIÖLD.—THE ARCTIC VOYAGES OF ADOLPH ERIC NORDENSKIÖLD, 1858—79. By ALEXANDER LESLIE. 8vo. 16s.

NORGATE (Kate).—ENGLAND UNDER THE ANGEVIN KINGS. In 2 vols. With Maps and Plans. 8vo. 32s.

NORRIS (W. E.).—MY FRIEND JIM. Globe 8vo. 2s.

—— CHRIS. Globe 8vo. 2s.

NORTON (the Hon. Mrs.).—THE LADY OF LA GARAYE. 9th Ed. Fcp. 8vo. 4s. 6d.

—— OLD SIR DOUGLAS. Crown 8vo. 6s.

OLD SONGS. With Drawings by E. A. ABBEY and A. PARSONS. 4to. Morocco gilt. 1l. 11s. 6d.

OLIPHANT (Mrs. M. O. W.).—A SON OF THE SOIL. Globe 8vo. 2s.

—— THE CURATE IN CHARGE. Globe 8vo. 2s.

—— FRANCIS OF ASSISI. Crown 8vo. 6s.

—— YOUNG MUSGRAVE. Globe 8vo. 2s.

—— HE THAT WILL NOT WHEN HE MAY. Globe 8vo. 2s.

—— SIR TOM. Globe 8vo. 2s.

—— HESTER. Globe 8vo. 2s.

—— THE WIZARD'S SON. Globe 8vo. 2s.

—— A COUNTRY GENTLEMAN AND HIS FAMILY. Globe 8vo. 2s.

—— THE SECOND SON. Globe 8vo. 2s.

—— NEIGHBOURS ON THE GREEN. Crown 8vo. 3s. 6d.

—— JOYCE. Crown 8vo. 3s. 6d.

—— A BELEAGUERED CITY. Cr. 8vo. 3s. 6d.

—— THE MAKERS OF VENICE: DOGES, CONQUERORS, PAINTERS, AND MEN OF LETTERS. Illustrated Crown 8vo. 10s. 6d.

—— THE MAKERS OF FLORENCE: DANTE, GIOTTO, SAVONAROLA, AND THEIR CITY. With Illustrations. Cr. 8vo. 10s. 6d.

—— ROYAL EDINBURGH: HER SAINTS, KINGS, PROPHETS, AND POETS. Illustrated by GEORGE REID, R.S.A. Med. 8vo. 21s.

Edition de Luxe. Sup. roy. 8vo. 50s. net.

—— AGNES HOPETOUN'S SCHOOLS AND HOLIDAYS. Illustrated. Globe 8vo. 2s. 6d.

—— THE LITERARY HISTORY OF ENGLAND IN THE END OF THE XVIII. AND BEGINNING OF THE XIX. CENTURY. 3 vols. 8vo. 21s.

—— SHERIDAN. Cr. 8vo. 1s. 6d.; sewed, 1s.

—— SELECTIONS FROM COWPER'S POEMS. 18mo. 4s. 6d.

—— KIRSTEEN. 3 vols. Crown 8vo. 31s. 6d.

OLIPHANT (T. L. Kington).—THE OLD AND MIDDLE ENGLISH. Globe 8vo. 9s.

—— THE DUKE AND THE SCHOLAR, AND OTHER ESSAYS. 8vo. 7s. 6d.

—— THE NEW ENGLISH. 2 vols. Cr. 8vo. 21s.

OLIVER (Prof. Daniel).—LESSONS IN ELEMENTARY BOTANY. Illustr. Fcp. 8vo. 4s. 6d.

—— FIRST BOOK OF INDIAN BOTANY. Illustrated. Extra fcp. 8vo. 6s. 6d.

OLIVER (Capt. S. P.).—MADAGASCAR: AN HISTORICAL AND DESCRIPTIVE ACCOUNT OF THE ISLAND AND ITS FORMER DEPENDENCIES. 2 vols. Medium 8vo. 2l. 12s. 6d.

ORCHIDS: BEING THE REPORT ON THE ORCHID CONFERENCE HELD AT SOUTH KENSINGTON, 1885. 8vo. 2s. 6d. net.

OSTWALD (Prof. W.). — OUTLINES OF GENERAL CHEMISTRY. Translated by Dr. J. WALKER. 8vo. 10s. net.

OTTÉ (E. C.).—SCANDINAVIAN HISTORY. With Maps. Globe 8vo. 6s.

OVID.—SELECTIONS. Edited by E. S. SHUCKBURGH, M.A. 18mo. 1s. 6d.

—— FASTI. Edited by G. H. HALLAM, M.A. Fcp. 8vo. 3s. 6d.

—— HEROIDUM EPISTULÆ XIII. Edited by E. S. SHUCKBURGH, M.A. Fcp. 8vo. 3s. 6d.

—— METAMORPHOSES. Books I.—III. Edited by C. SIMMONS, M.A.

—— STORIES FROM THE METAMORPHOSES. Edited by the Rev. J. BOND, M.A., and A. S. WALPOLE, M.A. With Notes, Exercises, and Vocabulary. 18mo. 1s. 6d.

—— METAMORPHOSES. Books XIII. and XIV. Ed. by C. SIMMONS. Fcp. 8vo. 3s. 6d.

—— EASY SELECTIONS FROM OVID IN ELEGIAC VERSE. Arranged and Edited by H. WILKINSON, M.A. 18mo. 1s. 6d.

OWENS COLLEGE CALENDAR, 1889—90. Crown 8vo. 3s. net.

OWENS COLLEGE ESSAYS AND ADDRESSES. By Professors and Lecturers of the College. 8vo. 14s.

OXFORD, A HISTORY OF THE UNIVERSITY OF. From the Earliest Times to the Year 1530. By H. C. MAXWELL LYTE, M.A. 8vo. 16s.

PALGRAVE (Sir Francis). — HISTORY OF NORMANDY AND OF ENGLAND. 4 vols. 8vo. 4l. 4s.

PALGRAVE (William Gifford).—A NARRATIVE OF A YEAR'S JOURNEY THROUGH CENTRAL AND EASTERN ARABIA, 1862—63. 9th Edition. Crown 8vo. 6s.

—— ESSAYS ON EASTERN QUESTIONS. 8vo. 10s. 6d.

—— DUTCH GUIANA. 8vo. 9s.

—— ULYSSES; OR, SCENES AND STUDIES IN MANY LANDS. 8vo. 12s. 6d.

PALGRAVE (Prof. Francis Turner).—THE FIVE DAYS' ENTERTAINMENTS AT WENTWORTH GRANGE. A Book for Children. Small 4to. 6s.

—— ESSAYS ON ART. Extra fcp. 8vo. 6s.

—— ORIGINAL HYMNS. 3rd Ed. 18mo. 1s. 6d.

—— LYRICAL POEMS. Extra fcp. 8vo. 6s.

—— VISIONS OF ENGLAND: A SERIES OF LYRICAL POEMS ON LEADING EVENTS AND PERSONS IN ENGLISH HISTORY. Crown 8vo. 7s. 6d.

—— THE GOLDEN TREASURY OF THE BEST SONGS AND LYRICAL POEMS IN THE ENGLISH LANGUAGE. 18mo. 4s. 6d. (Large Type.) Crown 8vo. 10s. 6d.

Edition de Luxe. 21s. net.

PALGRAVE (Prof. F. T.).—SONNETS AND
SONGS OF SHAKESPEARE. 18mo. 4s. 6d.

—— THE CHILDREN'S TREASURY OF LYRICAL
POETRY. 18mo. 2s. 6d.—Or in Two Parts,
1s. each.

—— HERRICK: SELECTIONS FROM THE LYRI-
CAL POEMS. 18mo. 4s. 6d.

—— THE POETICAL WORKS OF JOHN KEATS.
With Notes. 18mo. 4s. 6d.

—— LYRICAL POEMS OF LORD TENNYSON.
Selected and Annotated. 18mo. 4s. 6d.
Large Paper Edition. 8vo. 9s.

PALGRAVE (Reginald F. D.).—THE HOUSE
OF COMMONS: ILLUSTRATIONS OF ITS HIS-
TORY AND PRACTICE. Crown 8vo. 2s. 6d.

PALGRAVE (R. H. Inglis).—DICTIONARY OF
POLITICAL ECONOMY. Edited by R. H. I.
PALGRAVE.

PALMER (Lady Sophia).—MRS. PENICOTT'S
LODGER, AND OTHER STORIES. Cr.8vo. 2s.6d.

PALMER (J. H.).—TEXT-BOOK OF PRACTI-
CAL LOGARITHMS AND TRIGONOMETRY.
Crown 8vo. 4s. 6d.

PANSIE'S FLOUR BIN. By the Author
of "When I was a Little Girl," etc. Illustrated. Globe 8vo. 2s. 6d.

PANTIN (W. E. P.).—A FIRST LATIN VERSE
BOOK. Globe 8vo. 1s. 6d.

PARADOXICAL PHILOSOPHY: A SE-
QUEL TO "THE UNSEEN UNIVERSE." Cr.
8vo. 7s. 6d.

PARKER (Prof. W. K.) and BETTANY
(G. T.).—THE MORPHOLOGY OF THE SKULL.
Crown 8vo. 10s. 6d.

PARKER (Prof. T. Jeffery).—A COURSE OF
INSTRUCTION IN ZOOTOMY (VERTEBRATA).
With 74 Illustrations. Crown 8vo. 8s. 6d.

—— LESSONS IN ELEMENTARY BIOLOGY. Illustrated. Crown 8vo. [In the Press.

PARKINSON (S.).—A TREATISE ON ELE-
MENTARY MECHANICS. Crown 8vo. 9s. 6d.

—— A TREATISE ON OPTICS. 4th Edition,
revised. Crown 8vo. 10s. 6d.

PARKMAN (Francis). — MONTCALM AND
WOLFE. Library Edition. Illustrated with
Portraits and Maps. 2 vols. 8vo. 12s.6d. each.

—— THE COLLECTED WORKS OF FRANCIS
PARKMAN. Popular Edition. In 10 vols.
Crown 8vo. 7s. 6d. each; or complete,
3l. 13s. 6d.—PIONEERS OF FRANCE IN THE
NEW WORLD. 1 vol.—THE JESUITS IN
NORTH AMERICA. 1 vol.—LA SALLE AND
THE DISCOVERY OF THE GREAT WEST. 1
vol.—THE OREGON TRAIL. 1 vol.—THE
OLD RÉGIME IN CANADA UNDER LOUIS
XIV. 1 vol.—COUNT FRONTENAC AND NEW
FRANCE UNDER LOUIS XIV. 1 vol.—MONT-
CALM AND WOLFE. 2 vols.—THE CON-
SPIRACY OF PONTIAC. 2 vols.

PASTEUR — FAULKNER. — STUDIES ON
FERMENTATION: THE DISEASES OF BEER,
THEIR CAUSES, AND THE MEANS OF PRE-
VENTING THEM. By L. PASTEUR. Trans-
lated by FRANK FAULKNER. 8vo. 21s.

PATER (W.).—THE RENAISSANCE: STUDIES
IN ART AND POETRY. 4th Ed. Cr.8vo. 10s.6d.

—— MARIUS THE EPICUREAN: HIS SENSA-
TIONS AND IDEAS. 3rd Edition. 2 vols.
8vo. 12s.

—— IMAGINARY PORTRAITS. Crown 8vo. 6s.

—— APPRECIATIONS. With an Essay on
Style. 2nd Edition. Crown 8vo. 8s. 6d.

PATERSON (James).—COMMENTARIES ON
THE LIBERTY OF THE SUBJECT, AND THE
LAWS OF ENGLAND RELATING TO THE SE-
CURITY OF THE PERSON. 2 vols. Cr.8vo. 21s.

—— THE LIBERTY OF THE PRESS, SPEECH, AND
PUBLIC WORSHIP. Crown 8vo. 12s.

PATMORE (C.).—THE CHILDREN'S GAR-
LAND FROM THE BEST POETS. With a Vig-
nette. 18mo. 4s. 6d.
Globe Readings Edition. For Schools.
Globe 8vo. 2s.

PATTESON.—LIFE AND LETTERS OF JOHN
COLERIDGE PATTESON, D.D., MISSIONARY
BISHOP. By CHARLOTTE M. YONGE. 8th
Edition. 2 vols. Crown 8vo. 12s.

PATTISON (Mark).—MILTON. Crown 8vo.
1s. 6d.; sewed, 1s.

—— MEMOIRS. Crown 8vo. 8s. 6d.

—— SERMONS. Crown 8vo. 6s.

PAUL OF TARSUS. 8vo. 10s. 6d.

PAYNE (E. J.).—HISTORY OF EUROPEAN
COLONIES. 18mo. 4s. 6d.

PEABODY (Prof. C. H.).—THERMODYNAMICS
OF THE STEAM ENGINE AND OTHER HEAT-
ENGINES. 8vo. 21s.

PEDLEY (S.).—EXERCISES IN ARITHMETIC.
With upwards of 7000 Examples and Answers.
Crown 8vo. 5s.—Also in Two Parts. 2s. 6d.
each.

PEEL (Edmund).—ECHOES FROM HOREB, AND
OTHER POEMS. Crown 8vo. 3s. 6d.

PEILE (John).—PHILOLOGY. 18mo. 1s.

PELLISSIER (Eugène).—FRENCH ROOTS
AND THEIR FAMILIES. Globe 8vo. 6s.

PENNELL (Joseph).—PEN DRAWING AND
PEN DRAUGHTSMEN: Their Work and
Methods, a Study of the Art to-day, with
Technical Suggestions. With 158 Illustra-
tions. 4to. 3l. 13s. 6d. net.

PENNINGTON (Rooke).—NOTES ON THE
BARROWS AND BONE CAVES OF DERBYSHIRE.
8vo. 6s.

PENROSE (Francis).—ON A METHOD OF
PREDICTING, BY GRAPHICAL CONSTRUCTION,
OCCULTATIONS OF STARS BY THE MOON AND
SOLAR ECLIPSES FOR ANY GIVEN PLACE.
4to. 12s.

—— AN INVESTIGATION OF THE PRINCIPLES
OF ATHENIAN ARCHITECTURE. Illustrated.
Folio. 7l. 7s.

PERRAULT.—CONTES DE FÉES. Edited by
G. EUGÈNE FASNACHT. Globe 8vo. 1s. 6d.

PERRY (Prof. John).—AN ELEMENTARY
TREATISE ON STEAM. 18mo. 4s. 6d.

PERSIA, EASTERN. An Account of the Journeys of the Persian Boundary Commission, 1870—71—72. 2 vols. 8vo. 42s.

PETERBOROUGH. By W. Stebbing. With Portrait. Crown 8vo. 2s. 6d.

PETTIGREW (J. Bell). —The Physiology of the Circulation. 8vo. 12s.

PHAEDRUS.—Select Fables. Edited by A. S. Walpole, M.A. With Notes, Exercises, and Vocabularies. 18mo. 1s. 6d.

PHILLIMORE (John G.).—Private Law among the Romans. 8vo. 16s.

PHILLIPS (J. A.).—A Treatise on Ore Deposits. Illustrated. Medium 8vo. 25s.

PHILOCHRISTUS.—Memoirs of a Disciple of the Lord. 3rd Ed. 8vo. 12s.

PHILOLOGY.—The Journal of Sacred and Classical Philology. 4 vols. 8vo. 12s. 6d. each net.

—— The Journal of Philology. New Series. Edited by W. A. Wright, M.A., I. Bywater, M.A., and H. Jackson, M.A. 4s. 6d. each number (half-yearly) net.

—— The American Journal of Philology. Edited by Prof. Basil L. Gildersleeve. 4s. 6d. each (quarterly) net.

—— Transactions of the American Philological Association. Vols. I.—XX. 8s. 6d. per vol. net, except Vols. XV. and XX., which are 10s. 6d. net.

PHRYNICHUS. The New Phrynichus. A revised text of "The Ecloga" of the Grammarian Phrynichus. With Introductions and Commentary. By W. Gunion Rutherford, M.A. 8vo. 18s.

PICKERING (Prof. Edward C.).—Elements of Physical Manipulation. Medium 8vo. Part I., 12s. 6d.; Part II., 14s.

PICTON (J. A.).—The Mystery of Matter, and other Essays. Crown 8vo. 6s.

PIFFARD (II. G.).—An Elementary Treatise on Diseases of the Skin. 8vo. 16s.

PINDAR'S EXTANT ODES. Translated by Ernest Myers. Crown 8vo. 5s.

—— The Olympian and Pythian Odes. Edited, with Notes, by Prof. Basil Gildersleeve. Crown 8vo. 7s. 6d.

—— The Nemean Odes. Edited by J. B. Bury, M.A. 8vo. 12s.

PIRIE (Prof. G.).—Lessons on Rigid Dynamics. Crown 8vo. 6s.

PLATO.—Phædo. Edited by R. D. Archer-Hind, M.A. 8vo. 8s. 6d.

—— Timæus. With Introduction, Notes, and Translation, by the same Editor. 8vo. 16s.

—— Phædo. Ed. by Principal W. D. Geddes, LL.D. 2nd Edition. 8vo. 8s. 6d.

—— The Trial and Death of Socrates: Being the Euthyphron, Apology, Crito, and Phædo of Plato. Translated by F. J. Church. 18mo. 4s. 6d.

—— Euthyphro and Menexenus. Ed. by C. E. Graves, M.A. 18mo. 1s. 6d.

PLATO.—The Republic. Bks. I.—V. Edit. by T. H. Warren, M.A. Fcp. 8vo. 5s.

—— The Republic of Plato. Translated by J. Ll. Davies, M.A., and D. J. Vaughan, M.A. 18mo. 4s. 6d.

—— Laches. Edited by M. T. Tatham, M.A. Fcap. 8vo. 2s. 6d.

—— Phædrus, Lysis, and Protagoras. A New Translation, by J. Wright, M.A. 18mo. 4s. 6d.

PLAUTUS.—The Mostellaria. With Notes, Prolegomena, and Excursus. By the late Prof. Ramsay. Ed. by G. G. Ramsay, M.A. 8vo. 14s.

—— Miles Gloriosus. Edit. by Prof. R. Y. Tyrrell, M.A. 2nd Ed. Fcp. 8vo. 3s. 6d.

—— Amphitruo. Edited by Prof. A. Palmer, M.A. Fcp. 8vo. 3s. 6d.

PLINY.—Letters. Books I. and II. Edit. by James Cowan, M.A. Fcp. 8vo. 3s. 6d.

—— Letters. Book III. Edited by Prof. John E. B. Mayor. Fcp. 8vo. 3s. 6d.

—— Correspondence with Trajan. Ed., with Notes and Introductory Essays, by E. G. Hardy, M.A. 8vo. 10s. 6d.

PLUMPTRE (Prof. E. H.).—Movements in Religious Thought. Fcp. 8vo. 3s. 6d.

PLUTARCH. Being a Selection from the Lives in North's Plutarch which illustrate Shakespeare's Plays. Edited by Rev. W. W. Skeat, M.A. Crown 8vo. 6s.

—— Life of Themistokles. Edited by Rev. H. A. Holden, M.A. Fcp. 8vo. 3s. 6d.

—— Lives of Galba and Otho. Edited by E. G. Hardy, M.A. Fcp. 8vo. 5s.

POLLOCK (Prof. Sir F., Bart.).—Essays in Jurisprudence and Ethics. 8vo. 10s. 6d.

—— The Land Laws. 2nd Edition. Crown 8vo. 3s. 6d.

—— Introduction to the History of the Science of Politics. Crown 8vo. 2s. 6d.

—— Oxford Lectures and other Discourses. 8vo. 9s.

POLLOCK (W. H. and Lady).—Amateur Theatricals. Crown 8vo. 2s. 6d.

POLLOCK (Sir Frederick).—Personal Remembrances. 2 vols. Crown 8vo. 16s.

POLYBIUS.—The History of the Achæan League. As contained in the "Remains of Polybius." Edited by Rev. W. W. Capes. Fcp. 8vo. 5s.

—— The Histories of Polybius. Transl. by E. S. Shuckburgh. 2 vols. Cr. 8vo. 24s.

POOLE (M. E.).—Pictures of Cottage Life in the West of England. 2nd Ed. Crown 8vo. 3s. 6d.

POOLE (Reginald Lane).—A History of the Huguenots of the Dispersion at the Recall of the Edict of Nantes. Crown 8vo. 6s.

POOLE, THOMAS, AND HIS FRIENDS. By Mrs. Sandford. 2 vols. Crn. 8vo. 15s.

POPE.—THE POETICAL WORKS OF ALEX. POPE. Edited by Prof. WARD. Globe 8vo. 3s. 6d.

—— POPE. By LESLIE STEPHEN. Crown 8vo. 1s. 6d.; sewed, 1s.

POPULATION OF AN OLD PEAR TREE; OR, STORIES OF INSECT LIFE. From the French of E. VAN BRUYSSEL. Ed. by C. M. YONGE. Illustrated. Globe 8vo. 2s. 6d.

POSTGATE (Prof. J. P.).—SERMO LATINUS. A Short Guide to Latin Prose Composition. Part I. Introduction. Part II. Selected Passages for Translation. Gl. 8vo. 2s. 6d.— Key to "Selected Passages." Crown 8vo. 3s. 6d.

POTTER (Louisa).—LANCASHIRE MEMORIES. Crown 8vo. 6s.

POTTER (R.).—THE RELATION OF ETHICS TO RELIGION. Crown 8vo. 2s. 6d.

POTTS (A. W.).—HINTS TOWARDS LATIN PROSE COMPOSITION. Globe 8vo 3s.

—— PASSAGES FOR TRANSLATION INTO LATIN PROSE. 4th Ed. Extra fcp. 8vo. 2s. 6d.

—— LATIN VERSIONS OF PASSAGES FOR TRANSLATION INTO LATIN PROSE. Extra fcp. 8vo. 2s. 6d. (For Teachers only.)

PRACTICAL POLITICS. Published under the auspices of the National Liberal Federation. 8vo. 6s.

PRACTITIONER (THE): A MONTHLY JOURNAL OF THERAPEUTICS AND PUBLIC HEALTH. Edited by T. LAUDER BRUNTON, M.D., F.R.C.P., F.R.S., Assistant Physician to St. Bartholomew's Hospital, etc., etc.; DONALD MACALISTER, M.A., M.D., B.Sc., F.R.C.P., Fellow and Medical Lecturer, St. John's College, Cambridge, Physician to Addenbrooke's Hospital and University Lecturer in Medicine; and J. MITCHELL BRUCE, M.A., M.D., F.R.C.P., Physician and Lecturer on Therapeutics at Charing Cross Hospital. 1s. 6d. monthly. Vols. I.—XLIII. Half-yearly vols. 10s. 6d. [Cloth covers for binding, 1s. each.]

PRESTON (Rev. G.).—EXERCISES IN LATIN VERSE OF VARIOUS KINDS. Globe 8vo. 2s. 6d.—Key. Globe 8vo. 5s.

PRESTON (T.).—THE THEORY OF LIGHT. Illustrated. 8vo. 12s. 6d.

PRICE (L. L. F. R.).—INDUSTRIAL PEACE: ITS ADVANTAGES, METHODS, AND DIFFICULTIES. Medium 8vo. 6s.

PRIMERS.—HISTORY. Edited by JOHN R. GREEN, Author of "A Short History of the English People," etc. 18mo. 1s. each: EUROPE. By E. A. FREEMAN, M.A. GREECE. By C. A. FYFFE, M.A. ROME. By Prof. CREIGHTON. GREEK ANTIQUITIES. By Prof. MAHAFFY.

PRIMERS (HISTORY)—continued. ROMAN ANTIQUITIES. By Prof. WILKINS. CLASSICAL GEOGRAPHY. By H. F. TOZER. FRANCE. By CHARLOTTE M. YONGE. GEOGRAPHY. By Sir GEO. GROVE, D.C.L. INDIAN HISTORY, ASIATIC AND EUROPEAN. By J. TALBOYS WHEELER.

PRIMERS.—LITERATURE. Edited by JOHN R. GREEN, M.A., LL.D. 18mo. 1s. each: ENGLISH GRAMMAR. By Rev. R. MORRIS. ENGLISH GRAMMAR EXERCISES. By Rev. R. MORRIS and H. C. BOWEN. EXERCISES ON MORRIS'S PRIMER OF ENGLISH GRAMMAR. By J. WETHERELL, M.A. ENGLISH COMPOSITION. By Prof. NICHOL. QUESTIONS AND EXERCISES IN ENGLISH COMPOSITION. By Prof. NICHOL and W. S. M'CORMICK. PHILOLOGY. By J. PEILE, M.A. ENGLISH LITERATURE. By Rev. STOPFORD BROOKE, M.A. CHILDREN'S TREASURY OF LYRICAL POETRY. Selected by Prof. F. T. PALGRAVE. In 2 parts. 1s. each. SHAKSPERE. By Prof. DOWDEN. GREEK LITERATURE. By Prof. JEBB. HOMER. By Right Hon. W. E. GLADSTONE. ROMAN LITERATURE. By A. S. WILKINS.

PRIMERS.—SCIENCE. Under the joint Editorship of Prof. HUXLEY, Sir H. E. ROSCOE, and Prof. BALFOUR STEWART. 18mo. 1s. each: INTRODUCTORY. By Prof. HUXLEY. CHEMISTRY. By Sir HENRY ROSCOE, F.R.S. With Illustrations, and Questions. PHYSICS. By BALFOUR STEWART, F.R.S. With Illustrations, and Questions. PHYSICAL GEOGRAPHY. By A. GEIKIE, F.R.S. With Illustrations, and Questions. GEOLOGY. By ARCHIBALD GEIKIE, F.R.S. PHYSIOLOGY. By MICHAEL FOSTER, F.R.S. ASTRONOMY. By J. N. LOCKYER, F.R.S. BOTANY. By Sir J. D. HOOKER, C.B. LOGIC. By W. STANLEY JEVONS, F.R.S. POLITICAL ECONOMY. By W. STANLEY JEVONS, LL.D., M.A., F.R.S.

PROCTER (Rev. F.).—A HISTORY OF THE BOOK OF COMMON PRAYER. 18th Edition. Crown 8vo. 10s. 6d.

PROCTER (Rev. F.) and MACLEAR (Rev. Canon).—AN ELEMENTARY INTRODUCTION TO THE BOOK OF COMMON PRAYER. 18mo. 2s. 6d.

PROPERT (J. Lumsden).—A HISTORY OF MINIATURE ART. With Illustrations. Super royal 4to. 3l. 13s. 6d. Also bound in vellum. 4l. 14s. 6d.

4

PROPERTIUS.—SELECT POEMS. Edited by J. P. POSTGATE, M.A. Fcp. 8vo. 5s.

PSALMS (THE). With Introductions and Critical Notes. By A. C. JENNINGS, M.A. and W. H. LOWE, M.A. In 2 vols. 2nd Edition. Crown 8vo. 10s. 6d. each.

PUCKLE (G. H.).—AN ELEMENTARY TREATISE ON CONIC SECTIONS AND ALGEBRAIC GEOMETRY. 6th Edit. Crn. 8vo. 7s. 6d.

PYLODET (L.).—NEW GUIDE TO GERMAN CONVERSATION. 18mo. 2s. 6d.

RACINE.—BRITANNICUS. Ed. by EUGÈNE PELLISSIER, M.A. 18mo. 2s.

RADCLIFFE (Charles B.).—BEHIND THE TIDES. 8vo. 6s.

RAMSAY (Prof. William).—EXPERIMENTAL PROOFS OF CHEMICAL THEORY. 18mo. 2s. 6d.

RANSOME (Prof. Cyril).—SHORT STUDIES OF SHAKESPEARE'S PLOTS. Cr. 8vo. 3s. 6d.

RATHBONE (Wm.).—THE HISTORY AND PROGRESS OF DISTRICT NURSING, FROM ITS COMMENCEMENT IN THE YEAR 1859 TO THE PRESENT DATE. Crown 8vo. 2s. 6d.

RAWNSLEY (H. D.).—POEMS, BALLADS, AND BUCOLICS. Fcp. 8vo. 5s.

RAY (Prof. P. K.).—A TEXT-BOOK OF DEDUCTIVE LOGIC. 4th Ed. Globe 8vo. 4s. 6d.

RAYLEIGH (Lord).—THEORY OF SOUND. 8vo. Vol. I. 12s. 6d.—Vol. II. 12s. 6d.—Vol. III. (in preparation.)

RAYS OF SUNLIGHT FOR DARK DAYS. With a Preface by C. J. VAUGHAN, D.D. New Edition. 18mo. 3s. 6d.

REALMAH. By the Author of "Friends in Council." Crown 8vo. 6s.

REASONABLE FAITH: A SHORT RELIGIOUS ESSAY FOR THE TIMES. By "THREE FRIENDS." Crown 8vo. 1s.

RECOLLECTIONS OF A NURSE. By E. D. Crown 8vo. 2s.

REED.—MEMOIR OF SIR CHARLES REED. By his Son, CHARLES E. B. REED, M.A. With Portrait. Crown 8vo. 4s. 6d.

REMSEN (Prof. Ira).—AN INTRODUCTION TO THE STUDY OF ORGANIC CHEMISTRY. Crown 8vo. 6s. 6d.

—— AN INTRODUCTION TO THE STUDY OF CHEMISTRY (INORGANIC CHEMISTRY). Cr. 8vo. 6s. 6d.

—— THE ELEMENTS OF CHEMISTRY. A Text-Book for Beginners. Fcp. 8vo. 2s. 6d.

—— TEXT-BOOK OF INORGANIC CHEMISTRY. 8vo. 16s.

RENDALL (Rev. Frederic).—THE EPISTLE TO THE HEBREWS IN GREEK AND ENGLISH. With Notes. Crown 8vo. 6s.

—— THE THEOLOGY OF THE HEBREW CHRISTIANS. Crown 8vo. 5s.

—— THE EPISTLE TO THE HEBREWS. English Text, with Commentary. Cr. 8vo. 7s. 6d

RENDALL (Prof. G. H.).—THE CRADLE OF THE ARYANS. 8vo. 3s.

RENDU—WILLS.—THE THEORY OF THE GLACIERS OF SAVOY. By M. LE CHANOINE RENDU. Trans. by A. WILLS, Q.C. 8vo. 7s. 6d.

REULEAUX—KENNEDY.--THE KINEMATICS OF MACHINERY. By Prof. F. REULEAUX. Translated by Prof. A. B. W. KENNEDY, F.R.S., C.E. Medium 8vo. 21s.

REYNOLDS (J. R.).—A SYSTEM OF MEDICINE. Edited by J. RUSSELL REYNOLDS, M.D., F.R.C.P. London. In 5 vols. Vols. I. II. III. and V. 8vo. 25s. each.—Vol. IV. 21s.

REYNOLDS (H. R.).—NOTES OF THE CHRISTIAN LIFE. Crown 8vo. 7s. 6d.

REYNOLDS (Prof. Osborne).—SEWER GAS, AND HOW TO KEEP IT OUT OF HOUSES. 3rd Edition. Crown 8vo. 1s. 6d.

RICE (Prof. J. M.) and JOHNSON (W. W.).—AN ELEMENTARY TREATISE ON THE DIFFERENTIAL CALCULUS. New Edition. 8vo. 18s. Abridged Edition. 9s.

RICHARDSON (A. T.).—THE PROGRESSIVE EUCLID. Books I. and II. With Notes, Exercises, and Deductions. Illustrated. Globe 8vo.

RICHARDSON (Dr. B. W.).—ON ALCOHOL. Crown 8vo. 1s.

—— DISEASES OF MODERN LIFE. Crown 8vo. 6s.

—— HYGEIA: A CITY OF HEALTH. Crown 8vo. 1s.

—— THE FUTURE OF SANITARY SCIENCE. Crown 8vo. 1s.

—— THE FIELD OF DISEASE. A Book of Preventive Medicine. 8vo. 25s.

RICHEY (Alex. G.).—THE IRISH LAND LAWS. Crown 8vo. 3s. 6d.

ROBINSON CRUSOE. Edited by HENRY KINGSLEY. Globe Edition. 3s. 6d.—Golden Treasury Edition. Edit. by J. W. CLARK, M.A. 18mo. 4s. 6d.

ROBINSON (Prebendary H. G.).—MAN IN THE IMAGE OF GOD, AND OTHER SERMONS. Crown 8vo. 7s. 6d.

ROBINSON (Rev. J. L.).—MARINE SURVEYING: AN ELEMENTARY TREATISE ON. Prepared for the Use of Younger Naval Officers. With Illustrations. Crown 8vo. 7s. 6d.

ROBY (H. J.).—A GRAMMAR OF THE LATIN LANGUAGE FROM PLAUTUS TO SUETONIUS. In Two Parts.—Part I. containing Sounds, Inflexions, Word Formation, Appendices, etc. 5th Edition. Crown 8vo. 9s.—Part II. Syntax, Prepositions, etc. 6th Edition. Crown 8vo. 10s. 6d.

—— A LATIN GRAMMAR FOR SCHOOLS. Cr. 8vo. 5s.

—— AN ELEMENTARY LATIN GRAMMAR. Globe 8vo.

—— EXERCISES IN LATIN SYNTAX AND IDIOM. Arranged with reference to Roby's School Latin Grammar. By E. B. ENGLAND, M.A. Crown 8vo. 2s. 6d.—Key, 2s. 6d.

ROCKSTRO (W. S.).—LIFE OF GEORGE FREDERICK HANDEL. Crown 8vo. 10s. 6d.

ROGERS (Prof. J. E. T.).—HISTORICAL GLEANINGS.—First Series. Cr. 8vo. 4s. 6d. —Second Series. Crown 8vo. 6s.

—— COBDEN AND POLITICAL OPINION. 8vo. 10s. 6d.

ROMANES (George J.).—THE SCIENTIFIC EVIDENCES OF ORGANIC EVOLUTION. Cr. 8vo. 2s. 6d.

ROSCOE (Sir Henry E., M.P., F.R.S.).— LESSONS IN ELEMENTARY CHEMISTRY. With Illustrations. Fcp. 8vo. 4s. 6d.

—— PRIMER OF CHEMISTRY. With Illustrations. 18mo, cloth. With Questions. 1s.

ROSCOE (Sir H. E.) and SCHORLEMMER (C.).—A TREATISE ON CHEMISTRY. With Illustrations. 8vo.—Vols. I. and II. INORGANIC CHEMISTRY: Vol. I. THE NONMETALLIC ELEMENTS. With a Portrait of DALTON. 21s.—Vol. II. Part I. METALS. 18s.; Part II. METALS. 18s.—Vol. III. ORGANIC CHEMISTRY: Parts I. II. and IV. 21s. each; Parts III. and V. 18s. each.

ROSCOE—SCHUSTER.—SPECTRUM ANALYSIS. By Sir HENRY E. ROSCOE, LL.D., F.R.S. 4th Edition, revised by the Author and A. SCHUSTER, Ph.D., F.R.S. Medium 8vo. 21s.

ROSENBUSCH—IDDINGS.—MICROSCOPICAL PHYSIOGRAPHY OF THE ROCK-MAKING MINERALS. By Prof. H. ROSENBUSCH. Translated by J. P. IDDINGS. Illustrated. 8vo. 24s.

ROSS (Percy).—A MISGUIDIT LASSIE. Crown 8vo. 4s. 6d.

ROSSETTI (Dante Gabriel). — A RECORD AND A STUDY. By W. SHARP. Crown 8vo. 10s. 6d.

ROSSETTI (Christina).—POEMS. New and Enlarged Edition. Globe 8vo. 7s. 6d.

—— A PAGEANT, AND OTHER POEMS. Extra fcp. 8vo. 6s.

—— SPEAKING LIKENESSES. Illustrated by ARTHUR HUGHES. Crown 8vo. 4s. 6d.

ROUSSEAU. By JOHN MORLEY. 2 vols. Globe 8vo. 10s.

ROUTH (E. J.).—A TREATISE ON THE DYNAMICS OF A SYSTEM OF RIGID BODIES. 4th Edition, revised and enlarged. 8vo. In Two Parts.—Part I. ELEMENTARY. 14s.— Part II. ADVANCED. 14s.

—— STABILITY OF A GIVEN STATE OF MOTION, PARTICULARLY STEADY MOTION. 8vo. 8s. 6d.

ROUTLEDGE (James).—POPULAR PROGRESS IN ENGLAND. 8vo. 16s.

RUMFORD (Count).—COMPLETE WORKS OF COUNT RUMFORD. With Memoir by GEORGE ELLIS, and Portrait. 5 vols. 8vo. 4l. 14s. 6d.

RUNAWAY (THE). By the Author of "Mrs. Jerningham's Journal." Gl. 8vo. 2s. 6d.

RUSH (Edward).—THE SYNTHETIC LATIN DELECTUS. A First Latin Construing Book. Extra fcp. 8vo. 2s. 6d.

RUSHBROOKE (W. G.).—SYNOPTICON: AN EXPOSITION OF THE COMMON MATTER OF THE SYNOPTIC GOSPELS. Printed in Colours. In Six Parts, and Appendix. 4to.—Part I. 3s. 6d.—Parts II. and III. 7s.—Parts IV. V. and VI., with Indices. 10s. 6d.—Appendices. 10s. 6d.—Complete in 1 vol. 35s.

RUSSELL (W. Clark).—MAROONED. Crown 8vo. 3s. 6d.

—— DAMPIER. Portrait. Cr. 8vo. 2s. 6d.

RUSSELL (Sir Charles).—NEW VIEWS ON IRELAND. Crown 8vo. 2s. 6d.

—— THE PARNELL COMMISSION: THE OPENING SPEECH FOR THE DEFENCE. 8vo. 10s. 6d.

*Popular Edition.* Sewed. 2s.

RUSSELL (Dean). — THE LIGHT THAT LIGHTETH EVERY MAN: Sermons. With an Introduction by the Very Rev. E. H. PLUMPTRE, D.D. Crown 8vo. 6s.

RUST (Rev. George).—FIRST STEPS TO LATIN PROSE COMPOSITION. 18mo. 1s. 6d.

—— A KEY TO RUST'S FIRST STEPS TO LATIN PROSE COMPOSITION. By W. YATES. 18mo. 3s. 6d.

RUTH AND HER FRIENDS: A STORY FOR GIRLS. Illustrated. Gl. 8vo. 2s. 6d.

RUTHERFORD (W. Gunion, M.A., LL.D.). —FIRST GREEK GRAMMAR. Part I. Accidence, 2s.; Part II. Syntax, 2s.; or in 1 vol. 3s. 6d.

—— THE NEW PHRYNICHUS. Being a revised Text of the Ecloga of the Grammarian Phrynichus, with Introduction and Commentary. 8vo. 18s.

—— BABRIUS. With Introductory Dissertations, Critical Notes, Commentary, and Lexicon. 8vo. 12s. 6d.

—— THUCYDIDES. Book IV. A Revision of the Text, illustrating the Principal Causes of Corruption in the Manuscripts of this Author. 8vo. 7s. 6d.

RYLAND (F.).—CHRONOLOGICAL OUTLINES OF ENGLISH LITERATURE. Crn. 8vo. 6s.

ST. JOHNSTON (A.).—CAMPING AMONG CANNIBALS. Crown 8vo. 4s. 6d.

—— A SOUTH SEA LOVER: A Romance. Cr. 8vo. 6s.

—— CHARLIE ASGARDE: THE STORY OF A FRIENDSHIP. Crown 8vo. 5s.

SAINTSBURY (George).—A HISTORY OF ELIZABETHAN LITERATURE. Cr. 8vo. 7s. 6d.

—— DRYDEN. Crown 8vo. 1s. 6d.; sewed, 1s.

SALLUST.—CAII SALLUSTII CRISPI CATILINA ET JUGURTHA. For Use in Schools. By C. MERIVALE, D.D. Fcp. 8vo. 3s. 6d. The JUGURTHA and the CATILINE may be had separately, 2s. each.

—— THE CONSPIRACY OF CATILINE AND THE JUGURTHINE WAR. Translated into English by A. W. POLLARD, B.A. Crown 8vo. 6s. CATILINE separately. Crown 8vo. 3s.

—— BELLUM CATULINAE. Edited, with Introduction and Notes, by A. M. COOK, M.A. Fcp. 8vo. 2s. 6d.

SALMON (Rev. Prof. George).—NON-MIRACULOUS CHRISTIANITY, AND OTHER SERMONS. 2nd Edition. Crown 8vo. 6s.

—— GNOSTICISM AND AGNOSTICISM, AND OTHER SERMONS. Crown 8vo. 7s. 6d.

SAND (G.).—LA MARE AU DIABLE. Edited by W. E. RUSSELL, M.A. 18mo. 1s.

SANDEAU (Jules).—MADEMOISELLE DE LA SEIGLIÈRE. Ed. H. C. STEEL. 18mo. 1s. 6d.

SANDERSON (F. W.).—HYDROSTATICS FOR BEGINNERS. Globe 8vo. 4s. 6d.

SANDHURST MATHEMATICAL PAPERS, FOR ADMISSION INTO THE ROYAL MILITARY COLLEGE, 1881—89. Edited by E. J. BROOKSMITH, B.A. Cr. 8vo. 3s. 6d.

SANDYS (J. E.).—AN EASTER VACATION IN GREECE. Crown 8vo. 3s. 6d.

SAYCE (Prof. A. H.).—THE ANCIENT EMPIRES OF THE EAST. Crown 8vo. 6s.

—— HERODOTOS. Books I.—III. The Ancient Empires of the East. Edited, with Notes, and Introduction. 8vo. 16s.

SCHILLER.—DIE JUNGFRAU VON ORLEANS. Edited by JOSEPH GOSTWICK. 18mo. 2s. 6d.

—— MARIA STUART. Edited, with Introduction and Notes, by C. SHELDON. 18mo. 2s. 6d.

—— SELECTIONS FROM SCHILLER'S LYRICAL POEMS. Edit. E. J. TURNER and E. D. A. MORSHEAD. 18mo. 2s. 6d.

—— WALLENSTEIN. Part I. DAS LÄGER. Edit. by H. B. COTTERILL, M.A. 18mo. 2s.

—— WILHELM TELL. Edited by G. E. FASNACHT. 18mo. 2s. 6d.

SCHILLER'S LIFE. By Prof. HEINRICH DÜNTZER. Translated by PERCY E. PINKERTON. Crown 8vo. 10s. 6d.

SCHMID.—HEINRICH VON EICHENFELS. Edited by G. E. FASNACHT. 2s. 6d.

SCHMIDT—WHITE.—AN INTRODUCTION TO THE RHYTHMIC AND METRIC OF THE CLASSICAL LANGUAGES. By Dr. J. H. HEINRICH SCHMIDT. Translated by JOHN WILLIAMS WHITE, Ph.D. 8vo. 10s. 6d.

SCIENCE LECTURES AT SOUTH KENSINGTON. With Illustrations.—Vol. I. Containing Lectures by Capt. ABNEY, R.E., F.R.S.; Prof. STOKES; Prof. A. B. W. KENNEDY, F.R.S., C.E.; F. J. BRAMWELL, C.E., F.R.S.; Prof. F. FORBES; H. C. SORBY, F.R.S.; J. T. BOTTOMLEY, F.R.S.E.; S. H. VINES, D.Sc.; Prof. CAREY FORSTER. Crown 8vo. 6s.

Vol. II. Containing Lectures by W. SPOTTISWOODE, F.R.S.; Prof. FORBES; H. W. CHISHOLM; Prof. T. F. PIGOT; W. FROUDE, LL.D., F.R.S.; Dr. SIEMENS; Prof. BARRETT; Dr. BURDON-SANDERSON; Dr. LAUDER BRUNTON, F.R.S.; Prof. McLEOD; Sir H. E. ROSCOE, F.R.S. Illust. Cr.8vo. 6s.

SCOTCH SERMONS, 1880. By Principal CAIRD and others. 3rd Edit. 8vo. 10s. 6d.

SCOTT.—THE POETICAL WORKS OF SIR WALTER SCOTT. Edited by Prof. F. T. PALGRAVE. Globe 8vo. 3s. 6d.

—— THE LAY OF THE LAST MINSTREL, and THE LADY OF THE LAKE. Edited, with Introductions and Notes, by Prof. F. T. PALGRAVE. Globe 8vo. 1s.

SCOTT.—MARMION, and THE LORD OF THE ISLES. By the same Editor. Gl. 8vo. 1s.

—— MARMION. A Tale of Flodden Field in Six Cantos. Edited, with Introduction and Notes, by Prof. M. MACMILLAN, B.A. Globe 8vo. 3s.; sewed, 2s. 6d.

—— ROKEBY. By the same. Globe 8vo. 3s.; sewed, 2s. 6d.

—— THE LAY OF THE LAST MINSTREL. Edited, with Introduction and Notes, by Prof. G. H. STUART, M.A., and E. H. ELLIOT, B.A. Globe 8vo. Introduction and Canto I., sewed, 9d. Cantos I.—III., 1s. 3d. —Cantos IV.—VI. [In the Press.

—— THE LADY OF THE LAKE. By Prof. G. H. STUART, M.A. Globe 8vo.

SCOTT. By R. H. HUTTON. Crown 8vo. 1s. 6d.; sewed, 1s.

SCOTTISH SONG: A SELECTION OF THE LYRICS OF SCOTLAND. Compiled by MARY CARLYLE AITKEN. 18mo. 4s. 6d.

SCRATCHLEY—KINLOCH COOKE.—AUSTRALIAN DEFENCES AND NEW GUINEA. Compiled from the Papers of the late Major-General Sir PETER SCRATCHLEY, R.E., by C. KINLOCH COOKE. 8vo. 14s.

SCULPTURE, SPECIMENS OF ANCIENT. Egyptian, Etruscan, Greek, and Roman. Selected from different Collections in Great Britain by the SOCIETY OF DILETTANTI. Vol. II. 5l. 5s.

SEATON (Dr. Edward C.).—A HANDBOOK OF VACCINATION. Extra fcp. 8vo. 8s. 6d.

SEELEY (Prof. J. R.).—LECTURES AND ESSAYS. 8vo. 10s. 6d.

—— THE EXPANSION OF ENGLAND. Two Courses of Lectures. Crown 8vo. 4s. 6d.

—— OUR COLONIAL EXPANSION. Extracts from "The Expansion of England." Crown 8vo. 1s.

SEILER (Carl, M.D.).—MICRO-PHOTOGRAPHS IN HISTOLOGY, NORMAL AND PATHOLOGICAL. 4to. 31s. 6d.

SELBORNE (Roundell, Earl of).—A DEFENCE OF THE CHURCH OF ENGLAND AGAINST DISESTABLISHMENT. Crown 8vo. 2s. 6d.

—— ANCIENT FACTS AND FICTIONS CONCERNING CHURCHES AND TITHES. Cr. 8vo. 7s. 6d.

—— THE BOOK OF PRAISE. From the Best English Hymn Writers. 18mo. 4s. 6d.

—— A HYMNAL. Chiefly from "The Book of Praise." In various sizes.—A. In Royal 32mo, cloth limp. 6d.—B. Small 18mo, larger type, cloth limp. 1s.—C. Same Edition, fine paper, cloth. 1s. 6d.—An Edition with Music, Selected, Harmonised, and Composed by JOHN HULLAH. Square 18mo. 3s. 6d.

SERVICE (Rev. John).—SERMONS. With Portrait. Crown 8vo. 6s.

—— PRAYERS FOR PUBLIC WORSHIP. Crown 8vo. 4s. 6d.

SHAIRP (John Campbell).—GLEN DESSERAY, AND OTHER POEMS, LYRICAL AND ELEGIAC. Ed. by F. T. PALGRAVE. Crown 8vo. 6s.

—— BURNS. Crown 8vo. 1s. 6d.; sewed, 1s.

SHAKESPEARE.—The Works of William Shakespeare. Cambridge Edition. New and Revised Edition, by W. Aldis Wright, M.A. 9 vols. 8vo. 10s. 6d. each.—Vol. I. Jan. 1891.

—— Shakespeare. Edited by W. G. Clark and W. A. Wright. *Globe Edition.* Globe 8vo. 3s. 6d.

—— The Works of William Shakespeare. *Victoria Edition.*—Vol. I. Comedies.—Vol. II. Histories.—Vol. III. Tragedies. In Three Vols. Crown 8vo. 6s. each.

—— Shakespeare's Songs and Sonnets. Edited, with Notes, by F. T. Palgrave. 18mo. 4s. 6d.

—— Charles Lamb's Tales from Shakespeare. Edited, with Preface, by the Rev. A. Ainger, M.A. 18mo. 4s. 6d. *Globe Readings Edition.* For Schools. Globe 8vo. 2s.—*Library Edition.* Globe 8vo. 5s.

—— The Tempest. By K. Deighton. Globe 8vo. 1s. 9d.; sewed, 1s. 6d.

—— Much Ado about Nothing. By the same Editor. Gl. 8vo. 1s. 9d.; swd., 1s. 6d.

—— A Midsummer Night's Dream. By the same Editor. Gl. 8vo. 1s. 9d.; swd., 1s. 6d.

—— The Merchant of Venice. By the same Editor. Gl. 8vo. 1s. 9d.; swd., 1s. 6d.

—— Twelfth Night; or, What You Will. By the same Editor. Globe 8vo. 1s. 9d.; sewed, 1s. 6d.

—— The Winter's Tale. By the same Editor. Globe 8vo. 2s.; sewed, 1s. 9d.

—— King John. By the same Editor. 1s. 9d.; sewed, 1s. 6d.

—— Richard II. By the same Editor. Globe 8vo. 1s. 9d.; sewed, 1s. 6d.

—— Henry V. By the same Editor. Globe 8vo. 1s. 9d.; sewed, 1s. 6d.

—— Richard III. Edited by Prof. C. H. Tawney, M.A. Gl. 8vo. 2s. 6d.; swd., 2s.

—— Coriolanus. By K. Deighton. Globe 8vo. [Feb. 1891.

—— Julius Caesar. By the same Editor. Globe 8vo. 1s. 9d.; sewed, 1s. 6d.

—— Macbeth. By the same Editor. Globe 8vo. 1s. 9d.; sewed, 1s. 6d.

—— Hamlet. By the same Editor. Globe 8vo. 2s. 6d.; sewed, 2s.

—— Othello. By the same Editor. Globe 8vo. 2s.; sewed, 1s. 9d.

—— Cymbeline. By the same Editor. Globe 8vo. 2s. 6d.; sewed, 2s.

SHAKSPERE. By Prof. Dowden. 18mo. 1s.

SHANN (G.).—An Elementary Treatise on Heat in Relation to Steam and the Steam-Engine. Illustrated. Crown 8vo. 4s. 6d.

SHARP (W.).—Dante Gabriel Rossetti. Crown 8vo. 10s. 6d.

SHELBURNE. Life of William, Earl of Shelburne. By Lord Edmond Fitz-maurice. In 3 vols.—Vol. I. 8vo. 12s.—Vol. II. 8vo. 12s.—Vol. III. 8vo. 16s.

SHELLEY. Complete Poetical Works. Edited by Prof. Dowden. With Portrait. Crown 8vo. 7s. 6d.

—— Selections. Edited by Stopford A. Brooke. 18mo. 4s. 6d. Large Paper Edition. 12s. 6d.

SHELLEY. By J. A. Symonds, M.A. Crown 8vo. 1s. 6d.; sewed, 1s.

SHERIDAN. By Mrs. Oliphant. Crown 8vo. 1s. 6d.; sewed, 1s.

SHIRLEY (W. N.).—Elijah: Four University Sermons. Fcp. 8vo. 2s. 6d.

SHORTHOUSE (J. H.).—John Inglesant: A Romance. Crown 8vo. 6s.

—— The Little Schoolmaster Mark: A Spiritual Romance. Two Parts. Crown 8vo. 2s. 6d. each: complete, 4s. 6d.

—— Sir Percival: A Story of the Past and of the Present. Crown 8vo. 6s.

—— A Teacher of the Violin, and other Tales. Crown 8vo. 6s.

—— The Countess Eve. Crown 8vo. 6s.

SHORTLAND (Admiral).—Nautical Surveying. 8vo. 21s.

SHUCKBURGH (E. S.).—Passages from Latin Authors for Translation into English. Crown 8vo. 2s.

SHUCHHARDT (Carl).—Dr. Schliemann's Excavations at Troy, Tiryns, Mycenae, Orchomenos, Ithaca presented in the Light of Recent Knowledge. Translated by Eugenie Sellers. With Introduction by Walter Leaf, Litt.D. Illustrated. 8vo. [In the Press.

SHUFELDT (R. W.).—The Myology of the Raven (*Corvus corax Sinuatus*). A Guide to the Study of the Muscular System in Birds. Illustrated. 8vo. 13s. net.

SIBSON.—Dr. Francis Sibson's Collected Works. Edited by W. M. Ord, M.D. Illustrated. 4 vols. 8vo. 3l. 3s.

SIDGWICK (Prof. Henry).—The Methods of Ethics. 4th Edit., revised. 8vo. 14s.

—— A Supplement to the Second Edition. Containing all the important Additions and Alterations in the 4th Edit. 8vo. 6s.

—— The Principles of Political Economy. 2nd Edition. 8vo. 16s.

—— Outlines of the History of Ethics for English Readers. Cr. 8vo. 3s. 6d.

—— Elements of Politics. 8vo.

SIDNEY (Sir Philip). By John Addington Symonds. Cr. 8vo. 1s. 6d.; sewed, 1s.

SIME (James).—History of Germany. 2nd Edition. Maps. 18mo. 3s.

—— Geography of Europe. Globe 8vo. 3s.

SIMPSON (F. P.).—Latin Prose after the Best Authors.—Part I. Caesarian Prose. Extra fcp. 8vo. 2s. 6d.

Key (for Teachers only). Ex. fcp. 8vo. 5s.

SIMPSON (W.).—An Epitome of the History of the Christian Church. Fcp. 8vo. 3s. 6d.

SKRINE (J. H.).—UNDER TWO QUEENS. Crown 8vo. 3s.

—— A MEMORY OF EDWARD THRING. Crown 8vo. 6s.

SLIP IN THE FENS (A). Globe 8vo. 2s.

SMALLEY (George W.).—LONDON LETTERS AND SOME OTHERS. 2 vols. 8vo. 32s.

SMITH (Barnard).—ARITHMETIC AND ALGEBRA. New Edition. Crown 8vo. 10s. 6d.

—— ARITHMETIC FOR THE USE OF SCHOOLS. New Edition. Crown 8vo. 4s. 6d.

—— KEY TO ARITHMETIC FOR SCHOOLS. New Edition. Crown 8vo. 8s. 6d.

—— EXERCISES IN ARITHMETIC. Crown 8vo, 2 Parts, 1s. each, or complete, 2s.—With Answers, 2s. 6d.—Answers separately, 6d.

—— SCHOOL CLASS-BOOK OF ARITHMETIC. 18mo. 3s.—Or, sold separately, in Three Parts. 1s. each.

—— KEY TO SCHOOL CLASS-BOOK OF ARITHMETIC. In Parts I. II. and III. 2s. 6d. each.

—— SHILLING BOOK OF ARITHMETIC FOR NATIONAL AND ELEMENTARY SCHOOLS. 18mo, cloth.—Or separately, Part I. 2d.; II. 3d.; III. 7d.—With Answers, 1s. 6d.

—— ANSWERS TO THE SHILLING BOOK OF ARITHMETIC. 18mo. 6d.

—— KEY TO THE SHILLING BOOK OF ARITHMETIC. 18mo. 4s. 6d.

—— EXAMINATION PAPERS IN ARITHMETIC. In Four Parts. 18mo. 1s. 6d.—With Answers, 2s.—Answers, 6d.

—— KEY TO EXAMINATION PAPERS IN ARITHMETIC. 18mo. 4s. 6d.

—— THE METRIC SYSTEM OF ARITHMETIC. 3d.

—— A CHART OF THE METRIC SYSTEM OF ARITHMETIC. On a Sheet, size 42 by 34 in., on Roller mounted and varnished. 3s. 6d.

—— EASY LESSONS IN ARITHMETIC. Combining Exercises in Reading, Writing, Spelling, and Dictation. Part I. for Standard I. in National Schools. Crown 8vo. 9d.

—— EXAMINATION CARDS IN ARITHMETIC. With Answers and Hints. Standards I. and II. In box. 1s.—Standards III. IV. and V. In boxes. 1s. each.—Standard VI. in Two Parts. In boxes. 1s. each.

SMITH (Catherine Barnard).—POEMS. Fcp. 8vo. 5s.

SMITH (Charles).—AN ELEMENTARY TREATISE ON CONIC SECTIONS. 7th Edition. Crown 8vo. 7s. 6d.

—— SOLUTIONS OF THE EXAMPLES IN "AN ELEMENTARY TREATISE ON CONIC SECTIONS." Crown 8vo. 10s. 6d.

—— AN ELEMENTARY TREATISE ON SOLID GEOMETRY. 2nd Edition. Cr. 8vo. 9s. 6d.

—— ELEMENTARY ALGEBRA. 2nd Edition. Globe 8vo. 4s. 6d.

—— A TREATISE ON ALGEBRA. 2nd Edition. Crown 8vo. 7s. 6d.

—— SOLUTIONS OF THE EXAMPLES IN "A TREATISE ON ALGEBRA." Cr. 8vo. 10s. 6d.

SMITH (Goldwin).—THREE ENGLISH STATESMEN. New Edition. Crown 8vo. 5s.

—— COWPER. Crown 8vo. 1s. 6d.; sewed, 1s.

—— PROHIBITIONISM IN CANADA AND THE UNITED STATES. 8vo, sewed. 6d.

SMITH (Horace).—POEMS. Globe 8vo. 5s.

SMITH (J.).—ECONOMIC PLANTS, DICTIONARY OF POPULAR NAMES OF: THEIR HISTORY, PRODUCTS, AND USES. 8vo. 14s.

SMITH (Rev. Travers).—MAN'S KNOWLEDGE OF MAN AND OF GOD. Crown 8vo. 6s.

SMITH (W. G.).—DISEASES OF FIELD AND GARDEN CROPS, CHIEFLY SUCH AS ARE CAUSED BY FUNGI. With 143 new Illustrations. Fcp. 8vo. 4s. 6d.

SMITH (W. Saumarez).—THE BLOOD OF THE NEW COVENANT: A THEOLOGICAL ESSAY. Crown 8vo. 2s. 6d.

SNOWBALL (J. C.).—THE ELEMENTS OF PLANE AND SPHERICAL TRIGONOMETRY. 14th Edition. Crown 8vo. 7s. 6d.

SONNENSCHEIN (A.) and MEIKLEJOHN (J. M. D.).—THE ENGLISH METHOD OF TEACHING TO READ. Fcp. 8vo. Comprising—

THE NURSERY BOOK, containing all the Two Letter Words in the Language. 1d.—Also in Large Type on Four Sheets, with Roller. 5s.

THE FIRST COURSE, consisting of Short Vowels with Single Consonants. 7d.

THE SECOND COURSE, with Combinations and Bridges, consisting of Short Vowels with Double Consonants. 7d.

THE THIRD AND FOURTH COURSES, consisting of Long Vowels and all the Double Vowels in the Language. 7d.

SOPHOCLES.—ŒDIPUS THE KING. Translated from the Greek into English Verse by E. D. A. MORSHEAD, M.A. Fcp. 8vo. 3s. 6d.

—— ŒDIPUS TYRANNUS. A Record by L. SPEED and F. R. PRYOR of the performance at Cambridge. Illustr. Small folio. 12s. 6d. net.

—— By Prof. L. CAMPBELL. Fcp. 8vo. 1s. 6d.

SOUTHEY. By Prof. DOWDEN. Crown 8vo. 1s. 6d.; sewed, 1s.

SOUTHEY.—LIFE OF NELSON. Edit., with Introduction and Notes, by Prof. MICHAEL MACMILLAN, B.A. Gl. 8vo. 3s.; swd., 2s. 6d.

SPENDER (J. Kent).—THERAPEUTIC MEANS FOR THE RELIEF OF PAIN. 8vo. 8s. 6d.

SPENSER.—COMPLETE WORKS OF EDMUND SPENSER. Ed. by R. MORRIS, with Memoir by J. W. HALES. Globe 8vo. 3s. 6d.

SPENSER. By the Very Rev. Dean CHURCH. Cr. 8vo. 1s. 6d.; swd., 1s.—Library Ed., 5s.

SPINOZA: A STUDY OF. By JAMES MARTINEAU, LL.D. 2nd Ed. Cr. 8vo. 6s.

SPOTTISWOODE (W.).—POLARISATION OF LIGHT. Illustrated. Crown 8vo. 3s. 6d.

STANLEY (Very Rev. A. P.).—THE ATHA-NASIAN CREED. Crown 8vo. 2s.

—— THE NATIONAL THANKSGIVING. Sermons preached in Westminster Abbey. 2nd Ed. Crown 8vo. 2s. 6d.

—— ADDRESSES AND SERMONS DELIVERED AT ST. ANDREWS IN 1872-75 and 1877. Crown 8vo. 5s.

—— ADDRESSES AND SERMONS DELIVERED DURING A VISIT TO THE UNITED STATES AND CANADA IN 1878. Crown 8vo. 6s.

STANLEY (Hon. Maude).—CLUBS FOR WORKING GIRLS. Crown 8vo. 6s.

STATESMAN'S YEAR-BOOK (THE). A Statistical and Historical Annual of the States of the Civilised World for the year 1890. Twenty-seventh Annual Publication. Revised after Official Returns. Edited by J. SCOTT KELTIE. Crown 8vo. 10s. 6d.

STATHAM (R.).—BLACKS, BOERS, AND BRITISH. Crown 8vo. 6s.

STEBBING (W.)—PETERBOROUGH. Portrait. Crown 8vo. 2s. 6d.

STEPHEN (Sir J. Fitzjames, Q.C., K.C.S.I.). —A DIGEST OF THE LAW OF EVIDENCE. 5th Edition. Crown 8vo. 6s.

—— A DIGEST OF THE CRIMINAL LAW: CRIMES AND PUNISHMENTS. 4th Edition. 8vo. 16s.

—— A DIGEST OF THE LAW OF CRIMINAL PROCEDURE IN INDICTABLE OFFENCES. By Sir JAMES F. STEPHEN, K.C.S.I., etc., and HERBERT STEPHEN, LL.M. 8vo. 12s. 6d.

—— A HISTORY OF THE CRIMINAL LAW OF ENGLAND. 3 vols. 8vo. 48s.

—— THE STORY OF NUNCOMAR AND THE IM-PEACHMENT OF SIR ELIJAH IMPEY. 2 vols. Crown 8vo. 15s.

—— A GENERAL VIEW OF THE CRIMINAL LAW OF ENGLAND. 2nd Edition. 8vo. 14s.

STEPHEN (J. K.).—INTERNATIONAL LAW AND INTERNATIONAL RELATIONS. Crown 8vo. 6s.

STEPHEN (Leslie).—JOHNSON. Crown 8vo. 1s. 6d.; sewed, 1s.

—— SWIFT. Crown 8vo. 1s. 6d.; sewed, 1s.

—— POPE. Crown 8vo. 1s. 6d.; sewed, 1s.

STEPHEN (Caroline E.).—THE SERVICE OF THE POOR. Crown 8vo. 6s. 6d.

STEPHENS (J. B.).—CONVICT ONCE, AND OTHER POEMS. Crown 8vo. 7s. 6d.

STERNE. By H. D. TRAILL. Crown 8vo. 1s. 6d.; sewed, 1s.

STEVENSON (J. J.).—HOUSE ARCHITEC-TURE. With Illustrations. 2 vols. Royal 8vo. 18s. each. Vol. I. ARCHITECTURE. Vol. II. HOUSE PLANNING.

STEWART (Aubrey).—THE TALE OF TROY. Done into English. Globe 8vo. 3s. 6d.

STEWART (Prof. Balfour).—LESSONS IN ELEMENTARY PHYSICS. With Illustrations and Coloured Diagram. Fcp. 8vo. 4s. 6d.

—— PRIMER OF PHYSICS. Illustrated. New Edition, with Questions. 18mo. 1s.

STEWART (Prof. Balfour).—QUESTIONS ON STEWART'S LESSONS ON ELEMENTARY PHYSICS. By T. H. CORE. 12mo. 2s.

STEWART (Prof. Balfour) and GEE (W. W. Haldane).—LESSONS IN ELEMENTARY PRAC-TICAL PHYSICS. Crown 8vo. Illustrated. Vol. I. GENERAL PHYSICAL PROCESSES. 6s. —Vol. II. ELECTRICITY AND MAGNETISM. Cr. 8vo. 7s. 6d.—Vol. III. OPTICS, HEAT, AND SOUND.

—— PRACTICAL PHYSICS FOR SCHOOLS AND THE JUNIOR STUDENTS OF COLLEGES. Globe 8vo. Vol. I. ELECTRICITY AND MAGNETISM. 2s. 6d.—Vol. II. HEAT, LIGHT, AND SOUND.

STEWART (Prof. Balfour) and TAIT (P. G.). —THE UNSEEN UNIVERSE; OR, PHYSICAL SPECULATIONS ON A FUTURE STATE. 15th Edition. Crown 8vo. 6s.

STEWART (S. A.) and CORRY (T. H.).— A FLORA OF THE NORTH-EAST OF IRELAND. Crown 8vo. 5s. 6d.

STOKES (Sir George G.).—ON LIGHT. The Burnett Lectures. Crown 8vo. 7s. 6d.

STONE (W. H.).—ELEMENTARY LESSONS ON SOUND. Illustrated. Fcap. 8vo. 3s. 6d.

STRACHAN (J. S.) and WILKINS (A. S.).— ANALECTA. Passages for Translation. Cr. 8vo. 5s.

STRACHEY (Lieut.-Gen. R.).—LECTURES ON GEOGRAPHY. Crown 8vo. 4s. 6d.

STRAFFORD. By H. D. TRAILL. With Portrait. Crown 8vo. 2s. 6d.

STRANGFORD (Viscountess). — EGYPTIAN SEPULCHRES AND SYRIAN SHRINES. New Edition. Crown 8vo. 7s. 6d.

STRETTELL (Alma).—SPANISH AND ITAL-IAN FOLK SONGS. Illustrated. Royal 16mo. 12s. 6d.

STUART, THE ROYAL HOUSE OF Illustrated by Forty Plates in Colours drawn from Relics of the Stuarts by WILLIAM GIBB. With Introduction by J. SKELTON, C.B., LL.D., and Descriptive Notes by W. ST. J. HOPE. Folio, half morocco, gilt edges. 7l. 7s. net.

STUBBS (Rev. C. W.).—FOR CHRIST AND CITY. Sermons and Addresses. Cr. 8vo. 6s.

SURGERY, THE INTERNATIONAL ENCYCLOPAEDIA OF. A Systematic Treatise on the Theory and Practice of Sur-gery by Authors of Various Nations. Edited by JOHN ASHHURST, Jun., M.D., Professor of Clinical Surgery in the University of Penn-sylvania. 6 vols. Royal 8vo. 31s. 6d. each.

SWIFT. By LESLIE STEPHEN. Crown 8vo. 1s. 6d.; sewed, 1s.

SYMONS (Arthur).—DAYS AND NIGHTS: POEMS. Globe 8vo. 6s.

SYMONDS (J. A.).—SHELLEY. Crown 8vo. 1s. 6d.; sewed, 1s.

—— SIR PHILIP SIDNEY. 1s. 6d.; sewed, 1s.

TACITUS, THE WORKS OF. Transl. by A. J. CHURCH, M.A., and W. J. BRODRIBB, M.A.

THE HISTORY OF TACITUS. 4th Edition. Crown 8vo. 6s.

THE AGRICOLA AND GERMANIA. A Revised Text. With Notes. Fcp. 8vo. 3s. 6d. The AGRICOLA and GERMANIA may be had separately. 2s. each.

THE ANNALS. Book VI. With Introduction and Notes. Fcp. 8vo. 2s.

THE AGRICOLA AND GERMANIA. With the Dialogue on Oratory. Trans. Cr. 8vo. 4s. 6d.

ANNALS OF TACITUS. Translated. 5th Ed. Crown 8vo. 7s. 6d.

—— THE ANNALS. Edited by Prof. G. O. HOLBROOKE, M.A. 8vo. 16s.

—— THE HISTORIES. Edited, with Introduction and Commentary, by Rev. W. A. SPOONER, M.A. 8vo.

—— THE HISTORIES. Books I. and II. Ed. by A. D. GODLEY, M.A. Fcp. 8vo. 3s. 6d.

—— THE HISTORIES. Books III.–V. Edited by A. D. GODLEY, M.A. Fcp. 8vo. 3s. 6d.

TACITUS. By A. J. CHURCH, M.A., and W. J. BRODRIBB, M.A. Fcp. 8vo. 1s. 6d.

TAIT (Archbishop).—THE PRESENT POSITION OF THE CHURCH OF ENGLAND. Being the Charge delivered at his Primary Visitation. 3rd Edition. 8vo. 3s. 6d.

—— DUTIES OF THE CHURCH OF ENGLAND. Being Seven Addresses delivered at his Second Visitation. 8vo. 4s. 6d.

—— THE CHURCH OF THE FUTURE. Charges delivered at his Third Quadrennial Visitation. 2nd Edition. Crown 8vo. 3s. 6d.

TAIT.—THE LIFE OF ARCHIBALD CAMPBELL TAIT, ARCHBISHOP OF CANTERBURY. By the Very Rev. the DEAN OF WINDSOR and Rev. W. BENHAM, B.D. 2 vols. 8vo.

TAIT.—CATHARINE AND CRAWFURD TAIT, WIFE AND SON OF ARCHIBALD CAMPBELL, ARCHBISHOP OF CANTERBURY: A MEMOIR. Edited by the Rev. W. BENHAM, B.D. Crown 8vo. 6s.

Popular Edition, abridged. Cr. 8vo. 2s. 6d.

TAIT (C. W. A.).—ANALYSIS OF ENGLISH HISTORY, BASED ON GREEN'S "SHORT HISTORY OF THE ENGLISH PEOPLE." Revised and Enlarged Edition. Crown 8vo. 4s. 6d.

TAIT (Prof. P. G.).—LECTURES ON SOME RECENT ADVANCES IN PHYSICAL SCIENCE. 3rd Edition. Crown 8vo. 9s.

—— HEAT. With Illustrations. Cr. 8vo. 6s.

TAIT (P. G.) and STEELE (W. J.).—A TREATISE ON DYNAMICS OF A PARTICLE. 6th Edition. Crown 8vo. 12s.

TANNER (Prof. Henry).—FIRST PRINCIPLES OF AGRICULTURE. 18mo. 1s.

—— THE ABBOTT'S FARM; OR, PRACTICE WITH SCIENCE. Crown 8vo. 3s. 6d.

—— THE ALPHABET OF THE PRINCIPLES OF AGRICULTURE. Extra fcp. 8vo. 6d.

—— FURTHER STEPS IN THE PRINCIPLES OF AGRICULTURE. Extra fcp. 8vo. 1s.

TANNER (Prof. Henry). — ELEMENTARY SCHOOL READINGS IN THE PRINCIPLES OF AGRICULTURE FOR THE THIRD STAGE. Extra fcp. 8vo. 1s.

—— ELEMENTARY LESSONS IN THE SCIENCE OF AGRICULTURAL PRACTICE. Fcp. 8vo. 3s. 6d.

TAVERNIER (Baron): TRAVELS IN INDIA OF JEAN BAPTISTE TAVERNIER, BARON OF AUBONNE. Translated by V. BALL, LL.D. Illustrated. 2 vols. 8vo. 2l. 2s.

TAYLOR (Franklin). — PRIMER OF PIANO-FORTE PLAYING. 18mo. 1s.

TAYLOR (Isaac).—THE RESTORATION OF BELIEF. Crown 8vo. 8s. 6d.

TAYLOR (Isaac). — WORDS AND PLACES. 9th Edition. Maps. Globe 8vo. 6s.

—— ETRUSCAN RESEARCHES. With Wood-cuts. 8vo. 14s.

—— GREEKS AND GOTHS : A STUDY OF THE RUNES. 8vo. 9s.

TAYLOR (Sedley).—SOUND AND MUSIC. 2nd Edition. Extra Crown 8vo. 8s. 6d.

—— A SYSTEM OF SIGHT-SINGING FROM THE ESTABLISHED MUSICAL NOTATION. 8vo. 5s. net.

TEBAY (S.).—ELEMENTARY MENSURATION FOR SCHOOLS. Extra fcp. 8vo. 3s. 6d.

TEGETMEIER (W. B.).—HOUSEHOLD MAN-AGEMENT AND COOKERY. 18mo. 1s.

TEMPLE (Right Rev. Frederick, D.D., Bishop of London).—SERMONS PREACHED IN THE CHAPEL OF RUGBY SCHOOL. 3rd and Cheaper Edition. Extra fcp. 8vo. 4s. 6d.

—— SECOND SERIES. 3rd Ed. Ex. fcp. 8vo. 6s.

—— THIRD SERIES. 4th Ed. Ex. fcp. 8vo. 6s.

—— THE RELATIONS BETWEEN RELIGION AND SCIENCE. Bampton Lectures, 1884. 7th and Cheaper Edition. Crown 8vo. 6s.

TEMPLE (Sir Rd.).—LORD LAWRENCE. Portrait. Crown 8vo. 2s. 6d.

TENNYSON (Lord). — COMPLETE WORKS. New and enlarged Edition, with Portrait. Crown 8vo. 7s. 6d.

School Edition. In Four Parts. Crown 8vo. 2s. 6d. each.

—— POETICAL WORKS. Pocket Edition. 18mo, morocco, gilt edges. 7s. 6d. net.

—— WORKS. Library Edition. In 8 vols. Globe 8vo. 5s. each. Each volume may be had separately.—POEMS. 2 vols.—IDYLLS OF THE KING.—THE PRINCESS, AND MAUD. —ENOCH ARDEN, AND IN MEMORIAM.— BALLADS, AND OTHER POEMS. — QUEEN MARY, AND HAROLD.—BECKET, AND OTHER PLAYS.

—— WORKS. Extra Fcp. 8vo. Edition, on Hand-made Paper. In 7 volumes (supplied in sets only). 3l. 13s. 6d. — Vol. I. EARLY POEMS; II. LUCRETIUS, AND OTHER POEMS; III. IDYLLS OF THE KING, IV. THE PRINCESS, AND MAUD ; V. ENOCH ARDEN, AND IN MEMORIAM; VI. QUEEN MARY, AND HAROLD ; VII. BALLADS, & OTHER POEMS.

TENNYSON (Lord).—The Collected Works. Miniature Edition, in 14 vols., viz. The Poetical Works, 10 vols. in a box. 21s.—The Dramatic Works, 4 vols. in a box. 10s. 6d.

—— Lyrical Poems. Selected and Annotated by Prof. F. T. Palgrave. 18mo. 4s.6d. Large Paper Edition. 8vo. 9s.

—— In Memoriam. 18mo. 4s. 6d. Large Paper Edition. 8vo. 9s.

—— The Tennyson Birthday Book. Edit. by Emily Shakespear. 18mo. 2s. 6d.

—— The Brook. With 20 Illustrations by A. Woodruff. 32mo. 2s. 6d.

—— Selections from Tennyson. With Introduction and Notes, by F. J. Rowe, M.A., and W. T. Webb, M.A. Globe 8vo. 3s. 6d.

—— Enoch Arden. By W. T. Webb, M.A. Globe 8vo. [In the Press.

—— The Coming of Arthur, and The Passing of Arthur. By F. J. Rowe, M.A. Globe 8vo. 2s. [In the Press.

—— A Companion to "In Memoriam." By Elizabeth R. Chapman. Globe 8vo. 2s.

—— The Original Editions. Fcp. 8vo. Poems. 6s. Maud, and other Poems. 3s. 6d. The Princess. 3s. 6d. Idylls of the King. (Collected.) 6s. Enoch Arden, etc. 3s. 6d. The Holy Grail, and other Poems. 4s.6d. Ballads, and other Poems. 5s. Harold: A Drama. 6s. Queen Mary: A Drama. 6s. The Cup, and the Falcon. 5s. Becket. 6s. Tiresias, and other Poems. 6s. Locksley Hall sixty years after, etc. 6s. Demeter, and other Poems. 6s.

—— The Royal Edition. 1 vol. 8vo. 16s.

—— Selections from Tennyson's Works. Square 8vo. 3s. 6d.

—— Songs from Tennyson's Writings. Square 8vo. 2s. 6d.

TENNYSON FOR THE YOUNG. Selections from Lord Tennyson's Poems. Edited with Notes, by the Rev. Alfred Ainger, M.A. 18mo. 1s. net.

TENNYSON (Frederick).—The Isles of Greece: Sappho and Alcaeus. Crown 8vo. 7s. 6d.

TENNYSON (Hallam). — Jack and the Bean-stalk. With 40 Illustrations by Randolph Caldecott. Fcp. 4to. 3s. 6d.

TERENCE.—Hauton Timorumenos. Edit. by E. S. Shuckburgh, M.A. Fcp. 8vo. 2s. 6d.—With Translation, 3s. 6d.

—— Phormio. Edited by Rev. John Bond, and A. S. Walpole. Fcp. 8vo. 2s. 6d.

—— Scenes from the Andria. Edited by F. W. Cornish, M.A. 18mo. 1s. 6d.

TERESA (St.): Life of. By the Author of "Devotions before and after Holy Communion." Crown 8vo. 8s. 6d.

THACKERAY. By Anthony Trollope. Crown 8vo. 1s. 6d.; sewed, 1s.

THEOCRITUS, BION, and MOSCHUS. Rendered into English Prose, with Introductory Essay, by A. Lang, M.A. 18mo. 4s.6d. Large Paper Edition. 8vo. 9s.

THOMPSON (Edith).—History of England. New Edit., with Maps. 18mo. 2s.6d.

THOMPSON (Prof. Silvanus P.).—Elementary Electricity and Magnetism. Illustrated. New Edition. Fcp. 8vo. 4s. 6d.

THOMPSON (G. Carslake).—Public Opinion and Lord Beaconsfield, 1875—80. 2 vols. 8vo. 36s.

THOMSON (Hugh).—Days with Sir Roger de Coverley. Illustrated. Fcp. 4to. 6s.

THOMSON (J. J.).—A Treatise on the Motion of Vortex Rings. 8vo. 6s.

—— Applications of Dynamics to Physic and Chemistry. Crown 8vo. 7s. 6d.

THOMSON (Sir Wm.).—Reprint of Papers on Electrostatics and Magnetism. 2nd Edition. 8vo. 18s.

—— Popular Lectures and Addresses. In 3 vols.—Vol. I. Constitution of Matter. Illustrated. Crown 8vo. 6s.—Vol. III. Papers on Navigation.

THOMSON (Sir C. Wyville).—The Depths of the Sea. An Account of the General Results of the Dredging Cruises of H.M.SS. "Lightning" and "Porcupine" during the Summers of 1868-69-70. With Illustrations, Maps, and Plans. 2nd Edit. 8vo. 31s. 6d.

—— The Voyage of the "Challenger": The Atlantic. With Illustrations, Coloured Maps, Charts, etc. 2 vols. 8vo. 45s.

THORNTON (W. T.).—A Plea for Peasant Proprietors. New Edit. Cr. 8vo. 7s. 6d.

—— Old-Fashioned Ethics and Common-Sense Metaphysics. 8vo. 10s. 6d.

—— Indian Public Works, and Cognate Indian Topics. Crown 8vo. 8s. 6d.

—— Word for Word from Horace: The Odes Literally Versified. Cr. 8vo. 7s.6d.

THORNTON (J.).—First Lessons in Book-keeping. New Edition. Crown 8vo. 2s. 6d.

—— Key. Containing all the Exercises fully worked out, with brief Notes. Oblong 4to. 10s. 6d.

—— Primer of Book-Keeping. 18mo. 1s.

—— Key. Demy 8vo. 2s. 6d.

THORPE (Prof. T. E.).—A Series of Problems, for Use in Colleges and Schools. New Edition, with Key. 18mo. 2s.

THRING (Rev. Edward).—A Construing Book. Fcp. 8vo. 2s. 6d.

—— A Latin Gradual. 2nd Ed. 18mo. 2s.6d.

—— The Elements of Grammar taught in English. 5th Edition. 18mo. 2s.

—— Education and School. 2nd Edition. Crown 8vo. 6s.

—— A Manual of Mood Constructions. Extra fcp. 8vo. 1s. 6d.

—— Thoughts on Life Science. 2nd Edit. Crown 8vo. 7s. 6d.

—— A Memory of Edward Thring. By J. H. Skrine. Portrait. Crown 8vo. 6s.

**THROUGH THE RANKS TO A COM-MISSION.** New Edit. Cr. 8vo. 2s. 6d.

**THRUPP** (Rev. J. F.).—INTRODUCTION TO THE STUDY AND USE OF THE PSALMS. 2nd Edition. 2 vols. 8vo. 21s.

**THUCYDIDES.**—THE SICILIAN EXPEDITION. Books VI. and VII. Edited by the Rev. PERCIVAL FROST, M.A. Fcp. 8vo. 3s. 6d.

—— THE RISE OF THE ATHENIAN EMPIRE. Being Selections from Book I. Edited by F. H. COLSON, M.A. 18mo. 1s. 6d.

—— THE CAPTURE OF SPHACTERIA. Book IV. Chaps. 1—41. Edit. by C. E. GRAVES, M.A. 18mo. 1s. 6d.

—— BOOK II. Ed. by E. C. MARCHANT, M.A.

—— BOOK IV. By C. E. GRAVES. Fcp 8vo. 3s. 6d.

—— BOOK IV. A Revision of the Text, illustrating the Principal Causes of Corruption in the Manuscripts of this Author. By WILLIAM G. RUTHERFORD, M.A., LL.D. 8vo. 7s.6d.

—— Book VIII. Edited, with Introduction and Commentary, by H. C. GOODHART, M.A. 8vo.

**THUDICHUM** (J. L. W.) and **DUPRÉ** (A.).—TREATISE ON THE ORIGIN, NATURE, AND VARIETIES OF WINE. Medium 8vo. 25s.

**TODHUNTER** (Isaac).—EUCLID FOR COLLEGES AND SCHOOLS. 18mo. 3s. 6d.

—— KEY TO EXERCISES IN EUCLID. Crown 8vo. 6s. 6d.

—— MENSURATION FOR BEGINNERS. With Examples. 18mo. 2s. 6d.

—— KEY TO MENSURATION FOR BEGINNERS. By Rev. FR. L. MCCARTHY. Cr. 8vo. 7s. 6d.

—— ALGEBRA FOR BEGINNERS. With numerous Examples. 18mo. 2s. 6d.

—— KEY TO ALGEBRA FOR BEGINNERS. Cr. 8vo. 6s. 6d.

—— ALGEBRA FOR THE USE OF COLLEGES AND SCHOOLS. Crown 8vo. 7s. 6d.

—— KEY TO ALGEBRA FOR COLLEGES AND SCHOOLS. Crown 8vo. 10s. 6d.

—— TRIGONOMETRY FOR BEGINNERS. With numerous Examples. 18mo. 2s. 6d.

—— KEY TO TRIGONOMETRY FOR BEGINNERS. Crown 8vo. 8s. 6d.

—— PLANE TRIGONOMETRY FOR COLLEGES AND SCHOOLS. Crown 8vo. 5s.

—— KEY TO PLANE TRIGONOMETRY. Crown 8vo. 10s. 6d.

—— A TREATISE ON SPHERICAL TRIGONOMETRY FOR THE USE OF COLLEGES AND SCHOOLS. Crown 8vo. 4s. 6d.

—— MECHANICS FOR BEGINNERS. With numerous Examples. 18mo. 4s. 6d.

—— KEY TO MECHANICS FOR BEGINNERS. 6s. 6d.

—— A TREATISE ON THE THEORY OF EQUATIONS. Crown 8vo. 7s. 6d.

—— A TREATISE ON PLANE CO-ORDINATE GEOMETRY. Crown 8vo. 7s. 6d.

**TODHUNTER** (I.).—SOLUTIONS AND PROBLEMS CONTAINED IN A TREATISE ON PLANE CO-ORDINATE GEOMETRY. By C. W. BOURNE, M.A. Crown 8vo. 10s. 6d.

—— A TREATISE ON THE DIFFERENTIAL CALCULUS. Crown 8vo. 10s. 6d.

—— KEY TO TREATISE ON THE DIFFERENTIAL CALCULUS. By H. ST. J. HUNTER, M.A. Crown 8vo. 10s. 6d.

—— A TREATISE ON THE INTEGRAL CALCULUS. Crown 8vo. 10s. 6d.

—— KEY TO TREATISE ON THE INTEGRAL CALCULUS AND ITS APPLICATIONS. By H. ST. J. HUNTER, M.A. Cr. 8vo. 10s. 6d.

—— EXAMPLES OF ANALYTICAL GEOMETRY OF THREE DIMENSIONS. Crown 8vo. 4s.

—— THE CONFLICT OF STUDIES. 8vo. 10s. 6d.

—— AN ELEMENTARY TREATISE ON LAPLACE'S, LAMÉ'S, AND BESSEL'S FUNCTIONS. Crown 8vo. 10s. 6d.

—— A TREATISE ON ANALYTICAL STATICS. Edited by J. D. EVERETT, M.A., F.R.S. 5th Edition. Crown 8vo. 10s. 6d.

**TOM BROWN'S SCHOOL DAYS.** By An OLD BOY.

Golden Treasury Edition. 18mo. 4s. 6d.
Illustrated Edition. Crown 8vo. 6s.
Uniform Edition. Crown 8vo. 3s. 6d.
People's Edition. 18mo. 2s.

People's Sixpenny Edition. With Illustrations. Medium 4to. 6d.—Also uniform with the Sixpenny Edition of Charles Kingsley's Novels. Medium 8vo. 6d.

**TOM BROWN AT OXFORD.** By the Author of "Tom Brown's School Days." Illustrated. Crown 8vo. 6s.

Uniform Edition. Crown 8vo. 3s. 6d.

**TOURGÉNIEF.**—VIRGIN SOIL. Translated by ASHTON W. DILKE. Crown 8vo. 6s.

**TOZER** (H. F.).—CLASSICAL GEOGRAPHY. 18mo. 1s.

**TRAILL** (H. D.).—STERNE. Crown 8vo. 1s. 6d. ; sewed, 1s.

—— CENTRAL GOVERNMENT. Cr. 8vo. 3s. 6d.

—— WILLIAM III. Crown 8vo. 2s. 6d.

—— STRAFFORD. Portrait. Cr. 8vo. 2s. 6d.

—— COLERIDGE. Cr. 8vo. 1s. 6d. ; sewed, 1s.

**TRENCH** (R. Chenevix).—HULSEAN LECTURES. 8vo. 7s. 6d.

**TRENCH** (Capt. F.).—THE RUSSO-INDIAN QUESTION. Crown 8vo. 7s. 6d.

**TREVELYAN** (Sir Geo. Otto).—CAWNPORE. Crown 8vo. 6s.

**TRISTRAM** (W. Outram).—COACHING DAYS AND COACHING WAYS. Illustrated by HERBERT RAILTON and HUGH THOMSON. Extra Crown 4to. 21s.

**TROLLOPE** (Anthony).—THACKERAY. Cr. 8vo. 1s. 6d. ; sewed, 1s.

**TRUMAN** (Jos.).—AFTER-THOUGHTS: POEMS. Crown 8vo. 3s. 6d.

**TULLOCH** (Principal).—THE CHRIST OF THE GOSPELS AND THE CHRIST OF MODERN CRITICISM. Extra fcp. 8vo. 4s. 6d.

TURNER'S LIBER STUDIORUM. A Description and a Catalogue. By W. G. RAWLINSON. Medium 8vo. 12s. 6d.

TURNER (Charles Tennyson).—COLLECTED SONNETS, OLD AND NEW. Ex. fcp. 8vo. 7s. 6d.

TURNER (Rev. Geo.).—SAMOA, A HUNDRED YEARS AGO AND LONG BEFORE. Preface by E. B. TYLOR, F.R.S. Crown 8vo. 9s.

TURNER (H. H.).—A COLLECTION OF EXAMPLES ON HEAT AND ELECTRICITY. Cr. 8vo. 2s. 6d.

TYLOR (E. B.).—ANTHROPOLOGY. With Illustrations. Crown 8vo. 7s. 6d.

TYRWHITT (Rev. R. St. John). — OUR SKETCHING CLUB. 4th Ed. Cr. 8vo. 7s. 6d.

—— FREE FIELD. Lyrics, chiefly Descriptive. Globe 8vo. 3s. 6d.

—— BATTLE AND AFTER: Concerning Sergt. Thomas Atkins, Grenadier Guards; and other Verses. Globe 8vo. 3s. 6d.

UHLAND.—SELECT BALLADS. Edited by G. E. FASNACHT. 18mo. 1s.

UNDERHILL (H. G.).—EASY EXERCISES IN GREEK ACCIDENCE. Globe 8vo. 2s.

UPPINGHAM BY THE SEA. By J. H. S. Crown 8vo. 3s. 6d.

VAUGHAN (Very Rev. Charles J.).—NOTES FOR LECTURES ON CONFIRMATION. 14th Edition. Fcp. 8vo. 1s. 6d.

—— MEMORIALS OF HARROW SUNDAYS. 5th Edition. Crown 8vo. 10s. 6d.

—— LECTURES ON THE EPISTLE TO THE PHILIPPIANS. 4th Edition. Cr. 8vo. 7s. 6d.

—— LECTURES ON THE REVELATION OF ST. JOHN. 5th Edition. Crown 8vo. 10s. 6d.

—— EPIPHANY, LENT, AND EASTER. 3rd Edition. Crown 8vo. 10s. 6d.

—— HEROES OF FAITH. 2nd Ed. Cr. 8vo. 6s.

—— THE BOOK AND THE LIFE, AND OTHER SERMONS. 3rd Edition. Fcp. 8vo. 4s. 6d.

—— ST. PAUL'S EPISTLE TO THE ROMANS. The Greek Text with English Notes. 7th Edition. Crown 8vo. 7s. 6d.

—— TWELVE DISCOURSES ON SUBJECTS CONNECTED WITH THE LITURGY AND WORSHIP OF THE CHURCH OF ENGLAND. 4th Edition Fcp. 8vo. 6s.

—— WORDS FROM THE GOSPELS. 3rd Edition. Fcp. 8vo. 4s. 6d.

—— THE EPISTLES OF ST. PAUL. For English Readers. Part I. containing the First Epistle to the Thessalonians. 2nd Ed. 8vo. 1s. 6d.

—— THE CHURCH OF THE FIRST DAYS. New Edition. Crown 8vo. 10s. 6d.

—— THE CHURCH OF THE FIRST DAYS. Series I. THE CHURCH OF JERUSALEM. 3rd Edition. Fcap. 8vo. 4s. 6d.—III. THE CHURCH OF THE WORLD. Fcp. 8vo. 4s. 6d.

—— LIFE'S WORK AND GOD'S DISCIPLINE. 3rd Edition. Extra fcp. 8vo. 2s. 6d.

—— THE WHOLESOME WORDS OF JESUS CHRIST. 2nd Edition. Fcp. 8vo. 3s. 6d.

—— FOES OF FAITH. 2nd Ed. Fcp. 8vo. 3s. 6d.

—— CHRIST SATISFYING THE INSTINCTS OF HUMANITY. 2nd Edit. Ext. fcp. 8vo. 3s. 6d.

VAUGHAN (Very Rev. C. J.).—COUNSELS FOR YOUNG STUDENTS. Fcp. 8vo. 2s. 6d.

—— THE TWO GREAT TEMPTATIONS. 2nd Edition. Fcp. 8vo. 3s. 6d.

—— ADDRESSES FOR YOUNG CLERGYMEN. Extra fcp. 8vo. 4s. 6d.

—— "MY SON, GIVE ME THINE HEART." Extra fcp. 8vo. 5s.

—— REST AWHILE. Addresses to Toilers in the Ministry. Extra fcp. 8vo. 5s.

—— TEMPLE SERMONS. Crown 8vo. 10s. 6d.

—— AUTHORISED OR REVISED? Sermons on some of the Texts in which the Revised Version differs from the Authorised. Crown 8vo. 7s. 6d.

—— ST. PAUL'S EPISTLE TO THE PHILIPPIANS. With Translation, Paraphrase, and Notes for English Readers. Crown 8vo. 5s.

—— LESSONS OF THE CROSS AND PASSION. WORDS FROM THE CROSS. THE REIGN OF SIN. THE LORD'S PRAYER. Four Courses of Lent Lectures. Crown 8vo. 10s. 6d.

—— UNIVERSITY SERMONS, NEW AND OLD. Crown 8vo. 10s. 6d.

—— THE EPISTLE TO THE HEBREWS. With Notes. Crown 8vo. 7s. 6d.

VAUGHAN (D. J.).—THE PRESENT TRIAL OF FAITH. Crown 8vo. 9s.

VAUGHAN (E. T.).—SOME REASONS OF OUR CHRISTIAN HOPE. Hulsean Lectures for 1875. Crown 8vo. 6s. 6d.

VAUGHAN (Robert).—STONES FROM THE QUARRY: Sermons. Crown 8vo. 5s.

VELEY (Marg.).—A GARDEN OF MEMORIES; MRS. AUSTIN; LIZZIE'S BARGAIN. Three Stories. 2 vols. Globe 8vo. 12s.

VENN (John). — ON SOME CHARACTERISTICS OF BELIEF, SCIENTIFIC AND RELIGIOUS. Hulsean Lectures, 1869. 8vo. 7s. 6d.

—— THE LOGIC OF CHANCE. 2nd Edition. Crown 8vo. 10s. 6d.

—— SYMBOLIC LOGIC. Crown 8vo. 10s. 6d.

—— THE PRINCIPLES OF EMPIRICAL OR INDUCTIVE LOGIC. 8vo. 18s.

VERNEY (Lady).—HOW THE PEASANT OWNER LIVES IN PARTS OF FRANCE, GERMANY, ITALY, AND RUSSIA. Cr. 8vo. 3s. 6d.

VERRALL (A. W.).—STUDIES, LITERARY AND HISTORICAL, IN THE ODES OF HORACE. 8vo. 8s. 6d.

VERRALL (Mrs. M. de G.) and HARRISON (Miss Jane E.).—MYTHOLOGY AND MONUMENTS OF ANCIENT ATHENS. Illustrated. Crown 8vo. 16s.

VICTORIA UNIVERSITY CALENDAR, 1890. Crown 8vo. 1s. net.

VICTOR EMMANUEL II., FIRST KING OF ITALY. By G. S. GODKIN. 2nd Edition. Crown 8vo. 6s.

VIDA: STUDY OF A GIRL. By AMY DUNSMUIR. 3rd Edition. Crown 8vo. 6s.

VINCENT (Sir E.) and DICKSON (T. G.).—HANDBOOK TO MODERN GREEK. 3rd Ed. Crown 8vo. 6s.

**VIRGIL.**—The Works of Virgil rendered into English Prose. By Jas. Lonsdale, M.A., and S. Lee, M.A. Globe 8vo. 3s. 6d.

—— The Æneid. Transl. into English Prose by J. W. Mackail, M.A. Cr. 8vo. 7s. 6d.

—— Georgics, I. Edited by T. E. Page, M.A. 18mo. 1s. 6d.

—— Georgics II. Edited by Rev. J. H. Skrine, M.A. 18mo. 1s. 6d.

—— Æneid, I. Edited by A. S. Walpole, M.A. 18mo. 1s. 6d.

—— Æneid, II. Ed. by T. E. Page. 18mo. 1s. 6d.

—— Æneid, II. and III.: The Narrative of Æneas. Edit. by E. W. Howson, M.A. Fcp. 8vo. 2s.

—— Æneid, III. Edited by T. E. Page, M.A. 18mo. 1s. 6d.

—— Æneid, IV. Edited by Rev. H. M. Stephenson, M.A. 18mo. 1s. 6d.

—— Æneid, V.: The Funeral Games. Ed. by Rev. A. Calvert, M.A. 18mo. 1s. 6d.

—— Æneid, VI. Edit. by T. E. Page, M.A. 18mo. 1s. 6d.

—— Æneid, VII.: The Wrath of Turnus. Ed. by Rev. A. Calvert, M.A. 18mo. 1s. 6d.

—— Æneid, VIII. Ed. by Rev. A. Calvert. 18mo. 1s. 6d.

—— Æneid, IX. Edited by Rev. H. M. Stephenson, M.A. 18mo. 1s. 6d.

—— Æneid X. Edited by S. G Owen, M A. 18mo. 1s. 6d.

—— Selections. Edited by E. S. Shuckburgh, M.A. 18mo. 1s. 6d.

**VIRGIL.** By Prof. Nettleship. 8vo. 1s. 6d.

**VITA.**—Links and Clues. By Vita (the Hon. Lady Welby-Gregory). 2nd Edition. Crown 8vo. 6s.

**VOICES CRYING IN THE WILDERNESS.** A Novel. Crown 8vo. 7s. 6d.

**VOLTAIRE.**—Histoire de Charles XII., Roi de Suède. Edited by G. Eugène Fasnacht. 18mo. 3s. 6d.

**VOLTAIRE.** By John Morley. Gl. 8vo. 5s.

**WALDSTEIN (C.).**—Catalogue of Casts in the Museum of Classical Archæology, Cambridge. Crown 8vo. 1s. 6d.

Large Paper Edition. Small 4to. 5s.

**WALKER (Prof. Francis A.).**—The Wages Question. 8vo. 14s.

—— Money. 8vo. 16s.

—— Money in its Relation to Trade and Industry. Crown 8vo. 7s. 6d.

—— Political Economy. 2nd Ed. 8vo. 12s. 6d.

—— A Brief Text-Book of Political Economy. Crown 8vo. 6s. 6d.

—— Land and its Rent. Fcp. 8vo. 3s. 6d.

—— First Lessons in Political Economy. Crown 8vo. 5s.

**WALLACE (Alfred Russel).**—The Malay Archipelago: The Land of the Orang Utang and the Bird of Paradise. Maps and Illustrations. 10th Ed. Cr. 8vo. 6s.

—— The Geographical Distribution of Animals. With Illustrations and Maps. 2 vols. Medium 8vo. 42s.

**WALLACE (A. R.).**—Island Life. With Illustrations and Maps. Demy 8vo. 18s.

—— Bad Times. An Essay on the present Depression of Trade. Crown 8vo. 2s. 6d.

—— Darwinism. An Exposition of the Theory of Natural Selection, with some of its Applications. Illustrated. 3rd Ed. Cr. 8vo. 9s.

—— Contributions to the Theory of Natural Selection; and Tropical Nature and other Essays. New Edition. Extra crown 8vo. 6s.

**WALLACE (Sir D. Mackenzie).**—Egypt and the Egyptian Question. 8vo. 14s.

**WALPOLE (Spencer).**—Foreign Relations. Crown 8vo. 3s. 6d.

—— The Electorate and Legislature. Crown 8vo. 3s. 6d.

**WALPOLE.** By John Morley. Cr. 8vo. 2s. 6d.

**WALTON and COTTON—LOWELL.**—The Complete Angler; or, the Contemplative Man's Recreation of Izaak Walton and Thomas Cotton. With an Introduction by Jas. Russell Lowell. Illustrated. Extra crown 8vo. 2l. 12s. 6d. net.

Also an Edition on large paper, Proofs on Japanese paper. 3l. 13s. 6d. net.

**WANDERING WILLIE.** By the Author of "Conrad the Squirrel." Globe 8vo. 2s. 6d.

**WARD (Prof. A. W.).**—A History of English Dramatic Literature, to the Death of Queen Anne. 2 vols. 8vo. 32s.

—— Chaucer. Cr. 8vo. 1s. 6d.; sewed, 1s.

—— Dickens. Cr. 8vo. 1s. 6d.; sewed, 1s.

**WARD (Prof. H. M.).**—Timber and some of its Diseases. Illustrated. Cr. 8vo. 6s.

**WARD (John).**—Experiences of a Diplomatist. 8vo. 10s. 6d.

**WARD (T. H.).**—English Poets. Selections, with Critical Introductions by various Writers, and a General Introduction by Matthew Arnold. Edited by T. H. Ward, M.A. 4 vols. 2nd Ed. Crown 8vo. 7s. 6d. each.—Vol. I. Chaucer to Donne.—II. Ben Jonson to Dryden.—III. Addison to Blake.—IV. Wordsworth to Rossetti.

**WARD (Mrs. T. Humphry).**—Milly and Olly. With Illustrations by Mrs. Alma Tadema. Globe 8vo. 2s. 6d.

—— Miss Bretherton. Crown 8vo. 3s. 6d.

—— The Journal Intime of Henri-Frédéric Amiel. Translated, with an Introduction and Notes. 2nd Ed. Cr. 8vo. 6s.

**WARD (Samuel).**—Lyrical Recreations. Fcp. 8vo. 6s.

**WARD (W.).**—William George Ward and the Oxford Movement. Portrait. 8vo. 14s.

**WARINGTON (G.).**—The Week of Creation. Crown 8vo. 4s. 6d.

**WARREN HASTINGS.** By Sir Alfred Lyall. With Portrait. Cr. 8vo. 2s. 6d.

**WARWICK, THE KING-MAKER.** By C. W. Oman. With Portrait. Crown 8vo.

WATERTON (Charles).—WANDERINGS IN SOUTH AMERICA, THE NORTH-WEST OF THE UNITED STATES, AND THE ANTILLES. Edited by Rev. J. G. WOOD. With 100 Illustrations. Crown 8vo. 6s.

*People's Edition.* With 100 Illustrations. Medium 4to. 6d.

WATSON. A RECORD OF ELLEN WATSON. By ANNA BUCKLAND. Crown 8vo. 6s.

WATSON (R. Spence).—A VISIT TO WAZAN, THE SACRED CITY OF MOROCCO. 8vo. 10s.6d.

WEBSTER (Augusta).—DAFFODIL AND THE CROÄXAXICANS. Crown 8vo. 6s.

WELBY-GREGORY (The Hon. Lady).— LINKS AND CLUES. 2nd Edition. Crown 8vo. 6s.

WELCH (Wm.) and DUFFIELD (C. G.).— LATIN ACCIDENCE AND EXERCISES ARRANGED FOR BEGINNERS. 18mo. 1s. 6d.

WELLDON (Rev. J. E. C.).—THE SPIRITUAL LIFE, AND OTHER SERMONS. Cr. 8vo. 6s.

WELLINGTON. By GEO. HOOPER. With Portrait. Crown 8vo. 2s. 6d.

WESTBURY (Hugh).—FREDERICK HAZZLEDEN. 3 vols. Crown 8vo. 31s. 6d.

WESTCOTT (The Rt. Rev. Bishop.)—A GENERAL SURVEY OF THE HISTORY OF THE CANON OF THE NEW TESTAMENT DURING THE FIRST FOUR CENTURIES. 6th Edition. Crown 8vo. 10s. 6d.

—— INTRODUCTION TO THE STUDY OF THE FOUR GOSPELS. 7th Ed. Cr. 8vo. 10s. 6d.

—— THE GOSPEL OF THE RESURRECTION. 6th Edition. Crown 8vo. 6s.

—— THE BIBLE IN THE CHURCH. 10th Edit. 18mo. 4s. 6d.

—— THE CHRISTIAN LIFE, MANIFOLD AND ONE. Crown 8vo. 2s. 6d.

—— ON THE RELIGIOUS OFFICE OF THE UNIVERSITIES. Sermons. Cr. 8vo. 4s. 6d.

—— THE REVELATION OF THE RISEN LORD. 4th Edition. Crown 8vo. 6s.

—— THE HISTORIC FAITH. 3rd Edition. Cr. 8vo. 6s.

—— THE EPISTLES OF ST. JOHN. The Greek Text, with Notes. 2nd Edition. 8vo. 12s. 6d

—— THE REVELATION OF THE FATHER. Cr. 8vo. 6s.

—— CHRISTUS CONSUMMATOR. 2nd Edition. Crown 8vo. 6s.

—— SOME THOUGHTS FROM THE ORDINAL. Crown 8vo. 1s. 6d.

—— SOCIAL ASPECTS OF CHRISTIANITY. Cr. 8vo. 6s.

—— GIFTS FOR MINISTRY. Addresses to Candidates for Ordination. Crown 8vo. 1s. 6d.

—— THE EPISTLE TO THE HEBREWS. The Greek Text, with Notes and Essays. 8vo. 14s.

—— THE VICTORY OF THE CROSS. Sermons preached during Holy Week, 1888, in Hereford Cathedral. Crown 8vo. 3s. 6d.

WESTCOTT (Bishop). — FROM STRENGTH TO STRENGTH. Three Sermons (In Memoriam J. B. D.) Crown 8vo. 2s.

—— ESSAYS. Globe 8vo.

—— THOUGHTS ON REVELATION AND LIFE. Selections from the Writings of Canon WESTCOTT. Edited by Rev. S. PHILLIPS. Crown 8vo. 6s.

WESTCOTT (Bishop) and HORT (Prof.).— THE NEW TESTAMENT IN THE ORIGINAL GREEK. Revised Text. 2 vols. Crown 8vo. 10s. 6d. each.—Vol. I. Text.—Vol. II. The Introduction and Appendix.

—— THE NEW TESTAMENT IN THE ORIGINAL GREEK. An Edition for Schools. The Text revised by Bp. WESTCOTT and Dr. HORT. 18mo, 4s.6d. ; roan, 5s. 6d. ; morocco, 6s. 6d.

WETHERELL (J.).—EXERCISES ON MORRIS' PRIMER OF ENGLISH GRAMMAR. 18mo. 1s.

WHEELER (J. Talboys).—A SHORT HISTORY OF INDIA. With Maps. Crown 8vo. 12s.

—— INDIA UNDER BRITISH RULE. 8vo. 12s.6d.

—— COLLEGE HISTORY OF INDIA. Asiatic and European. Crown 8vo. 3s. 6d.

—— PRIMER OF INDIAN HISTORY, ASIATIC AND EUROPEAN. 18mo. 1s.

WHEN I WAS A LITTLE GIRL. By the Author of "St. Olave's." With Illustrations. Globe 8vo. 2s. 6d.

WHEN PAPA COMES HOME. By the Author of "When I was a Little Girl." With Illustrations. Globe 8vo. 4s. 6d.

WHEWELL. DR. WILLIAM WHEWELL, late Master of Trinity College, Cambridge. An Account of his Writings, with Selections from his Literary and Scientific Correspondence. By I. TODHUNTER, M.A. 2 vols. 8vo. 25s.

WHITE (Gilbert).—NATURAL HISTORY AND ANTIQUITIES OF SELBORNE. Edited by FRANK BUCKLAND. With a Chapter on Antiquities by Lord SELBORNE. Cr.8vo. 6s.

WHITE (John Williams).—A SERIES OF FIRST LESSONS IN GREEK. Adapted to GOODWIN'S Greek Grammar. Crown 8vo. 3s. 6d.

WHITE (Dr. W. Hale).—A TEXT-BOOK OF GENERAL THERAPEUTICS. Illustrated. Cr. 8vo. 8s. 6d.

WHITHAM (Prof. J. M.).—STEAM ENGINE DESIGN. Illustrated. 8vo. 25s.

WHITNEY (Prof. W. D.).—A COMPENDIOUS GERMAN GRAMMAR. Crown 8vo. 4s. 6d.

—— A GERMAN READER IN PROSE AND VERSE. With Notes and Vocabulary. Cr. 8vo. 5s.

—— A COMPENDIOUS GERMAN AND ENGLISH DICTIONARY. Crown 8vo. 7s. 6d.—German-English Part separately. 5s.

WHITTIER.—COMPLETE POETICAL WORKS OF JOHN GREENLEAF WHITTIER. With Portrait. 18mo. 4s. 6d.

WHITTIER.—THE COMPLETE WORKS OF J. GREENLEAF WHITTIER. 7 vols. Crown 8vo. 6s. each.—Vol. I. NARRATIVE AND LEGENDARY POEMS.— II. POEMS OF NATURE; POEMS SUBJECTIVE AND REMINISCENT; RELIGIOUS POEMS.—III. ANTI-SLAVERY POEMS; SONGS OF LABOUR AND REFORM.— IV. PERSONAL POEMS; OCCASIONAL POEMS; THE TENT ON THE BEACH; with the Poems of ELIZABETH H. WHITTIER, and an Appendix containing Early and Uncollected Verses.— V. MARGARET SMITH'S JOURNAL; TALES AND SKETCHES. — VI. OLD PORTRAITS AND MODERN SKETCHES; PERSONAL SKETCHES AND TRIBUTES; HISTORICAL PAPERS.—VII. THE CONFLICT WITH SLAVERY, POLITICS AND REFORM: THE INNER LIFE, CRITICISM.

WICKHAM (Rev. E. C.)—WELLINGTON COLLEGE SERMONS. Crown 8vo. 6s.

WICKSTEED (Philip H.).—ALPHABET OF ECONOMIC SCIENCE.—I. ELEMENTS OF THE THEORY OF VALUE OR WORTH. Globe 8vo. 2s. 6d.

WIEDERSHEIM—PARKER.— ELEMENTS OF THE COMPARATIVE ANATOMY OF VERTEBRATES. Adapted from the German of Prof. ROBERT WIEDERSHEIM, by Prof. W. NEWTON PARKER. Illustrated. Medium 8vo. 12s. 6d.

WILBRAHAM (Frances M.).—IN THE SERE AND YELLOW LEAF: THOUGHTS AND RECOLLECTIONS FOR OLD AND YOUNG. Globe 8vo. 3s. 6d.

WILKINS (Prof. A. S.).—THE LIGHT OF THE WORLD : AN ESSAY. 2nd Edition. Crown 8vo. 3s. 6d.

—— ROMAN ANTIQUITIES. Illustr. 18mo. 1s.

—— ROMAN LITERATURE. 18mo. 1s.

WILKINSON (S.). — THE BRAIN OF AN ARMY. A Popular Account of the German General Staff. Crown 8vo. 2s. 6d.

WILLIAM THE CONQUEROR. By EDWARD A. FREEMAN, D.C.L., LL.D. Crown 8vo. 2s. 6d.

WILLIAM III. By H. D. TRAILL. Crown 8vo. 2s. 6d.

WILLIAMS (Montagu).—LEAVES OF A LIFE. 15th Thousand. Crown 8vo. 3s.6d.; sewed, 2s. 6d.

WILLOUGHBY (F.).—FAIRY GUARDIANS. Illustrated by TOWNLEY GREEN. Crown 8vo. 5s.

WILSON (A. J.).—THE NATIONAL BUDGET; THE NATIONAL DEBT; RATES AND TAXES. Crown 8vo. 3s. 6d.

WILSON (Dr. George).—RELIGIO CHEMICI. Crown 8vo. 8s. 6d.

—— THE FIVE GATEWAYS OF KNOWLEDGE. 9th Edition. Extra fcp. 8vo. 2s. 6d.

WILSON. MEMOIR OF PROF. GEORGE WILSON, M.D. By HIS SISTER. With Portrait. 2nd Edition. Crown 8vo. 6s.

WILSON (Rev. Canon).—THE BIBLE STUDENT'S GUIDE. 2nd Edition. 4to. 25s.

WILSON (Sir Chas.).—CLIVE. With Portrait. Crown 8vo. 2s. 6d.

WILSON (Sir Daniel, LL. D.).—PREHISTORIC ANNALS OF SCOTLAND. With Illustrations. 2 vols. Demy 8vo. 36s.

—— PREHISTORIC MAN : RESEARCHES INTO THE ORIGIN OF CIVILISATION IN THE OLD AND NEW WORLD. 3rd Edition. With Illustrations. 2 vols. Medium 8vo. 36s.

—— CHATTERTON : A BIOGRAPHICAL STUDY. Crown 8vo. 6s. 6d.

—— CALIBAN : A CRITIQUE ON SHAKESPEARE'S "TEMPEST" AND "A MIDSUMMER NIGHT'S DREAM." 8vo. 10s. 6d.

WILSON (Rev. J. M.).—SERMONS PREACHED IN CLIFTON COLLEGE CHAPEL, 1879—83. Crown 8vo. 6s.

—— ESSAYS AND ADDRESSES. Cr. 8vo. 4s.6d.

—— SOME CONTRIBUTIONS TO THE RELIGIOUS THOUGHT OF OUR TIME. Crown 8vo. 6s.

—— ELEMENTARY GEOMETRY. Books I.—V. Containing the Subjects of Euclid's First Six Books, following the Syllabus of Geometry prepared by the Geometrical Association. Extra fcp. 8vo. 4s. 6d.

—— SOLID GEOMETRY AND CONIC SECTIONS. Extra fcp. 8vo. 3s. 6d.

WINGATE (Major F. R.).—MAHDIISM AND THE SOUDAN. Being an Account of the Rise and Progress of Mahdiism, and of subsequent Events in the Soudan to the Present Time. With 10 Maps. 8vo.

WINKWORTH (Catherine). — CHRISTIAN SINGERS OF GERMANY. Crown 8vo. 4s. 6d.

WOLSELEY (General Viscount).—THE SOLDIER'S POCKET-BOOK FOR FIELD SERVICE. 5th Edition. 16mo, roan. 5s.

—— FIELD POCKET-BOOK FOR THE AUXILIARY FORCES. 16mo, 1s. 6d.

WOLSEY (CARDINAL). By Prof. M. CREIGHTON. Crown 8vo. 2s. 6d.

WOLSTENHOLME (Joseph). — MATHEMATICAL PROBLEMS ON SUBJECTS INCLUDED IN THE FIRST AND SECOND DIVISION OF THE SCHEDULE OF SUBJECTS FOR THE CAMBRIDGE MATHEMATICAL TRIPOS EXAMINATION. 2nd Edition. 8vo. 18s.

—— EXAMPLES FOR PRACTICE IN THE USE OF SEVEN-FIGURE LOGARITHMS. 8vo. 5s.

WOOD (Andrew Goldie).—THE ISLES OF THE BLEST, AND OTHER POEMS. Globe 8vo. 5s.

WOOD (Rev. E. G.).—THE REGAL POWER OF THE CHURCH. 8vo. 4s. 6d.

WOODS (Miss M. A.).—A FIRST POETRY BOOK. Fcp. 8vo. 2s. 6d.

—— A SECOND POETRY BOOK. 2 Parts. Fcp. 8vo. 2s. 6d. each.

—— A THIRD POETRY BOOK. Fcp. 8vo. 4s.6d.

—— HYMNS FOR SCHOOL WORSHIP. 18mo. 1s. 6d.

WOOLNER (Thomas). — MY BEAUTIFUL LADY. 3rd Edition. Fcp. 8vo. 5s.

—— PYGMALION : A POEM. Cr. 8vo. 7s. 6d.

—— SILENUS : A POEM. Crown 8vo. 6s.

WOOLWICH MATHEMATICAL PA-
PERS. For Admission in the Royal Military Academy for the Years 1880 -88. Edit.
by E. J. BROOKSMITH, B.A. Cr. 8vo. 6s.

WORDS FROM THE POETS. With a
Vignette and Frontispiece. 12th Edition.
18mo. 1s.

WORDSWORTH. By F. W. H. MYERS.
Crown 8vo. 1s. 6d.; sewed, 1s.

—— SELECT POEMS. Edited by MATTHEW
ARNOLD. 18mo. 4s. 6d.
Large Paper Edition. 8vo. 9s.

—— THE RECLUSE: A POEM. Fcp. 8vo.
2s. 6d.

—— THE COMPLETE POETICAL WORKS. Copy-
right Edition. With an Introduction by
JOHN MORLEY, and Portrait. Cr.8vo. 7s.6d.

WORDSWORTHIANA: A SELECTION OF
PAPERS READ TO THE WORDSWORTH SO-
CIETY. Edited by W. KNIGHT. Crown
8vo. 7s. 6d.

WORSHIP (THE) OF GOD, AND FEL-
LOWSHIP AMONG MEN. By the late
Prof. MAURICE and others. Fcp. 8vo. 3s. 6d.

WORTHEY (Mrs.).—THE NEW CONTINENT:
A NOVEL. 2 vols. Globe 8vo. 12s.

WRIGHT (Rev. Arthur).—THE COMPOSITION
OF THE FOUR GOSPELS. Crown 8vo. 5s.

WRIGHT (Miss Guthrie).—THE SCHOOL
COOKERY-BOOK. 18mo. 1s.

WRIGHT (Rev. Josiah).—THE SEVEN KINGS
OF ROME. Abridged from the First Book of
Livy. 8th Edition. Fcp. 8vo. 3s. 6d.

—— FIRST LATIN STEPS. Crown 8vo. 3s.

—— ATTIC PRIMER. Crown 8vo. 2s. 6d.

—— A COMPLETE LATIN COURSE. Crown
8vo. 2s. 6d.

WRIGHT (Lewis).—LIGHT. A Course of
Experimental Optics, chiefly with the Lan-
tern. With Illustrations and Coloured
Plates. Crown 8vo. 7s. 6d.

WRIGHT (W. Aldis).—THE BIBLE WORD-
BOOK. 2nd Edition. Crown 8vo. 7s. 6d.

WURTZ.—A HISTORY OF CHEMICAL THE-
ORY. By AD. WURTZ. Translated by
HENRY WATTS, F.R.S. Crown 8vo. 6s.

WYATT (Sir M. Digby).—FINE ART: A
Sketch of its History, Theory, Practice, and
Application to Industry. 8vo. 5s.

XENOPHON.—THE COMPLETE WORKS.
Translated by H. G. DAKYNS, M.A. 4
vols. Crown 8vo.—Vol. I. THE ANABA-
SIS AND BOOKS I. AND II. OF THE HEL-
LENICA. 10s. 6d.—Vol. II. HELLENICA
III.—VII., and the rest of the Works
bearing on History, viz. the two Polities—
ATHENIAN and LACONIAN, the AGESILAUS,
and the Tract on REVENUES. With Maps
and Plans.

—— ANABASIS. Selections from Book I. For
the Use of Beginners, with Notes, Vocabulary, and Exercises, by W. WELCH, M.A.,
and C. G. DUFFIELD, M.A. 18mo. 1s. 6d.

—— ANABASIS. Book I. chaps. 1—8. For
the Use of Beginners. Edited by E. A.
WELLS, M.A. 18mo. 1s. 6d.

XENOPHON.—ANABASIS. Book I. With
Notes and Vocabulary, by A. S. WALPOLE.
18mo. 1s. 6d.

—— ANABASIS. Book II. Edited by A. S.
WALPOLE, M.A. 18mo. 1s..6d.;

—— ANABASIS. Book III. Edited by Rev.
G. H. NALL, M.A. 18mo. 1s. 6d.

—— ANABASIS. Book IV. Edited by Rev.
E. D. STONE, M.A. 18mo. 1s. 6d.

—— ANABASIS. Books I.—IV. Edited, with
Notes, by Professors W. W. GOODWIN and
J. W. WHITE. Fcp. 8vo. 3s. 6d.

—— SELECTIONS FROM BOOK IV. OF THE
ANABASIS. Edited by Rev. E. D. STONE,
M.A. 18mo. 1s. 6d.

—— CYROPÆDIA. Books VII. and VIII.
Edited by Prof. ALFRED GOODWIN, M.A.
Fcp. 8vo. 2s. 6d.

—— SELECTIONS FROM THE CYROPÆDIA.
Edit. by Rev. A. H. COOKE. 18mo. 1s. 6d.

—— HELLENICA. Books I. and II. Edited
by H. HAILSTONE, M.A. With Map.
Fcp. 8vo. 2s. 6d.

—— HIERO. Edited by Rev. H. A. HOLDEN,
LL.D. Fcp. 8vo. 2s. 6d.

—— MEMORABILIA SOCRATIS. Edited by
A. R. CLUER, B.A. Fcp. 8vo. 5s.

—— OECONOMICUS. Edited by Rev. H. A.
HOLDEN, LL.D. Fcp. 8vo. 5s.

YONGE (Charlotte M.). — NOVELS AND
TALES. Crown 8vo. 3s. 6d. each.

1. THE HEIR OF REDCLYFFE.
2. HEARTSEASE.
3. HOPES AND FEARS.
4. DYNEVOR TERRACE.
5. THE DAISY CHAIN.
6. THE TRIAL: MORE LINKS OF THE
   DAISY CHAIN.
7. PILLARS OF THE HOUSE. Vol. I.
8. PILLARS OF THE HOUSE. Vol. II.
9. THE YOUNG STEPMOTHER.
10. CLEVER WOMAN OF THE FAMILY.
11. THE THREE BRIDES.
12. MY YOUNG ALCIDES.
13. THE CAGED LION.
14. THE DOVE IN THE EAGLE'S NEST.
15. THE CHAPLET OF PEARLS.
16. LADY HESTER: AND THE DANVERS
    PAPERS.
17. MAGNUM BONUM.
18. LOVE AND LIFE.
19. UNKNOWN TO HISTORY.
20. STRAY PEARLS.
21. THE ARMOURER'S PRENTICES.
22. THE TWO SIDES OF THE SHIELD.
23. NUTTIE'S FATHER.
24. SCENES AND CHARACTERS.
25. CHANTRY HOUSE.
26. A MODERN TELEMACHUS.
27. BYWORDS.
28. BEECHCROFT AT ROCKSTONE.
29. MORE BYWORDS.
30. A REPUTED CHANGELING.

—— THE POPULATION OF AN OLD PEAR-
TREE; OR, STORIES OF INSECT LIFE. From
the French of E. VAN BRUYSSEL. Illustrated. Globe 8vo. 2s. 6d.

—— THE PRINCE AND THE PAGE. Globe
8vo. 4s. 6d.

YONGE (Charlotte M.).—A BOOK OF GOLDEN DEEDS. 18mo. 4s. 6d.

*Cheap Edition.* 18mo. 1s.

*Globe Readings Edition.* Globe 8vo. 2s.

—— P's AND Q's; OR, THE QUESTION OF PUTTING UPON. Illustrated. Gl. 8vo. 4s. 6d.

—— THE LANCES OF LYNWOOD. Illustrated. Globe 8vo. 2s. 6d.

—— LITTLE LUCY'S WONDERFUL GLOBE. Illustrated. Globe 8vo. 4s. 6d.

—— THE LITTLE DUKE. Illustrated. Globe 8vo. 2s. 6d.

—— A STOREHOUSE OF STORIES. 2 vols. Gl. 8vo. 2s. 6d. each.

—— A BOOK OF WORTHIES : GATHERED FROM THE OLD HISTORIES AND WRITTEN ANEW. 18mo. 4s. 6d.

—— CAMEOS FROM ENGLISH HISTORY. Extra fcp. 8vo. 5s. each.—Vol. I. FROM ROLLO TO EDWARD II.—Vol. II. THE WARS IN FRANCE. —Vol. III. THE WARS OF THE ROSES. —Vol. IV. REFORMATION TIMES.—Vol. V. ENGLAND AND SPAIN. — Vol. VI. FORTY YEARS OF STUART RULE (1603—1643).— Vol. VII. THE REBELLION AND RESTORA- TION (1642—78).

—— SCRIPTURE READINGS FOR SCHOOLS AND FAMILIES. Globe 8vo. 1s. 6d. each; also with Comments, 3s. 6d. each.—GENESIS TO DEUTERONOMY.—Second Series: JOSHUA TO SOLOMON.—Third Series: KINGS AND THE PROPHETS.—Fourth Series: THE GOS- PEL TIMES.—Fifth Series: APOSTOLIC TIMES.

—— FRANCE. 18mo. 1s.

—— HISTORY OF FRANCE. Maps. 18mo. 3s. 6d.

YONGE (Charlotte M.).—THE LIFE OF JOHN COLERIDGE PATTESON. 2 vols. Crown 8vo. 12s.

—— THE PUPILS OF ST. JOHN. Illustrated. Crown 8vo. 6s.

—— PIONEERS AND FOUNDERS; OR, RECENT WORKERS IN THE MISSION FIELD. Crown 8vo. 6s.

—— THE STORY OF THE CHRISTIANS AND MOORS IN SPAIN. 18mo. 4s. 6d.

—— HISTORY OF CHRISTIAN NAMES. New Edition, revised. Crown 8vo. 7s. 6d.

—— THE HERB OF THE FIELD. A New Edition, revised. Crown 8vo. 5s.

—— THE VICTORIAN HALF-CENTURY. Crown 8vo. 1s. 6d. ; sewed, 1s.

—— THE TWO PENNILESS PRINCESSES: A STORY OF THE TIME OF JAMES I. OF SCOT- LAND. 2 vols. Crown 8vo. 12s.

YOUNG (E. W.).—SIMPLE PRACTICAL ME- THODS OF CALCULATING STRAINS ON GIR- DERS, ARCHES, AND TRUSSES. 8vo. 7s. 6d.

ZECHARIAH. THE HEBREW STUDENT'S COMMENTARY ON ZECHARIAH, HEBREW AND LXX. By W. H. LOWE, M.A. 8vo. 10s. 6d.

ZIEGLER.—A TEXT-BOOK OF PATHOLOGI- CAL ANATOMY AND PATHOGENESIS. By ERNST ZIEGLER. Translated and Edited for English Students by DONALD MAC- ALISTER, M.A., M.D. With Illustrations. 8vo. — Part I. GENERAL PATHOLOGICAL ANATOMY. 2nd Edition. 12s. 6d.—Part II. SPECIAL PATHOLOGICAL ANATOMY. Sections I.—VIII. 2nd Edition. 12s. 6d. Sections IX.—XII. 8vo. 12s. 6d.

MACMILLAN AND CO., LONDON.

J. PALMER, PRINTER, ALEXANDRA STREET CAMBRIDGE.

VI/30/1/91

2266 0

Milton Keynes UK
Ingram Content Group UK Ltd.
UKHW051925240624
444478UK00004BA/49